Management Information Systems

Dr. P. Mohan

Professor,
Department of Commerce and Management Studies,
University of Calicut,
Kerala – 673635.

Himalaya Publishing House
ISO 9001:2008 CERTIFIED

First Edition	:	1996	**Ninth Edition**	: 2007
Second Revised Edition	:	1998	**Tenth Edition**	: 2008
Third Revised Edition	:	1999	**Eleventh Revised Edition**	: 2012
Fourth Revised Edition	:	2002	**Twelfth Edition**	: 2013
Fifth Revised Edition	:	2003	Edition	: 2015
Sixth Edition	:	2004	Reprint	: 2017
Seventh Edition	:	2005	Reprint	: 2018
Eighth Edition	:	2006	Edition	: 2021

Published by	:	Mrs. Meena Pandey for **Himalaya Publishing House Pvt. Ltd.,** "Ramdoot", Dr. Bhalerao Marg, Girgaon, **Mumbai - 400 004.** Phone: 022-23860170/23863863, Fax: 022-23877178 **E-mail: himpub@vsnl.com; Website: www.himpub.com**
Branch Offices	:	
New Delhi	:	"Pooja Apartments", 4-B, Murari Lal Street, Ansari Road, Darya Ganj, New Delhi - 110 002. Phone: 011-23270392, 23278631; Fax: 011-23256286
Nagpur	:	Kundanlal Chandak Industrial Estate, Ghat Road, Nagpur - 440 018. Phone: 0712-2738731, 3296733; Telefax: 0712-2721216
Bengaluru	:	No. 16/1 (Old 12/1), 1st Floor, Next to Hotel Highlands, Madhava Nagar, Race Course Road, Bengaluru - 560 001. Phone: 080-22286611, 22385461, 4113 8821, 22281541
Hyderabad	:	No. 3-4-184, Lingampally, Besides Raghavendra Swamy Matham, Kachiguda, Hyderabad - 500 027. Phone: 040-27560041, 27550139
Chennai	:	8/2 Madley 2nd street, T. Nagar, Chennai - 600 017. Mobile: 09320490962
Pune	:	First Floor, "Laksha" Apartment, No. 527, Mehunpura, Shaniwarpeth (Near Prabhat Theatre), Pune - 411 030. Phone: 020-24496323/24496333; Mobile: 09370579333
Lucknow	:	House No 731, Shekhupura Colony, Near B.D. Convent School, Aliganj, Lucknow - 226 022. Mobile: 09307501549
Ahmedabad	:	114, "SHAIL", 1st Floor, Opp. Madhu Sudan House, C.G. Road, Navrang Pura, Ahmedabad - 380 009. Phone: 079-26560126; Mobile: 09377088847
Ernakulam	:	39/104 A, Lakshmi Apartment, Karikkamuri Cross Rd., Ernakulam, Cochin - 622011, Kerala. Phone: 0484-2378012, 2378016; Mobile: 09387122121
Bhubaneswar	:	Plot No. 214/1342, Budheswari Colony, Behind Durga Mandap, Bhubaneswar - 751 006. Phone: 0674-2575129; Mobile: 09338746007
Indore	:	Kesardeep Avenue Extension, 73, Narayan Bagh, Flat No. 302, IIIrd Floor, Near Humpty Dumpty School, Indore - 452 007 (M.P.). Mobile: 09303399304
Kolkata	:	108/4, Beliaghata Main Road, Near ID Hospital, Opp. SBI Bank, Kolkata - 700 010, Phone: 033-32449649, Mobile: 7439040301
Guwahati	:	House No. 15, Behind Pragjyotish College, Near Sharma Printing Press, P.O. Bharalumukh, Guwahati - 781009, (Assam). Mobile: 09883055590, 08486355289, 7439040301
DTP by	:	HPH, Editorial Office, Bhandup (Swapnali)
Printed at	:	M/s. Sri Sai Art Printer, Hyderabad. On behalf of HPH.

DEDICATED TO MY TEACHERS

PREFACE

Information systems have become a strategic resource for organisations. It is almost impossible to run a business without having proper information systems. Even small and micro enterprises are discovering the potential of information systems for enhancing competitiveness of business. Data is the key raw material for information. So, proper capturing and storage of data is a fundamental activity in information systems. Processing and communicating information and protecting the information resources from possible threats are the other key activities in information systems management. A proper understanding of the subject of information systems will enable a person to design and implement the right kind of information systems in organisations.

Usually, information systems literature is loaded with technical stuff. Care has been taken to keep the subject simple and easy to understand. This book covers most of the non-technical subjects in the area of information systems. This edition of the book contains a lot more content than the last. Addition to content includes CRM, Supply Chain Management and IS audit.

This book is organised into twenty-two chapters. The first four chapters discuss the concepts and structure of information systems. Chapters five to eight give an introduction to specific information systems like TPS, DSS, ES and ERPS. Chapters nine and ten cover essentials of CRM and Supply Chain Management respectively. Chapter eleven presents electronic commerce. Chapter twelve discusses the role of computers in MIS. Chapters thirteen to eighteen deal with planning, designing and implementing information systems. Chapter nineteen is on social and legal aspects of computerisation. Chapters twenty and twenty-one deal with networking and the Internet. The book concludes with chapter twenty-two which introduces IS Audit. IT Act 2000 is given in the appendix.

I hope this book will be well received by the teachers and students of the subject. I would welcome suggestions from the students and teachers for improving the work.

Dr. P. Mohan

ACKNOWLEDGEMENTS

This book was first published in 1996. It is gratifying to note that this book is still much in demand in many states in the country. It was because of the pressing demand from students of various programmes of study, I decided to revise it after nearly 10 years. There was a lot of updating to be done and it is a pleasure to note that most of the content has been reviewed and revised.

As a teacher of the course 'Management Information Systems' for nearly two decades, I have benefited a lot from my interaction with the MBA and M.Com. students in the Department of Commerce and Management Studies, University of Calicut. I would like to thank them for keeping me interested in the subject.

Mr. Habeeb K. Thangal, Asst. Librarian, Department of Commerce and Management Studies was always helpful in locating and issuing me reference materials for this work. I wish to acknowledge here his sincere help.

I would like to thank those who sent me their comments about the earlier editions that helped me a lot in updating and adding content to this book and I have, therefore, included in this revised edition a few new chapters like CRM, Supply Chain Management and IS Audit.

I would like to thank Mr. Neeraj Pandey of Himalaya Publishing House Pvt. Ltd., for his interest in the work and keeping the pressure on me to complete the work in time.

I am grateful to Ms. Niranjana and Ms. Vijayalakshmi, both research scholars at DCMS, University of Calicut, for helping me with proof correction of this book.

Finally, I wish to thank my wife and children who spared me long hours for completing this work and sustaining my interest in this work.

Calicut

May 5, 2012

Dr. P. Mohan

CONTENTS

DETAILED CONTENTS

1

CHAPTER

Information System

Business management is a complex process. Complexity is caused by uncertainly about future. Uncertainly and available information are inversely correlated. If uncertainly is high, information available is low and vice versa. If complexity experienced is more, information required is more as it implies that the manager has less information on hand for decision-making and vice versa. Size and complexity are positively correlated. Larger the size of an organisation, larger is the complexity that decision-makers face in organisations. Information plays a crucial role in all kinds of organisations. It brings clarity to thoughts. Such clarity results in better decisions and actions. Decision-making is a major activity in any organisation. It requires a lot of relevant information.

In the past information reporting in business firms and organisations was not as frequent as it is today. Internal reporting was carried out manually and hence it involved a lot of paper work. The reports were prepared periodically like half yearly, quarterly and monthly. The reports gave limited and delayed information on management performance. The required data is collected each time when a report is to be prepared. But, with computerised information systems, data is collected routinely and stored for future use.

Initially, computers were used to prepare payroll and inventory management. Later, applications were developed for almost every information need in organisations. Different information systems like transaction processing system, office automation, information reporting system, decision support system, and expert system were developed for organisational implementation. The term 'management information system' is used to mean broadly all these information systems. Information systems designed to provide information needed for effective decision making by managers, are called management information systems. The objective of MIS is to provide management with accurate and timely information necessary for decision making.

Need for Information Systems

Every business firm has three types of flows — physical flow, finance flow and information flow. Physical flow is represented by the raw materials moving through the production processes into finished goods. It flows from raw material producer — manufacturer — distributor — wholesaler — retailer chain to the consumer. Money flows from consumer to retailer, wholesaler, producer and raw material producer. Finance flow, thus, is a reverse flow. Information flow tracks the other two flows and supports all operations of a firm.

If finance is the life blood of business, management information system is the nervous system of business. When a business firm is small in size, its operations are in a limited area and the owner-manager will know almost everything about his business. But, growth brings complexity. Organisational structure undergoes major change. Ownership and management are separated. Owners and managers have to depend on reported information. Complexity calls for information to understand and solve problems.

Planning, coordination and control are essential functions of a manager. Decision making is another pervasive function in organisations. These are all information intensive activities. Nothing gets done in the absence of relevant information. In the absence of information, organisations suffer paralysis.

In an organisation, there are many centres of information generation. There are cost centres, revenue centres and investment centres in any business organisation. Cost centre accumulates cost. For example, each machine centre is a cost centre. It uses raw materials and converts raw materials into finished or semi finished goods. At every stage, it adds to cost. Revenue centre besides incurring cost earns revenue as well. It is responsible for both cost and revenue. Investment centre takes decisions on asset acquisition also that generates revenue in future.

Each centre generates a lot of data and information. Each one communicates the information with many other centres in the organisation and some with even information centres outside the organisation. Thus viewed, any business firm is a network of information centres. This information is critical for coordination and control of business firms. Planning requires forecast. Forecasting needs a lot of data about the phenomenon to be predicted. Control is a process of minimising the negative deviation of the actual from the planned outcome.

Information systems generate the required information and supplies it to the users in time to enable decisions or actions to be taken. In the absence of the right information, it is nearly impossible to run business firms.

Business organisations always had some kind of information systems, though manual and mostly informal. But the significance of information system was not fully recognised until the advent of computers with incredible processing capabilities. The computer was initially used to process accounting transactions and this function was called electronic data processing (EDP). Gradually other transactions and data processing operations were also computerised. Later the EDP department started to generate periodic standardised reports to operating managers for effective planning and control activities. When the EDP department went beyond the routine data processing operations and began to support managers with information to locate and fix problems, it came to be called computer-based information system or management information system. Management information system has now become largely formal, and an important field of study.

Information system generates information from data. Data is in the form of raw material and it is subjected to some manipulation to generate useful information. If a system generates information for managerial use in planning and control, it is called management information system (MIS). Managers at all levels of the organisation require a steady flow of information for effective and efficient functioning. But they are not to be flooded with irrelevant and unnecessary information. It is the function of management information system to determine the information needs of decision makers in the organisation in advance and to meet such needs by the provision of timely, relevant and reliable information. Management information is reported on an exceptional basis to facilitate taking managerial decisions or actions.

The following example will help us in understanding the concept of information and information system.

Mr. Raju, a long-time customer, rings up Mr. Hari, Sales Manager of a large pharmaceutical company located in Chennai and asks him for supplying 5000 vials of insulin the same day. Mr. Hari does not know how much insulin he has in stock. He tells Mr. Raju to call after 15 minutes, as he wants tó check the stock before confirming the order. Mr. Hari sends his sales officer to ascertain the stock of insulin. Mr. Raju calls Mr. Hari again after 30 minutes, but Mr. Hari cannot give an answer as he is yet to get the stock details of insulin and the pending orders. Mr. Raju rings up Mr. Sankar, Sales Officer of another pharmaceutical company in Chennai, which is also one of Raju's suppliers, and enquires about the availability of insulin. Mr. Sankar taps in the product name into his computer and gets insulin stock and price details from the stock database. He informs Mr. Raju that he has enough stock and he can deliver the product the same day. Mr. Sankar bags the order after verifying the customer's credit status. The order is passed electronically to the despatch department. The despatch department packs the cartons and gives them to the delivery department. The sales invoice is generated and customer and stock files are updated to show the current status. Mr. Raju is informed of the time of delivery at his office.

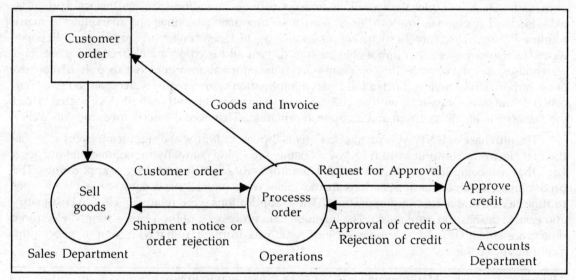

Fig. 1.1: A Section of Order Processing System

Now you can appreciate the change in decision behaviour of people in organisations with computer-based information systems and of those without them. With information available on tap, decisions can be quicker and the increased efficiency results in better performance.

The organisation needs to employ some technology for it. It should have networked computers in the Sales Department, Operations Department, Inventory Department and Accounts Department that can communicate with each other. The transaction data must be entered into the databases immediately on effecting transactions so that the data is current. The database must have files on customers to track sales, collections, credit limit sanctioned, current balances etc. Similarly, data on inventories, orders pending delivery, production schedules, etc. must be available in the database. There must be applications (programs) that can generate this kind of information for managerial use. Otherwise, Mr. Sankar cannot confirm the order for fulfilment immediately.

EVOLUTION OF MIS

Information system is as old as recorded human history. The earliest use of information system so far discovered was in a Sumerian temple way back in the third millennium B.C. The Sumerians used clay tablets for recording receipts and issues of grain to individuals out of temple grain store. The data storage requirement was little in those days. Information system had its fast growth in the last few centuries. The Industrial Revolution gave it a great fillip. Thereafter business started growing and along with growth, business complexity also increased. Modern systems of state administration also required the business of keeping accounts and reporting to various groups interested in the business. More commercial laws were enacted to bring control over business and industry. Accounting systems, fast growth of organisations, professionalism, and advances in information technology among others have ensured the fast growth of information systems in the recent past.

Until a few hundred years ago all businesses were mostly local and small in operations. A single individual performed all activities by himself. He procured goods, stored them for a while and exchanged or sold them to others. There was practically no need for record keeping. He knew how much of stock he had, how much surplus he had made etc. But over the years business grew in size and complexity: from sole trading firms to global corporations, from one or two commodities to several thousand products, from localised operations to global operations with production facilities and marketing in many countries! The chief executive of such a big corporation has to depend on reports, mostly periodic paper reports, for information. It is impossible for him to visit all his corporation's facilities, plants and warehouses, etc., and observe things for himself. It is the information system that keeps him informed of his corporation's activities. Such a full-fledged information system requires an organised system to collect data at source measured with precision, process it immediately and keep all files updated to feed the managers with most current and accurate information. That needs massive investment as well.

The purchase of UNIVAC I by the US Census Bureau in 1951 was a significant event as it was the first electronic computer produced by a business machine company for commercial purpose. Until that year computers were used only in laboratories for scientific and defence applications. The predominant commercial applications in the 1950s were payroll processing, billing and other routine clerical and accounting operations. These applications were relatively easy to cost-justify and easy to design and implement. The business data processing of the 1950s is termed electronic data processing (EDP) and later the word 'electronic' was dropped from it with computer becoming a commonplace thing.

Period	Major Focus	Main Functions
1950s - 1960s	EDP	Transaction Processing, record keeping and accounting
1960s - 1970s	IRS	Information Reporting
1970s - 1980s	DSS	Decision Support
1980s - 1990s	EIS & KBS	Special Information needs of top management and use of artificial intelligence for problem solving

Fig. 1.2: Changing Role of Information Systems

During the 1960s great advances took place in hardware and software such as development of high level languages and huge and fast access secondary storage devices. These advances led to the development of management information system and it became widespread during the late 1960s. This system was later referred to as information reporting system as it was mainly producing reports for managerial purposes.

During the 1970s further advances in hardware and software, such as microcomputers, interactive display devices, user-friendly software and improvements in database technology, paved the way for decision support system. Another development of this period was the increasing appearance of office automation technologies that included word processing, desktop publishing, and electronic mail among others. During the 1980s information technology gained much in importance as a strategic resource. In the past two decades, information technology has brought about dramatic changes in communication and business processes so much that they have changed lifestyles of people worldwide very significantly.

The executives of firms were still not happy with the IRS, MIS and DSS. They wanted systems exclusively designed for them. That led to the development of executive information system. It contained database, and analytical and presentation tools required to make relevant information available to the executives of firms. It provides critical information to executives like corporate and business level performance, competitor moves and consequences, economic and industry environmental changes and their effects etc. for strategic planning.

Another great change was happening in the computing industry with the introduction of artificial intelligence. Expert systems and knowledge management systems were developed using artificial intelligence capabilities. The expert system provides expert advice anytime the executive wants it in its domain. Similarly, knowledge management systems support capturing and managing valuable knowledge inside firms. Such systems facilitate knowledge sharing among employees about best industry practices, best ways of customer problem handling etc.

Another major development in information systems domain was the emergence of enterprise resource planning systems (ERP). A common database formed the core of such monolithic information system. It captures and stores all transaction data and allows easy access to data and sharing of data across functions. The package contains many modules for firms to choose from and install. It is a massive software package and addresses all transaction processing needs in a firm. With a common database and easy access to data from any function or department in a firm, it seamlessly integrates an organisation.

GROWTH OF MANAGEMENT INFORMATION SYSTEM

Management Information System (MIS) as a discipline is a study of generation, storage and communication of information and its impact on people and organisations. It is concerned with the organisation and its functions. The discipline is influenced by a number of other related disciplines such as computer science, management science, political science, organisational theory, sociology, psychology and operations research. The fast growth of MIS in the last few decades has been largely due to the following factors:

1. Growth of management theory and techniques.
2. Growth of management accounting and its applications in business.
3. Changes in the production and distribution methods and the consequent changes in organisational structure.
4. Development of Management Science (Operations Research).
5. Introduction of computer into business data processing and the advances in information technology.
6. Growth of the Internet and popularity of World Wide Web (WWW).

Management Theory and MIS

Business management is a profession calling for sharp skills of various kinds like problem solving skills, interpersonal skills, etc. Management is the single most important factor in business success. A lot of theories have been written about management seeking to impart right kind of theoretical understanding to the future managers to grapple with daunting problems. A plethora of management techniques has been developed to solve management problems. Modern managers require information that helps them in locating and fixing problems before they arise. They have to act proactively for that. The right kind of information equips them in their pursuit of business excellence. MIS is oriented towards achieving management goals and objectives. MIS derives its strategy from business strategy and backs achievement of business goals with IS capabilities.

Management Accounting and MIS

Management accounting has a repertoire of tools and techniques for managers to analyse financial data, past and projected, for making right decisions. It projects trends in costs and prices, calculates profitability of products, analyses product mix profitability and meets financial information needs. These tools and techniques are widely used in MIS.

Organisation Structure and MIS

Business growth necessitated changes in the structure of business firms from simple to complex ones with proper checks and balances. Sole trader was sole owner and manager of business when small size was the order of the day. Later ownership was separated from management. When owners' managerial skills proved inadequate to manage business they hired managers. Several layers of management were created to adequately supervise and control business. From single owner/single employee firm to millions of owners' and millions of employees' firm, the transition brought about radical changes in the structure and reporting requirements of organisations. MIS has become an integrating force in modern organisations by facilitating free flow of information throughout the multi-layered organisations.

Organisations are created for certain purposes and achieving these purposes requires bringing people together to work for common goal. The purpose necessitates some production and distribution activities to be undertaken and these production and distribution functions generally decide the nature and size of organisations. Thus the organisational purpose is the starting point for organisation structure design. The structure design takes into account such factors as the kind of processing facilities, resources and people required for the effective functioning of the organisation. Apart from the internal factors, there are a number of external factors which are also important in organisational structure design such as the economic, political, cultural and competitive forces. For effective management of the organisation, several layers of management have to be created and supported with information and data analysis facilities. The more the number of layers, the more the complexity of organisations. Greater the complexity, greater is the role of MIS.

MIS has a crucial role in keeping the organisation integrated by providing facilities for information exchanges. It takes care of information flows, up and down the management hierarchy besides the lateral and external flows. It collects data extensively and generates meaningful information for specified end-users. At every higher level of the hierarchy such information is summarised to meet specific information needs of users and with each such summarisation at higher levels the breadth of information gets widened.

MIS structure in organisations depends on the role assigned to it and the level of sophistication reached by it. In a large organisation with a full fledged information system the MIS may be given a functional subsystem status, as production or marketing is, with the Chief Information Officer becoming a member of the top management.

Management Science and MIS

Another notable contribution to MIS came from the discipline of Management Science. The Management Science or Operations Research is the application of Mathematical and Statistical tools and techniques to business problem solving.

Management Science had impressive growth in the last century. During the World War II, many statistical tools were designed, tested and successfully employed in military warfare. After the war, the Statistical and Mathematical tools were applied in business for greater efficiency of operations. Management Science or Operations Research required file keeping on every significant data item and, thus, reinforced the role of MIS in business management.

MIS extensively employs Management Science concepts, tools and techniques such as linear programming, inventory modelling, queuing theory, simulation techniques, decision theory, game theory and replacement theory. Management Science supplies a variety of models and techniques, which help in designing systems that make structured decisions or assist managers in making unstructured decisions. MIS stores many models in its model base so that managers can draw upon this model base to manipulate data retrieved from the database for analysing decision situations and generating optimum solutions.

Information Technology and MIS

The computer is a tool for rapid calculations. It has massive information storage and retrieval facilities. Growth in computing technology made modern MIS possible. With its fast processing capability, information could be generated and updated without any loss of time in processing. Over the years computing power increased manifold and, wonderfully enough, cost dropped with large-scale production bringing this wonder machine within the reach of any business. Large-scale use of computers in information system resulted in accurate and speedy information leading to greater efficiency in resource use. The speed, accuracy and the retrieval facility in computer make it a pivot in modern MIS. Along side revolutionary changes taking place in information technology facilitated rapid growth of MIS. Face to face contact, control and evaluation of subordinates are essential to effective and efficient management. The advances in information technology have enabled managers to interact face to face with subordinates or superiors far away through videoconference, videophone etc. The following developments in information technology have great impact on the way business is organised and run.

1. Continuing decline in hardware prices
2. Technological advances in hardware, software and telecommunications
3. Wide spread use of microcomputers,
4. Dramatic increase in end-user computing, and,
5. Advances in database technologies and storage devices

Growth of the Internet and Popularity of WWW

The Internet has brought about revolutionary changes in communication. The WWW offers a huge repository of information accessible any time from anywhere. The Web's capability to track user preferences and habits is unparalleled in the history of data generation and communication. It has made information search quick and easy. The Internet technologies are rapidly finding applications in organisational information systems. The Web has made the Internet a global electronic marketplace. Businesses are migrating on to the Net for commerce and communication.

THEORIES OF EVOLUTION OF MIS

There are a few theories or models of evolution of information system in organisations. They give us some frameworks to understand how information systems evolved over time. The stages theory, Dickson's systems hierarchy theory and Benefit and Beneficiary Matrix are useful in this respect. Let us briefly discuss these theories.

Stages Theory of MIS Growth

One way to study the evolution of MIS is to look at the various stages of its growth within an organisation. Nolan and Dickson Model[1] analyses the growth stages of information systems in firms. This model divides life cycle of organisational information systems into six stages such as initiation, contagion, control, integration, data administration and maturity.

Stage I: Initiation

In the initial stage, computers are introduced into the organisation and a small number of people use them for some data processing needs. The organisation sets up a data processing department under its accounting department with a small number of people such as a supervisor, one data entry clerk and, sometimes, an operator. The applications computerised during this stage are highly structured and labour intensive like payroll processing, accounts receivable, accounts payable, general ledger etc. System development is characterised by trial and error methods. Systems analysis and design uses some crude tools and project implementation always took more time than the estimated one. The staff of the data processing department is learning about the potential of new technology. The users do not know what to expect from the system and hence are not dissatisfied with what system support they are getting in the initiation stage.

Stage II: Contagion

The contagion stage is a period of unbridled growth. The number of users and applications multiply and costs rise rapidly. Specialists, who are Mathematicians or technology oriented, handle the computers in this stage. The users get increasingly enthusiastic about the uses of information systems. They demand more applications. The computer department in this stage is called EDP Department. The EDP department gets more attention. EDP staff makes tall claims about the potential of information systems and of even information systems replacing managers.

Stage III: Control

This stage is characterised by missed deadlines and cost overruns of information system projects. Senior managers take control of EDP function and EDP budgets are closely scrutinized. The user community becomes comfortable with sophisticated technology. They demand more sophisticated applications.

EDP function gets a new name Management Information system and is assigned a manager to the function. Better controls are introduced on applications and uses leading to more efficient use and cost effectiveness.

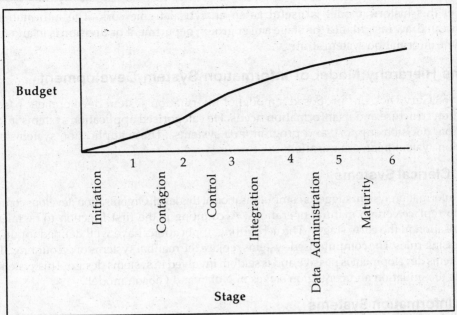

Fig. 1.3: Stages of Information System

Stage IV: Integration

MIS function gets centralised. The centralisation of MIS function results in data and systems integration. The DBMS and fourth generation languages (4GLs) facilitated the integration of data systems. The cost of hardware and software falls and t he organisation acquires microcomputers and microcomputer based software. Spreadsheet applications become popular with users in addition to developing their own applications using 4GLs.

Management Information System becomes Information System and a separate Department is created with more decentralised structure. Information System Manager's power gets weakened during this stage as users become aware of the potential of information systems and develop their own applications. Both users and information system department initiate system development during this period.

Stage V: Data Administration

During this stage, information gets recognised as an organisational resource and information resource management gains in importance. Systems are designed to give organisation-wide access to information so that information resources are more efficiently used. The user gets more control over information system and is responsible for the use of information resources.

Stage VI: Maturity

At this stage, information is recognised as a strategic resource and the organisation develops an information systems strategy to support corporate strategy. The information systems manager becomes Chief Information Officer (CIO). The CIO becomes part of senior management and guides the organisation in using information technology for gaining competitive advantage.

The model is dated. A new organisation does not go through these stages now. It can develop sophisticated information systems with the latest hardware and software to meet its information needs. Yet this historic model is useful as an analytical framework. The information system managers can draw insight into the stage a user group, department or division is in and to develop appropriate information system strategy.

Systems Hierarchy Model of Information System Development

In 1968 Gary Dickson[2] proposed a model of information system development based on the organisation structure and its information needs. He categorised application systems into clerical, information, decision support, and programmed systems. These application systems constitute information system in an organisation.

Level 1. Clerical Systems

The information system suggests computerisation at this level. Organisation develops computerised systems to replace certain manual operations. Accounting is the first function to be taken up for computerisation in the early stages. The accounting applications have well defined inputs, outputs and processing rules. The computerised systems replace the manual systems of accounting. The users' role in systems development is passive and is seldom involved in systems design. This system roughly represents the initiation and contagion stages in Nolan and Gibson model.

Level 2. Information Systems

Information system does not generate any information at this level. The system provides summarised data to the managers who, in turn, convert it into information for control or decision-making. The system stores and retrieves data on request by managers. The user plays only a minor role in systems development. This level represents the control stage in Nolan and Gibson model.

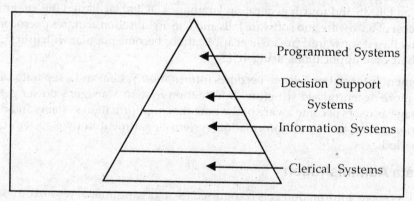

Fig. 1.4: Systems Hierarchy

Level 3. Decision Support Systems

At this level, applications are developed to address decision problems. The Application systems at this level are interactive manager-machine systems. They provide facilities to decision makers to analyse data using models to arrive at better solutions for unstructured problems. Decision making at this level is less structured. It involves some fixed decision rules and heuristic inputs. The system stores the decision rules and the manager provides the heuristics into the decision making process. The system does not make decisions but facilitate decision-making. The manager arrives at the decision after many iterative interactions with the system. The user managers and the information systems professionals develop the decision support systems jointly.

Level 4. Programmed Systems

These systems help in arriving at decisions after applying a set of decision rules. Artificial Intelligence concepts are used to develop these programmed systems. Information systems manager becomes a member of top management. He advices the top management on ways to strategically use information systems to gain competitive advantage for the organisation. The programmed systems require the information systems manager to be very proactive.

Benefit/Beneficiary Matrix

Cyrus Gibson and Michael Hammer[3] developed this model. It uses a domain scheme to categorize an organisation's need for information systems.

Domain 1: Domain 1 contains functional units as the beneficiaries and efficiency and effectiveness as the benefits.

Domain 2: Individual users are the beneficiaries in Domain 2. Individual managers define their information needs to improve their decision effectiveness. Managers use spreadsheet to improve their decisions. Clerical workers use tools like word processing to improve speed and accuracy.

Beneficiary / Benefits	IT as a Strategic Advantage weapon		
	Individual	Functional Units	Whole organisation
Efficiency Effectiveness Transformation	Domain 2	Domain 1	Domain 3

Fig. 1.5: Benefit/Beneficiary Matrix

Domain 3: The potential of information systems to create external linkages and strengthening such linkages is recognised. The strategic use of information systems transforms the organisation internally and externally. Organisations use information systems to gain strategic advantage. For example, online processing of transactions creates linkages for customers with sales, production and shipping.

Use of Benefit/Beneficiary Matrix

The matrix captures the evolutionary development of information systems in an organisation. It points out the possibility of strategic transformation of organisation using information systems. The matrix enables a manager to position the problem in one of the nine cells in the matrix and to focus on appropriate technology to solve the problem.

Beneficiary / Benefits	Individual	Functional	Whole organisation
Efficiency	Task mechanisation	Process automation	Boundary expansion
Effectiveness	Work improvement	Functional enhancement	Service enhancement
Transformation	Role expansion	Functional redefinition	Product innovation

Fig. 1.6: Use of Benefit/Beneficiary Matrix

MIS Processes

MIS is a discipline that deals with information generation, storage and its communication and use.

Its processes can broadly be classified as:

Data-related process: Management process needs relevant information. Large organisations need large amount of information. Data is the raw material for Information. Information needs specify data needs. Once, data required is determined, data sources have to be identified. A process for data capturing, cleaning, structuring and storing data is to be put in place for routine data cycles. Creation and population of databases is a key task in this area.

Storage related: Data is a reusable resource. It can be used again and again. Larger the data, more is the value of information generated from it. Therefore, each data item must be appropriately stored. The storage should facilitate retrieval. Databases are created to store data into tables. Database management systems facilitate data storage and retrieval.

Information related process: Information is processed data. Each information need, if anticipated at the design stage of information system, can be met from the organisation's databases. Each information need calls for a relevant data set. The relevant data set is drawn from the database or databases and it is processed into appropriate information product like enquiry response, its report etc.

Security related: Data and information resources have to be properly protected against accidental or wanton destruction. Natural calamities like earthquake, flood etc. can cause loss of data. Deliberate attempts to access data without authorization are also a cause for concern. It may be to cause destruction of vital data or misuse of such data may cause damage to the organisations. Hence, adequate security measures have to be taken to protect sensitive data and information resources of organisations.

Communication-related: Information is structured into some forms like report. The information is to be communicated to the user who has requested for such information. It is only when information reaches the user in the right time, right form and right measure, the requester can act on that information and generate value from it for the organisation. Communication enables value creation from information use.

Usage related: Value of information depends on its use. If that right information is supplied to the user, he can apply the information to use. Such usage of information generates value for the organisation. Hence, adequate infrastructure should be created and made available for the people to access information and use it. To encourage such use of information, the information products must be designed in such a way that it entirely meets the information needs of such information users.

Definition of MIS

MIS is a man-machine system that produces information for use in managerial problem solving and decision-making. A full-fledged MIS provides for capturing of data at source with desirable accuracy and processing them to generate information in a usable form for managers. The purpose of management information is to highlight a situation requiring managers' attention and action. The system collects data at source about every transaction in every area of activity and stores them for present or future use. The data items are processed and the information is either stored or communicated to the users.

All management functions require a steady stream of information to enable managers to be informed of the organisation and its environment. Without it, the planning and control activities will break down. Management information system ensures that the information flows in the organisation are unhindered and every authorised user is supplied with the information he needs from the system.

Davis and Olson[4] define management information system as "an integrated, user-machine system for providing information to support operations, management, and decision-making functions of an organisation. The system utilises computer hardware and software; manual procedures; models for analysis, planning, control and decision-making, and a database".

Jerome Kanter[5] defines it as "a system that aids management in making, carrying out and controlling decisions".

Robert J. Thierauf and George W. Raynolds[6] define MIS concept as " a collection of subsystems and related program parts or modules that are interconnected in a manner which fulfils the information requirements necessary to plan, organise, direct and control business activities. It is a system for producing and delivering timely information that will support management in accomplishing its specific tasks in an enterprise".

Management information system is an information technology project implemented for collecting, processing, storing and disseminating data in the form of information needed to carry out the functions of management. Information system generates information from data. Data is in the form of raw material. It is not useful in that form. So it has to be made useful by applying procedures to generate information. The raw data is manipulated using arithmetic operations, sorting, grouping, summarising etc. The outcome from data processing is information.

If a system generates information for managerial use in planning and control, it is called management information system (MIS). Managers at all levels of an organisation require a steady flow of information for effective and efficient functioning. But they are not to be flooded with irrelevant and unnecessary information. It is the function of management information system to determine the information needs of decision makers and other information users in the organisation in advance and to meet such needs by the provision of timely, relevant and reliable information. Management information is reported on an exceptional basis to facilitate taking managerial decisions or actions.

MIS: Different Views

MIS has been viewed both in a narrow sense and in a broad sense. In the narrow sense, it is a component of the information system that meets the requirements of middle and lower levels of management. It produces reports, periodic and ad hoc, for these managers to achieve optimum use of resources. It corresponds to information reporting system in this sense.

The broader approach to MIS accommodates electronic data processing, process control systems, office automation systems, decision support systems, expert systems, executive information systems and other knowledge based systems. It draws heavily on management theory, industrial engineering, operations research, computer science and accounting. As per this view, MIS encompasses all the above information systems. This book takes the second approach to MIS for discussion.

Functions of MIS

The Management Information Department in an organisation provides a variety of services relating to computer and telecommunications services, application software design and development, and software training to user departments. These services encompass personal computers, networks, printers, servers, and more. The MIS department consults with other departments to analyse and select proper IT solutions for specific applications, provides internet access, computer training and support, and mobile computing solutions for user departments. Some of the specific funcations are:

- Data gathering and storage
- Data processing
- Information reporting
- Information support to users
- Communication of information
- Database design and maintenance
- Network design and maintenance, and,
- Protection of information resources.

Role of MIS

Organisations are created for certain purposes and achieving these purposes requires bringing people together to work for common goal. The purpose necessitates some production and distribution activities to be undertaken and these production and distribution functions generally decide the nature and size of organisations. Thus, the organisational purpose is the starting point for organisation structure design. The structure design takes into account such factors as the kind of processing facilities, resources and people required for the effective functioning of the organisation. Apart from the internal factors, there are a number of external factors which are also important in organisational structure design such as the economic, political, cultural and competitive forces. For effective management of the organisation, several layers of management have to be created and supported with information and data analysis facilities. The more the number of layers, the more the complexity of organisations. Greater the complexity, greater is the role of MIS.

MIS has a crucial role in keeping the organisation integrated by providing facilities for information exchanges. It takes care of information flows, up and down the management hierarchy besides the lateral and external flows. It collects data extensively and generates meaningful information for specified end-users. At every higher level of the hierarchy such information is summarised to meet specific information needs of users and with each such summarisation at higher level the breadth of information gets larger.

MIS structure in organisations depends on the role assigned to it and the level of sophistication reached by it. In a large organisation with a full-fledged information system, the MIS may be given a functional subsystem status, as production or marketing is, with the Chief Information Officer becoming a member of the top management.

Objectives of MIS

The overarching objective of MIS is to ensure long-term survival of the organisation. The system handles data, information and knowledge which are critical resources for effective decision-making and control of operations. The other specific objectives of MIS in any organisation are:

- To build competency of the organisation
- To enable the organisation to gain strategic advantage
- To reduce cost of operations and improve employee productivity
- To enhance decision effectiveness

- To improve team collaboration
- To increase organisation's reach, and,
- To integrate the organisation through seamless information flows and enable effective management of its operations.

To achieve the above objectives an MIS of any organisation has to do the following:

- Aligning MIS objectives with organisation's objectives
- Identifying need for information and system support for users
- Designing and implementing systems to meet such needs
- Business process redesigning to radically improve business efficiency
- Developing and populating databases with transaction data
- Collecting relevant data, in addition to transaction data, from inside or outside the organisation to support higher level information needs
- Generating information to meet user needs to make effective decisions or planning or control actions.
- Communicating such information and extending data analysis facility to decision makers in the organisation.
- Designing and implementing security measures for protecting data and other resources of the system

Components of MIS

The components of MIS are hardware, software, data, people and networks. These components when assembled into a system creates an organisation-wide information machine that can meet information needs of management and operating personnel.

Hardware resources: The hardware resources include central processing units and peripherals like input-output devices and storage devices.

Software resources: These resources include system software, application software and procedures.

People resources: These include users, system programmers, analysts, designers, system administrators, database administrators and system manager.

Network resources: These include network infrastructure and communication technologies. Information systems are integrated with network resources. Networks and communication technologies are vital these days for communication and commerce.

Data resources: These resources are central to information systems. Every transaction that an organisation carries out generates data. It has to be stored for future use. Information is generated from data. Data resources are captured, structured and stored into compact databases for easy retrieval.

CHARACTERISTICS OF MIS

Management information system has a number of characteristic features. The purpose of MIS is to enhance organisational effectiveness through information support. It derives its goals from organisational goals. Yet, it has acquired a strategic dimension since the middle of 1980s. To guide strategy formulation for gaining competitive advantage, the information systems need to be very sophisticated. Jerome Kanter[7] identifies some of the features of MIS, which are briefly discussed below.

1. **MIS is management oriented/directed:** MIS is designed to meet the information needs of the management at all levels so that the organisational objectives are achieved. Since MIS requires heavy planning and investment, management is deeply involved in the design, implementation and maintenance of the system.

2. **Business driven:** MIS is a support function. Its purpose is to meet information needs of the organisation and its stakeholders. The business philosophy and goals of the organisation drive MIS. The information system strategy is derived from the corporate strategy. So, MIS is business driven.

3. **Integrated system:** MIS views organisation's information needs from a system's point of view. It blends together databases of all subsystems of the business system and through information interchange integrates the organisation.

4. **Avoids redundancy in data storage:** Since MIS is an integrated system, it avoids unnecessary duplication and redundancy in data gathering and storage. Since some data redundancy is desirable, the purpose is not to eliminate redundancy but to minimise it.

5. **Heavy planning:** Design and implementation of MIS require detailed and meticulous planning of such activities as acquisition and deployment of hardware and software, hiring and training of personnel, planning data processing operations, information presentation and feed back.

6. **Common database:** The database is central to any information system. It stores transaction data for present and future uses. Applications access this database for relevant data to process transactions or to generate information. The system maintains general databases so that any functional subsystem can access the database.

7. **Flexibility and ease of use:** The MIS is designed flexible enough to accommodate new requirements. The system is easy to operate so that not much computer skills are required on the part of the user to access database for information or for carrying out special analysis of data.

8. **Distributed systems:** Most organisations have their offices, sales outlets, etc. geographically spread over a wide area. These offices work mostly independently of its headquarters. But information has to be routinely exchanged between offices. Most big organisations develop distributed systems to meet the information processing requirements of their various constituents.

9. **Information as a resource:** MIS views information as an organisational resource. Organisations centralise information resources for providing greater access to them. They design systems to share information resources across functions and offices for increasing the return form investment in information resources.

SUBSYSTEMS OF MIS

The management information system is a federation of many subsystems. The subsystems can be seen as organisational function subsystems or basic activity subsystems. Management information system has several functional subsystems depending upon the stage of its growth and the role assigned to it. If an organisation structures its MIS department functionally, it may have subsystems as shown below.

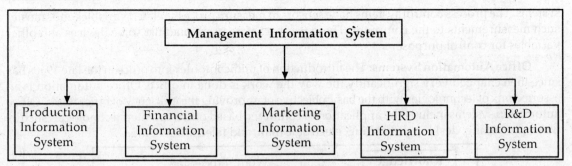

Fig. 1.7: Functional Subsystems of MIS

The production information system tracks production data, generates production-related reports and provides them to target users. Similarly marketing information system gathers data about sales, stock, distribution costs, promotion costs, media effectiveness and so on. It meets the information requirements of marketing managers primarily and provides access for other managers to its database.

The financial information system keeps data on customer credit, accounts payable, accounts receivable, cash management, fund allocation, etc. HRD information system is concerned with the personnel functions such as hiring and training of personnel, fixation and payment of wages and salary etc. Similarly, R&D information system takes care of data on R&D activities.

Basic Subsystems of MIS

The basic subsystems of MIS are transaction processing subsystem, information reporting subsystem, decision support system and office automation subsystem. They may also include process control systems and knowledge based systems.

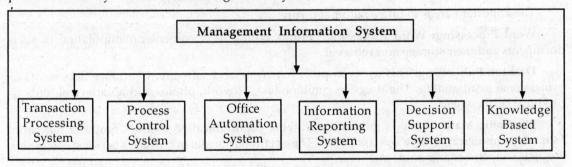

Fig: 1.8: Basic Activity Subsystems of MIS

Transaction Processing System: The Transaction Processing System (TPS) is developed to support day-to-day operations. The system maintains detailed records of all transactions and enables mangers to track the organisation's activities. It comprises routine data processing operations that include accounts receivable, accounts payable, inventory control, payroll processing, customer order processing and many others. These were the major applications of computer during the 1950s.

Process Control Systems: In process industries such as those producing cement, steel, paper and chemical products, the physical production flow is controlled by computerised process control systems. The process control systems have sensors to measure process-related variables and transfer such measurements to the computer. These feedbacks are used to adjust some devices and other variables for control purpose.

Office Automation Systems: The introduction of minicomputer into office in the late 1960s has since then changed very significantly the way the work is done in office. Office automation is an assorted mix of technologies with the basic objective of improving the efficiency of office work. Office automation systems include the application of computer-based office-oriented technologies such as word-processing, desktop publishing, electronic mail, and teleconferencing.

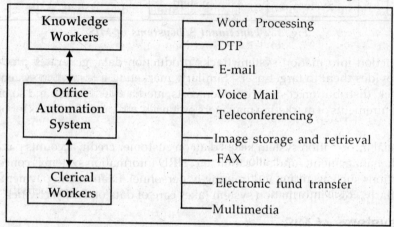

Fig. 1.9: Office Automation Systems: Tools and Systems

Source: Modified from Gupta, Uma G., Management Information Systems, A Managerial Perspective, Galgotia Publications, New Delhi, 1998 p. 60.

The important areas in office automation are:

Word Processing: Word processing permits typing in documents, manipulation of such documents and their storage and retrieval.

Desktop Publishing: This uses computer hardware and software to produce documents of professional print quality. The user can combine text, artwork, photos and a variety of fonts to produce the document.

Electronic Mail: E-mail is the fastest growing communication mode. Computer networks facilitate communication between computers. The electronic transfer of messages between computers is quick, convenient and economic.

Facsimile (FAX): The FAX machine sends and receives text and images. The text and images are converted into digital form and at the receiving end it is converted back into text and image form.

Voice Mail: Voice mail sends digitised speech over phone to a mailbox and the message is digitally stored at the receiving end, which can be accessed using telephone.

Teleconferencing: It is the use of telecommunications technology to see people face to face without their physical proximity to each other. The participants gather in specially equipped rooms capable of simultaneous audio and video transmission.

Spreadsheet: Electronic spread sheet permits easy data entry and analysis. Spreadsheet allows storage, analysis and presentation of data. It has a large number of statistical, mathematical and financial tools to analyse data and charting tools to present data.

Image Storage and Retrieval Systems: These systems convert paper documents into electronic files and images for easy storage and retrieval.

Calendar: Calendar software enables users to schedule activities and events. It can also create 'To Do List' and reminders.

Electronic Fund Transfer: It is a facility to transfer funds between accounts of customers with banks. At the point of sale counter customer presents his card and keys in a code and if the card and code tally; the bill amount is transferred to the account of the retailer and the customer's account is updated.

Database Management: Database Management system provides electronic storage of large amount of data. Tables can be created, modified and updated as and when needed. With database management system, it is possible to generate reports, to run queries to get information and to view lists meeting some criteria (like a list of customers with annual transaction value of above ₹ 5 lakh and without any payment default).

Multimedia Systems: The multimedia systems store, retrieve and process different types of data such as text, graphics, audio, video and animation. They facilitate information storage, retrieval and presentation in a variety of impressive ways.

Information Reporting Systems

This system generates reports in pre-planned formats and summarises the data generated by the transaction processing subsystem in creating these reports. These reports usually contain routine summary and control information. They may be classified into regular, *ad-hoc* or exception reports.

Regular Reports

These reports are periodical, say, weekly, monthly, quarterly, etc., and are usually associated with a cycle of activities such as payroll.

Adhoc Reports

These reports are not planned in advance and have to be designed and produced depending upon user-requests.

Exception Reports

These reports present only exceptional matters to the manager. They provide enough details to the manager to apprise him/her of the problem and permit intervention.

TPS and IRS – A Comparison

The TPS generates raw data as a result of transaction processing. For example, when stores are requested by various production centres, processing these requests generates data like the quantity issued to various production centres. Analysis of this data results in information that is presented in reports to managers for use. IRS uses this data for generation of information.

Decision Support System (DSS)

Decision Support System assists managers in making unstructured decisions. The system enables them to interact with the database, model base and other software and generate the information they need rather than depend on some reports produced according to some planned information needs. Please see Chapter Six for more details.

Other Knowledge-based Systems

The other knowledge-based systems include expert systems, executive information systems and business intelligence systems.

Expert Systems

Expert systems have evolved out of the work on artificial intelligence over the past several years and are finding increasing applications in business. The system gathers together a database of knowledge or expertise to offer advice or solution for problems in a particular area by emulating the abilities and judgements of human experts. It accumulates all the expert knowledge in a given area so that the advice or solution offered is better than that of a single consultant or expert. It guides users through problems by asking them a set of questions about the problem. The answers given are checked against the rule base in the system to draw appropriate conclusions from the problem situation. Expert systems are particularly useful in dealing with unstructured problems.

Intelligent Information System

Intelligent information system is specially designed to meet managers' information needs mainly for long-range planning. The term 'intelligence' in this context does not include business espionage. Intelligent information system systematically gathers and analyses data about:

- social and cultural trends
- political environment,
- legal environment
- regulatory environment
- economic environment
- competition in the industry
- technology
- products and
- markets.

This database is expanded to include data on such aspects in many countries to enable the managers to track investment opportunities globally. Most of such data is available from the publication of Government agencies, industry and trade associations, business journals, newspapers and market research reports. The system collects data from internal and external sources and is organised as either a formal or an informal system. The key element here is the specification of information needs for planning and budgeting. Depending upon these needs various analyses of data are performed to reveal patterns and trends to guide the long range planning. This area has been well taken care of by the executive information systems.

EXECUTIVE INFORMATION SYSTEMS (EIS)

The executives are the managerial personnel at the top of the management pyramid who are responsible for fixing organisational goals and guiding the business organisation towards such goals. They formulate strategic plans and broad organisational policies. The decisions of executives have great impact on organisations. Errors are costly and may end up in business failure. The information requirements of executives are different from other levels of decision-makers in the organisation.

Executive Information System is to support executive decision making in the organisation. Most executives have a network of people to collect information. Secretarial assistance is also available to them to gather data, arrange meetings with experts, etc. They have staff members to analyse problems, evaluate alternatives and make recommendations to them. Their information requirements are dominated by external information such as regulatory information, customer information, competitor information and quality of service. The sources of information to them include telephone calls, letters, memos, reports, dailies and periodicals, and social contacts. Most of which originate outside the organisation. Organisational database is designed to meet information needs of all the people in the organisation. But it normally does not store information originating through the above sources. EIS is therefore tailored to meet information needs of the top management of the organisation.

EIS provides database support and interaction facility for the executive to try out his/her ideas and solutions. It contains special databases and model base which can provide current status, past and projected trends, model support for analysis, graphic displays, etc. It has fast response capability and greater user friendly features. One of the benefits of EIS is that the executive can access reliable information a lot more quickly. Information is stored in organisational databases but rarely such information is suitable for executive users. They may require combining information from a number of databases and also information from external databases. The EIS database is designed to meet the executive information needs. It also uses a number of presentation techniques to highlight information for executive attention.

EIS is also a solution to the problem of executive information over-load. If a decision-maker is provided with too much of irrelevant, unfocused and poorly presented information, the result is information overload. EIS provides focused and relevant information using attractive presentation techniques. It helps the executive in getting a conceptual view of business and in developing improved plans and control techniques.

INFORMATION RESOURCE MANAGEMENT (IRM)

IRM is a concept that focuses on the information that is produced by a system. Information, its availability and its usage are given primacy in IRM. Computer systems are important as generators of information. The emphasis in IRM is managerial and not technical, that is on managing information efficiently. IRM-oriented firms see information as a key resource and invest on information technology with a long-term perspective to gain a competitive advantage over rival firms. In fact, IRM is a reaction of managers to technician's dominance of information systems. The early information system specialists promised great capabilities that information systems could possess. But little effort has been devoted to ensure that every one has access to whatever information is available in the organisation and the benefit from the use justified its cost of generation, storage and communication. The department that is in need of some information may not be aware of the existence of the same information elsewhere in the organisation. So it managed to do without that information or duplicated the effort by independently generating that information.

These problems of traditional approaches have forced managers to focus on information as a resource of the entire organisation. This concept is beginning to alter attitudes towards information systems.

The features of IRM are:

- information is viewed as a resource
- it is seen as an organisational resource
- it comes from many sources, not just from traditional data processing
- its focus is on effectiveness of information use in the organisation

Information – Similarities with Other Resources

1. It has a cost
2. It has a return on investment
3. Its efficient use requires good organisation for its use.
4. There is an opportunity cost of not having information.

Differences from Other Resources

1. It can be reused indefinitely
2. The marginal cost per additional usage is low
3. It is intangible.

The IRM is a perspective; it is also an approach to organising and integrating ingredients of information system. IRM's focus in on management of these ingredients and the information of the organisation in a co-ordinated manner.

The Ingredients of IRM

All the information resources of an organisation should be within the purview of an IRM activity. These include:

- business data processing
- data management
- systems and applications development within an MIS context
- networking
- office automation and word processing
- end-user computing, and,
- information centres.

The task of IRM is to integrate and co-ordinate the above activities for the entire organisation. Thus, IRM is an all encompassing, information focused concept that involves no less than organising all aspects of the information activities and flows.

Realising the significance of IRM to the organisation, many firms have given a top berth to the chief information officer of the organisation and he/she reports directly to its chief executive officer.

Customer Relationship Management

It is an area where information and communication technology is extensively used. Websites, call centres, toll free numbers etc. are deployed to provide maximum comfort to customers. Satisfied customers bring more customers to a firm. So, it makes a lot of sense to increase the level of customer experience at every customer touch point. E-CRM is an integrated software solution to manage a firm's interactions with customers. For more details please see the chapter on Customer Relationship Management.

Supply Chain Management

Supply chain is a set of integrated and coordinated processes that are employed to fulfil customer orders at a profit to the firm and its partners. Supply chain management involves trade-offs between cost and responsiveness. Coming together of different firms in a supply chain eliminates many transaction costs. The purpose of a supply chain is to deliver more value to customers at lower costs. This results in more profits which are shared by the firms in the supply chain.

The success of a supply chain depends on reliable forecast of demand and planning supply, production and logistics operations accordingly. The tasks involved are very complex. There are a host of software solutions available for managing supply chains. For more details please see the chapter on Supply Chain Management.

ROLE OF MANAGEMENT INFORMATION SYSTEM

Information system is assigned a strategic role in the highly competitive business world. Information system is the most integrating force in an organisation. Its role has changed drastically over the years from one of reporting post mortem information for control purposes to future information for planning and forward control apart from continuing to meet other traditional information needs.

According to James O'brien[8] management information system performs three major roles such as:

(a) support to business operations,

(b) support to managerial decisions, and,

(c) gaining strategic competitive advantage.

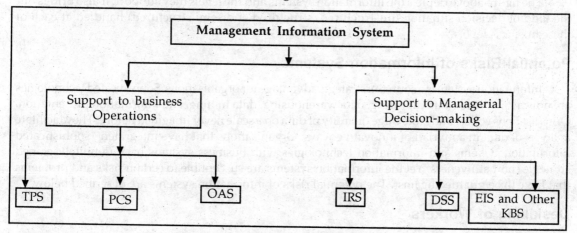

Fig. 1.10: Role of Management Information System

Source: Adapted from James A.O'Brien, "Management Information System, A Managerial End User Perspective", p. 36.

The systems which support business operations include transaction processing system (TPS), process control systems (PCS) and office automation systems (OAS).

Support to managerial decision making in the organisation is extended through information reporting systems (IRS) which is often referred to as MIS, decision support systems (DSS), executive support system (ESS) and other knowledge-based systems (KBS).

Information Systems and Management Levels

A number of information systems have evolved to support managerial functions at various levels of management. They include transaction processing system, office automation system, information reporting system (or MIS), decision support system, executive support system etc. These systems support business processes at various levels of the organisational hierarchy.

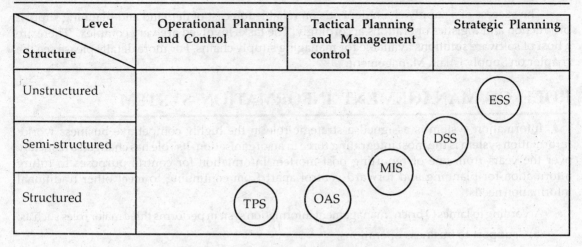

Level / Structure	Operational Planning and Control	Tactical Planning and Management control	Strategic Planning
Unstructured			ESS
Semi-structured		DSS	
	MIS		
Structured	TPS OAS		

Fig. 1.12: Information Systems and Management Levels

The figure above depicts the information systems and the levels they support. It also brings out the kind of decision situation (unstructured, structured and semi structured) handled at each of these business levels.

Potential Risks of Information Systems

Information system is a source of strategic advantage for organisations. Sophisticated technologies are now available for data capturing, data warehousing, data mining, and information presentation. Organisations collect and store huge quantity of data on a scale never imagined before. They facilitate analysis of data in a myriad of innovative ways. Organisations that have integrated sophisticated information systems and information technologies with business systems have definitely gained strategic competitiveness. Yet the information systems are susceptible to certain risks and problems that have to be guarded against. The potential risks of information systems are described below[9].

Deskilling of Workers

Information system uses innovative technologies for data processing, storage and retrieval. For example, the office automation technologies raise productivity and improve profits. It makes some of the skills of workers obsolete. Often, it results in surplus hands and the organisation finds it difficult to give them meaningful work. These workers have to be either retrained for deployment in other activities or retrenched.

Information Overload

Advances in information technologies make information generation, storage and communication much easier and quicker than before. Huge secondary and primary storage capacity comes handy for capturing and storing massive quantity of data. Online transaction processing yields huge quantity of data about customers, products and markets. The variety and quantity of information that can be generated by the information systems these days is enormous. If decision-makers are provided with the information so generated, they will not be able to digest them; it results in information overload for them.

Employee Mistrust

Information technologies have great potential and can replace routine manual jobs. The employees are sceptical about these technologies and do not cooperate in implementing them. The mistrust arises because of a fear that these technologies will eventually replace them. Since some companies use these technologies for tracking employee activities, it further increases the mistrust.

Increased Competitive Pressure

Organisations that use sophisticated information technologies are often found to be successful. They derive competitive advantage from the use of these technologies and integrate customers and suppliers more closely with their business systems. Organisations that do not employ these sophisticated technologies or less successful in integrating these technologies with business systems come under greater competitive pressure.

Poor Returns from IT Investment

Organisations originally expected good returns from investment in information technology and invested large capital in IT. Information system is only a support service. The returns have to come from the business the organisation is in. Organisations that invested large sums in IT are disappointed by the poor returns from that investment.

Challenges in Developing Information System

Developing an information system for an organisation is a difficult and challenging problem for the information system personnel. Very few organisations complete the information system projects on time and within the budget.

Security Breaches

The information system function has the responsibility to protect information system assets from theft and security breaches. Ensuring security of ever evolving information technology systems is both difficult and expensive.

Relationship between Decision-making and MIS

Decision-making is a pervasive function of management. Decisions commit resources to projects. Thus, decisions carry risk. Any decision should minimise adverse effects and maximise favourable or desirable effects. Decision-making is a process where a plan of action conceived today is to be implemented in the future to produce a desired outcome. Decision-making is always risky as the uncertain future may produce an adverse result.

Decisions are needed to solve problems or exploit opportunities. Decision situations may fall into any of the three situations: uncertain, risk or certain. The objective of decision-making in each situation is different from the others. Information helps in accurately forecasting the relevant future and enabling an organisation to devise a strategy that is the best in the given situation.

Steps in decision-making are as follows:

- Problem identification and definition
- Design of alternatives
- Evaluation of alternatives

- Choice of the best alternative
- Implementation of the decision
- Follow up.

Each step in decision-making is information intensive. An organisation may experience certain symptoms of a problem. Problem identification needs a lot of data and data analysis. MIS applications churn the data to identify useful trends and patterns in the data. Such data analysis locates the problem and helps in designing alternative solutions to the problem identified. Evaluation of alternatives needs information about the outcome from each alternative. That alternative which maximises the desired outcome is the decision to be implemented. Problem solving includes additionally implementation and follow-up.

Benefits of MIS

1. Efficiency improvement. MIS helps an organisation in achieving superior efficiency. Operating cost declines due to computer based applications. The business processes are reengineered to improve efficiency of transaction processing.

2. Better communication. MIS generates and communicates information as a routine. Users can access databases, run query and request for reports.

3. Better control over organisational processes. With MIS, it is possible to access any kind of control information. For example, a bank can generate a list of defaulters in seconds which would have taken weeks together earlier. Such timely information facilitates effective control.

4. Alters basis of competition. Information technology is a source of competitive advantage. It changes basis of competition. For example, National Stock Exchange of India became the largest stock exchange in India in a matter of a few years of its setting up. Its extensive use of information technology was the major reason for its success.

5. More effective planning: MIS improves the quality of plans by providing relevant information for sound decision-making

6. MIS reduces information overload. MIS supplies the right information to users. Users, if needed, can access the database and generate the relevant information. There is a limit to the amount of information that one can efficiently process and use. Too much of information results in information overload to the recipient. If it results in overload, information cannot benefit the organisation through appropriate decisions and actions.

7. Decentralization made possible: MIS enables an organisation to decentralize its operations and still retain effective control from head quarters.

8. Effective coordination. By ensuring free flow of information within an organisation and also between trading partners, MIS enables an organisation to effectively coordinate its operations.

9. Tracking performance. With computer-based information systems, it is possible to analyse performance of any business unit on a real-time basis.

10. Effective and timely business decisions. MIS gives a capability to business firms to track market changes and its performance in the market place enabling it to take appropriate and quick decisions.

Role of Chief Information Officer

Since information system has gained the status of a strategic tool to gain competitive advantage, it has made it a necessity to have a senior managerial staff to develop and maintain information systems in organisations. Large organisations created the position of Chief Information Officer (CIO) to head the information system function. The CIO reports directly to the president of the organisation.

The CIO is responsible for creation and maintenance of information systems at personal level, work group level and enterprise level. His tasks include cultivating a culture of productive use of information, better decision-making and gaining competitiveness through the use of information technologies. He must ensure compatibility of information systems in various departments of the organisation and train people in efficient use of information resources. His specific responsibilities include the following:

- Supervision of enterprise-wide data management, office automation systems and technical aspects of communication
- Reporting to senior management and particularly to the CEO about matters concerning information system, and,
- Active participation in the formulation of company's strategic plan and long-term policies
- Identifying and designing new strategic applications and training users in such systems for gaining greater efficiency in business processes.

Though the CIO is solely responsible for all information system activities, the co-operation of all the people inside the organisation and those outside who interact with the organisation is needed for the system to be efficient and effective.

ENTERPRISE INFORMATION SYSTEMS

The piecemeal solutions developed in the early part of the information system era for meeting information needs of decision-makers were fragmented in nature. They could not be integrated into a single system permitting free flow of information across functions and divisions of business firms.

The fragmented and functionally compartmentalised Information systems of the day are giving way to totally integrated information systems that facilitate seamless communication of information. Software systems such as ERP integrate organisations seamlessly. Within the organisation, all the functional subsystems merge into a single enterprise information system. Functional information systems lose their individual identity and they are integrated into a more elaborate enterprise wide information system. Computer networks and Internet infrastructure facilitate this integration. With an enterprise information system in place, information flows freely across functions and information truly becomes an organisational resource to guide decisions and actions.

Enterprise Information Portals

Companies develop enterprise information portals to share information resources with employees and clients. Enterprise information portals are centralised Internet-based gateways. These gateways enable a company's employees, trade partners and clients to access the company's internal knowledge base and external information resources and selected applications. The company controls access to the resources. EIP contains search, content management, collaboration, application integration, personalisation and security.

Digital Firms

Information technology is a tool that facilitates information and business processes of a firm both internally and externally. Information technology has become an essential infrastructure for doing business. For example, any new bank has to have a networked banking and Internet banking capability to enter the banking industry in the country. The new banks have set up high quality IT infrastructure and any new entrant into this industry has to match the IT infrastructure of the existing banking firms to deliver the minimum threshold level of service quality.

On top of a firm's IT infrastructure, the Internet and Internet technologies provide a cost-effective infrastructure to integrate organisations across functions, divisions and nations. Internet technologies help organisations in integrating their internal processes and external processes. This IT infrastructure enables seamless integration of the business firm with its suppliers, customers and business partners leading to the emergence of digital firms.

The digital firms can radically cut their cost of business operations and communications. These firms use Internet extensively for communication and transactions with suppliers, business partners and customers. Intranet technologies facilitate internal communication and smooth flow of information internally. More evolved digital firms use the Internet as e-commerce platform. The Internet based e-commerce helps in cutting cost of promoting business, locating customers, selling and delivering goods to customers.

Conclusion

Information system is as old as recorded human history. The introduction of computer into data processing has revolutionised the business information systems. The increase in business complexity and the capability of information systems to provide a competitive edge to the firm have made MIS an inevitable component of modern business systems. Information technology has redefined business and is radically influencing the way business is managed the world over. It has become a great strategic tool for business competence. The role of information system is becoming all pervasive. It affects activities of organisations at all levels and opens up opportunities for business growth and survival.

QUESTIONS

1. Define Management Information System?
2. What is the scope of MIS?
3. What are the basic subsystems of MIS?
4. Explain the characteristics of MIS?
5. What is DSS?
6. What is IRM?
7. What is Expert System?
8. What is the role of Executive Information System in a business firm?
9. Briefly explain the evolution of MIS?
10. Describe the various types of management information systems.
11. What is Office Automation? Describe some of the areas in office automation.
12. Describe the role of management information systems in a business organisation.
13. Explain the use of intelligent information system.
14. Explain the use of office automation technology for business management.
15. What is the role of CIO in organisations?
16. What is a digital firm? How does it use information technology?

REFERENCES

1. Nolan, Richard L. and Gibson, Cyrus F, "Managing Four Stages of EDP Growth", *Harvard Business Review*, Jan-Feb, 1974 pp. 76-78.

2. Dickson, Garry W., Management Information Systems: *Evolution and Status, in Advances in Computers,* M.Youts (ed.), Academic Press, New York, 1981.

3. Cyrus F.Gibson and Michael Hammel, "Now That the Dust Has Settled. A Clear View of the Train", Indications Vol. 2, No. 5, July 1985 Index Group Inc., Cambridge.

4. Davis, Gordon B, and Olson, Malgrethe H, *Management Information Systems*, McGraw-Hill Book Company, Singapore, 1984 p. 6.

5. Kantor, Jerome, *Managing With Information*, Prentice Hall of India, New Delhi, 1996.

6. Thierauf, Robert J. and Reynolds, George W.

7. Kantor, Jerome, *Ibid*, pp. 16-20.

8. O'Brien, James A., *Management Information System A Managerial End User Perspective*, Galgotia Publications Private .Limited, New Delhi, 1996, p. 36.

9. Gupta, Uma G., *Management Information Systems, A Managerial Perspective,* Galgotia Publications, New Delhi, 1998, pp. 23-24.

Case 1.1: First Bank

First Bank* is a leading old generation private sector bank in India with a large number of branches in India and a few offices outside the country. It implemented core banking solution (CBS) a few years back in all its branches across the country. The integrated software enabled the bank to launch innovative banking services like 'Anytime, Anywhere Banking', Internet banking and mobile banking.

The audit wing of the bank detected a fraud committed by a branch manager. He granted loans beyond his limits to a construction firm. The same property was hypothecated to the bank for multiple loans from different branches. The branch manager of the First Bank was an office bearer of the national level officers association of bank employees. He threatened audit officers not to report the irregularity. Under the manual system it was not detected nor reported. Once the data conversion and migration to CBS happened, the fraud came to light. An inquiry was ordered into the fraud. After the protracted inquiry and appeal process, it was established that the branch manager was guilty on several counts. He exceeded his powers in granting loans to the firm and influenced other branch managers to lend multiple loans to the same firm violating the loan norms. The bank's exposure to the firm was around ₹ 65 crore and the firm's operations were not comfortable financially. It was a criminal act and the management of the bank dismissed the branch manager from service.

* Name has been changed for anonymity.

Questions:

1. What are the advantages of computerisation of the bank's branches and offices?
2. How was the fraud suppressed earlier? How did it come out later?
3. Discuss the changes that accompany implementation of integrated software systems in an organisation.

2

CHAPTER

Concepts of Information

INTRODUCTION

Information is analogous to light. When light is present, objects are visible. Information presents a picture of reality to a user who is not aware of that reality. Like light, too little or too much of information vitiates the picture of reality conveyed. Information is a precious organisational resource. It is a resource like materials and money. It evolves from data and becomes knowledge for decision-makers. Its value depends on how quickly it is generated from relevant data and how fast it is used in decision and control actions. Information may have low value, moderate value and high value depending on the person using it and the purpose of use. If higher level managers use it to solve organisation wide problems, the impact is sure to be great.

In simple terms, information is processed data. 'Data' is the raw material for generating information. The data needs some processing to render it usable. When the data is processed and placed in a context, it becomes meaningful. That is, the context gives meaning to information. Removed from the context, it ceases to be meaningful or the meaning gets distorted.

The purpose of information is to reduce uncertainty about decision situations and consequences. Information is vital for survival of business firms. As the size and complexity of business unit grow, managers may increasingly rely on reported information for decisions and actions. Information helps in understanding and analysing problems and opportunities. It raises the level of confidence with which the decisions are made as it increases the domain of certainty. Since the user of information places so much trust in the information reported, generation and communication of information assume great importance.

Data and Information

Data is the result of measurements of various attributes of entities such as product, student, inventory and employee. The measurements may be recorded in alphabetical, numerical, image, voice or other forms. Thus, the raw and unanalysed numbers and facts about entities constitute data. On the other hand, information results from data sets when they are organised or structured in some meaningful ways. The processed data has to be placed in a context for it to derive meaning and relevance. Relevance in turn adds to the value of information in decisions and actions. Data processing requires some infusion of intelligence (that is, meaning, purpose and usefulness) into data to generate information. The application of intelligence may be in the form of some principles, knowledge, experience and intuition to convert data into information.

Differences between Data and Information

Though the words 'data' and 'information' are often used interchangeably, there is clear distinction between the two. Some of the major differences are as follows:

- Data is fact but information though based on data is not fact
- Data in the raw form has limited use, information has extensive use
- Data does not make sense to users, information is highly sensible
- Though information arises from data, all data does not become information. There is a lot of selective filtering of data before processing it into information
- Data is the result of routine recording of events and activities taking place. Generation of information is user-driven which is not always automatic
- Data is independent of users whereas information is user dependent. Most information reports are designed to meet anticipated information needs of a user or a group of users. That is, information for one user is very likely to be data for other users.

Knowledge and Wisdom

Knowledge represents a higher level of understanding of phenomenon. It involves rules, patterns, trends and decisions. Knowledge calls for higher level thinking and use of analytical skills.

Wisdom is distilled experience. It cannot be taught. It has to be acquired through one's own experience. It is useful in creating new knowledge.

Definition of Information

The term 'information' is a very common word and it conveys some meaning to the recipient. It is very difficult to define it comprehensively. Yet, Davis and Olson[1] give a fairly good definition. They define information as "data that has been processed into a form that is meaningful to the recipient and is of real or perceived value in current or prospective actions or decisions".

This implies that information is:

- Processed data
- It has a form
- It is meaningful to the recipient
- It has a value, and,
- It is useful in current or prospective decisions or actions.

BUSINESS DATA PROCESSING

Business data processing is concerned with abstracting meaningful information from large volumes of data. Production Manager of a company is asked by Managing Director to suggest ways of controlling production costs. For this task, details like inventory items, descriptions, quantity, supplier etc constitute data. When average consumption in quantity per unit of output, average cost of materials per unit of output, cost per unit of procuring material from each supplier etc. are meaningful information for controlling costs. Whether the message presented is data or information depends on the user and context of decision-making. For example, the information presented to the Production Manager may be data to Marketing Manager if he wants to fix price of the end-product.

He/she will need more information to fix the price like total cost of the product per unit, mark-up or margin required on sales, prices charged by competitors, cost and profit at various levels of capacity utilisation etc.

Business data processing is a major application of computers. In business data processing, huge quantity of data forms input and the processing results in collapsing the data into small quantity of meaningful information to the users. Such data processing systems need the facility to handle a number of data files simultaneously for input-output operations. The programming language COBOL was developed in the 1960s to address the needs of business data processing.

Steps in Data Processing

Once the information needs are identified, we need to follow certain steps to locate data sources, generate information and communicate it. The basic steps are:

- **Identifying the data:** Accuracy of information depends on accurate data input. Once certain information needs are determined, the data for generating that information needs to be identified. The first step in data processing, therefore, is to locate data sources for the information. Accurate, adequate and relevant data must be used as input.

- **Designing forms:** The next step is to design forms for data entry. The forms are linked to databases so that it becomes easy to enter data into the system.

- **Entering data:** Once the input forms are designed, the actual data must be keyed into the forms. Data entry personnel do this task. This task is monotonous, but the work has to be done very carefully to avoid any incorrect data.

- **Validation:** The data entered must be valid. Certain validation procedures may be built into the code so that input forms do not accept any incorrect data.

- **Storage:** The next step is to organise and store the data in appropriate databases to facilitate easy storage and retrieval of data. It should also take care of data security, particularly in a multi-user environment.

- **Processing the data:** The next step is to retrieve the appropriate data for the information required and process it. The operations to be performed to generate information depend on the nature of data and the information required. For example, if Production Manager wants only to know the quantity of stock of a particular item, it requires only a query on the database once it is populated and updated with transaction data. On the other hand, if Finance Manager is asked by the top management to suggest pruning the product mix of the company by dropping a few products, he needs to present his logic based on some meaningful analyses like contribution per unit of product, return on assets, return on investment, margin on sales etc. This requires drawing lot of sales and cost data from the database and computing various ratios etc. for the products considered for dropping.

- **Generating reports and communicating them:** The information must be meaningfully presented to the users. Each user may want the information in a particular format. So applications must be developed to generate reports for the users. The report may be presented in the form of print-out, on screen display, etc.

Data Processing and Information Processing

Data, as it arises, is ill-structured. Forms, vouchers etc. are designed to capture data at source. The captured data is structured for storage or further processing. The database is a huge repository for transaction data. Data is retrieved from database for processing it into information. A series of operations are performed on the data to generate information. The type of operation to be performed on the data like aggregation, summarisation, calculation, etc., depends on the type and quality of information required.

Information processing includes the traditional data processing as well as processing text, images, audio, video and animation. The focus of information processing is on creation of information products for users.

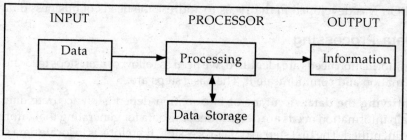

Fig. 2.1: Model of Information Generation with Storage

FEATURES OF INFORMATION

Information possesses some features or attributes that give it value and usefulness. Some of the important features of information are:

(i)   Information adds to a representation
(ii) It corrects or confirms previous information
(iii) It has surprise element or news value
(iv) It reduces uncertainty
(v)   It has value in decision-making
(vi) It is reusable

Dimensions of Information

Information has many facets and some of these facets or dimensions of interest to information system people are[2]:

• economic dimension,
• business dimension, and
• technical dimension.

The Economic Dimension

The economic dimension includes both the cost of information and its benefits from use. The cost of information consists of the cost to acquire data, the cost to maintain data, and the cost·for generating and communicating information.

The cost is related to accuracy, speed of generation etc., of information. If the system has to be more reliable and accurate, the costs have to be higher. In a given system, beyond a certain level of accuracy the cost will rise rapidly. Costs are also related to the response time required to generate information and communicate it. For real time systems, where response time is low, the costs are very high.

The Business Dimension

The characteristics of information required by managers at different levels of hierarchy are different. The characteristics of information for top management are in striking contrast with those of operating level management. The characteristics of information for middle management lie somewhere between the two. The top management requires information that is:

- future oriented,
- external,
- unstructured,
- non programmable, and
- inexact.

Whereas the operating management needs information that is:

- historical,
- internal,
- structured,
- programmable, and
- exact.

Since the top management is concerned with strategic planning and giving direction to the organisation, it requires environmental information. The information that the top management needs cannot be foreseen and planned or some of its needs may be too infrequent to justify designing and putting in place a system to generate such information. It means that the information the top management requires is unstructured. Since it is unstructured, its generation cannot be programmed. Top level managers do not require very high accuracy of such information as they are looking for some clues into the shape of things to come in future. Some trends and patterns in the data and projected information about the environment are useful for their functioning.

Operations management requires information about operations just finished or just to be started. Mostly their information concerns with operations just completed like information about a shift of production such as units of raw materials consumed, budgeted output, actual output, wastage, machine idle time and labour idle time. Such information is used for immediate control actions and as it arises internally, it is relatively easy to ensure accuracy. As this information is structured, which is generated from the routine transaction data, generation of such information can be programmed.

The Technical Dimension

The technical dimension of information depends on the quality and reliability of technology used for data processing and information communication. It is also concerned with the database that is vital for any information system. The database is an orderly collection of centrally controlled data that minimises data redundancy, facilitates storage of massive data, quick retrieval of data and ensures data security. The technical considerations of database are its capacity, response time, data interrelationships, security and validity. The technical considerations of information are:

— **Capacity:** This refers to the content of information. Information reports should be concise and clear. It should not overload the user with unnecessary details.

—**Security:** This aspect emphasises the privacy and security of data. Information systems must have adequate safeguards against unauthorised access, hacking and other misuse of database and facilities.

—**Validity:** The data must be validated before it enters the database. The quality and quantity of input data determines the quality of information. Adequate procedures must be built into the applications for validation of input data at data entry points.

— **Response Time:** This is the time taken by the system to respond to the user requests for information or support. The response time depends on the technical capacity of the system and the volume of such transactions to be processed by the system per unit of time. The advances in computing technology, database technology, networking technology and communication technology have made it possible to develop systems with real-time response capability at affordable costs for organisations.

TYPES OF INFORMATION

Information broadly falls into two classes on the basis of its intrinsic nature and organisational use: planning information and control information. The strategic level management is mostly concerned with planning information and its requirement for control information is very limited as most of the control function is exercised at lower levels. On the other hand, the operational level management requires a large amount of control information and small amount of planning information.

Differences between Planning and Control Information

(1) Planning information cuts across all organisational divisions and provides information about a few divisions or the entire organisation. Control information relates to functions or divisions or such small area of responsibility.

(2) Planning information covers a wider time span whereas the control information relates to a short time span say a shift to a few months at the most.

(3) Trends and patterns are more important in planning information. Finer details are important in control information.

(4) In the case of planning information the purpose is to guide planning by projecting trends and patterns whereas that of control information is to invite managerial intervention to correct a deviation.

The planning information can also be classified into three categories such as strategic, tactical and operational information based on who uses it and what impact its use produces in the organisation.

Strategic Information

Strategic information pertains mostly to the organisation as a whole and its environs such as information about population changes, natural resources, new technologies, new products, competitors, political, legal and economic changes, and so on. Top management needs strategic information for its long-term planning which affects the whole or a significant part of the organisation over a fairly long period of time.

Tactical Information

Tactical information is required for short-term planning by middle level managers. Sales analyses and forecasts, and cash flow projections are examples of tactical information. This information arises mostly from current internal activities. Some tactical information arises externally such as competitor information. Its impact is short term and affects only a department or a small area of activity.

Operational Information

Operational information relates to a very short period of time that may be a few hours to a few weeks. It may be about current stock levels of inventory, outstanding orders from customers, work schedule for next shift, etc. This information can be generated from current activity data arising from internal sources. It is of immediate use and is of interest to a few people. Such information covers only a limited area of operation of the organisation; for example, a shift of production.

External and Internal Information

There is another way of classifying information based on the source of such information: external and internal. The external information originates outside the organisation. Market research information, competitor information and database services which an organisation gets from information services firms are examples of external information. The reliability of externally originating information is difficult to establish. The credibility of information source may be a surrogate for the reliability of information. Internal information originates inside the organisation. Most of the data for internal information results from transaction processing. The transaction data is structured and stored in databases and they are available for tap any time. The organization has absolute control over its accuracy, reliability, security and availability.

Horizontal, Vertical and Lateral Information

Similarly, information can be classified into vertical and horizontal based on its flow within an organisation. Information flowing up or down the organisation hierarchy is called vertical flow of information. For example, orders and decisions communicated downward, reports originating from lower levels and flowing to higher levels of an organisation are vertical flows of information. When information flows from peer to peer at the same level, the flow is called lateral. For example, information flows between marketing manager, finance manager, personnel manager and production manager are lateral in nature.

Information Products

Information system generates and communicates the output from data processing activities. The output from such processing activity takes the shape of messages, images, forms and reports. Most of the information queries are responded to with video displays of status information and presentation of available information. Such output that is displayed on the monitor or printed on paper is called information product.

Information Theory

Norbert Weiner developed the information theory. He developed the concept of cybernetics. The cybernetic systems are automated systems that control their own actions using feedback. Information theory evaluates communication of information at three levels.

- the technical level
- the semantic level, and,
- the effectiveness level.

At the technical level the concern is how information can be transmitted accurately. The focus is on the use of redundancy; that is, the repetition of part or whole of the message for effectiveness in communication. Such redundancy ensures the communication of message by reducing the chance of noise which distorts it. The message may contain more information than is required to convey the message to the recipient. For example, along with sales for the four quarters, a graph of the sales data for the quarters and the total sales for the year may be furnished to a sales manager for better understanding of trends, etc.

At the semantic level, the concern is how the transmitted symbols convey the right meaning to the recipient. Presentation methods can ensure that the messages are correctly interpreted by reducing the chance of misinterpretation or misuse. For example, the message that the number of customer complaints received by the marketing department has doubled over the last two years may not present the right information unless it is presented with the growth in customers and sales. If sales have increased five fold in the last two years, the doubling of the number of complaints means that the firm is doing better than before in customer care.

At the effectiveness level, the stress is on quality of information and how it influences behaviour of its recipient. The bare information has to be supplemented with summaries and graphic presentation, etc., for communicating the message more effectively.

Information in Mathematical Theory of Communication

Mathematical theory mainly explains the coding scheme for the contexts of information. Different combinations of binary digits are used to identify a particular message from a set of messages. Binary digits, 1 and 0, represented by the presence and absence of a signal, are used in coding of messages. The binary digits are called bits. If there are only two messages, a two-bit code is used to identify messages.

Mathematical Definition of Information

Information in the Mathematical theory of communication is the average number of binary digits which must be transmitted to identify a given message from the set of all possible messages to which it belongs.

"Let us consider a communication system in which the allowable messages are $M_1, M_2,...$ with probabilities of occurrence $p_1, p_2,...$ subject to $P_1 + P_2 + ... = 1$. Let the transmitter select message M_k of probability P_k. Let us further assume that the receiver has correctly identified the message. Then we shall say, by way of definition of 'information', that the system has conveyed an amount of information given by $I_k = \log_2 1/P_k$.[3] A greater amount of information has been conveyed when the receiver correctly identifies a less likely message. When two independent messages M_K and M_l are correctly identified, we can prove that the amount of information conveyed is the sum of the information associated with each of the messages individually.

Average Information and Entropy

Suppose we have M different and independent messages $M_1, M_2 ...$ with probabilities $P_1, P_2,...$ and suppose further that during a long period of transmission a sequence of L messages has been generated. Then, if L is very large we may expect that in that message sequence we transmitted P_1L messages of M_1, P_2L messages of M_2, etc. The total message in that sequence will be:

$$I_{total} = P_1L \log_2 1/P_1 + P_2L \log_2 1/P_2 + ...$$

The average information per message interval represented by the symbol H will then be:

$$H = I_{total}/L$$

$$= P_1 \log 1/P_1 + P_2 \log 1/P_2 + ...$$

$$\sum_{k-}^{M} P_k \log_2 1/P_k$$

This average information is called entropy. The entropy for extremely likely and extremely unlikely messages is zero. Entropy is a term used in information theory to describe the uncertainty surrounding an event (for example a business decision) and information about that event. Entropy is a quantitative measure of uncertainly. Uncertainty and information are closely related. Entropy is the minimum when complete certainty exists regarding the actual outcome of an event. It increases as the number of outcomes increases.

Redundancy

Redundancy represents duplication of information. The same information may be stored or communicated using different messages. This results in redundancy. Redundancy in database, by storing the same data in multiple locations, results in wastage of storage space. Redundancy also creates problem when updating of file is done. Updating of all the files containing the same data has to be done together. If this is not done, the database will have inconsistent data.

Usually redundancy is built into information systems so as to facilitate error detection through the transmission of parity bits. For example, a parity bit introduced into the coding system to check errors in transmission of code.

The code used for communication can also have redundancy. Redundancy in coding can be calculated using the formula

R = 1 – (lr/lc)

Where R = Redundancy

1 = Constant

lr = Information capacity required

lc = Information capacity of the code used.

For example, a code with 8 bits can code 256 possibilities. The same code may be used at times to differentiate among 128 possibilities. The redundancy in this case is:

lr $= \log_2 (128)$ i.e., = 7

lc $= \log_2 (256)$ i.e., = 8

R $= 1 - (7/8)$

$= 1/8$ or 0.125.

Information Overload

Advances in IT are making information systems more user-friendly than ever before. The system churns out information reports of various kind for users. Since the information system people want to satisfy the users with its capability to produce information, these reports contain lot of information: some essential and the rest "just in case needed". The decision maker is often flooded with information.

Information overload is a state when a user is presented with too much information. It will be impossible to find out which information is relevant to the problem context and which is not. Overload causes a barrier to understanding the information presented and confuses the user. It often results when unfocused and irrelevant information is presented. It may also result from poor presentation of information. Information overload defeats the purpose of information system and it should be avoided or minimised.

Information overload does not improve quality of managerial decisions or actions. Since, it leads to inefficient information use, it does not generate value. Hence, a firm must take steps to avoid information overload. At the organisation level, data reduction, data summarisation, message modification, information filtering and inferences are some techniques for reducing information overload. At the level of user, that is, decision-maker, attempt has to be made to reduce the information overload. Setting clear information objectives in terms of what specific information is needed and the extent of detail needed, improving reading and note-taking skills so that key information is not missed in detailed report, and setting aside some time to choose the kind of information and information sources for tailored information requirements are some steps that will help a manager in tackling information overload at user level.

DATA REDUCTION

Data has to be collected from various records, measurements and observations made from the environment, etc. In order to store and use it efficiently, it is required to sort the data and only useful non-redundant data is entered into the system. For example, the quantity sold and sale price are enough for customer billing. There is no need to enter the total amount of the transaction as this can be calculated easily from these basic data items.

The data collected has to be classified into say cost data, sales data, service data, etc. The classification made will depend very much upon the organisation and its needs. The data also needs to be coded. For example, in an automobile plant store there will be a lot of shafts. A unique product coding system has to be used to identify each type of shaft in the store.

The data will then have to be organised and stored into files, tables, lists, database, etc. When information is required, it is generated by processing, summarising and filtering the data. Summarising of information is a process of aggregation. For example, the process of getting weekly sales report given daily sales figures is one of summarising. Filtering is a process by which irrelevant data is segregated and removed. For example, obtaining the list of products whose monthly sales turnover exceeds ₹ 10,000. Here all items that do not satisfy this criterion are removed.

The amount of data that is to be collected and processed into information at various levels of a business firm is staggering. The information system should be designed to gather relevant data and screen out irrelevant data. Substantial economy can be achieved if the amount of data collected and processed is reduced through such screening out. One method for such data reduction is filtering. For example, in collecting data for control purpose, data of operations within the permitted range of variation is not gathered. Only data pertaining to activities out of range is collected and processed into control information.

Data reduction can be effected in two ways: Transformation and Compression.

Transformation effects reduction by changing the physical form in which data exists thus saving storage space or through more effective data transmission. Changing the form of data also results in substantial compression of data. Compression reduces the physical size of data. Data reduction through compression can be effected in two ways. One is to physically compress the size of data. Data Compression is a technique that saves storage space by eliminating gaps, empty fields, redundancy or unnecessary data to shorten the length of records or blocks. Another method is sampling. Randomly selected sample may contain all the features of the population and hence statistical sampling reduces the mass of data to be processed. Instead of collecting, processing and storage of data about the entire population, only data about the sample is collected and stored.

Compaction is yet another form of data reduction. Through compaction, data that is not considered relevant for a purpose is deleted. Compaction techniques can be used in data storage and data transmission. The data compression is achieved through:

- Elimination of redundant data items
- Suppression of repeated characters
- Removing empty spaces in files
- Substituting commonly used data items, etc.

Information Filtering

Information industry is virtually facing an information explosion and every organisation that matters records enormous volume of data. Sophisticated information systems convert the vast data resources into information easily and quickly. If such information is presented without checking its relevance to a decision-maker, he/she will be faced with an information deluge. If too much information is presented to a person, he/she might experience an information overload. When a person suffers from information overload, much of the information presented may not be noticed or properly perceived. Information filtering reduces the volume of information flow upwards.

Brevity is an essential characteristic of information and in its absence the user may be misled or is likely to miss the vital facts of the problem being presented. Organisations have systems to scan information at every level and controlling the flow of it upwards. Information filtering is a technique that trims irrelevant information before it reaches the managers. In organisations the information is summarised at every higher level for superiors' convenience. Thus, each level in the hierarchy functions as a filter station and exercises discretion as to what information should go up to the superior and when and how. The purpose of this filtering is to avoid overloading of superiors with irrelevant information. Thus, the managers are provided with information pertinent to the problem to be solved or action to be taken.

The information filtering permits managers in exercising control over the information flows in the organisation. It also minimises the pressure on communication channels and the expenditure of money and time on generation and distribution of trivial information. It can also be harmful to the organisation as some vital information may not reach the superior if it reflects badly on the manager responsible for reporting or if he/she thinks that the information is not of any consequence. Thus, personal bias of the subordinate as well as his/her tendency to withhold information that puts him/her in bad light may deny the organisation the benefit of some critical information.

A manager has to be cautious about this risk in filtered information and he can call for additional information or observe things to ensure that he/she is not fooled by his subordinate. In computerised information systems, this risk can be minimised by retaining unfiltered information in the database. The manager can examine the full information in the database, if needed, to ensure that he/she is getting all the essential information.

Data Summarisation

Data summarisation reduces the volume of data for transmission without affecting its essential meaning. Classification is a formal way of summarisation of data. The accounting system summarises information into sales for a quarter, etc. Depending upon the user's requirement, the level of aggregation is done. For example, for the top management sales of various years may be furnished, for the marketing manager sales of a quarter by product, sales territory, etc., may be furnished to enable him to see the finer details for decisions and controls. The summarisation rises progressively from operations level to strategic planning level of management.

At the supervisory level of management, information is presented in great detail. For higher level management, summary of such information is presented. The summarisation is done in many ways. Aggregation is the most popular form of summarisation of information., Aggregation is the process of combining information originating at higher levels of organisations such as departments level, divisional and organisational level. For example, sales of various products of a company in various sales territories under a region are added to give aggregate sales figure for a quarter to the sales manager.

Statistics are yet another important form of summarisation. Averages, means, medians, ratios, and standard deviations are some of the often-used summary statistics. These statistics provide information about a set of transactions or other detailed data. A statistical sample can also be used as a summary of large amounts of data.

Inferences

Inferences are drawn usually from a large volume of data and such inferences are communicated in place of the original data. This technique reduces the volume of data transmission substantially. The inferences are drawn based on statistical analysis of data or they may be drawn intuitively. The problem with inferences is that the user gets only the inferences and does not know any thing about the data on which the inferences are based. Inferences often turn out to be highly subjective and personal. The quality of inference depends on a person's ability to see patterns, trends and relationships in the data available and to make an objective evaluation of them in the context of the problem.

QUALITY OF INFORMATION

Quality is fitness for use, or reliability. Quality of information is difficult to be measured. Since quality is related to use, one may have to ask the user about the quality of information he/she is getting. The user may be asked to rate it. If a user is satisfied with the information currently provided, he/she may rate it high and vice versa. Usually the more accurate the information, the higher is its quality, but quality is also influenced by other attributes of information. Apart from accuracy, some of the other attributes of information are brevity, timeliness, action orientation, being current and rarity.

The attributes of information which influence the quality of information can be classified into three categories such as time related, content related and form related.

(1) **Time-Related Attributes**

    i. **Timeliness.** Information should be available when needed.

    ii. **Currency.** The information should be up-to-date when needed.

    iii. **Frequency.** The information should be available as frequently as needed

    iv. **Time period.** The time period may be past, present and future as needed by the user.

(2) **Content-Related Attributes**

    i. **Accuracy.** The information should be free from errors

    ii. **Relevance.** The information should be specific to the needs of the recipient

    iii. **Completeness.** All the information required must be provided to the user when needed.

    iv. **Brevity.** Information needed must be provided in the right measure. Too much information may confuse the recipient.

(3) **Form-Related**

    i. **Clarity.** The form in which information is served must be easy to understand.

    ii. **Detail.** The level of summary or detail as required by the user must be met

    iii. **Order.** There should be a predetermined order for providing information.

    iv. **Presentation.** The presentation may be in narrative, numeric or graphic form, etc.

    v. **Media.** The media may be paper documents, video displays, etc., as needed by the user.

If the information provided has these attributes in the required measure, that information has quality.

Roman R. Andrus suggests a utility approach to evaluating quality of information. He says that information can be evaluated in terms of its utilities. He mentions four utilities which information may have:

    i. **Form utility:** The closer the form matches the decision-maker's requirement, the greater is its value.

    ii. **Place utility:** Information has greater value if it can be had or accessed easily.

    iii. **Time utility:** If information is available when needed, its value is greater.

    iv. **Possession utility:** The possessor of information influences its value by controlling its flow to others in the organisation.

Age and Quality of Information

Management information system collects data and stores it in databases on a routine basis. A large part of such data is updated on a periodical basis. Such periodically updated data has a time factor associated with it. Generation of information from such stored data takes some time. The length of this time that spans from the occurrence of the event and the use of information about the event decides the age of that information.

The factors that lead to delay in generating information from data about events are the information interval and the processing delay.[3] Information has a time period embedded like one week, one month or a quarter, etc., which is the information interval. The data processing takes some time to convert raw data into information for users. The sum of the information interval and the processing time is the age of information.

In the fast-changing world of today, the age of information has a lot of effect on its quality. In the high-tech industry, the quality of information deteriorates very quickly with age. This is due to many reasons. Some of them are:

(i) The environment is changing fast and therefore, what was true a year or say 6 months back might not be the same today with the passage of time.

(ii) More people are likely to have that information; this takes away the competitive edge that information can provide.

The Information systems must be designed to capture and provide timely and relevant information to the user in the minimum possible time.

VALUE OF INFORMATION

Information is a resource and has a cost for its acquisition and maintenance. For deciding on whether some information is to be acquired or not one has to know its value. The value of information is derived indirectly from the change in decision behaviour due to provision of information. The change in performance with provision of fresh information has to be measured to know the gain from its use. The cost of information must be deducted from the gain to arrive at its value. The decision maker must determine the value of information by studying the sensitivity of the decision to the additional information desired. One must also ensure that the information is timely, adequate, usable, reasonably accurate and pertaining directly to the problem on hand. That is, the decision-maker must know the incremental cost of additional information and the incremental gain from improved decisions. One must ask for further information or more accurate information only if one is sure that it will produce more gain than its cost.

To be of value information should have the following properties:

- availability,
- relevance,
- usefulness
- timeliness
- accuracy
- consistency, and,
- comprehensibility.

Decision-making requires information relevant to the problem on hand to analyse the problem and arrive at a solution. But decision-makers are often provided with too much of irrelevant information which results in information overload. It might cause the decision-maker to overlook serious problems.

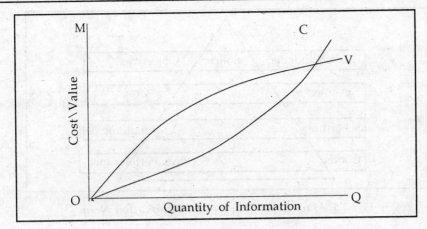

Fig. 2.2: Quantity and Value of Information

OC measures cost of information and OV measures the value of information. The figure reveals that increasing amount of information initially increases the pay off and eventually decreases it due to overload of information and high cost of information.

For increasing the value of information the following aspects of information must be considered:

(i)   only information relevant and appropriate to a manager's problem context must be provided,

(ii)   the information must be available timely for the manager to use immediately,

(iii)   reasonable accuracy and reliability of information must be ensured,

(iv)   the information must be in a form readily usable by the manager.

(v)   the information must be adequate to give a fair understanding of the problem or opportunity at hand.

MANAGEMENT INFORMATION

Management information has two major components: one is the information that arises from the internal data processing and the other is externally originating. Internal information arises from the routine data processing activity in the organisation and it summarises the organisation's operations. It contributes to formulation of policies and making of decisions by managers. The management has total control on such data originating internally and can insist on certain degree of accuracy of internal information depending upon its use. The source documents can be verified for correctness of information, if required. The other source of management information is the environment. Environmental information is diverse and subjective. Management has little control over such information that arises outside the organisation and cannot be sure of its accuracy. Reliability of the information source is a major concern in external information. If the source is reliable, the information is supposed to be accurate. Yet, it is critical for long-term decisions. Managers combine environmental information with the internally generated information to properly evaluate problem situations and arrive at solutions. Managers should be provided with a continuous feedback of information so as to know whether a decision has been carried out or whether the plans and budgets are adhered to or not, etc. Though, the microcomputer has brought processing power within the reach of all managers and information virtually on their finger tips, they still prefer paper reports for routine and pre-planned information requirements. These reports carry information for specific purposes.

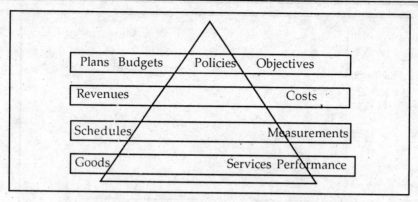

Fig. 2.3: Management Levels and Information Needs

Application of Information Concepts to Information System Design

The information theory provides some valid insights that are valuable for information system design. Some of these useful concepts are as follows:

Information reduces uncertainty and it positively influences the choice of alternatives in decision situations. The information theory approach focuses the attention of the systems designer not only on the value of information in decision-making but also on its cost of acquisition.

Redundancy is built into communication system to ensure correct transmission of messages. It can be effectively used to overcome noise and improve the probability of messages being received and interpreted correctly. Concepts of information presentation such as summarisation and message routing are relevant in designing information systems. The quality of information received cannot be directly measured. The user's perception of quality may provide guidelines to the designer in improving the information system.

Information has value only if it changes decision behaviour. It forces the system design team to look at the needs and use of information and fine tune the system to increase its utility to the users. The concepts of age and interval of information are useful to the designers in designing flexible information system.

Information system should keep information flowing to users but it should not result in information overload. Filtering can be exercised at lower levels to remove irrelevant information being reported to higher levels of management.

Information should be presented in a form needed by the user. It should not require further processing for his/her need.

Information system should give summarised information but facilities should be available for the user to check the detailed information, if needed.

Information system should take care of individual differences in information need and use. It should accommodate some special information needs of decision-makers.

Information Processing and Organisational Responses

The amount of information to be processed in an organisation depends on many factors. Davis and Olson[4] classify these factors into three such as task uncertainty, number of units relevant for decision and interdependence of organisational units.

If an activity is well understood, little uncertainty prevails about carrying out the activity. The activity can be planned in advance. If the activity is uncertain there is need for greater amount of information as the activity progresses for effective performance of it.

If the number of units involved in a decision, such as departments, products and clients, is greater, the larger the amount of information needed for decisions.

If the organisational units are not interdependent, the amount of information to be exchanged for co-ordination among them is less. If they are interdependent, large amount of information is needed to co-ordinate the activities.

Organisational responses to such information processing load include:

1. Operational procedures and decision rules
2. Hierarchy of authority
3. Self organising subsystems
4. Slack resources
5. Self contained structures
6. Vertical information systems
7. Lateral organisational forms.

The operating procedures and decision rules decrease the need for information exchange by laying down clear-cut guidelines for activities. Situations not covered by operating procedures and decision rules are taken up on an exceptional basis with the higher levels in the hierarchy. Self-organising systems, which are given reasonable autonomy, reduce the need for communication. Slack resources reduce the necessity for communication.

Conclusion

Information is processed data and serves current or prospective use. It reduces uncertainty and enables informed decision-making. It has a cost for acquisition, storage and maintenance. It is regarded as a resource and its value depends on the difference between its costs and benefits from its use. Only if the benefits are greater than the costs, acquisition of that information is economically justified. Too much of information does not improve the quality of decision. Therefore, there is a need to provide only relevant information in the right measure to the decision-makers to have maximum pay-off from information use in organisations.

QUESTIONS

1. What is information?
2. What are the characteristics of information?
3. What is information overload? How can it be checked?
4. What are the types of information?
5. How are the information requirements of top management different from those of bottom level management?
6. What are the differences between planning information and control information?
7. What is entropy?
8. What is redundancy in information system?

9. What is data reduction? How is it done?
10. How do you determine the value of information?
11. How do you assess the quality of information?
12. Mention some of the information concepts that can be applied to better information system design?
13. What are the factors that affect the quality of information?

REFERENCES

1. Davis, Gordon B. and Olson, Malgrethe H., *Management Information Systems,* McGraw-Hill Book Company, Singapore, 1985, p. 200.
2. Kanter, J., *Managing With Information,* Prentice Hall of India, New Delhi, pp. 8-9.
3. Taub, Herbert and Schilling, Donald L., *Principles of Communication System,* McGraw-Hill, New Delhi, pp. 512-515.
4. Davis, Gordon B. and Olson, Malgrethe, *op.cit.,* p. 341.

Case 2.1: PMS at MM HOSPITAL

MM Hospital (MMH) started in the year 2002 with around ₹ 150- crore investment. It had about 150 doctors and around 1,000 other employees. The HR function is organised with a lean structure: one senior manager who reports to the GM of the hospital, one Asst. Manager and two officers. The hospital is administered by a team of senior doctors and management professionals with right mix of professional skills and experience. It adopts good management practices in all departments and creates a highly conducive environment for employees to work. HR department has been asked by the management to implement a performance management system (PMS). It has already implemented a performance appraisal system for employees. A team has been formed with two senior members of HR Department (Senior Manager and Asst. Manager) and two senior members from the MIS department to prepare a detailed report on how to implement the PMS.

As a first step the team conducted a few workshops for its employees on key result area-based (KRA-Based) performance management system. It also held several rounds of interviews with many department heads and officers. Having won the support of most of its employees, MMH started to design a performance management system.

Having implemented a Hospital information management system (HIS), the hospital had plenty of data with it. But except many standard and routine reports, nothing much has been done with the data.

The team met a few times and discussed the concepts and methodologies. Yet, it could not resolve a few issues which are given below.

- How to decide performance criteria for each position in the hospital?
- How to fix performance criteria for team tasks?
- Where to collect the data for analysis of performance?
- What are the key indicators of performance to be reported to the Managing Director?
- Should the report be sent to department heads?
- How frequently the reports should be prepared and sent?
- Should it be printed or displayed on screen?
- Can the HIS help in providing all the data for the performance management system?

As a secretary to the team, you are asked to draft the final report of the Team on How to implement PMS in MMH.

CHAPTER 3

System Concepts

INTRODUCTION

A system is a set of interrelated components working together as an integrated unit to achieve common goal(s). It is derived from the Greek word "systema" meaning organised relationship among functioning units or components. A system is actually a set of nested subsystems. The subsystems are structured into a hierarchy with specific roles in the system. When the subsystems play their respective roles in a coordinated way, the system reaches its goals. A system needs to exchange a lot of information with its subsystems for such coordination and ordered execution of tasks for reaching the goals. Examples for systems include almost everything like home, village, college, hospital, state administration, education, automobile and military. A college has subsystems like academic, administration, examination, sports, residential and healthcare components constituting the basic subsystems.

The subsystems within a system are orderly arranged according to a design and each subsystem has a definite function to perform in the system. The components forming a system are called sub systems. Each such subsystem can further be divided into lower level units. This process of dividing system into lower level units is called factoring of a system and this can be carried on until we get a unit that is easy to manage.

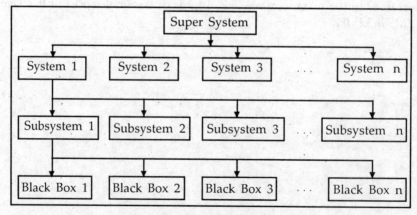

Fig. 3.1: Hierarchy of Systems

A system can be defined as an organised or complex whole, an assemblage or combination of things or parts forming a complex or unitary whole. The system may be physical or abstract. Physical systems are made up of objects such as land, building, machines, people and other tangible objects. The abstract systems are made up of concepts or events. Physical systems produce some outputs, which may help to achieve its defined objective. Organisations are more meaningfully defined as an array of components designed to accomplish a particular objective according to a plan.

System Elements

A system is a collection of related elements. These elements take the form of input, process and output and can be represented as in the following figures:

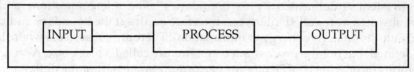

Fig. 3.2: Simple System Model

Figure 3.2 presents a simiplified moodel of a system, with single input and single output.

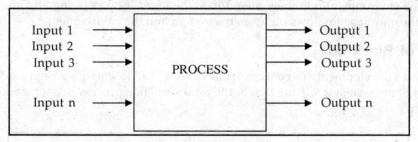

Fig. 3.3: System with Many Inputs and Many Outputs

Figure 3.3 presents a system with multiple inputs and multiple outputs.

Systems, Subsystems and Components

System has many layers and at every level a system can be perceived to be part of a still larger system. It also means that at every level a subsystem can be a system relative of the objective. That is, it is the objective that decides the system, subsystems, their functions and the systems environment. The system's environment is outside the system and the system boundary separates the system from its environment. Open systems interact with other systems in the environment and exchange inputs and outputs. The boundaries of open systems are relatively flexible whereas those of closed systems are rigid. Total system is determined by definition. When the total system is determined, the inputs of each segment can be specified in relation to the objectives of the total system. Once this is done, it is possible to analyse the functions and relationships among the parts and those of the parts in relation to the whole.

The components that constitute the whole are called subsystems. Each subsystem has a well-defined role in the total system design and if it fails in performing the assigned role, it will affect the performance of the system. If its failure leaves the system unaffected, then that component does not belong to the system.

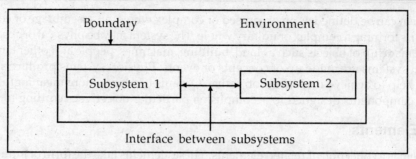

Fig. 3.4: Boundary, Interface and Environment of System

Each subsystem is delineated by its boundaries[1]. The interconnections and interactions between the subsystems are called interfaces. Interface occurs at the boundary and takes the form of inputs and outputs (material, energy or information). There are subsystems where the inputs and outputs are defined, but not the process; such systems are called a black box. A basic unit or black box that performs or provides the facility for performing some part of the defined transformation process can be defined as component; for example, a class room in case of an educational system.

A system permits flows of information, energy and other resources to ensure its survival. The flow from the environment into the system forms the input for processing and after the input is processed, the output again flows out from the system into the environment.

Concept of Black box

In systems development, the concept of black box is used to simplify design work. Initially the process part of the system is left out; that is, the transformation process is assumed to be black box or unknown.

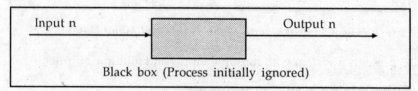

Fig. 3.5: Concept of Black Box

The output of the system is defined first. Once the output requirements are clearly defined, the designers turn to identifying and defining input requirements to generate the specified output. After defining the output and input, the last step in design is to specify the black box operation. The black box represents the conversion process. The steps in conversion are specified to convert the specified input into the specified output. This approach to the systems design is highly scientific and is often used in information system design.

CHARACTERISTICS OF SYSTEMS

Systems possess some characteristics that enable them to be distinguished from components. They are:

   (i)   Objective orientation,

  (ii)   Components

(iii)   Structure (i.e., design of components in a particular arrangement),

(iv)   Interaction

(v)   Interdependence.

(vi)   Inputs of information, energy and materials,

(vii)   Processing of inputs, and,

(viii)   Outputs or results.

Systems Theory and Systems Approach

The Systems theory conceptualises interrelationships among complex phenomena and integrates them into a systematic whole. It provides systematic theoretical framework for describing general relationships of the empirical world. The systems theory has heavily drawn on the Vitalist theory of deductive reasoning, which states that[2]:

1.   The whole is primary and the parts are secondary

2.   Integration is the condition of the inter relatedness of the many parts within

3.   The parts constitute an indissolvable whole such that no part can be affected without affecting the other parts

4.   Parts play their role in light of the purpose for which the whole exists

5.   The nature of the part and its functions are derived from its position in the whole and its behaviour is regulated by the whole-to-part relationship

6.   Everything should start with the whole as a premise and the parts and their relationships should evolve.

The systems approach is a framework that includes concepts such as systems theory, systems philosophy, systems management and systems analysis. Systems philosophy is a way of thinking. It relates complex ideas, principles and laws meaningfully and finds a logical order in everything in this universe.

Systems management is a practical application of systems theory to organisational units. Systems management has four decision stages such as:

• systems determination

• systems design and creation

• systems operation and control, and

• systems review and evaluation.

When a decision is taken to form a particular business, (that is, systems determination), the next stage is to synthesise the subsystems and components into the system and defining their role in the hierarchy into which these are structured to form the total system. Next stage is to operate the system with inputs and control the system as it operates. The last stage is to review the system and evaluate it continuously so that system functions efficiently and effectively.

The systems analysis is part of decision-making in all the four stages of systems management. Systems analysis constructs models to analyse systems and improve quality of decision-making. Thus, systems analysis is the application of modelling with the objective of optimising or problem solving.

TYPES OF SYSTEMS

Systems can be classified into a number of groups; some of them are explained below:

1. **Conceptual and Empirical:** Conceptual system is a theoretical framework that may or may not have any counter part with real world. Examples, economic theory, theology, etc. Empirical systems are generally concrete operational systems made up of people, machines, materials and energy. Empirical systems may be derived from or based upon conceptual systems. Examples are production system, examination system, etc.

2. **Natural and Artificial Systems:** Natural systems abound in nature such as solar system and water system. They are not the result of human effort. Artificial systems are man-made. Examples of artificial systems are transport system, communication system, etc.

3. **Social and Machine systems:** Systems made up of people may be viewed purely as social system. Business organisations, government agencies, political parties, etc., are examples of social systems. Machine system is made up of machine or machines only. Such systems would have to obtain their own inputs and maintain themselves. Solar power system may be put in this category except for its creation. Most empirical systems are Man-machine or socio-technical systems with people and machines forming part of the system.

4. **Open and Closed Systems:** Open systems interact with the environment and exchange information, material or energy with environment. They are difficult to study. Examples for open systems are biological systems, organisational systems, etc. A closed system is self-contained and does not interact with its environment. It has a well-defined boundary that keeps the environment from influencing the system directly. Most computer systems may be considered as closed systems.

5. **Adaptive and Non-adaptive systems:** A system that reacts to its environment in such a way as to improve its functioning is called an adaptive system. Most biological systems are adaptive systems. They change with the changes in their environment to ensure their survival. A non-adaptive system does not change with changes in its environment. It is free from its environmental influences and may degenerate eventually.

6. **Probabilistic and Deterministic Systems:** This classification of systems is based on their predictability of outcomes. In a probabilistic system some states can be predicted from the previous state only with a certain amount of error. For example, in an inventory system, the average stock, and average demand, may be predicted but the exact values of these factors at any given time cannot be known in advance. Deterministic systems are perfectly predictable. That is, it is possible to predict the outputs accurately from the inputs. For example, a given electric motor and an input of a particular voltage will produce an output of a known number of revolutions per minute (rpm).

7. **Permanent and Temporary Systems:** Systems enduring for a long time relative to the people belonging to the system are called permanent systems. Most man-made systems are permanent systems. Temporary systems are designed to last only for a limited period of time. Once the purpose is achieved such systems cease to exist.

8. **Stationary and non-stationary Systems:** Systems whose properties and operations do not vary significantly or change in repetitive cycles are called stationary systems; for example an automatic production system. The properties and operations of non-stationary systems change very frequently.

Subsystem

Each system seems to be nested in a larger system; smaller systems within a system are called subsystems. Super systems refer to extremely large and complex systems. Systems exist at an infinite number of levels of scale. For example, the system of education can be classified into global education system, national education system, state education system, district education system, block education system, panchayat education system and so on. Each subsystem may have many inputs and many outputs. Between subsystems many interconnections are required for the exchange of input and output. The number of interconnections or interfaces rapidly rises when the number of subsystems rises. Algebraically, the number of interconnections in a system is $N = 1/2\ N(N-1)$. Thus, a system with eight subsystems will have 28 interconnections, and a system with ten subsystems will have 45 interconnections. Though not all subsystems interconnect with all others, yet very large number of interconnections exist in most systems. Since such large number of interconnections cause problems in the normal functioning of a system, steps are taken to reduce them. The need for forming subsystems arises because of the following reasons:

- Simplification
- Decoupling, and,
- Decomposition.

Simplification

Most systems are complex with large number of interrelated and interdependent elements. The complex systems are broken down into lower level systems to simplify design, operation and control of systems.

Decoupling

Subsystems of a system constantly interact with each other for inputs and passing of outputs. If subsystems are tightly coupled or connected, close co-ordination is necessary for the smooth functioning of the system. For example, exact matching of output of one subsystem with the input of the next subsystem requires detailed planning and close co-ordination. This kind of co-ordination is very difficult to obtain always. It is therefore common to decouple subsystems. Some of the techniques of decoupling are described below.

Stack capacity is one way of decoupling. For example, if a machine centre stocks raw materials enough for a couple of days, even if raw material is not issued to it from the store, for a day or two, it does not affect its functioning. Similarly stocking some processed goods at machine centre A enables it to transfer output to machine centre B (which forms input to machine centre B) without any pressure on it to immediately process and transfer output to B. This kind of decoupling reduces the need for communication and co-ordination among subsystems.

Standardisation is another technique of decoupling that enables subsystems to plan and organise their processes without continual reference to other subsystems.

Advantages of Decoupling

Decoupling allows subsystems more independence in planning and control. Decoupling by increasing flexibility and independence may encourage initiative and self-reliance within individual subsystems. It is likely that with some decoupling of subsystems, the system as a whole is better able to deal with random and probabilistic movements.

Decomposition

This is a process of breaking down a system into hierarchical subsystems. The purpose of decomposition is to make components efficient and effective. The systems can be decomposed into subsystems vertically or horizontally or both.

CONTROL IN SYSTEMS

Control is necessary to ensure proper operation of a system. Feedback process is added to basic system model to achieve this purpose. Feedback in organisational systems is normally provided through information systems. It involves comparing actual output with the standard and in case of difference, input is sent to the process to modify the operations so that the output conforms to the standard.

To be successful any system must produce outputs that meet its objectives. To ensure this compliance, planning must be done and at the time of execution of plan, control should be exercised to ensure conformity with plans. A vital element in any planning process is controls and control systems necessary to achieve the objective.

Steps in Control

Control is the activity that measures deviation from planned performance, and initiates corrective action, if required. The steps involved are:

- setting up a standard specifying expected performance. Examples: a budget, a decision rule or an operation procedure
- measurement of actual performance
- comparison of the actual with the standard
- reporting of deviation to a control unit (say a manager)
- a set of actions the control unit can choose from to change performance if it is unfavourable.
- a procedure for higher level action if the control unit fails in producing correct performance.

Feedback Loops

Feedback is defined as the return of part of the output of a system into the input for purpose of modification and control of output as in electronic amplifiers, automatic machines, etc. The feedback may be negative or positive. Control is exercised in organisational systems by information feedback loops. The feedback can be positive or negative.

Negative Feedback

Feedback that seeks to dampen and reduce fluctuations around a norm or standard is termed negative feedback. The corrective action would be in opposite direction to the error. Negative feedback tends to smooth out fluctuations and enables the system to conform to norms and standards.

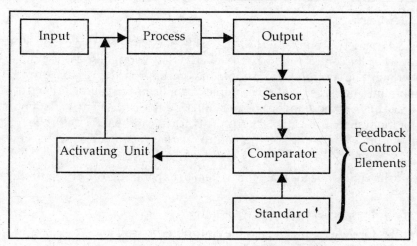

Fig. 3.6: Negative Feedback Control

Positive Feedback

Positive feedback causes the system to repeat or amplify an adjustment or action. It acts in the same direction as the measured deviation. For example, if advertisement spending brings more sales than the target sales, positive feedback causes the advertisement spending to be increased further.

Types of Control Systems

Feedback is the key to system control. Information about the transformation process is fed to the control centre, may be a manager or a computer system, so that the processing can be assessed and corrected, if needed. The control systems can be classified into the following three categories.

Closed Loop System

It is a system where feedback, based on output measurement, is fed back to make appropriate alterations to the input. For example, stock level control system has planned level of stock for each item. The actual stock level of each item is measured and compared with the planned level. Adjustments are made to bring stock level up or down to conform to the planned level.

Open Loop System

These are systems where no feedback loop exists and control is external to the system; that is, control is not an integral part of it. Control action is not automatic and may be made without monitoring the output of a system. An example may be a heating system without an automatic thermostat. Control is exercised externally by turning the heating system on and off at appropriate intervals.

Cybernetic System

Cybernetics is the science of communication and control. Systems embodying feedback control are commonly called cybernetic systems. But strictly the term should be used for exceedingly complex probabilistic self-regulating systems.

Law of Requisite Variety

The law of requisite variety propounded by Ross Ashby states that complete control of a system can be achieved only when the control system has as much variety in response as the number of ways the system can go wrong. The control system should have an appropriate response to each control situation. Business organisations, being highly complex, cannot ensure complete control of system with a few controls like budget and standards. There must be at least as many variations of control as there are ways for the system to go out of control. This also means that the controller of a system must be able to determine variations of the control variable and introduce system change instructions for such change.

The law of requisite variety means that for a system to be controlled, every controller must be provided with:

(i)   enough control responses to meet any situation

(ii) decision rules for generating all possible control responses, and

(iii) the authority to become a self-organising system in order to generate control responses.

Computer controlled open systems are useful for generating control responses in expected situations, and in case of unexpected situations it is better to leave it to a human decision maker.

Control in Information Systems

Management information system provides extensive support to management in its planning and control activities. The plans set the standard for achievement. Later the system measures and compares actual achievement with standard. The differences are analysed and the causes are identified for managerial control of such variances. The information system monitors performance on a continuous basis and reports to management on an exceptional basis.

SYSTEM CONCEPTS APPLIED TO MIS

MIS is a system just like any other system. The system concepts are used in designing, implementing and maintenance of MIS. MIS design uses structured design approach which requires delineation of subsystems and setting up of interfaces. The concept of black box is useful in defining systems. Inputs and outputs of each subsystem are defined and proper relationship established between subsystems.

Knowledge on the methods of decoupling of information systems and its impact on subsystems is useful in designing systems. The degree of decoupling of subsystems depends on the nature of each subsystem. In case of relatively less interdependent systems a fairly high degree of decoupling can be achieved without much cost. Decoupling has significant impact when highly interdependent subsystems are decoupled.

MIS as a System

A system receives input, processes it and outputs the results. MIS receives data and procedures as input and produces information from data according to the instructions. The simple information system comes close to the basic system model of input, process and output. But in the case of MIS all inputs do not arise all on a sudden. Data emerges all the time and they are captured and stored as they occur. So the stored data also becomes input to the system and the processed data is also stored awaiting future use. Thus the storage function is added to the basic system model of input, process and output.

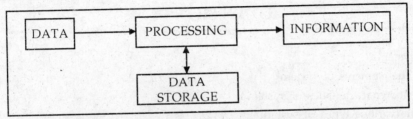

Fig. 3.7: Information System Model with Storage

MIS is a man-machine system designed to generate certain information outputs to meet information needs of managers. This system can be divided into functional subsystems and application subsystems. The functional subsystems include hardware, software, and data communication and database subsystems. The basic system model is helpful in understanding the functioning of subsystems. The application subsystems include transaction-processing subsystem, enquiry processing subsystem, etc.

Information Systems Analysis and Design

Systems analysis is the process of gathering of facts, analysing them to locate problems, and using the information to suggest improvements to the system. A system study is initiated to gather such facts about the system. Systems analysts perform this job. They not only help solve current problems but also help in expansion of the system. For example, if an educational institution wants to computerise its admission system, the first step is to invite an analyst to perform the system study.

Several questions are answered at this stage such as:

(i)   How does the current system function?

(ii) Is a change in the present system required?

(iii) What are the problems of the present system?

(iv) Whether a computerised system is feasible?

The analysts need also to find out the way the files are maintained, issue of admission notice, weight given for candidates, how data is stored, etc. This accumulation of study facts is called system study. Analysts, working with managers and employees in the organisation, recommend the alternative system designs. For more details on systems analysis and design please see chapters fifteen and sixteen.

Conclusion

System is an integrated whole. The systems theory is based on the Vitalist theory of deductive reasoning. Systems are of different types such as open system, closed system, natural system, artificial system, social system and technical system. It is one of the modern approaches to complex phenomena and takes a whole approach to problems. Its focus is on the whole, though made up of components, retaining its integrity and the components functioning smoothly to ensure accomplishment of the whole's goal. MIS is a system in all respects and the system concepts are highly useful in designing and implementing MIS.

QUESTIONS

1. What is system?
2. What are the elements of system?
3. What are the characteristics of system?
4. Explain the various types of system?
5. What is subsystem? What is black box?
6. Describe how an analysis of system is important to information system development.
7. What are the methods of decoupling of system?
8. What is feedback? What are the types of feedback?
9. Describe the elements of negative feedback control system.
10. What is law of requisite variety?
11. Explain how the system concepts are useful in designing and implementing MIS.
12. Explain the important system characteristics.
13. What do you understand by systems approach to problem solving? How is it applicable to development of MIS?
14. Explain the concept of black box.

REFERENCES

1. Davis, Gordon B, and Olson, Malgrethe H, *Management Information Systems*, McGraw Hill Book Company, Singapore, 1984, p. 271.
2. Johnson, Richard A., *et al.*, *Management, Systems, and Society: An Introduction*, Goodyear Publishing Company, California, 1976, pp. 57-60.

Case 3.1: Public Distribution System in India

Public Distribution System (PDS) is an antipoverty programme of the Government of India which was started in 1954 o tackle poverty and food shortages in different parts of the country. The objective was to supplement the open market with a network of retail outlets to supply food and essential commodities throughout the country. PDS provides essential food items such as rice, wheat, sugar and edible oils and non-food items like kerosene, standard cloth etc., through a rationing system to around 160 million households in the country at subsidised prices. PDS has around 500,000 outlets called fair price shops (FPS). The Central Government builds and maintains huge stock of food materials as buffer and it has a salubrious effect on food prices and food security in the country. Today, PDS is perhaps the largest such intervention anywhere in the world.

PDS is a joint programme of the centre and states. Procurement, transportation and warehousing are with the centre. It also allocates food and other essential articles to the states based on a set of entitlement criteria. Food Corporation of India carries out most of the responsibilities for the Central Government like procurement, warehousing and trasnportation. The state governments are having the operational responsibility of issuing ration cards, allocation of items within the state and supervision of the FPSs.

Central Ministry of Civil Supplies decides the allocation to each state and moves the quantity of food and other essential commodities to the warehouses in the state. The state Civil Supplies Department in turn makes allotment to Talukas. Taluk supply office allots quantity to each FPS. FPS owners take delivery of the food and essential commodities from the FCI warehouses and distribute to the cardholders as per their entitlements.

In 1996, targeted PDS was introduced to make it more effective. It divided the beneficiaries into two groups – Above Poverty Line (APL) and Below Poverty Line (BPL) families. The BPL families were entitled to get more quantity of food and other essential commodities at very low prices. It was further extended by adding one more layer of the 'poorest of the poor' called Antyodaya Anna Scheme (AAY) comprising the poorest 10 million of the 65.2 million BPL families identified for PDS.

Poor quality, leakage, pilferage, diversion to open market, lack of means of transportation, non-issue of ration cards to many families, etc., are some of the problems that cripple PDS in India. There are complaints about the working of PDS. The food materials released from the FCI go downs are not reaching the beneficiaries in the same quality and quantity. Even BPL and AAY cardholders are not even aware of their entitlement properly. There is leakage somewhere. Even when there is surplus food grains production, some parts of the country face shortage of food as the transportation of food materials to those parts is not done when needed. The system is run without much reliable data from procurement to distribution to card holders.

Questions:

1. Do you think PDS is a system? Why?
2. Can you identify the components and hierarchy of PDS?
3. What are the objectives of PDS? What responsibilities emerge from those objectives and how are they shared by the different organisations involved in it?
4. Can an MIS help running of such a huge system like the PDS in India?
5. How can you design IS solutions to meet the problems that PDS faces?

Structure of Management Information Systems

4
CHAPTER

INTRODUCTION

Every system has a definite structure; that is, a design according to which the components are synthesised into a functioning whole. Identification of the components of a physical system, like a desktop computer, is easy. Management information system is different from most other physical systems due to the difficulty in identifying its physical boundaries and properties. MIS captures, stores and processes data into a form that users specify. Much of the output from it is produced through user interaction with the systems. Hence, there is difficulty in defining the structure of MIS. Yet, it is possible to take a multiple view based approach to understand the components and functions of MIS. The structure of MIS can, thus, be described from different angles such as formal and informal systems, physical components of the system, and functional subsystems. Let us see some of these approaches to MIS structure to understand it better.

Formal and Informal Information Systems

Management Information System gathers data from internal and external sources. Transaction processing system generates bulk of the data used by MIS. Transaction data is internally captured and stored when transactions like purchases, wage payment, etc., are processed. The external data sources may be people like customers, suppliers, managers, workers, etc., and media like magazines, trade journals, newspapers, Government publications, etc. MIS regularly and systematically collects data and processes it into information to support managerial functions.

The classification of information system into formal and informal information systems is based on whether the information process uses the formal facilities for data capture, processing, storing and communicating of information. If the data processing uses the media officially prescribed and laid down, that part of MIS is formal. The formal part of MIS is strictly defined with procedures for access and updating through an authorisation system. The security aspects of the formal MIS are formally spelt out in detail. The formal component accounts for a lion's share of the organisational MIS. Formal MIS means an information system which is formally organised to provide information to different users for attaining higher levels of efficiency in their respective area of responsibility and to ensure effective functioning of different subsystems of the organisation so as to achieve the organisational objectives.

The informal MIS does not have any well-defined routine or procedure. Managers' conversation with customers over telephone may give them some information about competitors' products, price, etc. or it may be a supplier at a social gathering with whom a manger talks which gives him some useful information. Informal information is accessible to any user in the organisation regardless of his hierarchical position in the firm. There is no formally laid down or rigid procedure for information gathering or sharing in the organisation. The information is neither systematically arriving nor regular in its flow.

From the formal information system the top management requires internal information such as past sales, sales trends, distribution costs, production data and cost as well as external information such as environment of business, market conditions, economic fluctuations, money value fluctuations, Government regulations, etc. The informal system helps in getting some data that is otherwise not available on the internal and external environs of the firm.

Both formal and informal components are to be integrated into the organisational MIS. But there is a question of accuracy of such informally generated information. If the source of data is internal, it can be checked for accuracy. But external data accuracy is difficult to ensure. Users of such information have to be careful about the authenticity of the information. But it often gives a hint to the decision-maker about the business and its environment.

Public and Private Information Systems

If the access to the information system, subject to the security procedures, is available to every one in the organisation, it is called public information system. Most of the formal information is in the public domain of the information system.

In the private part of the information system certain files are not available to others in the organisation and certain files may be shared with trusted persons discriminatingly. These files may be created and maintained by a manager or managers for their own private use and may or may not use the formal channel and secretarial service for gathering data, and creating and maintaining such private files. For example, a marketing manager may maintain a secret file on his sales staff for his use, which he/she may not make available to any other in the organisation.

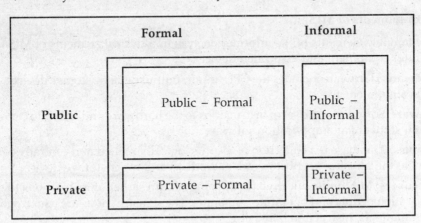

Fig. 4.1: Public/Private and Formal/Informal Components of Information System

By combining the public/private and formal and informal dualities, we have four components of information system structure. These are public formal, public informal, private formal and private informal components. In the public formal component, we have information that is collected, processed and stored for access to all the users in the organisation subject, of course, to the security restrictions. Public informal component of information system represents that part of the information that is informally gathered but is available to the users in the organisation for use. The private formal part of the information system refers to the information that is formally generated but is available only to the person who gathers and keeps it. In the private-informal component of information system represents information that is informally gathered and is available to only the user who maintains it.

MULTIPLE APPROACHES TO STRUCTURE OF MIS

The MIS can be described using several approaches like the components, decision support, managers' activity and organisational function. Gordon B. Davis and Malgrethe Olson[1] suggest a multiple approach to the structure of MIS. According to them the structure can be described using four approaches and they synthesised these approaches into a conceptual structure for organisational information system. These approaches to MIS are as follows:

1. operational elements of MIS,
2. management activity
3. decision support, and,
4. organisational function.

These approaches are explained in the following sections.

1. Operational Elements of MIS

Davis and Olson divide the operational elements of MIS into three classes such as:

- Physical components
- Processing functions and,
- Output to users.

(a) Physical Components of MIS

These are tangible elements of the information system. Physical elements of MIS refer to the physical computer equipment and associated devices.

    i. **Hardware:** Hardware includes the CPU, input/output devices, storage devices, communication equipment, etc.

    ii. **Software:** Software is the set of instructions to the hardware and falls into two categories, system software and application software.

    iii. **Database:** Database is a collection of records logically related and centrally controlled. It refers to the physical set of stored data on disks and other storage devies.

    iv. **Procedures:** MIS for its effective functioning requires a set of instructions to users, data preparation people and operating personnel. These instructions are usually contained in users' manuals, instruction book, etc.

    v. **People:** Users and Operations Personnel. The users include all information users in the organisation and outside. The operations personnel constitute the people element of information system. They include computer operators, systems analyst, programmers, data preparation people, data administrators, etc.

    vi. **Networks:** The networks are the enabler of real-time communications. The network infrastructure helps in integrating systems and facilitates online transactions.

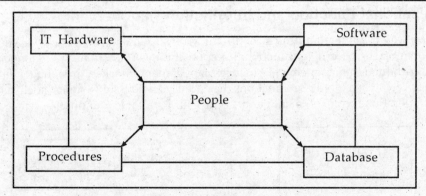

Fig. 4.2: Physical Components of MIS

(b) Processing Functions

Another way of understanding information system is to look at the processing functions that include:

i.   **Processing transactions:** Transaction is an activity and is the source of all internal data. The information system measures and records all transactions. This transaction data becomes the basis for all the internally generated information.

ii. **Maintaining master files:** Master files store relatively permanent data. Each transaction may necessitate updating of master files. Information system has the facility to update master files by incorporating new transaction data.

ii. **Producing reports:** Report generation is an integral process of MIS. Information system generates reports to provide information to users at different levels of management periodically or on special requests.

iv. **Processing inquiries:** The Information system provides responses to inquiries coming into it such as, say, stock available at a warehouse, the customer orders pending, and shipments during the last week.

v.   **Process interactive support application:** The Information system provides interactive facility to users. They can use models of various kinds, use the database and generate alternative solutions interactively.

(c) Outputs for users

Information system can be understood from the outputs provided by it to users. They include:

i.   **Transaction documents:** Transactions when processed result into some physical documents like sales invoice, payroll cheques, customer bills, purchase orders, etc.

ii.   **Reports:** Information System provides periodic and ad-hoc reports to provide users with information.

iii. **Enquiry responses:** Each enquiry is processed and the system generates a response for the user.

iv.   **Output of interactive support application:** The system's interactive facility enables users to draw on the database and manipulate the data with the aid of models. Such interactive operation results into some outputs to the users.

2. Organisational Function and Information Requirement

Another way to understand the structure of MIS is to look at the support given by it to the management in carrying out its functional responsibilities. Functionally, management can be divided into production management, Finance Management, Marketing Management, Personnel Management, etc. Each of these functions has four activity subsystems such as transaction processing, operational control, managerial control and strategic planning.

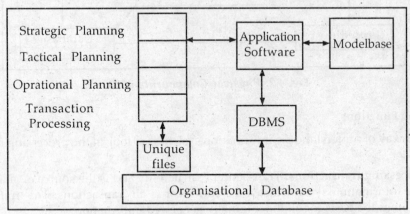

Fig. 4.3: A Model of Functional Information Subsystem

(*Source:* Adapted from Gordon B. Davis and Malgrethe H. Olson, *Management Information Systems*, McGraw Hill Book Company, Singapore, 1984.)

Production Subsystem

The transactions for the transaction processing function in the production subsystem are production orders, assembly orders, finished part tickets, scrap tickets, and time keeping tickets. Operational control management requires detailed reports comparing actual performance with the production schedule and highlighting areas where bottlenecks occur.

Management control level requires summary reports which compare overall planned or standard performance with actual performance. Strategic planning requires information about mergers and acquisitions, alternative manufacturing approaches, alternative approaches to automation, etc.

Marketing Subsystem

Transactions in the marketing subsystems are sales orders, promotion orders, etc. The operational control level of management is concerned with hiring and training of sales force, day-to-day scheduling of sales and promotion efforts, periodic analysis of sales volumes by region, product, customer, etc. Managerial control level compares overall performance against a marketing plan. Strategic planning level considers new markets and new marketing strategies. This level requires information about customer analysis, competitor analysis, income projection, demographic projections and technology projections.

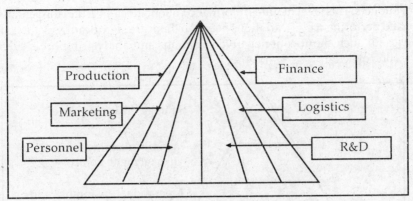

Fig. 4.4: Organizational Function Subsystems

Personnel Subsystem

The transactions in the personnel subsystem are employment requisitions, job description, training specification, personnel data, pay rate changes, hours worked, pay-cheques, benefits, and termination notices. Operational control level requires information about decision procedures for action such as hiring, training, termination, changing pay rates and issuing benefits. Management control level requires information about employees hired, cost of recruiting, composition of skills inventory, cost of training, salary paid, distribution of wage rates, etc. Strategic planning level requires information for evaluating alternative strategies for recruiting, salary, benefits and retaining personnel.

Finance Subsystem

Transactions in the finance subsystem are processing credit applications, sales, billings, collection, payment vouchers, cheques, journal vouchers, ledgers, and stock transfers. Operational control requires information about daily error and exception reports, records of processing delays, records of unprocessed transactions, etc. Management control requires information on budgeted and actual financial resources, cost of processing accounting data and error rates, etc. Strategic planning requires information to evolve alternative strategy to adequately finance the firm, a long range tax planning policy to minimise taxes, planning of systems for cost accounting and budgeting.

A big organisation can have more subsystems like R&D, information processing, logistics and even top management can be seen as a subsystem each having operational level, management control level and strategic planning level management.

3. Levels of Management Activity and Information Requirements

Anthony[2] has divided management activities into three categories: strategic planning, tactical planning and management control, and operational planning and control. At the strategic planning level fixing of the broad goals, policies and general guidelines for the organisation are the responsibilities of management. Strategic planning level requires information about the organisation and its environment. It requires competitor information, industry information, economic and political information, information about current performance of the organisation and new investment opportunities, etc.

At the management control and tactical planning level the responsibilities are concerned with raising and utilisation of resources efficiently and effectively. The activities include acquisition of resources, acquisition tactics, plant location, new product development, and establishing and monitoring of budgets. This level requires information about the targets and the actuals corresponding to these expected performances if variations between them are significant. An analysis is carried out to fix the causes for such significant negative variations and analysis report is submitted to these managers for control action.

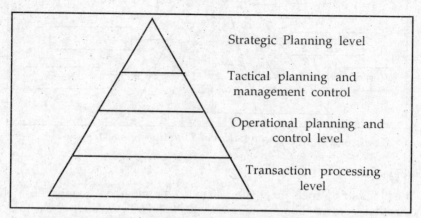

Fig. 4.5: Levels of Management

At the Operational planning and control level the responsibilities of management include effective and efficient use of existing facilities and resources, and to carry out activities within budget constraints. It requires very short-term information relating to a day to a week. It is mostly concerned with the current or the next shift of operations. It requires information about resources of all kinds, production targets, sales targets for a day or two, people availability, etc. It also requires information about pre-established rules and procedures and all its information requirements can be met from internal sources. Since the data for this information arises internally, a high degree of accuracy and effective control on its timely availability can be ensured.

Characteristics of Information for Different Management Levels

Gorry and Morton[3] conceptualise the character of information required by different levels of management as follows.

Table 4.1: Character of Information for Different Levels of Management

Character	Operational Planning and Control	Tactical Planning and Management Control	Strategic Planning
Source	Mostly internal	-	Mostly external
Level of aggregation	Very low	-	High level of aggregation
Accuracy	Very high	-	Not much
Scope	Narrow	-	Wide
Time	Historical	-	Futuristic

As Table 4.1 reveals, the character of information required by different levels of management varies widely. The strategic planning level sets the corporate goals and strategies to achieve them. The information required for strategic planning is mostly externally originating in nature, future oriented and very wide in scope. On the other hand, the operations planning and control level management needs exact and detailed information about its area of operations for planning and controlling activities in that area. For example, sales order processing needs information about actual inventory of finished goods, backlog of orders, goods that will be available from production, customer credit limits, delivery schedules, payment information etc.

4. Decision Support

Decision situations are broadly classified into structured and unstructured on the basis of whether the procedure can be well defined or not. In case of structured decisions, MIS provides the entire information required for making them and it can even handle such decisions automatically. In the case of unstructured decisions, the users cannot even specify the information requirements at the various decision stages and hence MIS cannot anticipate information requirements for such decisions. Hence, the system extends facilities to the managers to interact with the database and model base for analysing the problem and explore feasibilities of alternative solutions. For a detailed discussion on DSS, please refer Chapter Six.

SYNTHESIS OF MIS STRUCTURE

Davis and Olson[4] combined all the four approaches to MIS structure into a conceptual structure for an organisational MIS. Conceptually each functional subsystem is having its own files. The organisational MIS is having a database, models for planning, decisions and investment in the model base and commonly shared application software. The common database is managed by database management software (DBMS). Conceptually it is a federation of subsystems integrated through the database software.

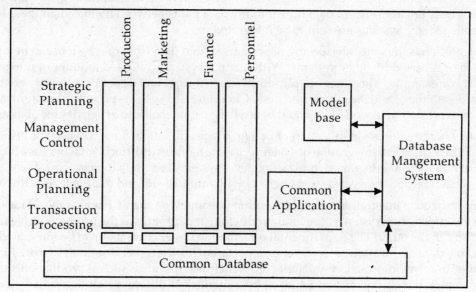

Fig. 4.6: Conceptual Structure of Organisational MIS

Source: Adapted from Gordon B. Davis and Malgrethe H. Olson, *Management Information Systems,* McGraw Hill Book Company, Singapore, 1984, p 47.

Physical Structure

The physical structure of MIS would be identical with the above conceptual structure if all applications consisted of completely separate programs, used by only one function. But in practice several activity subsystems have similarity of processing requirements and therefore they can use the same application software and hardware facilities.

It is very difficult, and in fact impossible, to develop a totally integrated single MIS for any organisation. What is found feasible and adequate is a kind of federation of subsystems designed to meet the information requirements of activity centres.

Integrating applications across the organisation through a single database and common interface brings about organisational integration. ERP is such an information technology solution to integrate organisation across functions and divisions.

EXTENT OF INTEGRATION OF INFORMATION SYSTEMS

Integration of information systems is one of the key concepts of MIS. Systems are interrelated to one another and interact with one another in many ways underlining the need for integration. Integration is possible through data flows throughout the systems. This can be done particularly when data files of one system are required to be accessed by another system or systems and generation of the same data by the latter system or systems is very expensive or impossible. Systems can also be integrated when they use the same data source for data capturing or they provide data to the same system. When any of the relations mentioned above exists, the system is said to be interacting with other system or systems. These interactions help in establishing linkages between systems. These linkages ensure data flow into the data paths between them. When these linkages are established, the systems are said to be integrated.

Integration is thus the interlocking of systems so that data from one system can be routinely passed to or received by other systems. With manual systems a limited amount of integration is possible. For example, when files are physically carried from one desk to another where they are combined with the files at the transferred desk. Computerised systems permit automatic transfer of data from workstation to workstation and hence they are amenable to a high degree of integration.

Integration requires identification of potentially useful interactions. This can be achieved by a systems investigation. Integration of systems may be hierarchical, horizontal or cross-functional. In case of hierarchical integration, transaction level systems feed data to managerial level systems or vice versa. The bottom level system interacts with middle level and middle level with top level.

The horizontal integration takes place within a chain of command. For example, data is passed among the information systems of several production departments as the products move from one department to the other. The departmental information systems are likely to be integrated so that production data is transferred from one department to the other routinely. Cross-functional integration involves information systems of different functional areas such as production, marketing and personnel. Integration can be achieved by a number of different techniques. An elementary method is to establish standard procedures such as the procedure to regularly transfer data from one system to another. Integration can be accomplished when managers freely communicate among themselves. In computer systems, integration can be achieved by automated responses to internal conditions in certain situations. For example, when to place stock replenishment order. Organisational database, which is a common data pool, provides another opportunity to integrate systems.

Integration of information systems is a matter of degree. A totally integrated MIS is out of reach for most organisations. Not only cost is high but also the complexity of information systems increases due to a high degree of integration. The major benefit of integration is improved data flows within an organisation. More information will be available timely for managerial decisions. Another benefit is that it forces managers to share information of one system with those of other systems. A careful trade off between the costs and benefits of integration should be struck to achieve an optimum level of systems integration.

Enterprise Resource Planning System is a dream come true for information system people. It integrates information resources into a single comprehensive database across various functions, offices, factories, etc. All information flowing through an organisation is integrated, and updating information is automated using integrated modules.

MAN-MACHINE INTERACTION

The purpose of information systems is to provide timely information to managers for decision-making. Information is at the base of communication. The data does not become information until it is communicated in a useful form to the persons who need it. The managers are provided with interfaces to interact with the systems. The interface is the contact point of the system with the user.

Managers interact with the system in several ways. One is as an input provider to the system. For example, a decision of a manager to increase sales price of a product. Information accessing is another mode of interaction. A third mode of interaction is managers designing information systems for their own use by writing simple computer programs at their terminals. Continuous interaction with computer files is yet another mode of interaction. A manager might initiate a dialogue with the system by seeking a general type of data, say data about product life cycle. The computer may respond with a series of questions and may finally provide product life cycle information that is available within the system.

Despite such manifold modes of interaction with the system, most managers spend much less time interacting with the system. One reason could be their feeling of frustration about using computer systems particularly when they feel that it requires a great deal of training for effective use. Another reason is difficulty in locating the information though they know what information they need. But with user-friendly systems and productivity languages (non-procedural languages) attempts are being made to reduce this social distance between managers and computer systems.

Modularity

Though the three levels of management are separated in terms of their activities and time horizon, information required at some of these levels may originate from the same source. Managers at different levels and in different functional departments can share the same information resource or hardware or software. The source of most data can be identified to a particular customer order.

The system design employs modular structure. A module is a small set of instructions. It is easy to design and test such modules. These modules are invoked for individual applications. Common modules can be designed to meet processing requirements of a few subsystems. The structured approach to system design employs modular concept widely to facilitate smooth and early completion of projects.

Under the modular concept information system modules are identified by factoring the system, which is carried on until it results into a set of compact and manageable units. For example, the marketing function can be factored into four modules such as product, price, promotion and distribution. Each of these modules can be further divided into minor and basic modules. This approach can be applied in analysing and designing systems. An important advantage is in programming as the job can be divided into modules and distributed among a group of programmers. It is possible to modify any module without affecting any other module. After all modules are designed, coded and tested, they are then logically integrated into a system.

INFORMATION NETWORK

Information flows in all directions in an organisation. It is this information flow which keeps organisations united and integrated. It flows from one person to another, from one place to another through what is described as loops. Forrester visualised organisation as an information network. He observes that enterprises are very complex and multi-loop interconnected systems. Decisions are taken at multiple points in an organisation. Such decisions require a lot of information: background information, analysis information, projection information, etc. Each decision when implemented generates large amount of information, which can be used at several decision points again. This structure of interconnected information feedback loops, when taken together, describes the total system. The interlocking network of information channels emerges at various points to control physical processes such as the hiring of employees, erection of plants and production and distribution of goods.

Every action point in the system is backed up by local decision point whose information sources reach into other parts of the organisation and the surrounding environment. Management is a process of converting information into action. Forrester conceptualises six information feedback networks in an industrial setting viz. materials, orders, money, personnel, capital equipment and information.

Conclusion

MIS can be described using several concepts of MIS organisation such as the formal and informal systems, public and private systems, etc. MIS can be viewed as a federation of subsystems. It has a number of functional subsystems like finance, production, marketing, etc., and basic subsystems like transaction processing, office automation, process control, information reporting, decision support and knowledge-based subsystems. No single view gives a clear perspective of organisational MIS. So a synthesis of these approaches is helpful in understanding MIS better. Davis and Olson have given a conceptual structure by synthesising four approaches to MIS such as the physical components of MIS, management activity subsystems, functional subsystems of management and decision support to management. Information system specialists promised a monolithic MIS for organisations; but it has not yet materialised. A modular structure with subsystems integrated into a federation is found to be acceptable and practical.

QUESTIONS

1. Explain how formal information system is different from the informal information system?
2. What is public information system? How is it different from private information system?
3. "Planning information is different from control information". Do you agree?

4. "Information requirements of top management are different from that of bottom level management". Substantiate.

5. How does MIS provide decision support to top mar.agement?

6. What are the physical components of MIS?

7. Explain briefly how MIS supports functions of management?

8. What is systems integration? What are the methods of systems integration?

9. What is information network?

10. "MIS is a confederation of subsystems." Elaborate.

11. "The physical structure of MIS need not be the same as the conceptual structure." Do you agree?

12. How does information requirement change with levels of management?

13. What do you understand by a synthesis of MIS structure? When will the physical structure be the same as the conceptual structure?

REFERENCES

1. Davis, Gordon B, and Olson, Malgrethe H, *Management Information Systems*, McGraw Hill Book Company, Singapore, 1984, pp. 28-48.

2. Anthony, Robert N., *Planning and Control Systems: A Framework for Analysis*, Harvard University Press, Cambridge, 1965.

3. G.A. Gorry and M.S. Scott Morton, *"Framework for Management Information Systems"*, Sloan Management Review, Fall 1971, p. 59.

4. Davis, Gordon B, and Olson, op. cit.

Transaction Processing System

5 CHAPTER

INTRODUCTION

Business transactions are certain events that occur routinely in a business firm such as purchase and issue of raw materials. The nature and volume of transactions depend on the type and size of business. The transactions are to be recorded to measure efficiency of operations and resource use. The transaction processing system (TPS) is the most important source of data for a business firm.

The transaction processing system (TPS) is the earliest form of computerised management information system. Originally, business transactions were processed manually. This was partly replaced by machine-assisted data processing systems. Gradually, electronic data processing was introduced to record business transactions. TPS is today an integral part of computer-based information systems. It is very difficult to imagine an organisation without a functional TPS. For example, if an airline reservation system breaks down for a day or two, it will cripple the airlines company and the flights will be in disarray causing untold miseries to customers.

In a business firm, there are three types of flows in and out of the firm: physical, financial and information flows. The physical flow is represented by the flow of inputs into the organisation and its various processes within the firm and the flow of the output out of the firm. The second is the reverse flow of money and its equivalent. It starts from customer and ends with the supplier. The third is information flow. Information flow tracks the physical and financial flows.

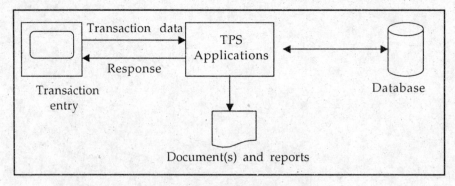

Fig. 5.1: Transaction Processing

The physical flow of input and output is measured and recorded. Similarly the finance flow is also recorded. These records are the sources of data for information corresponding to the physical and financial flows.

The operations management takes care of the physical flow of resources, the accounting and finance management takes care of the financial flow and the transaction processing system takes care of the information flow. The transaction processing system processes all transactions and records them. This results in generation of transaction data which is structured and stored in databases. Apart from recording routine transactions, TPS also updates master files and databases.

TRANSACTION PROCESSING CYCLE

Transaction processing is a basic activity in organisations. It is a routine and repetitive activity that triggers a few other activities like updating database and generation of documents forming a cycle. The transaction processing cycle consists of six steps such as:

1. data entry
2. input data validation
3. transaction processing and validation of results
4. file and database maintenance
5. document and report generation, and,
6. inquiry processing.

The transactions are measured in some convenient unit for recording such as money unit for expenses, hours in case of labour, etc. Data pertaining to the transaction must be entered into the system. The source of this data usually is a document such as sales order from customers, invoice from suppliers, etc. These are called source documents and they provide the basic data for TPS. The data is entered using either the traditional data entry methods or the direct data entry methods. In the former method the source documents like purchase order are prepared and usually accumulated into batches. The direct entry method uses automated systems for data capturing and recording. Point of sale terminals, optical scanners and MICR devices are used in capturing data and transferring data to computers in real time for transaction processing.

Input data validation is the next step in TPS. It checks the accuracy and reliability of data by comparing it with range data or standards, etc. It involves error detection and error correction. Checking for errors include checking the data for appropriate format, missing data and inconsistent data. If the data value falls outside the normal range it is invalid. For example, if a firm's orders for materials in kilograms ranging from 100 to 1,000 kilograms and if that range is accepted as normal data range for purchase orders, then this range is coded into the program for validation checking. That is whenever a purchase order is prepared, as soon as quantity is entered in the appropriate column, the system checks whether the quantity entered is between 100 and 1,000. Otherwise, it will give an error message as "Check the Quantity Entered, it is out of range" or some other error message as is coded.

Processing of transaction data is the next step. This involves some computation, checking and comparing etc. For instance, if it is a credit sale transaction, then the total value of the transaction has to be computed, the system should check whether the value is within the credit limit sanctioned to the customer, it should check the availability of stock, delivery date possible, etc.

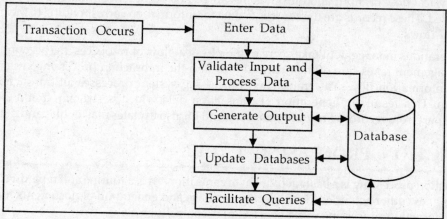

Fig. 5.2: Steps in Transaction Processing

Once the transaction is processed, certain output needs to be generated. The output may be some documents like sales invoices, pay slips, etc., or screen displays or the output data may be used to update related databases. Files and databases have to be updated with each transaction or each batch of transactions. In case of applications that are not time critical, the transactions may be processed in batch mode. Certain systems like airline reservation require updating with every transaction for giving status information in real time. Direct data entry devices have to be used to capture transaction data and update related files and databases to provide current information to users.

Inquiry processing is another activity of transaction processing system which involves providing information on current status like inventory levels, customer credit limit, dues from a particular customer, inbound supply, etc. The inquiry response is pre-planned and the on-screen display or output is formatted for the convenience of the requester.

A business transaction with a customer involves a product or service that a customer wants and the business provides for a price. The TPS supports the delivery process. To complete a transaction with an external entity like customer, supplier, etc., a series of activities is involved such as checking of account, current inventory balance, delivery time and price. For instance, the transaction at a bank counter involves checking of account balance, withdrawal of money or deposit of money. In the case of some transactions, an activity serves as a trigger and a series of activities follow it. For example, a sales order from a customer is followed by a number of activities; some of these are queries like:

- Checking whether the customer is an existing or a new customer,
- Checking customer's credit limit to know whether the transaction is within the permitted credit limit or not,
- Checking inventory balance to know whether the order can be fulfilled within the time the customer needs it,
- Checking production schedule to know how much will be added to finished stock at the end of a production period,
- Checking of back orders to know how much stock will be left to meet this sale order.
- Once this querying is over and if adequate stock is available for meeting the order, the sales order is approved and the transaction is processed. This involves:

- Debiting customer account with the value of goods
- Crediting sales file with the value of goods
- Updating inventory file with the quantity of stock sold
- Generating a packing list for the Dispatch department to assemble the order
- Generating documents like sales invoice, bill of exchange, etc.
- Packing the goods and handing them to the delivery staff, and,
- Delivering the goods.

TPS actually tracks the workflows. Each operation of the workflow is recorded. At each of these points in the sales order processing, the information about the state of the order is recorded.

FEATURES OF TPS

TPS is a fundamental activity subsystem of information system and plays a very critical role in any organisation. Some of the major features of TPS are as follows:

Integration Tool

TPS integrates the various departments in an organisation. Each department will generate data and this transaction data flows into a centralised database. The common database provides the raw data for information generation for various decision makers. TPS, thus, integrates the various functional units of an organisation.

Links Customers with the Organisation

TPS also connects customers with the organisation's warehouse, plant and management. If TPS fails, it may cut the link with customers and organisation cannot transact business with them.

Inputs

Processing involves sorting, listing, merging, updating, etc. The inputs are transaction data like customer code, name, product, quantity, price, etc.

Output

The output includes invoice, sales reports, lists, summaries, and inquiry responses. These are the results of enquiry processing, report processing and interactive processing.

The users

TPS is designed to support lower level management. The transactions are highly structured and routine in nature. Applications are developed to facilitate data capture and recording. Mostly, operations personnel and supervisors are the users of transaction processing system.

User Department Specific

TPS is designed for each department to cater to its special data processing needs. Thus, production department will have a TPS for processing transactions in that department, marketing department will have another TPS for it and so on.

Highly Structured

TPS is highly structured. Business transactions are routine events with relatively very high frequency like those of inventory management, payroll processing, accounting, etc. Hence, these are early candidates for computerisation in most business firms.

Scope for Cost Savings

Since manual transaction processing requires too many hands and often inefficient, most organisations computerise transaction processing. This results in cost savings and drastic improvement in efficiency of service and information availability.

TRANSACTION DOCUMENTS

Processing of transactions results in certain documents. These documents may be classified into any of the following types.

  (a) **Informational documents:** These documents just inform that something has taken place or is taking place. For example, a sale confirms that the order has been received from the customer and has been verified.

  (b) **Action oriented documents:** These documents need to be acted upon. For example, a purchase order initiates a purchase. Similarly, a production order instructs the production department to start production of the products mentioned in the production order.

  (c) **Investigational Documents:** These are generated on an exceptional basis. For example, whenever operations are not conforming to the range of deviations permitted, the variations are tracked and analysed. A report is generated to enable the control point to take corrective action.

The reports or outputs generated by the TPS can also be classified into the following categories.

  (a) **Pre-planned Reports:** Formats of these reports are pre-designed. These reports are frequently generated to meet information requirements of planning and control of actions. Most of these reports are periodic in nature like daily report, weekly report, monthly report etc. For example, weekly sales analysis report submitted to the sales manager helps him to know whether the sales targets for the week were met or not. If the targets were not met, the reasons for failure to meet the target are also analysed and mentioned in the report. This enables a manager to take corrective action.

  (b) **Pre-planned Enquiries:** For the smooth and efficient functioning of any business, a lot of status information will be needed. For example, if a sale order comes from a customer, the sales clerk needs some status information about the stock of that particular inventory item, pending orders, credit limits in case of credit transaction etc. before he confirms the order. Most of this type of status information needs can be met through built in query facility.

  (c) *Ad hoc* **Reports and Inquiry Responses:** These reports and inquiries are infrequent or are not anticipated. They are needed to take some non-routine decisions or actions. For example, at the time of wage negotiation with its workers, if a firm is considering a new incentive scheme to workers, the personnel manager/the finance manager may want to know the implications of this decision in terms of financial obligations. This information need cannot be anticipated in advance. Hence, such unique information needs have to be met by ad hoc reports and enquiry facility.

(d) **User machine dialogue results:** For interactive decision making like in DSS, the decision maker has to enter into a dialogue with the system to generate more useful information. The results are interactively generated and displayed on the screen.

TRANSACTION PROCESSING MODES

Transactions may be processed individually or in batches. Similarly, the processing may be done at local offices or at the head quarters of organisations. The type of processing depends on a set of factors like the volume of data, complexity of data processing operations, processing time constraints, computational demands and the degree of decentralisation of authority. Thus, the processing modes are as follows.

(a) **Batch Processing:** Under this method, transactions are accumulated into batches which are processed periodically. Most organisations handle a large number and variety of transactions every day such as cash sales, credit sales, sales commission, customer credit, consignment sale, advertising, etc., in marketing area. An efficient way to process these transactions is to collect all transactions of the same type for a particular period of time and process them as one batch of transactions. Thus, all sales transactions of a day of a particular product are processed once in a day or period. All these transactions are entered into the system at one time. This enables data processing personnel to better control the entire processing cycle for that type of transaction, and leads to more efficient scheduling of computer time.

(b) **On-line Processing:** The term on-line refers to the fact that the input/output files, data files and related equipment are connected to the computer such that a transaction may be entered at once or information may be retrieved immediately any time. Each transaction is entered into the system as and when it arises. There is no waiting for a minimum number of transactions to enter transaction data into the system.

(c) **On-line, Real time Processing:** If the transaction is processed one by one as it occurs without any loss of time between the event and recording of the event, the processing is in on-line, real time mode. It means that the files for the transaction type are kept on-line, that is electronically connected to the computer, and the transaction is processed quickly, for example, airline reservation.

The concept of real time means that data is entered relatively quickly as it arises and updated information is available without loss of any time between data entry and information retrieval. Real time processing usually requires dedicated terminals connected to the central computer. An input transaction triggers an immediate processing of data with the response being returned in seconds, for example, online stock trading.

(d) **Distributed Processing:** This arose out of the need to channel data processing power to where data actually arises and where it can be processed more efficiently. That is, some processing power is distributed to local or regional level offices by installing computers there rather than centralising it at the head quarters. The detailed information required for daily operations remains at the local level and the summary information required at higher levels for planning and controlling overall operations is forwarded to the central computer.

Online Transaction Processing Systems

Airlines reservation system, online securities trading system, electronic banking, railway reservation system, Hotel room booking system, etc., are examples of online transaction processing systems.

Airlines Reservation System

Online airlines reservation system requires a central computer with networked terminals at booking offices, which may be spread over a wide geographical area. Each booking clerk can access the flight database and check flights, routes, type of seats available, etc. On request by a customer, the booking clerk blocks seats, if available. The flight database is updated with the seats booked. If the applications are critical, adequate security measures are taken to guard against data loss due to system break down or more, etc. Normally, critical online applications like airline reservation, and securities trading, run on two or more servers, one server mirrors the other. If one server fails, the other server takes over processing to ensure uninterrupted access to the system.

Online Security Trading

The National Stock Exchange[1] (NSE) and the Bombay Stock Exchange (BSE) provide online security trading facilities in India. NSE has an automated online trading system with offices in about 390 cities all over the country. Millions of security transactions are processed every day. Set up in 1993 by financial institutions, NSE happens to be the first stock exchange in the world to have used satellite communication system for trading. Through 1,777 satellite dishes, over 3,000 computer terminals are connected into NSE's VSAT network. Thus NSE's VSAT network is the first high speed private network in India and the first extended C-band VSAT network in the world. At the trading counters, operators enter client transactions into the system. The clients may want to buy or sell securities.

For example, if Mr.Ajayan wants to sell 100 shares of Reliance Industries Limited, he will give the order over telephone to the operator at the counter of the broking firm or he will personally walk into the counter and give the order to the operator. The operator will ask for his member code, name of security, quantity, transaction type (buy or sell), etc., and the details are entered into the system. The system confirms the order entry by a message from the host computer at the NSE or if buy or sell transaction is effected, the details of transaction appears on the screen like member code, security name, quantity sold, price at which it was sold, etc., within two seconds.

If Mr. Ajayan visits the trading counter, where he has opened a trading account, during NSE's trading hours, he can see on the terminal the price at which the shares of Reliance Industries are traded at present and make a decision on holding or selling them. A lot of user-friendly information is also displayed on the screen for member clients. This has brought about complete transparency in, and improved efficiency of, securities trading.

Online systems normally have huge processing and storage capacity to provide fast response. Since the system is vulnerable to hacking, etc., adequate security measures are taken to prevent such unauthorised access to these systems. NSE has located its disaster and recovery centre at Chennai to minimise the risk of system failure due to natural calamities, enemy bombing of facility in case of a war, etc.

FUNCTIONAL TPS

Each functional area is provided with a TPS to process transactions in that area. Thus, an organisation will have functional transaction processing systems like:

Sales and marketing TPS,

Manufacturing TPS,

Finance/Accounting TPS,

HRM TPS, and,

Other types of TPS.

Each functional TPS will have applications for various types of transactions. For example, the HRM TPS will have many modules such as time keeping, leave processing, selection, training and placement, and payroll, retirement. Let us take payroll processing to understand the transaction processing within the module.

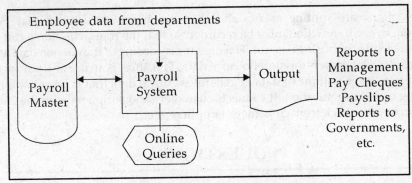

Fig. 5.3: Payroll Processing

Payroll processing is done every month in every organisation that pays its salary to its employees monthly. Payroll processing needs data about the employees such as their attendance, leave, and output. from each department. It draws relatively permanent data from employee master file and uses the transaction data from the other departments in producing pay slips and pay cheques. Such transaction data required for payroll processing includes hours or days worked, leave availed, and the output generated.

Electronic Broking

NSE started screen based trading in securities in India for the first time in 1993. Later BSE also moved over to screen-based trading. But NSE continued to innovate in securities trading. It started offering Internet-based trading in securities in 1999.

The Internet has revolutionised online broking industry. Online brokerage has increased substantially over the last few years globally. Online securities trading in India is yet to become popular. Cochin based M/s. Geojit Securities Limited was the first stock broking firm to start electronic broking in India. Internet-based electronic stock trading offers a number of advantages to the investor such as simplicity, lower brokerage charges and operation from home. Internet-based e-broking has brought in a new class of investors who cannot maintain regular contact with a broker. For example, the NRIs find it extremely convenient to trade in securities on Indian stock exchanges like BSE and NSE. Both BSE and NSE have online trading systems.

Online Banking

Modern generation banks compete among themselves in offering the best of services to their customers. These banks offer online banking. Some of the traditional banks also have started online banking facilities, though not in full mode. Online banking brings banks to the customers. The customers with a computer at home or office can log onto the site of the bank via telephone cable and transact business.

The online services on offer vary from bank to bank. But all the online banks allow customers to check account balances, transfer funds between accounts and applying for loan, etc. These services are available 24 hours-a-day. Web-based Internet banking allows banks to offer online banking services at very low costs.

Conclusion

The transactions are routine events and they are highly structured that permits easy computerisation. Every transaction must be recorded so that the transaction data can be analysed to know how efficiently the business is run. TPS does the recording of transaction data and updating of related databases. Database is the storehouse of data. TPS, thus, is an integral part of information system. It generates huge volume of data. It generates critical data that is essential for the day-to-day functioning of any organisation. It connects customers and suppliers with the enterprise and becomes a source of feedback from customers, suppliers, etc.

QUESTIONS

1. What is transaction processing? How critical is it for a business firm?
2. What is online processing? What are the advantages of online processing?
3. Explain the modes of transaction processing.
4. Explain the steps in transaction processing cycle.
5. Explain some applications where online processing is used.
6. What are the requirements for online trading?
7. Explain how payroll processing is done.
8. Explain the features of TPS.

REFERENCE

1. http://www.nse-india.com

Case 5.1: Hotel Heritage

The Hotel Heritage is centrally located in the city of Calicut. The Hotel has seven departments such as front office, restaurant, banquet, stores, housekeeping, accounts and room service. The Hotel has 49 centrally air-conditioned deluxe rooms and 42 well furnished non air-conditioned rooms.

For holding meetings and conferences, the Hotel has two conference halls with a capacity of 100 and 300 people and a boardroom. It also has a multi-cuisine restaurant, catering coffee shop and 24 hour room service.

Heritage started building its information technology infrastructure in 1997 with an initial investment of ₹ 5 lakh. Today, it has 15 Pentium III computers and a server connected using UTP cable into a LAN with Novel Netware as the network operating system. The Hotel is planning to spend more on IT infrastructure and to set up a website to provide customers Internet access for room reservation, cancellation, conference booking and other services.

Most of the routine transactions with customers have been computerised and more applications are being developed to computerise all of its transaction processing activities. Apart from transaction processing, currently a few reports are also generated for management. The use of computers has increased the efficiency and accuracy of billing operations. It also helps the Hotel in tracking and controlling its inventory. Besides software problems, poor security of the data and low reliability of the network are problems vexing the management.

Questions:

1. Do you think the Hotel's IT infrastructure is adequate for its size and operations?

2. The Hotel is planning to provide facility for room reservation and cancellation through the Internet. What facilities should the Hotel set up to offer this capability to enable customers to access its reservation system over the Internet.

3. What additional security measures can be suggested to improve the Hotel's data security and system reliability?

6 CHAPTER

Decision Support Systems

INTRODUCTION

Management Information system consists of several information systems like transaction processing system, information reporting system, decision support system and executive support system. Every information system aims at meeting information needs of specific users. Decision Support System is different from other information systems in that it does not provide any information directly, but provides some capabilities to the user to analyse the decision problem and generate some meaningful information for decision-making.

A decision support system is a computer application that helps users analyse problems and make business decisions more confidently. It uses data routinely collected in organisations and special analysis tools to provide information support to complex decisions. For example, a firm's sales department may be interested in analysing various sales decision options. The decision support application might gather data, present the data graphically and help in evaluating various options. It may use past sales figures, project sales based on sales assumptions for each alternative considered and display information graphically. It may also use artificial intelligence to enhance its decision support capability.

Decision Support System assists managers in making unstructured decisions. The system enables them to interact with the database, model base and other software. It enables the users to generate the information they need rather than depend on some reports produced according to some anticipated information needs. DSS is more suited to handling unique and non-routine decision problems. In many situations the problem itself may not be easily identified. Similarly, identifying alternatives, identifying outcomes of each alternative considered, evaluation of alternatives, etc., pose problems to the decision maker. Each problem might require a different approach to problem definition, analysis and resolution. Not only that it is difficult to solve such problems, it is also possible that the decision process and solution vary with the decision maker.

DSS is designed to support managerial decision-making, usually, at middle and top levels of management. Decisions made at the top level are mostly futuristic and non-repetitive in nature. Such decision situations are highly uncertain and even specification of information requirements for decisions is difficult. They are classified as non-programmable or unstructured decision situations. The impact of such decisions will be seen throughout the organisation and cost of a wrong decision is usually very high, for example a decision to sell off a line of business.

This is in sharp contrast to programmable or structured decisions where the decision procedure can be well defined and every information requirement can be pre-specified. Most of the decisions taken at lower levels of management fall into this category. For example, a decision to replenish stock of an inventory item is a highly structured decision taken at the operational level. DSS is intended to help managers making unstructured decisions. The system includes a database, various models (Mathematical models for optimisation etc.) and an interface for the manager (usually a terminal) to interact with the system. The manager takes data from the database, selects appropriate model or models and analyses the data using these models to know the probable results of various actions.

DSS is thus an interactive computer system with many user-friendly features aimed at helping non-computer specialist managers in making plans and decisions on their own. With the recent advances in computing technology, particularly the powerful microcomputer and interactive devices, the use of DSS is expanding rapidly as these managers find it easy to access databases and model base for retrieving and analysing data.

DSS contains a database, models and data manipulation tools to help decision makers. It is useful where decisions are semi-structured or unstructured. The decision rule for a structured decision can be pre-specified. Hence it is possible to automate such problem solving.

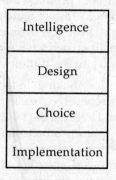

Fig. 6.1: Herbert Simon's Decision Model

Intelligence activities are targeted at discovering problems of organisations. The information reporting system can handle most of these information requirements. In the design phase, alternative solutions to the problem identified are generated. This stage requires more focused information and more intelligence based systems like DSS and Knowledge-based systems. Choice phase involves selecting the right alternative. This requires thorough evaluation of the consequences of all the alternatives under consideration in terms of risk and return, and its impact on problem area.

Information Requirements at Various Stages of Decision-making and the Type of Systems

Stage	Information required	Example System
Intelligence	Exception reporting	IRS
Design	Simulation prototype	DSS, KWS
Choice	'What if' analysis	DSS, large models
Implementation	Graphics, charts	Microcomputer and mainframe decision aids

Source: "A Framework for Management Information Systems", Kenneth C. Laudon et. al., Sloan Management Review, 13, No.1, (Fall 1971).

Decision implementation is a critical phase. Managers are anxious about the results of decision implementation right from day one of implementation. In this phase, managers call for information on implementation of decision such as stage of implementation, time and cost involved, implementation constraints, and impact of implementation.

Decision Structure and Information Support

In the case of structured decisions, decision rule for all the four stages of decision-making in Simon's decision model can be specified in advance. For example, in the case of inventory reordering problem, information requirement and decision rule for all the four stages can be pre-specified. If decision rule for none of the above stages of decision-making can be pre-specified, then it is an unstructured decision. If decision rule can be pre-specified for one or more of the above stages, but not for all, then it is a semi-structured problem. DSS is designed to help the decision maker at each of the four stages of decision-making where decision procedure is uncertain.

Yet, DSS can support repetitive or non-repetitive decision-making. It provides capabilities for repetitive decision-making by defining procedures and formats. For example, an insurance agent may use a DSS package to help clients in choosing insurance schemes. With the privatisation of insurance in the country, innovative insurance products are being introduced. An investor will find it difficult to properly identify an insurance product matching his or her requirements. The agent can carry a laptop with a DSS for insurance products to his clients. The DSS can be used by the sales agent to demonstrate to the clients the details of each scheme in terms of risk covered, bonus, maturity value, premiums, etc., and help the clients arrive at their decisions to purchase insurance policy.

DSS can also help non-routine decision-making. In fact its utility is high when non-repetitive decisions are made. For solving a non-repetitive problem, the DSS provides data, models and interface methods to the user to select and analyse data. For example, a marketing manager might want to analyse the potential demand for new products that the company is planning to introduce. The marketing manager can use a DSS to forecast the demand using relevant data about the market obtained from some database service firms like Centre For Monitoring Indian Economy. The analysis will provide new insights into the market behaviour and product performance that will help the manager in introducing new products into the market.

Decision-making and Problem Solving

Decision-making and problem solving are closely related. But, there is a difference between them. Problem solving involves decision-making and implementation of the solution to address the problem which is sought to be solved. Thus, decision-making has only three out of the five stages of the following model and problem solving has all the five stages of the model.

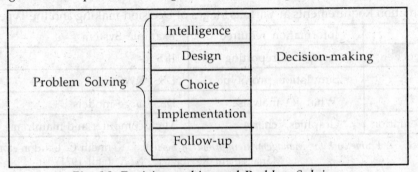

Fig. 6.2: Decision-making and Problem Solving

TYPES OF DSS

Basically, there are two types of DSS. One is data-driven DSS and the other is model-driven DSS. The data driven DSS helps in generating useful information from huge quantity of data in organisational databases, data warehouses and websites. Data mining techniques are employed to generate useful information. The model-driven DSS contains mathematical models to carry out 'what if' analysis and sensitivity analysis.

CHARACTERISTICS OF DSS

1. It is designed and run by managers
2. It contains a database drawn from internal files and external environment.
3. It focuses on decision processes rather than on transaction processing.
4. It is concerned with a small area of managerial activity or a small part of a large problem.
5. It permits managers to test the probable results of alternative decisions.
6. It supports decision-making, usually in solving semi-structured complex problems.
7. It helps in refining managerial judgment applied to problem solving.
8. It improves managerial decisions and thereby managerial effectiveness.
9. The decision maker retains control over decisions throughout the decision process.

COMPONENTS OF DSS

Managers use decision support systems generally for complex problem solving. Problem situation has to be understood properly. The appropriate variables and their interrelationships have to be explored and analysed. Therefore, DSS software needs to have a lot of flexibility in data selection, analysis and presentation. Components of DSS include the following[1]:

1. **DSS Database:** DSS requires a database of its own. It can use data in organisational database. But this will slow down the application. There is also a risk of DSS applications modifying data in the organisational database. Hence, DSS generally uses data from its own database built up from transaction data drawn from organisational database and other relevant data collected from outside.

2. **Model base:** It contains a collection of mathematical and analytical models that the DSS user may want to analyse the data. Each DSS is designed for a specific purpose such as fire fighting, diagnostics, oil exploration, etc. Hence, the models in the model base will vary from DSS to DSS. Generally, it contains statistical models, optimisation models, forecasting models etc.

3. **The hardware:** DSS requires hardware to provide the capability to the users to interact with the database and models using DSS applications.

4. **The user interface:** The user interface of DSS supports the interaction between the user and the data using the models.

5. **Analysis tools:** These include many tools which can be used at any level of management.

DSS TOOLS FOR DIFFERENT LEVELS OF MANAGEMENT

DSS tools can be applied to problems at all levels of management. The tools used at the three levels of management in an organisation are as follows:

(a) DSS Tools for Operational Management

- Material Requirement Planning
- Linear programming
- Queuing theory
- Analysis of variance
- Correlation analysis
- Descriptive statistics like mean, median, etc.

(b) DSS Tools for Tactical Planning and Management Control

- Dynamic programming
- Regression analysis
- Correlation analysis
- Factor analysis
- Multidimensional scaling
- Game theory
- Discriminant analysis
- Non-linear programming
- Network analysis

(c) DSS Tools for Strategic Planning

- Expert systems
- Natural language systems

DSS CAPABILITIES

DSS has acquired many capabilities over the years. Some of the major capabilities are as follows:

What if analysis: This helps in analysing the cause-effect relationship of variables. For example, if advertisement budget for a year is increased by 30% what will be its effect on total sales that year?

Model building: Model building is a central task in most decision support systems. It involves mathematically specifying the relationship between variables. For example, a sales forecasting model based on advertisement expenditure will specify the relationship between sales and advertisement in terms of mathematical statement as:

Sales= 10.94 x Advertisement expenditure.

It means sales turnover will be 10.94 times the advertisement expenditure for the period.

Sensitivity analysis: It is the process of analysing the effect of changes in input parameters on outcome. The input variables are changed over a reasonable range to determine their influence on outcome. It may be one-way or multi-way sensitivity analysis. In one-way sensitivity analysis, the effect of one parameter (say, advertisement) on an outcome variable (say, sales) is analysed. The amount of advertisement will be varied in a range like last year's spending plus 10%, 20%, 30%, etc. In a multi-way sensitivity analysis, the effect of multiple input variables are analysed to determine their impact on outcome variable. For example, what should be the cost of financing a project to get a return on investment of 20% after meeting costs of interest and other operations?

The sensitivity analysis helps the decision-makers to identify variables with large impact on outcome or target variable. That is, the factors which contribute to output variability and the extent of contribution. Such understanding of the degree of relationship between variables helps in revising the mathematical model and predicting outcomes better. By reducing uncertainty about decision situations, it leads to improved decision quality.

Risk analysis: This facility provides a useful probability distribution to the decision maker to assess the risk involved. For example, a probability distribution of profit helps the decision maker to expect certain profit level with certain probability.

Goal seeking analysis: This facility is the reverse of 'what if' analysis. It answers questions like what should be the price per unit to generate a profit of ₹ 10,00,000 from a project. This facility is normally available in spreadsheets. For example, if a person takes a car loan of ₹ 200,000 repayable on monthly basis over five years, the equated monthly instalment will be ₹ 4,488 at 12% interest per annum. If he can repay only ₹ 4,000 a month, at what interest rate he should borrow? This question can be answered using Goal seek, that is, @7.42%.

Optimisation analysis: Optimisation technique identifies the values of one or more target variables meeting certain constraints.

Graphic capability: This facility portrays data in the form of charts, graphs and diagrams to reveal underlying trends and patterns.

Exception reporting analysis: This facility tracks exceptions like overdue accounts, production runs that result in more power consumption than estimated, sales men who could not meet sales targets etc.

Hardware capabilities: It can be implemented on a wide range of hardware configurations ranging from PC to mainframes.

Access to database: DSS accesses data stored in databases and also in external files. DSS tools have the capability to maintain internal files once data is retrieved from other sources.

GROUP DECISION SUPPORT SYSTEM (GDSS)

GDSS is designed to support joint decision making by two or more individuals. The decisions involved in GDSS are mostly unstructured. The group may make decisions in several settings like board rooms, conferences, videoconferences, etc. The decision makers are in different places, yet the GDSS software brings them together in group decision making environment. GDSS provides support by facilitating electronic exchange of comments, views, suggestions and approval or disapproval. The system consists of advanced presentation devices, access to database and facilities for the decision makers to communicate electronically. All the participants in the group decision making are provided with computer-based support that includes data management, retrieval, graphical presentation tools, decision analysis capability, modelling, etc.

Typical GDSS capabilities include[2]

Display: A work station screen or previously prepared presentation material.

Electronic brainstorming: Participants communicate comments electronically.

Topic Commenting: Participants add comments to ideas suggested by others.

Issue analysis: Participants identify and consolidate key items generated during electronic brainstorming.

Voting: Participants use the computer to vote on topics with a choice of prioritisation methods.

Alternative evaluation: The computer ranks alternative decisions based on preferences entered by participants.

MIS and DSS

MIS and DSS are information systems. They have a lot in common. They can be differentiated to perceive the subtle differences between them. They differ on information form, format, content and processing methodology. In this context, MIS is used in a narrow sense of IRS.

MIS provides routine information to decision-makers about the performance of the organisation. The focus of DSS is to extend information and decision support to managers. It requires problem analysis, solution development and testing, etc.

MIS uses simple arithmetical models for analysing data and reporting. DSS needs more complex modelling for data analysis.

The report formats in MIS are pre-specified and fixed. DSS needs flexible format to analyse data in different ways and display results.

MIS has built-in periodic reports and exception reports. Reports have only background building role in DSS. The decision maker needs capability to analyse data in an interactive mode to try solutions and their results.

Business Intellignce System

The term 'business intelligence' was first used by Hans Peter Luhn, a researcher with IBM in a 1958 article. He defined business intelligence (BI) as 'the ability to apprehend the interrelationships of presented facts in such as way as to guide action towards a desired goal'. BI system is an assortment of applications and technologies for gathering, storing, analysing and reporting useful information to make more insightful decisions. It uses a variety of tools to analyse data differently to support strategic, tactical and operational decision making.

BI uses both structured and unstructured data. The former type resides in traditional databases and is fairly easy to search. But unstructured data is rarely used fully. Business firms have huge amount of valuable information, used only once, held in the form of emails, memos, reports, web pages, presentations, image and video files, marketing materials, press releases, etc. They are not structured properly and hence traditional data processing cannot access such data for processing. BI systems have tools to extract such data and analyse them. BI tools include spreadsheets, reporting and querying software, OLAP, data mining, process mining, decision engineering, etc.

Online Analytical Processing (OLAP)

OLAP is a processing method that enables users to selectively extract data from different objects and view them from different angles. The data for such analytical processing should be stored in multidimensional databases (two dimensional in relational databases) for easy querying, analysis and presentation. Using the Open Database Connectivity, data can be imported from traditional databases into OLAP databases.

OLAP services have the following features:

- Easy-to-use user interface and wizards.
- A flexible, robust data model for cube definition and storage.
- Write-enabled cubes for "what if" scenario analyses.
- Scalable architecture that provides a variety of storage scenarios

These features enable the OLAP software to respond quickly to queries.

Data Mining

Business firms capture huge amount of data about customers and business environment on a regular basis. Most of the transaction data is structured and stored in organisational databases. But there are many other attributes of such data which are not stored in traditional databases. They are huge in quantity and are warehoused by large firms. Such warehoused data does not have proper structure to be searched and processed in the traditional data processing way. Data mining is the process of generating business intelligence from large data sets, drawn from databases and data warehouses, for managerial decision-making. The data mining process reveals broad trends and hidden patterns in the data which are extremely useful for strategic and tactical planning and control. That is, it is a process of knowledge discovery from data sets which otherwise remain unexplored.

It extracts patterns from large data sets using tools from statistics, artificial intelligence and database management. Advances in computer science have made complex analysis of large data sets possible. For example, neural networks, clustering, genetic algorithm and decision tree tools have enhanced the capability of data mining to identify and test hidden patterns in the data.

Data Mining Process

Data mining process can be subdivided into three stages: pre-processing, data mining and result validation.

(a) **Preprocessing:** It is the first stage in data mining. Data sets from data warehouse are drawn and arrayed. They must be adequate to give some patterns in them.

(b) **Data mining:** Data mining process has four sets of tasks.

- **Association rule learning:** It is a search for any significant relationship between variables. For example, in a supermarket it was found that beer and baby napkins were bought together by customers frequently. This finding can help the supermarket in its merchandising decisions.

- **Clustering:** It is the process of identifying groups and structures in the data that are similar.

- **Classification:** This involves applying known structures to the new data sets. It classified the data sets in new ways to analyse possible interrelationships.

- **Regression:** This task identifies a regression function that fits with the data set with least error.

(c) **Result validation:** It is the final phase in knowledge discovery. The data mining process generates some trends and patterns which may hold true with the data set chosen for it. The same may not be true with the entire data sets. So, this phase tests whether the results apply equally to larger sets of data.

Conclusion

DSS is a part of organisational MIS. MIS reports are still necessary for managers to monitor the ongoing operations. DSS complements the reports by enabling managers to make less structured decisions with greater confidence. DSS contains models, specialised database and user interface. It helps the decision-maker to interact with the data using the models and generate information for solving semi-structured and unstructured problems. GDSS supports joint decision-making by two or more individuals involving mostly unstructured problems in an organisational setting.

QUESTIONS

1. What is DSS? How does it improve decisions?
2. What is structured decision? How is it different from unstructured decisions?
3. Describe the characteristics of DSS.
4. Explain the components of DSS.
5. Discuss the role of DSS in decision-making.
6. Explain the DSS tools that are used at various levels of management.
7. What is GDSS? Differentiate it from DSS?
8. Discuss the types of decision situations handled by various levels of management and the information system that can support their information needs.
9. Explain the various capabilities that GDSS has and how they help group decision-making.

REFERENCES

1. Kenneth C. Laudon and Jane P. Laudon, *Management Information Systems*, Prentice Hall of India, New Delhi, 1999, p. 615.
2. Steven Alter, *Information Systems*, Addison Wesley, New Delhi, 2000, p. 126.

7 CHAPTER

Expert Systems

INTRODUCTION

Expert systems have evolved out of the work on artificial intelligence over the past few decades and are finding increasing applications in business. The system gathers together a database of knowledge or expertise to offer advice or solution for problems in a particular area by emulating the abilities and judgments of human experts. It accumulates all the expert knowledge in a given area so that the advice or solution offered is better than that of a single consultant or expert. It guides users through problems by asking them a set of questions about the problem. The answers given are checked against the rule base in the system to draw appropriate conclusions from the problem situation. Expert systems are particularly useful in dealing with unstructured problems.

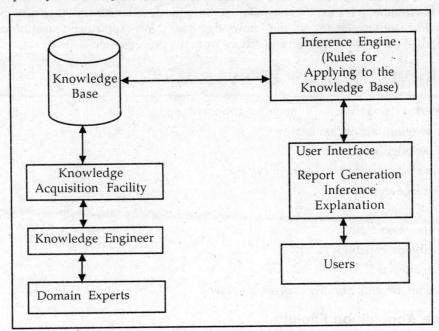

Fig. 7.1: Conceptual Structure of Expert Systems

Expert Systems were originally introduced by researchers in the Stanford Heuristics Programming Project. Principal contributors to this project were Bruce Buchanan, Edward Shorliffe, Randall Davis, William VanMelle, and Carli Scott. Expert systems were the first truly successful forms of artificial intelligence software. Dendral and Mycin were the expert systems software packages developed in the early days of expert system development.

Expert System was originally developed to replicate abilities of human experts. The system captures and stores human knowledge in an area of expertise, called domain, and uses it to solve problems which otherwise requires the help of human experts. The solution suggested by the system is expected to be superior to that by any single expert.

Expert systems are designed to solve real problems in a particular domain that normally would require a human expert. It can solve many types of problems. It is designed to solve some problems very effectively. But it cannot solve every problem one might encounter in an area.

Developing an expert system involves extracting relevant knowledge from human experts in the area of problem, called domain experts. Such knowledge is often heuristic in nature. That is, it is some useful knowledge based on some 'rules of thump' rather than absolute certainties. Acquisition of such rules of thumb and storing them in knowledge base are serious tasks in building a knowledge base. A knowledge engineer does this job of knowledge acquisition and building a knowledge base.

A wide variety of methods are available to simulate the consultation process that a consultant or subject matter expert uses. It involves creation of a knowledge base which uses some knowledge representation formalism to capture knowledge of the expert and a process of gathering the knowledge from experts and codifying it according to the formalism adopted.

The expert system consists of two major parts: the development environment and the consultation environment. The expert system builder uses the development environment to build the components and store expertise into the knowledge base. Non-expert users use the consultant environment to get the expert opinion and advice from the expert system.

COMPONENTS OF EXPERT SYSTEM

The expert systems have the following components:
1. Knowledge acquisition facility
2. Knowledge base
3. Knowledge-based management system
4. Inference engine,
5. Work space
6. Explanation facility
7. Reasoning capability and,
8. User interface.

These components are briefly explained below.

Knowledge Acquisition Facility

Domain experts acquire expertise in their area of expertise over a long period. The expertise may be the result of their constant interaction with similar experts, observation and personal experience in the domain. Capturing expertise is one of the most difficult tasks of building knowledge base. This facility adds new knowledge and rules to the existing knowledge base and ensures its growth to meet emerging needs. Usually a knowledge engineer takes care of this task. He identifies and interacts with the domain experts to gather expertise.

Knowledge Base

Knowledge base is just like the database of information system. It stores knowledge and rules and explanations associated with the knowledge. Knowledge representation is a major task in expert system building. The knowledge must be meaningfully represented in the system so that the system can relate to real world problems.

The knowledge base includes three types of knowledge such as:

- Factual knowledge
- Heuristic knowledge, and,
- Meta knowledge.

The factual knowledge consists of facts about the domain, say, finance, medicine, or design. Heuristic knowledge relates to the rules associated with a domain or problem area. Meta knowledge enables the expert system to use and analyse facts, extract those facts and specify the route to a solution. It refers to the ability of an expert system to learn from its own experience.

The knowledge base contains data and facts relevant to a problem area. The most common way to represent knowledge in expert systems is in the form of rules such as if....then statements. Semantic networks and frames are other forms of knowledge representation in expert systems. The inference engine contains reasoning methods. It is a piece of software that probes the user and searches the knowledge base for the appropriate solution. The user interface links the user with the expert system. It sets up screens for user-interaction with the system. Such interaction leads to identification and solution of problems.

Knowledge-base Management System

It is similar to a database management system in an information system. Its major task is to update the knowledge base with knowledge and rules.

Workspace

The workspace or black board is a memory area used for describing the current problem, and storing intermediate results.

Explanation Facility

Most expert systems have explanation facilities. It explains how recommendations are derived. The user can know how the expert system arrived at the solution, why some alternatives were rejected, why some information was asked for, etc. The explanation facility answers these questions by referring to the system goals, data input and the decision rules. For example, in case of loan proposal evaluation, the expert system's explanation facility will clarify on probing why one application was approved and why another was rejected. In case of a medical expert system such as Mycin, this facility explains how it arrived at a diagnosis. The explanation facility builds confidence in the user about the expert system and the solution it provides to problem.

Reasoning Capability or Knowledge Refinement

The expert system has the capability to analyse why its solution failed or succeeded and ways of improving its solution.

Inference Engine

The inference engine works like the model base in decision support system. It manipulates a series of rules using forward chaining and backward chaining techniques. In forward chaining the inference engine poses a series of if ... then condition checking. Based on the responses a particular solution is suggested. In backward chaining technique, the inference engine starts with the goal and checks whether the conditions leading to that goal are present.

User Interface

The system provides an interface for the users to interact with the system to generate solutions. It is similar to the dialogue facility in decision support system. The artificial intelligence technology tries to provide a natural language interface to users.

Components of Expert System – An Alternate Approach

Another way to analyse expert system components is to look at the physical ingredients of the system as follows.

Hardware

Expert system shells operate on all types of hardware such as micro-computers, minicomputers and mainframe computers. Since microcomputers have become ubiquitous, it has become the standard hardware platform.

Software

Two types of software are needed for expert system: symbolic programs and expert system shells. The expert systems were developed in symbolic programming languages. They have facility to process symbols rather than numbers. Expert system shells consist of a set of programs that provide an environment to declare rules and other knowledge. The shell also acts as an interface between the user and the expert system.

Knowledge

Expert system stores knowledge for decision-making. The knowledge may be represented in a meaningful way such as rule-based format or frame-based or a combination of both so that it can be retrieved to solve real-life problems.

People

Expert system requires some personnel with some expertise.

Knowledge engineers

Knowledge engineers are responsible for creating an expert system. They interview domain experts and build knowledge base of the system. Their tasks are acquiring knowledge, modelling knowledge, and encoding knowledge.

Procedures

Both the users and expert system operators have to follow certain procedures for working with the expert system. The procedures for normal operations and recovery operations have to be developed and maintained.

Characteristics of Expert System

The following are some of the characteristics of Expert System.

- Expert system is capable of handling challenging decision problems and delivering solutions.
- Expert system uses knowledge rather than data for solution. Much of the knowledge is heuristic-based rather than algorithmic.
- The knowledge is encoded and maintained separately from the control program.
- Expert system has the capability to explain how the decision was made. It can also state why a particular piece of information was needed for the solution.

When an Expert System can be Used

An expert system can be used for problem solving if the following conditions are met:

- The problem cannot be specified in terms of a well-defined algorithm.
- The problem requires consistency and standardisation.
- The domain or problem area is narrow or limited.
- When the task is hazardous.
- There is scarcity of experts in the area.
- The problem involves complex logic or a large number of rules.
- Human experts have successfully solved similar problems.

ADVANTAGES OF EXPERT SYSTEM

Expert System is an application area of artificial intelligence. Its purpose is to analyse how human experts make decisions and replicate this decision capability at affordable costs for organisations. Its advantages are:

- It enhances decision quality.
- It reduces the cost of consulting experts for problem solving.
- It provides quick and efficient solutions to problems in narrow area of specialisation.
- It offers high reliability of expert suggestions or decisions.
- It gathers scarce expertise and uses it efficiently.
- It can tackle very complex problems that are difficult for human experts to solve.
- It can work on standard computer hardware.
- It can not only give solutions, but also the decision logic and how the solution was arrived at. Hence, the explanation facility permits a review of the decision and its logic.

LIMITATIONS OF EXPERT SYSTEMS

Expert System is not the result of a one-shot development. It is subjected to an iterative process of problem identification and refinement. Once the system is found to be working satisfactorily, it is implemented for consultation and decision-making. Some of the limitations of expert systems are:

- It is difficult to extract expertise from human experts and hence the knowledge base may not be complete.

- Each problem situation is different from problem to problem. Hence the solution suggested by a human expert is bound to be different from expert system solution.

- Expert system is effective in solving specific problems in narrow domains. It fails in properly analysing problems in a larger area and in suggesting solutions.

- The cost and time required for developing an expert system are very high. Hence, expert system is not affordable for most firms.

- Expert systems are expensive to build and maintain. In many cases the system has to be developed for the organisation. If packages are installed they may have to be customised for the requirement of the organisation.

- It is impossible to build any useful expert system as the expert system cannot capture all the assumptions on which real-life decisions are based.

- It takes long period of time to develop and fine tune an expert system.

- Large expert systems are difficult to develop and maintain.

APPLICATIONS OF EXPERT SYSTEM

There is still difficulty in designing and developing expert systems that can provide reliable and accurate solutions. As such definitive answers cannot be expected from expert systems, but they are certainly capable of providing probabilistic recommendations. Expert system is available in many application areas like medicine, financial services, human resource management, quality control, agriculture, education, oil prospecting, fire fighting, accounting, investment management, criminal investigation, environment management, computer games, etc. Advances in this area are improving the expert systems. Today, expert system is a tool for managerial decision making. Some examples of expert system are discussed below.

Business Insight

This expert system offers facility for strategic analysis. It is based on knowledge from over thirty business experts. It identifies strength, weaknesses, inconsistencies, etc., and gives a thorough explanation. Business Resource Inc., developed this system.

Forecast Pro

It is a business forecasting expert system. The expert system examines data and the program helps the users in forecasting using statistical tools like exponential smoothing, regression, Box-Jenkin, etc. This software is from Business Forecast Systems.

Prospector

It is designed for use in prospecting for minerals. It recommends probable sites for mineral deposits.

Mycin

It is a famous expert system for medical diagnosis. It diagnoses blood infections and recommends treatment.

Conclusion

Expert system is an extension of the artificial intelligence. The system is designed for mimicking experts in their area of expertise. It collects and stores knowledge and rules in its knowledgebase. A user interface is provided to the user to interact with the inference engine in generating solutions and getting explanations. Expert systems are useful in tackling complex problems without the help of experts. They are used in a wide variety of applications such as diagnosis, design, planning, forecasting and control. Even though it is extremely useful for decision-making, it has its own limitations.

QUESTIONS

1. What is expert system? What is its role in organisations?
2. Explain the structure and components of expert system.
3. Illustrate with an example the usefulness of expert system.
4. What are the advantages and limitations of expert system?
5. Explain the characteristics of expert system.
6. Explain the desirability of an expert system for a business firm.
7. Explain the working of an expert system.
8. What is knowledge base in expert system? How is it developed? How is it used in problem solving?
9. "Expert system cannot replace human decision makers". Do you agree? Illustrate your answer.

REFERENCE

1. http://wwww.cee.hw.ac.uk

Case 7.1: MYCIN: A Case Study

Mycin was an expert system developed at Stanford in the 1970s. Its job was to diagnose and recommend treatment for certain blood infections. To do the diagnosis "properly" involves growing cultures of the infecting organism. Unfortunately this takes around 48 hours, and if doctors waited until this was complete their patient might be dead! So, doctors have to come up with quick guesses about likely problems from the available data, and use these guesses to provide a "covering" treatment where drugs are given which should deal with any possible problem.

Mycin was developed partly for exploring how human experts make these rough (but important) guesses based on partial information. However, the problem is also a potentially important one in practical terms – there are lots of junior or non-specialised doctors who sometimes have to make such a rough diagnosis, and if there is an expert tool available to help them, then this might allow more effective treatment to be given. In fact, Mycin was never actually used in practice. This was not because of any weakness in its performance – in tests it outperformed members of the Stanford medical school. It was as much because of ethical and legal issues related to the use of computers in medicine.

Anyway Mycin represented its knowledge as a set of IF-THEN rules with certainty factors. The following is an English version of one of Mycin's rules:

IF the infection is primary –bacteremia

AND the site of the culture is one of the sterile sites

AND the suspected portal of entry is the gastrointestinal tract

THEN there is suggestive evidence (0.7) that infection is bacteroid.

The 0.7 is roughly the certainty that the conclusion will be true given the evidence. If the evidence is uncertain the certainties of the bits of evidence will be combined with the certainty of the rule to give the certainty of the conclusion.

Mycin was written in Lisp, and its rules are formally represented as Lisp expressions. The action part of the rule could just be a conclusion about the problem being solved, or it could be an arbitrary lisp expression. This allowed great flexibility, but removed some of the modularity and clarity of rule-based systems, so using the facility had to be used with care.

Anyway, Mycin is a (primarily) goal-directed system, using the basic backward chaining reasoning strategy that we described above. However, Mycin used various heuristics to control the search for a solution (or proof of some hypothesis). These were needed both to make the reasoning efficient and to prevent the user being asked too many unnecessary questions.

One strategy is to first ask the user a number of more or less preset questions that are always required and which allow the system to rule out totally unlikely diagnoses. Once these questions have been asked the system can then focus on particular, more specific possible blood disorders, and go into full backward chaining mode to try and prove each one. This rules out a lot of unnecessary search, and also follows the pattern of human patient-doctor interviews.

The other strategies relate to the way in which rules are invoked. The first one is simple: given a possible rule to use, Mycin first checks all the premises of the rule to see if any are known to be false. If so there's not much point using the rule. The other strategies relate more to the certainty factors. Mycin will first look at rules that have more certain conclusions, and will abandon a search once the certainties involved get below 0.2.

A dialogue with Mycin has three main stages. In the first stage, initial data about the case is gathered so the system can come up with a very broad diagnosis. In the second more directed questions are asked to test specific hypotheses. At the end of this section a diagnosis is proposed. In the third section questions are asked to determine an appropriate treatment, given the diagnosis and facts about the patient. This obviously concludes with a treatment recommendation. At any stage the user can ask why a question was asked or how a conclusion was reached, and when treatment is recommended the user can ask for alternative treatments if the first is not viewed as satisfactory.

Enterprise Resource Planning Systems

8
CHAPTER

INTRODUCTION

Enterprise Resource Planning (ERP) is the logical extension of Material Requirements Planning I (MRP I) and Manufacturing Resource Planning II (MRP II). ERP packages are designed to model and automate many of the basic business processes in a firm. These software systems replace the legacy software system that the firms employ for automating transaction processing and information support. It is an integrated suite of cross functional applications which are modular in design. It gives the firm an integrated, real-time view of its business processes and tracks resources like cash, raw materials, production, finished inventory, etc.

ERP package contains techniques and methodologies for seamlessly integrating information flows in an organisation. They integrate all types of information like financial and accounting information, customer information, human resource information and supply chain information. It provides operational, tactical and strategic information for improving productivity, quality and competitiveness of a firm. It covers the entire organisation including the supply chain and brings about a total change in the working of the firm. ERP uses cutting-edge technology as well as the best management practices from well-run companies in the world. The advances in networking and communication technologies facilitated the smooth introduction of this massive software into business firms. ERP implementation in large organisations is a complex process. Yet, if a comprehensive ERP is implemented in a business firm, it leads to improved operational efficiency, centralised tracking of business performance and improved transparency.

The enterprise is made up of people with common goals. For achieving those goals it employs some resources like money, materials, workforce and technology. Planning is the process of forecasting future and preparing to use the resources for achieving the stated goals with minimum use of resources. Thus enterprise resource planning is the method of effective planning of all the resources of the enterprise to achieve its goals with minimum effort and resource use.

Seamless integration of firm is a major purpose of ERP. Large business firms collect and store huge quantity of data. The data is stored in databases on many or even hundreds of computers spread over many functions, plants and offices in different parts of the country or even globe. These databases are designed mainly to support some activities at these respective facilities. Maintaining these separate computer systems is an expensive proposition. Data transfer between these computer systems is problematic as these databases are designed to meet information needs of certain applications or activities.

ERP is an attempt at integrating fragmented information systems at the enterprise level. The integrated system permits communication between applications without any hitch. Thus, a customer order processing system can talk to any other application system like inventory system, production scheduling system or finance and accounting system so that the customer requests can be attended to more quickly.

To offer fast responsiveness to customer requests, the firm has to cut its cycle time. This requires rapid product development, flexible production systems, fast and efficient logistics, and efficient operations. No firm can do it without having quick access to accurate information about all internal functions and the entire supply chain activities. ERP provides a solution to this kind of information needs with a centralised database that integrates the various functions like production, marketing, logistics, human resources and finance.

At the core of the ERP is a single comprehensive database: a huge repository of data which stores data from all organisational activities in a single database system. Updating of this database is automatic and hence information is updated with every change in transaction data. Thus, when a sales person enters requirements of a customer into his laptop, the system produces details of the order like product configuration, price, delivery data, etc. If the customer accepts the price and terms of the deal, the sales person presses a key to record order acceptance. The system records the order after checking credit limit of the customer. It automatically updates all related information in the database. It schedules production, reserves necessary materials from the inventory for meeting the order, orders for necessary parts from suppliers, and schedules the assembly of the final products. It works out actual product cost and profits. It updates accounts payable, accounts receivable, balance sheet, etc. Thus the system automatically updates all related information automatically once a basic transaction data is entered into it.

ERP System permits centralisation of control over information and ensuring greater discipline over the entire organisation. Most organisations which have implemented ERP system have drastically cut the order processing and shipping time.

EVOLUTION OF ERP

As business organisations grow in size they undergo structural changes from simple organisation to functional, from functional to divisional or matrix. Large organisations create many divisions and many functions within each division to facilitate management. Such compartmentalisation of organisation results in creating organisational silos that are insulated from other parts of the organisation. This hinders integration of the organisation and sharing of information across functions and divisions. ERP is an answer to such problems of organisational communication and information sharing as it integrates every function and division in the organisation.

Three types of flows can be identified in a manufacturing organisation: flow of materials, flow of information, and flow of costs. The first is a physical flow and the other two are basically information flows.

Flow of Materials

The material flow consists of a chain of activities like procurement, production, inventory and sales. The raw materials are converted into useful products and they are moved into warehouses from where products are transferred to distribution channels that finally deliver to consumers. Flow of materials is a physical flow and it is easy to identify.

Flow of Information for Planning and Control

Production planning prepares schedules of production based on estimated market demand. Production control ensures that the actual production and the targeted production do not vary; if they differ it calls for correction to minimise such variations. Manufacturing planning and control system provides information for all the production and control activities. The flow of information is mostly invisible; but a large chunk of such information is summarised and presented to decision makers in the form of screen displays and printed reports.

Flow of Costs

Ultimately, a business firm must generate surplus value. For ascertaining efficiency of resource use the firm must accumulate costs.

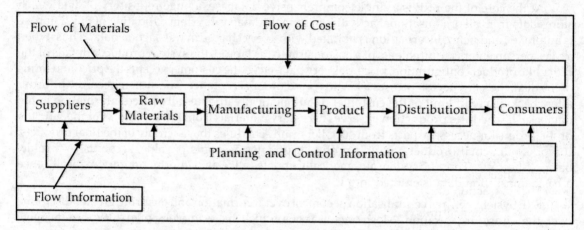

Fig. 8.1: Flow of Materials, Costs and Information in a Manufacturing Firm

Manufacturing organisations had some common problems in the inventory area, particularly when the production process is complex. Production plans are tied to customer orders. When customer orders change, the production plans are revised. The original inventory plans have to be redrawn due to changes in production plans.

There is greater need for integrating customers and suppliers with production process. The customers and suppliers must be integrated with the organisation to ensure fast delivery of customised products. ERP provides this capability to integrate suppliers and customers with its business processes.

In the 1960s materials requirement planning technique was developed to manage inventory. This technique exploded the end product into detailed schedule of purchase orders or production orders taking into account inventory on hand. This reduced the production and delivery lead times by coordinating with suppliers. It resulted in reduced inventory and increased efficiency. In the 1980s manufacturing requirement planning (MRP II) evolved as a logical extension of material requirement planning. MRP II included engineering, finance, human resources, project management, etc. Thus, it covered the entire gamut of operations of an enterprise leading to the use of the more appropriate name ERP. ERP is basically extension of MRPII. Let us now discuss the activities of MRP II.

MRP II ACTIVITIES

Manufacturing Resource Planning (MRP II) aims at planning of all the resources of a manufacturing firm. The activities MRP II comprises are[1]:

1. **Strategic and business planning:** Strategic and business planning is based on detailed environmental analysis and business forecasting. The corporate strategy provides basic inputs to MRP II. The strategy identifies products and markets, technologies and sets goals and objectives for the business. This covers a time span of three to five years.

The business planning is the process of preparing business plans for achieving the strategic objectives. This spans a period of one year to one and half years. The business planning deals with product market strategies (such as new product development, distribution strategies and product positioning), annual sales plan, make or buy decisions, process technologies, capacity decisions, human resource decisions, capital and investment planning, cost and quality control, etc.

2. **Demand management:** Demand management activities are carried out to ascertain market trends and changes with a view to ascertain the demand for firm's products. It helps in avoiding any last minute changes in master production schedule and sales and operations plans. Demand management activities are aimed at stimulating demand for a product, fulfilling consumer demand and providing after sales service to consumers. The specific activities include:

- Promotion, pricing and product mix decisions
- Forecasting demand
- Customer order servicing that includes receiving and responding to customer enquiries, and checking availability of products.
- Order delivery date promising
- Customer order entry
- Distribution requirement planning
- Other customer contact activities.

3. **Sales and operations planning:** Sales and operations planning derives operational plans from business plans. It focuses on managing rates of manufacture to meet targeted inventory and backlog levels. It provides the framework for the preparation of master production schedule. All the functional departments take part in sales and operations planning and hence it ensures coordination among functional departments. The specific activities in sales and operations planning are:

- Review and revision of sales forecasts based on recent sales data.
- Review of current inventory and backlog levels
- Demonstrated capacities
- Revision of production rates based on constraints such as material and capacity availability.
- Development of contingency plans based on expected variations of sales and manufacturing plans.
- Presentation of alternatives to the top management for review and approval.

4. **Master production scheduling with rough-cut capacity planning:** Master production scheduling is a statement of production by item, quantity and date. This involves trade off between manufacturing and marketing. Preparation of MPS is a challenging activity that tries to balance the demands of the marketplace with that of the resources of the firm.

5. MRP I: MRP I is a computerised inventory control and production planning system. It prepares schedule for each item of production and recommends the release of work orders and purchase orders. It also issues rescheduling notices when necessary. MRP I determines what to order, when to order, how much to order and when to schedule delivery. MRP I ignores capacity constraints.

Objectives of MRP I

- Determine requirements to support MPS
- Maintain the lowest possible inventory
- Schedule production
- Keep schedules valid and updated against changes in various factors.
- Explode Bill of Material (BOM) to determine quantities of raw materials, base components, fabricated components, assemblies, etc.
- Estimate gross requirements
- Find net requirements by deducting material available and scheduled to be received form gross requirements. This process is called netting
- Specify order quantity, that is lot sizing.
- Prepare manufacturing calendar. This calendar shows days of manufacturing excluding weekly off days, periods of plant shut down, etc.
- Offset lead time and plan orders
- Incorporate scrap, shrinkage or yield.

6. Capacity Requirements Planning: Capacity requirements planning takes into account planned orders and work in progress to ascertain the availability of resources to execute the production plan in more details than the rough-cut capacity planning. It produces a report showing the capacity required by machine centre and time when needed to actually execute the MRP I plan. It also reports machine centres overloaded and idling for various time periods. The production planners can use this information in smoothing the workflow. Based on material requirements plan, capacity requirement plans are developed that detail the capacity requirements such as labour, capital, machine or equipment time needed, etc.

7. Vendor Requirements Planning: Once the material requirements are identified, they must be communicated to the suppliers. Similarly the material and capacity plans are communicated to the plant. MRP I specifies material requirements by components and raw material. The purchasing function uses this information to identify and select vendors for planned acquisition. Once the suppliers are selected, contracts are negotiated with the suppliers for the required supplies. Supplier schedules are drawn up and communicated to the suppliers. The suppliers are issued schedules rather than a single purchase order each time. The schedules list the requirements and time when needed etc. which the suppliers have to adhere to.

8. Shop floor control: This component of MRP II is responsible for execution of the firm's production plan. The task includes[2]:

- Reviewing and releasing work to the shop
- Monitoring and controlling lead times
- Establishing and receiving order priorities
- Making detailed schedules

- Planning capacity at each work centre
- Controlling queue time and work in progress
- Receiving feedback on the status of production activity
- Disposing orders
- Recording performance or actual results and comparing them with the standards and targets.

MRP II is actually a software based manufacturing information system that supports forecasting of demand, production planning, production scheduling, purchase planning and control, production activity control, etc. The software integrates finance, marketing and operations, and derives finance requirements from production plans .

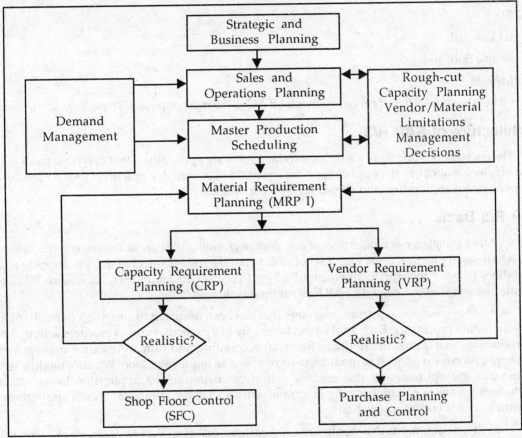

Fig. 8.2: MRP II - A Framework

(*Source: Manufacturing Resource Planning*, Khalid Sheikh, Tata McGraw-Hill Publishing Company Limited, New Delhi, 2001, p 64).

An integrated ERP system manages the business processes required to fulfil each customer order and assesses its impact on materials and production. ERP is a package software solution, not a custom-built solution specifically developed for a firm.

POPULAR ERP PACKAGES

The following are some of the popular enterprise resource planning software packages currently available in the market:

SAP R/3

Baan

Mfg Pro

Oracle Applications

Marshall

BPCS

JD Edwards

People Soft, and,

MAMIS

Of the above, SAP R/3 from Germany's SAP AG. is the most popular ERP package in the world.

Architecture of SAP R/3

The package is made up of a suite of standard software applications that carry out tasks in the most efficient manner as the applications are based on best industry practices. SAP R/3 is based on open system architecture and client/server technologies.

SAP R/3 Basis

SAP R/3 installation includes a set of components forming the core of the system. It is referred to as R/3 Basis. It provides users with a set of tools to build a suite of integrated applications that can be modified to match the exact requirements of a firm. Every SAP R/3 implementation needs R/3 Basis module that supplies the elements SAP R/3 runtime system.

SAP R/3 application is a set of programs that has been designed to support a particular kind of business data processing. Each application takes care of a particular area of business activity such as production, marketing, distribution, financial accounting and human resource management. Each application has a number of modules to form a specific implementation. Within a module some components are optional and this enables a firm to customise the application to its specific requirements. Each application is fully integrated with R/3 Basis. This permits each application to communicate with other applications.

The ERP package needs to be configured and customised to suit the requirements of a particular business firm. SAP experts, called Application Developers, configure and customise the package to suit the specific requirements of client firm.

FUNCTIONALITIES OF SAP R/3

SAP R/3 supports many functions in an organisation. Some of these functionalities of this package and the modules under them are mentioned below.

Financial Accounting

    Accounts receivable

    Accounts payable

    Legal consolidation

    General ledger

    Special purpose ledger

Controlling

    Product cost Controlling

    Activity Based Costing

    Overhead Cost Control

    Sales and Profitability Analysis

    Project Control

Project System

    Basic Data

    Operational Structure

    Project Planning

    Approval

    Project Execution/Integration

    Information System

Industry Solutions

    Public Sector

    Telecom

    Banks

    Oil

    Hospital

    Real Estate Management

Human Resources

    Personnel Planning and Development

- Organisational Management
- Workforce Planning
- Personnel Development
- Seminar and Convention Management
- Room Reservations Planning

Personnel Administration

- Employee Management
- Compensation Administration
- Benefits
- Time Management
- Applicant Manager
- Incentive Wages
- Travel Expenses
- Payroll

Plant Maintenance

Equipment and Technical Objects

Maintenance Order Management

Preventive Maintenance

Maintenance Projects

Service Management

Plant Maintenance Information System

Production Planning

Basic Data

Sales and Operations Planning

Materials Requirements Planning

Production orders

Assembly Orders

Product Costing

Repetitive Manufacturing

Kanban/JIT Production

Production Planning for Process Industries

Plant Data Collection

Information System

Materials Management

Material Requirements Planning

Purchasing

Invoice Verification

Inventory Management

Warehouse Management

Electronic Data Interchange

Information System

Sales and Distribution

   Master Data

   Basic Functions

   Sales

   Shipping

   Billing

   Sales Support

   Information System

   Electronic Data Interchange

Quality Management

   Planning Tools

   Inspection Processing

   Quality Certificates

   Quality Notifications

   Quality Control

Baan

Baan is a popular ERP package form the Netherlands based Baan company. Baan is based on open architecture that offers flexibility to clients in migrating to newer technologies and products. It can be scaled to meet the requirements of small, medium and large firms.

The company sells a family of related products such as BaanCoporate Solutions, BaanERP, BaanFrontOffice, and BaanSupplyChain Solutions.

Baan ERP MODULES

It consists of a number of interdependent components that can be configured to meet a firm's business needs. BaanERP includes the following modules Manufacturing, Finance, Project, Distribution and Tools. These modules are detailed below.

Manufacturing Module

Since it is based on open architecture Baan can be integrated with other popular Computer Aided Design packages.

- Bill of Materials
- Cost Price Calculation
- Engineering Change Control
- Engineering Data Management
- Hours Accounting
- Product Classification·
- Product Configuration

- Production Control
- Production Planning
- Project Budgeting
- Project Control
- Repetitive Manufacturing
- Routings
- Shop Floor Control
- Tools Requirements
- Planning and Control
- Capacity Requirements Planning
- Master Production Scheduling
- Material Requirements Planning

Finance Module

- Accounts Payable
- Accounts Receivable
- Financial Budgets System
- Cash Management
- Financial Reporting System
- Fixed Assets
- General Ledger
- Cost Accounting
- Sales Invoicing

Project Module

- Project Budget
- Project Estimating
- Project Invoicing
- Project Monitoring
- Project Planning
- Project Progress
- Project Recuirements Planning

Distribution Module

- Sales Management
- Purchase Management
- Warehouse Management

Tools Module

- Open System Tools
- Client/Server Tools
- End User Tools
- Developer Tools
- Documentation Tools
- Translation Tools
- Software Distribution
- Implementation Tools

INFORMATION INTEGRATION THROUGH ERP

ERP takes a holistic view of the business. It has a single centralised database that stores all the data. Physically the data may be stored on multiple computers in multiple offices but the software integrates them into a single database to facilitate smooth information flows.

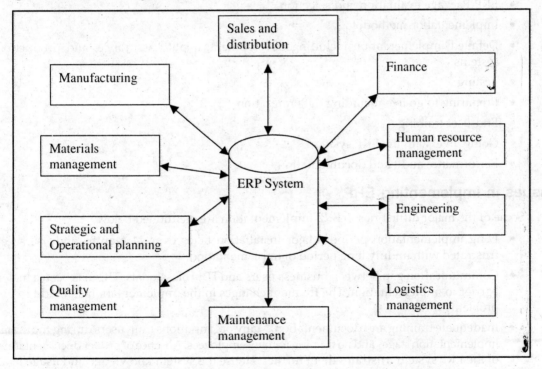

Fig. 8.2: Integration of Functions Using Centralised Database

ERP IMPLEMENTATION

ERP implementation introduces a major change in the organisation in the way it transacts business, captures data, processes and shares information. Since it involves huge investments and taking care of the finer aspects of implementation, involvement of management and employees at all levels is a pre-condition for implementation success. The implementation takes a long period of time as well. A typical ERP implementation project involves the following[3]:

- ERP readiness assessment
- Preparing the organisation for ERP
- ERP feasibility study
- Process modelling and documenting the 'as is' processes and 'to be' processes along with BPR.
- Detailed plan for ERP Implementation
- Selection of ERP Implementation consultant. ERP consultants are experts in developing techniques and methodologies for implementing ERP packages. They manage and control the ERP implementation project. The consultants take upon themselves the responsibility for implementing each phase of the implementation process. They being outsiders are in a better position to impartially question the current business practices of the client firm and decide on whether to carry them over to the new system or drop them. They are paid well for their service in implementing ERP.
- ERP Package evaluation and selection.
- Implementation methodology
- Detailed implementation including development, quality assurance, and production systems
- Testing
- Preparing to go live including data migration
- End-user training
- Going 'live' with the ERP system
- Performance audit and documentation

Issues in implementing ERP

Some of the major difficulties in ERP implementation are mentioned below.

- Long implementation period. Major installation takes over 24 months and users get frustrated with unduly long period of implementation.
- Communication gap between business users and IT professionals. This has been a major barrier to implementation. The frequent changes in the implementation staff add to the problem further.
- Inadequate training and documentation. Many organisations train users during the initial implementation stages and no training for new employees. Absence of proper documentation of the ERP system frustrates them further. Hence the system knowledge and usage tend to decline over a period of time.
- Constraints on customisation imposed by vendors. The ERP package can be customised, but the vendors warn the clients against major changes to the software package. They caution the clients that touching the core of the package may cause malfunctioning of the package. This limits the scope for any significant customisation of the software to user requirements.

- Shortage of consultants with adequate implementation experience. ERP consultants guide its implementation. But there is shortage of consultants with enough implementation experience to effectively oversee the implementation process.

ERP CONFIGURATION AND CUSTOMISATION

An organisation can implement all modules or any selected modules. The package is configured for an organisation by setting parameter values. ERP Implementation is not as easy as installation of any other off-the-shelf packages. It would normally require changing some of the existing processes and procedures. This is because of the ERP packages being modelled on best industry practices. Of course, it is possible to customise the package to meet the specific needs of the organisation that is implementing a package. Customising involves writing new modules and integrating it with the package. But the software package is too complex and hence most ERP software vendors do not allow touching the core of the package; that is they permit only a limited amount of customisation.

ERP software is based on best industry practices. Hence implementation of ERP involves BPR and configuration. The firm's business practices have to be synchronised with the business practices built into the ERP package. Wherever the current practice deviates from the corresponding business practice in the ERP, the consultant and client firm's management have to decide whether to remodel the current practice or change the software in the ERP to customise it. The ERP developers will identify business practices that do not go with the ERP package being implemented. For instance, a firm may have a personnel hiring practice that cannot be configured into the system. The developers are experts in the package and they need to tell the management about the process changes required to implement the ERP.

Some companies have software for helping configuration. For instance, SAP AG has developed industry specific templates as part of accelerated SAP solutions that can be used for configuring the ERP for a particular firm in that industry. Similarly, Baan has developed an automatic configuration tool called Orgware.

Benefits of ERP

ERP implementation offers many advantages to a firm, some direct and some indirect. The direct benefits include improved efficiency, improved quality of decisions, reduced cycle time and improved response time to customer queries. The indirect benefits include improved corporate image, satisfied customers and improved customer goodwill among others[4].

An integrated information system like ERPS offers the following specific benefits.

1. **No duplication of data.** Basic data is not duplicated. It is entered only once and in one place. Any application can access that data from anywhere in the organisation.

2. **Centralised control.** Data management can be centralised and the centralised system can permit sharing of data across applications.

3. **Consistency of data.** The system obviates duplication of data. Data is entered only once and all related information is updated automatically. Therefore, the database is not affected by any data inconsistency.

4. **Improved business performance.** ERP reduces cycle time and inventory levels. It improves the level of customer service and customer responsiveness.

5. **Quick access to transaction data.** It provides instant access from anywhere in the organisation to the transaction data across the functions and divisions.

6. ERP facilitates introduction of supply chain management.

7. ERP saves lot of time for operating managers who can spend the time on more productive activities.

DISADVANTAGES OF ERP

ERP is certainly an excellent software package that can address many of the concerns of management like integration, access and security of information resources. Yet, it has some disadvantages that may limit its use. Some of them are mentioned below:

- Vendors offer limited customisation of the ERP package. So business firms may have to develop their own ERP or develop modules for the level of customisation required.

- Since the ERP package is based on best industry practices, most firms will have to reengineer their business processes before ERP implementation. It may cause loss of competitive advantage to some firms.

- ERP implementation takes unduly long period of time. Such protracted implementation disturbs normal working of firms under ERP implementation.

- ERP packages are too rigid and inflexible. Hence, it is very difficult for many firms to adapt to the specific workflow and business processes embedded in the package.

- Holding back of any information by any of the departments or functions in a firm affects the system's effectiveness adversely.

- The total cost of Implementation of ERP package in a firm is very large. Though cost effective micro-ERP packages are available, many small firms may not have the resources to implement it.

Cost of ERP Implementation

ERP is one such application software that no manufacturing firm can ignore. It gives the management at all levels an advantage of seeing things from close quarters. Business firms that successfully implemented ERP packages have gained the power of integrated information and its impact on accurate business planning and effective controls. Yet, very often the true cost of ERP implementation is underestimated. The total cost includes the costs of software, hardware, data conversion, training and business process redesign. Typically, the hardware and software costs are around one-third of the total cost of implementation. Training cost and data conversion cost may account for a quarter of total expenses. The business process redesigning costs nearly 2/5 of the total cost.

Conclusion

ERP is an integrated suite of applications for business management. ERP implementation touches every aspect of business and information processes. Since ERP is designed on best industry practices, its implementation in specific firms will involve redesigning business processes to get better benefits from its implementation or customising the software to match its specific requirements. Most installations require both changing the business processes and customisation. Hence, BPR becomes a tool for ERP implementation process. The focus of ERP is on linking business applications across functions to seamlessly integrate the information flows through a centralised database. Information flows freely in such an integrated firm from one part of it to any other part of the firm when and where the information is needed. It thus smoothens business processes and raises the level of customer comfort in dealing with the firm.

QUESTIONS

1. What is ERP? How is BPR related to it?
2. What is MRP I? How is it different from MRP II?
3. Trace the evolution of ERP and explain its relationship with MRP II.
4. What is the need for configuration of ERP package?
5. What are the advantages and disadvantages of ERP?
6. Explain the common functionalities of ERP packages.
7. Discuss the stages in the ERP implementation in a firm.

REFERENCES

1. Khalid Sheikh, *Manufacturing Resource Planning*, Tata McGraw-Hill Publishing Company Limited, New Delhi, 2001, pp. 63-64.
2. Khalid, p. 462.
3. Khalid, p. 518.
4. Leon, Alexis, *Enterprise Resource Planning*, Tata McGraw-Hill Publishing Company Limited, New Delhi, 1999, p. 119.

Case 8.1: Micro ERP at FC Hypermarket

Set up in 2009, FC Hypermarket is one of the first hypermarkets in South India. It is located on the ground floor of FC Shopping Mall Building. The Shopping Mall started functioning in 2008 with 2.5 lakh sq ft of space. It has parking space for 300 cars and provides all modern amenities. The FC Hypermarket deals in thousands of products. The hypermarket was completely computerised. The management wanted a software solution for its business. It looked at the options available. SAP and Tally. ERP were the two choices considered by the management. Both were expensive and inflexible for the hypermarket's requirement. So, it was decided to hire a consultant to design, develop and install a custom package. Soware Software Solutions Pvt. Limited was hired to do it. The team from the software company set on its task. It identified the specific needs of the hypermarket and developed an ERP package to exactly meet the requirements of the client firm. It included modules on sales management, inventory management, employee compensation, consumer details management, cost control, purchase management, etc. Everything except accounting was taken care of by the software. Tally was used for accounting. The package is user-friendly and easy to update with modifications to the code.

The management identified the following benefits to the hypermarket because of the custom-made software package:

- Easy MIS reports for effective management of operations
- Complete tracking of revenue and cost
- Customer relationship management
- Inventory management including inventory tracking and analysis of fast moving, slow moving and dead items
- Cost control and cost reduction
- Improved efficiency
- Low cost of acquisition and low maintenance cost of the software

The employees were given 15-day training in the use of the new package. Follow-on training was also arranged to update their software skills to increase the benefits of the software package.

After a couple of months of use, it was found that certain reports which the management wanted could not be generated with the package. The package does not have data recovery capability in case of software failure or system crashing. The software does not have an Internet interface. So the hypermarket cannot contact customers via email or take orders online. The company has not hired any IT professional to update the software package.

Yet, the management is happy with the customised software package as it cost the company only a fraction of the cost of SAP ERP package.

Questions:

1. Do you think the decision of the management was right to go for a custom-made ERP package? Why?
2. What are the advantages of the present ERP package? Could the hypermarket have enhanced the features of the package? If so, how?
3. Can a Small business afford to implement SAP ERP package? Why?
4. Can the ERP software implemented in the hypermarket meet its future needs, say, in the next five years? How?

Customer Relationship Management

9
CHAPTER

INTRODUCTION

Successful business firms have recognised the fact that customers are their most valuable asset. CRM philosophy anchors on this fact. Hence, the task of marketing function is winning and satisfying customers. Satisfied customers buy products again and again. Keeping the customers satisfied is, therefore, the responsibility of the marketing function. This might appear to be simple. But the task is very difficult. It is not just the quality of products and services that is required to achieve it, but a host of other factors like personal interaction and communication with customers. Building long-term relationship with customers helps the firm in lowering cost of sales and in improving customer retention. Customer relationship management focuses on bringing delight to customers through customised products, support services and constant flow of communications between the firm and its customers. E-CRM is an integrated system of software tools and databases to acquire new customers and serve existing customers better.

Meaning

Winning business firms are more efficient in acquiring, keeping and growing customers. They improve customer base by lowering rate of customer defection and increasing the longevity of customer relationship. The value of a business firm depends on its customer base. Based on lifetime value of its customer, a firm can segregate high value and low value customer groups. Each customer group may have a set of characteristics that distinguishes it from other groups. The firm needs a lot of customer-specific information to identify customer characteristics. The type of customers and their buying behaviour strongly influence a firm's turnover and profitability.

The philosophy of CRM is based on the tenet that winning a new customer is at least five times as costly as retaining an existing customer. Hence, the focus of CRM is on matching firm's performance with the expectations of customers, so that they remain loyal to the firm. But, the level of expectations of customers does not remain constant. It changes due to several factors like superior product offerings by competing firms. Value of a product or benefit to customers depends on benefits and price. If a product gives more benefit than its cost, the product gives more value to customers. Here, mere satisfaction of expectations is not enough. The firm has to exceed expectations of customers. When a firm delivers more value to customers than they expect, the firm is bringing delight to them. Through such improved value delivery, the firm is trying to differentiate itself from competing firms. If a firm succeeds in differentiating its product or service, then it is perceived as not having a real substitute. Hence, the firm does not face much competition when its products are perceived to be different by customers.

Definitions

The core of CRM is to understand customer values and deliver those values profitably. It is defined as "a business strategy to acquire, grow and retain profitable customer relationships with the goal of creating a sustained competitive advantage".

Another definition of CRM goes as follows. "CRM is a state of being that puts customer at the centre of an organisation's universe. The promise at the end of this road is customer nirvana – loyal and satisfied customers being serviced at the lowest cost channels and providing companies with an ongoing source of revenue".

ROLE OF CRM

Relationship is moving centre-stage in building competitive advantage for firms. Customers are individuals and they expect the employees to take proper care of them. It requires a lot of information about each customer. Building customer database is, therefore, an essential requirement for CRM. The transactional database of an organisation contains huge quantity of data about customers and their buying behaviour. CRM can win and sustain customer loyalty. Loyal customers make repeated purchases from the same firm. It is possible to project the value of lifetime business with a customer. Based on such customer characteristics, it can classify customers into certain groups. Given this kind of information about customer groups, a firm can customise its products and services to meet the requirements of the selected groups of customers profitably. There will be unprofitable customer groups. The business firm can reduce cost of selling products and services to such groups as they may not be very fussy about quick delivery or other customer services.

The importance of CRM is much greater in e-commerce and m-commerce environment. Customers cannot feel the product and buy it. They need much information before, during and after a purchase decision is taken. Hence, the firm needs to make available the required information to the customers to keep them comfortable at each of the stages in purchasing.

Software solutions are available for a firm to implement CRM. With software solutions, the CRM processes are well established. The employees are adequately trained at the time of implementation to meet and exceed customer expectations.

The role of CRM can be understood from what it can do for a business firm in improving its customer relationship and business prospects. The following points reveal the role of CRM.

- By capturing, tracking and analysing customer service data, CRM enables a firm to identify product performance issues.
- Customer data will help a firm in identifying new product development opportunities
- Customer data will enable a firm to identify product training opportunities for customers and generate revenue from such opportunities.
- Data on customer service history will help a firm to anticipate customer need for new products or services and proactively solve customer needs.
- Provide personalised services to customers based on their behaviour and responses.
- It seeks to manage effectively the firm's interactions with customers, clients and sales prospects. It employs technology solutions to organise, automate and synchronise business processes like sales, marketing, customer service and technical support.

CRM involves the following steps:

- **Information collection.** Accurate customer data should be collected and stored for CRM use.
- **Information analysis.** Based on customer behaviour and loyalty status, customers are classified into segments sharing common characteristics.
- **Personalised marketing.** Based on the information about customer segments, products or services are offered to each individual customer to increase satisfaction with the product or service.

ADVANTAGES OF CRM

CRM is beneficial to firms and customers of the firms that implement it. Some of the advantages of CRM to the firm and its customers are as follows:

For the firm

- Staying ahead of competition is becoming increasingly difficult with superior quality of products and services alone. CRM can enable a firm to compete effectively by winning loyal customers and retaining them for long.
- CRM can differentiate a firm and its offerings from those of other competitors. Strategic differentiation through CRM can be based on core product or services, total cost of ownership or total relationship and customer experience.
- CRM can deliver more benefits to a firm from improved customer retention and selling more to its customers over a long period of relationship with them.
- CRM puts customer interests first and hence keeps the processes customer focused, and,
- CRM can improve both top line (sales turnover) and bottom line (profits) of a firm.

For customers of the firm

- Easy to do business with the business firm
- Quick response to customer order
- Customised products and services, and,
- Consistently high quality of service

Disadvantages

The disadvantages of CRM may be seen as disadvantages to firms and disadvantages to customers.

Firms

- CRM implementation is difficult and expensive. It has two parts: one, technology and the other CRM practices. Technology changes frequently and the organisation will also be growing. Updating of technology presents its own problems. Implementing CRM practices in an organisation is a still more challenging task.
- CRM projects fail in generating adequate return on investment.
- Implementation of CRM software and its maintenance needs a lot of managerial effort. If the management does not adequately support it with funds and leadership, CRM projects

may fail in producing the expected results. For example, ICICI Bank implemented CRM of Siebel Systems. But it was difficult for the company to maintain the technology in the face of its fast growth. So, it worked with Infosys to develop an improved version of the CRM software that is cost effective for ICICI Bank.

- It requires organisational change that may not be that easy to implement.
- Any strategic advantage that CRM may deliver to a firm may be lost when competitors also implement the same software solutions.

Customers

- Privacy is compromised as the firm gathers a lot of personal data, which may be misused by its employees.
- Less profitable customers may be ignored or their interests neglected by a firm that focuses on high value customers. Hence, some customers may feel alienated or discriminated against.

CRM SOFTWARE

SAP, Oracle, Salesforce.com, Microsoft and Amdocs are the leading players in CRM with large market share of e-CRM. Together they account for above 50% of the global CRM software market. CRM software modules include, among others, sales force automation (SFA), marketing, customer service and support, analytics and collaboration.

Sales Force Automation

SFA involves using software to streamline sales process so as to minimise the time sales representative has to spend with clients. SFA improves productivity of sales representatives and therefore, they can serve more clients than before. SFA has contact management system for tracking and recording every stage, from initial contact to final disposition, in the sales process for each client.

With CRM solutions, a firm will get all kinds of information and support for winning, serving and retaining customers. The sales, marketing and support team will get the help needed to target, close and retain customers.

Marketing

CRM software helps a firm in identifying potential clients and generating leads for the sales team. It is capable of tracking multichannel campaigns like email, social media, telephone and direct mail.

Customer Service and Support

CRM improves quality of customer experience with the firm and it helps the firm in retaining customers. It can extend support to customers anytime, anywhere.

Appointments

Sales, customer service and support personnel have to frequently fix appointment with customers. CRM's automated appointment fixing process saves a lot of time for such personnel.

Analytics

CRM software has analytics capabilities built into applications for sales, marketing and service. CRM is a technology supported, customer-centric way of doing business. It has the business process at its core. It gathers and consolidates information about customers, sales and marketing process, responsiveness and market trends.

Collaboration

CRM employs collaboration tools for the various departments of a business enterprise to cooperate among them to fulfil customer orders without any hassle.

CRM PACKAGES

Some of the CRM packages available in the market are mentioned below. They include CRM from SAP, Oracle and Microsoft.

Oracle Siebel CRM

Oracle Siebel CRM is a set of very popular CRM solutions and their functionalities are described below

Sales

Oracle's Siebel Sales applications improves sales effectiveness in real time by accelerating the quote-to-cash process, aligning sales channels, increasing pipeline and win rates, and raising average transaction values. It has comprehensive, industry-specific sales force automation capabilities and proven mobility solutions for disconnected access.

Marketing and Loyalty

Oracle's Siebel Enterprise Marketing Suite is a comprehensive closed-loop solution that empowers B2B and B2C organisations across industries to achieve excellence in marketing. Tailored to the needs of business and consumer marketers across more than 20 industries, the Siebel Enterprise Marketing Suite delivers actionable insight to all members of the marketing organisation.

Contact Service and Centre

Oracle's Siebel Contact Center and Service product family helps firms deliver quicker, better and more-efficient customer service. Whether a company needs hosted, mobile, or on-premise solutions, these applications provide optimal resource deployment, speedy issue resolution, one-and-done request handling, and powerful tracking and analytics capabilities. As a result, firms can increase customer satisfaction while cutting costs at all touch points around the globe.

Self Service and E-Billing

Oracle Self-Service offers complete solution for allowing customers to do business anytime, anywhere. Oracle's customer self-service offerings transform customer relationships, improve profitability, and increase customer loyalty.

Contact centre infrastructure

Oracle Contact Center Anywhere (formerly Telephony@Work CallCenterAnywhere) is a pre-integrated, multichannel contact center platform that takes communications from anywhere and routes them to anywhere. This platform includes queuing and routing of traditional phone calls in addition to e-mail, chat, fax, and web callback requests. It also provides blended predictive and preview dialing, interactive voice response (IVR), multichannel reporting, tools for supervisors to manage the call center, and call recording — for a comprehensive, unified solution.

Oracle Contact Center Anywhere increases agent, supervisor, and administrator productivity by extending the call center beyond the limits of traditional infrastructure. Agents can work efficiently from anywhere in the world with 360-degree views into customer interactions and real-time business intelligence. Supervisors are empowered with instantly customisable screens and real-time tools for monitoring and coaching agents, no matter where they are located. And, administrators can adapt to changing needs with real-time administration tools for implementing moves, adds, and changes.

SAP CRM

SAP Customer Relationship Management (SAP CRM) application is part of the SAP Business Suite. It enables a business firm not only to address its short-term imperatives — to reduce cost and increase decision-making ability — but also to achieve differentiated capabilities in order to compete effectively over the long-term.

With SAP CRM, marketers gain the essential business insights needed to make intelligent decisions, sharpen their focus on customers to drive demand and increase customer retention, and better manage marketing resources to do more with less. Key SAP CRM marketing capabilities include:

1. Marketing resource and brand management
   - Manage and optimise the use of marketing resources including budgets, people, time, and assets.
   - Align all activities and resources around strategic marketing goals.
   - Gain visibility and control into marketing processes.
   - Accurately manage the marketing budgets and costs.
   - Increase brand awareness with proper usage and consistency across enterprise and third-party agencies.
   - Facilitate collaboration among team members and coordinate marketing activities across the enterprise.

2. Segment and list management
   - Manage enterprise customer and prospect data without the need for IT support.
   - Define accurate segments with a consolidated view of all relevant enterprise customer data.
   - Gain insights into customer segments with data visualisation features.
   - Easily perform segmentation using an interactive, drag-and-drop interface.

3. Campaign management
   - Make relevant and personalised real-time offers through inbound marketing channels.
   - Execute marketing activities through all inbound and outbound interaction channels: direct mail, e-mail, phone, web, fax, and SMS.
   - Build customer relationships with dialog marketing that builds on previous interactions to make the follow up interactions more relevant and personalised.

- Leverage online marketing channels to plan, develop, and execute e-mail marketing campaigns.

4. Loyalty management
   - Create specific loyalty programs by defining customer tier levels, points management, and partner management capabilities.
   - Define loyalty rewards program rules, conditions, and offers using the flexible CRM rules builder.
   - Drive loyalty program membership with membership-handling capabilities; robust point management, tier management, and card-handling capabilities across multiple channels.
   - Process points accruals and redemptions with the scalable loyalty-processing engine.

5. Trade promotion management
   - Optimise allocated trade funds to best generate sales volumes and to maximise brand awareness.
   - Centrally plan and align all trade activities with the SAP Trade Promotion Management application.
   - Accurately develop sales volume forecasts and financial accruals with downstream performance data.
   - Close the loop on trade claim payments and deductions.
   - Automate trade settlements and redemption processes with integration to financials, close the loop on trade activities, and track plan and actual figures.
   - Gain insight into trade promotional effectiveness at multiple planning levels: product, category, account, and segments.

6. Lead management
   - Maintain a single source of all enterprise lead information.
   - Automated the entire lead life-cycle process from lead generation, prioritisation, distribution, and follow-up processes.
   - Extend lead management process to partner organisations to increase conversion rates.

7. Marketing analytics
   - Understand the effectiveness of marketing activities.
   - Convert reports and data into actionable insights.
   - Evaluate effectiveness of various marketing activities, channels, and tactics
   - Use advanced analytical algorithms to cluster, classify, and segment customer base.
   - Predict customer behaviours, anticipate their needs, and create more relevant, targeted messages.

SAP CRM supports key sales processes of client business firms, including:

1. Sales planning and forecasting
   - Enhance performance with coordinated planning and execution of sales activities across all channels.
   - Provide a complete picture of projected revenue and anticipated sales volume over time.
   - Increase the accuracy of demand plans and sales forecasts.

2. Territory management
   - Optimise account coverage and distribution of sales resources across clearly defined territories.
   - Improve resource utilisation with clear visibility into assignments and availability.
   - Place the right resources in the right locations at the right time to optimise team performance.
3. Accounts and contacts management
   - Provide a single, comprehensive view of all information necessary to manage sales accounts.
   - Capture, monitor, and track all critical information about prospects, customers, and partners.
   - Access key contacts, critical relationships, detailed customer profiles, and the status of all recent interactions at anytime and from any location.
4. Activity management
   - Focus the collective energy of sales team on actions proven to promote profitable business.
   - Foster efficient team collaboration with better transparency and coordination of sales activities.
   - Manage customer visits, account profiles, and activity-driven sales processes.
   - Seamlessly synchronise e-mail, contacts, calendar entries, and tasks with leading groupware solutions.
5. Opportunity management
   - Track, qualify, and distribute leads to the most appropriate sales professionals.
   - Monitor the conversion of opportunities into revenue.
   - Identify stalled deals, monitor quota attainment, simulate strategies to push deals through the sales cycle faster, and scrutinise the quantity and quality of sales opportunities with pipeline performance management.
6. Quotation management and order capture
   - Guide sales professionals through the product configuration process to ensure that complex product and service recommendations fully meet customer requirements.
   - Ensure consistent, accurate, and up-to-date pricing — regardless of the sales channel.
   - Generate accurate quotes, capture customer orders, confirm product availability, and track orders through to the fulfilment process.
   - Integrate end-to-end business processes to optimise supply chain planning, synchronise billing activities, and ensure the efficient fulfilment of customer orders.
7. Sales contract management
   - Develop and manage long-term customer contracts, incorporate customer agreements into ongoing customer processes, and monitor the sales process from inquiry to completion.
   - Seamlessly integrate with back-end financial and accounts receivable processes to generate invoices, process payments, credit returns, and process claims.

8. Sales performance management

   - Increase revenue and profitability by strategically employing incentive compensation to align the goals of individual sales professionals with those of the organisation.

   - Develop, implement, and manage compensation plans to retain and motivate sales professionals to succeed– allowing them to track performance and simulate potential compensation of deals in the pipeline.

9. Sales analytics

   - Monitor the overall health of business by creating accurate forecasts, proactively monitoring pipeline performance, effectively managing budgets, and properly allocating resources to meet revenue goals.

SAP CRM reduces service costs while enhancing customer satisfaction by increasing efficiency and delivering consistent high-quality service.

The application supports the following key business processes:

1. Sales and marketing for service

   - Develop and execute targeted, installed-base marketing campaigns.

   - Generate and process service contract quotations, and service orders.

   - Conduct solution-based selling.

2. Service contract management

   - Manage service contracts, automatically verify entitlement, manage service-level agreements, and alert agents when a customer's contract is about to expire.

   - Support a variety of service contracts, including standard parts and labour contracts and usage-based contracts.

3. Customer service and support

   - Access information on service histories, contracts and service entitlements, service levels, installed base, and warranties through an easy-to-use interaction centre screen.

4. Return and depot repair

   - Automate the entire return and depot repair process, including creating the return materials authorisation (RMA), billing and shipping repaired products to customers, and issuing and tracking loaner units as necessary.

5. Field service management

   - Organise, plan, and dispatch service resources to meet service demands using Gantt charts, geo-maps, or a powerful optimisation engine.

   - Execute and confirm service orders as well as manage van-stock spare parts with mobile devices.

6. Warranty and claim management

   - Manage the entire warranty and claims process, from return merchandise authorisation (RMA) to receipt and inspection.

   - Coordinate with third-party logistics providers to ensure timely customer credits and avoid unnecessary goodwill allowances.

7. Installation and maintenance

   - Track customers' installed base of products and their configuration with graphical hierarchical representation.

- Predict impact of new product installation for fast and accurate service.
- Minimise downtime with planned maintenance service.

8. Parts logistics and finance
   - Manage parts inventory and parts procurement with native integration to SAP ERP logistics capabilities.
   - Streamline invoicing, revenue recognition, and cost allocation with native integration to SAP ERP financial capabilities.

9. Service analytics
   - Identify problems and trends, and take corrective action if needed.
   - Gain additional insights by leveraging solutions from SAP BusinessObjects.

10. E-service
    - Provide a secure, personalised portal for customer support and service over the Web.
    - Enable customers to troubleshoot their product issues, create service requests, register products and warranties, and track orders.

11. Channel service
    - Manage and assign external resources to customer services orders.
    - Enable third-party technicians to receive, execute, and confirm service orders.

12. IT service management
    - Streamline IT helpdesk operations with ITIL-compliant solution for incident, problems, request for change, and so on.
    - Provide transparency and increase customer satisfaction with service-level management, knowledge articles, and analytics.
    - Ensure alignment between IT operations and business priorities through native integration between SAP CRM and SAP ERP.

With SAP CRM, supports partner channel management processes including:

1. Partner management
   - Manage channel partner relationships throughout the entire partner life cycle.
   - Recruit new partners, plan and forecast channel sales and revenues, segment partner base for more effective partner programs and management, manage partner compensation plans, and track partner training and certifications.

2. Channel marketing
   - Motivate partners to sell products and services rather than competitive offerings.
   - Provide relevant information to partners, maintain consistent branding, engage in joint marketing campaigns with partners, and manage channel marketing funds and partner Use functionality to manage content, catalogs, collateral, campaigns, and leads — as well as personalisation features and a partner locator — to drive demand for products through channel partners.

3. Channel sales
   - Give partners and direct sales force the same knowledge, tools, and expert advice.
   - Gain insight into demand across all selling channels to effectively forecast future business.

- Enable a full range of channel sales processes, including account and contact management, activity management, opportunity management, deal registration, and pipeline forecasting.

4. Partner order management

- Optimise partner ordering processes and include partners in collaborative selling across organisational boundaries.
- Enable a complete set of channel order management processes including quote and order management, interactive selling and configuration, pricing and contracts, and point of sale (POS) and channel inventory management.
- Empower end customers to order products and services across demand network and support distributed, order-management scenarios.

5. Channel service

- Ensure consistent and timely service to end customers by providing partners with the tools and expertise to manage problem resolution and ongoing service relationships.
- Enable a range of channel service business processes, including knowledge management, service resource planning, service order management, live partner support, warranty management, and complaints and returns management.

6. Partner and channel analytics

- Get a broad range of standard reports and analyses to determine partner coverage and gaps, partner and channel performance, revenue and sales statistics, the return on partner investments, gross margins with partners, and partner utilisation.
- Provide channel partners with reports and analyses relevant to their business incentives.

Microsoft Dynamics CRM

Microsoft Dynamics CRM is customer relationship management (CRM) software used to create a clear picture of customers. Its sales, marketing and customer service modules drive measurable improvements, enhance relationships and increase profitability.

NetSuite CRM+ Software

NetSuite is web-based SaaS (Software as a service) CRM system and it provides a complete view of a firm's customers and prospects. NetSuite helps sales and service teams in selling more effectively, improving customer service, and increasing revenue. The NetSuite CRM+ Software modules include:

- Sales force automation
- Sales force automation: order management
- Sales force automation: Upsell/Cross-sell
- Sales force automation: incentive management
- Customer support and service
- Partner relationship management
- Real-time dashboards
- Business intelligence

- Marketing automation
- Productivity tools
- Document management and publishing
- Self-service customer portal
- Website and analytics
- Job and Project tracking

Conclusion

CRM is a strategic initiative to gain long-term customer patronage for a firm. Winning and retaining profitable customers becomes the core concern of CRM initiatives. Retaining a customer is preferred to winning a new customer. Therefore, CRM initiatives aim at lowering customer defection. Though firms expect good returns from their investment on CRM implementation, most CRM projects have failed in delivering expected benefits.

QUESTIONS

1. What is CRM?
2. What are the advantages of CRM?
3. What are the disadvantages of CRM?
4. Explain the role of CRM.
5. "CRM can contribute to sales and profitability." Substantiate.

REFERENCES

1. Kotler, Philip, *Marketing Management*, Pearson Education, New Delhi 2005 p. 52.
2. Bob Thomson, *Successful CRM: Turning Customer Loyalty into Profitability*, E-Business, July 2005 p. 26.
3. Shamez S. Dharamsi and Brad Connard, *CRM Concepts for Effective Services Marketing*, Sbusiness, July/August 2003 p. 82.
4. http://www.oracle.com/us/products/applications/siebel/contact-center-service/038145.htm
5. www.sap.com/solutions/business-suite/index.epx

Case 9.1: HIS at Unity Hospital

The Unity Hospital was started in 2002 by a group of medical professionals. It is a small 50 bed hospital with three major departments General Medicine, Gynaecology and Paediatrics. The hospital has 12 doctors, 45 nurses and 15 other employees. It has a lab, a scanning centre and pharmacy store. Canteen service is outsourced. The hospital has grown significantly in the last eight years. The hospital gets around 15,000 new patients a year.

Till 2010 end, the hospital had no computer. Everything was manually done. In the early 2011, the management decided to implement a Hospital Information System (HIS). It looked for a few vendors and checked the features and costs. Finally, they chose HIS from Software Associates, Calicut and negotiated a deal with them. The software and the hardware cost them nearly ₹ 2,00,000 and the software was implemented in just 15 days.

The hospital started registration of patients. The patients have to give details for registration and a card was issued to them. Earlier this was not done. But the hospital started charging a nominal fee of ₹ 20 for registration.

Mr. M.M. Surendran, Manager of the Hospital, says, "It was a mess earlier with files all over and difficult to trace transactions. Now, it is quite easy to retrieve transaction data, check drug availability and stock in the pharmacy and room availability for in-patients, etc., it also realised a lot of space as most of the physical files have been eliminated. The waiting time for patients has come down for reception counter service. It is also easy now to trace patient history, treatment and payment."

The billing and accounts are accurate. Any transaction can be retrieved for verification. Pharmacy stock verification is facilitated, and the pharmacy staffs were asked to bill all drug sales, internal and external.

Questions:

1. What are the benefits of HIS for Unity Hospital?
2. How much investment the hospital made and how much gain it had in the first year?
3. What problems you anticipate for Unity Hospital in the future?

10
CHAPTER

Supply Chain Management

INTRODUCTION

Delivering superior customer experience needs cooperative and coordinated effort from vendors, manufacturers, distributors, wholesalers and retailers. Together they create and deliver value to identified base of customers. Competition is becoming intense globally. In some industries like the automobile, the competition is among supply chains. So, the survival of a group of cooperating firms in an industry depends on the agility of their supply chain. There is enormous pressure on companies to lower costs and improve customer service and responsiveness.

Supply chain management involves designing a network of facilities, forecasting sales, managing procurement, vendor relations and logistics. It has become too complex to be managed manually. Software solutions are deployed in most of the supply chain activities like supply and demand planning and forecasting, sourcing and procurement, supply chain execution and enterprise asset management. Software solutions for Supply chain management include SAP APO, Oracle APS, i2, Manugistics, SAP SRM, Ariba, Oracle Retail, Sterling Commerce, PkMS, Maximo, SAP PM and Oracle eAM.

SUPPLY CHAIN

Supply chain includes all the firms that are involved in producing and delivering products and services to fulfil customer orders. It includes raw material suppliers, manufacturers, stockists, distributors, wholesalers and retailers who cooperate and coordinate the flow of products and services to customer end.

"Supply chain is a set of three or more companies directly linked by one or more of the upstream and downstream flows of products, services, finances and information from a source to a customer".[1]

SUPPLY CHAIN DRIVERS

Supply chain performance hinges on four factors – design of a network of facilities, inventory level and policies, transportation design and information.[2]

Facilities: Facilities include production plants and storage sites. Decisions on type of facilities, capacity and flexibility of facilities have critical impact on supply chain efficiency and effectiveness.

Inventory: Inventory includes raw materials, work-in-progress and finished products within a supply chain. Inventory policies have significant impact on supply chain's efficiency and responsiveness. With large inventory at retailer, most customer orders can be fulfilled. But, it increases the cost of operations in the supply chain. With low inventory, efficiency increases but responsiveness drops. Managing efficiency and responsiveness at optimal levels is therefore a major task in supply chain management.

Transportation: It moves goods from place to place. There are many modes of transport. Each mode of transport has certain characteristics. For example, water transport is the least cost mode but it is very slow. On the other hand, air transport is the fastest while it costs very high. Again, it is a trade-off between efficiency and responsiveness that is to be made.

Information: Information is a key resource which improves both efficiency and responsiveness. For example, a reliable forecast of the demand for the next season will help the supply chain in producing what is needed and when it is needed. It avoids excess stocking and stock outs. Hence, it enhances efficiency and responsiveness of the entire supply chain. Thus, information is a key driver of the supply chain performance.

SUPPLY CHAIN PROCESSES

Traditionally independent firms performed different processes of a supply chain like supply of raw materials, production, marketing and selling, distribution and customer service. Instead of leaving these processes to independent firms, it is possible for a firm to vertically integrate all these processes. That is, a firm like Reliance Industries will have raw materials to marketing and selling under a single company management. These processes are integrated in a supply chain differently from vertically integrated firms. That is, Supply chain approach is something that is between independent firms and vertically integrated firm. The firms in a supply chain cooperate and coordinate their functions in a synchronised way to meet customer orders with target service levels and costs. It is a very different kind of collaborative structure that is fast evolving to respond quickly to market needs and changes.

The following are the major processes in supply chain management.

- Customer service management
- Demand management
- Order fulfilment
- Manufacturing flow management
- Supplier relationship management
- Product development and commercialisation
- Returns management
- Customer relationship management

SUPPLY CHAIN DECISIONS

There are four types of decisions to be made in a supply chain. They are about location, production, inventory and transportation.

Location of Facilities

Decisions on location of facilities like production centres, storage and sourcing points are very important to network design. The objective is to minimise cost. Facilities should be laid out in such a way that overall cost of procurement, production and distribution is optimal.

Production Decisions

The products to be produced, which plants to produce which products and in what quantity, which distribution centre is to be served from each of the production facilities and which retailers to be served from which distribution centres, etc., are important to supply chain management.

Inventory Decisions

How much inventory is to be carried at each stage of the supply chain is a key decision. Inventory carrying cost varies between 20% to 40% of inventory cost. Hence, the objective of supply chain management is to have adequate inventory to avoid excess stocks or stock-outs.

Transportation Decisions

Another key decision in configuring supply chain is the mode of transportation to be used. It accounts for roughly 30% of total logistics cost. Different modes of transpiration offer different levels of responsiveness and efficiency. A variety of options for transportation may help in configuring it according to customer requirements.

SUPPLY CHAIN MANAGEMENT

Supply chain involves integration of key business processes across firms that cooperate in designing, sourcing, producing, delivering and servicing products and services ordered by customers. The functions of supply chain management include processes like supply planning, demand planning, manufacturing and distribution across a supply chain. The firms joining a supply chain concentrate on some key processes and together they produce and deliver value to customers.

"Supply chain management is the systemic, strategic coordination of the traditional business functions and the tactics across these business functions within a particular company and across businesses within the supply chain, for the purposes of improving the long-term performance of the individual companies and the supply chain as a whole".[3]

For supply chain effectiveness and profitability there should be a system of monitoring of supply chain performance. It requires frequent reporting on performance metrics like cost, customer service, productivity measures, asset measurement and quality.

The major activities involved in supply chain management can be grouped under five heads like forecasting and planning, sourcing, manufacturing, logistics and reverse logistics.

Forecasting and Planning

Forecasting demand and planning operations accordingly is a key activity in supply chain management. The performance of the supply chain depends on accurate forecast of demand and how the supply chain manages to meet that demand. It requires a set of performance metrics to track and monitor the supply chain.

Sourcing

Any supply chain has a set of suppliers to ensure regular supply of materials, components and subassemblies to the manufacturing firm. Suppliers have a key role in supply chain operations. Identifying and selecting suppliers and developing long-term relationship with them through suppler relationship management is an important supply chain activity.

Manufacturing

SCM schedules production, testing, packaging and shipping activities. Each production facility will have certain quantity of products assigned to it for manufacturing. Quality standards have to be strictly adhered to. Manufacturing requires a number of metrics to report its performance to supply chain managers.

Logistics

This includes transporting, warehousing, packing, and delivering products. Policies on stocking and mode of distribution, etc., are aimed at meeting comfortable customer order fulfilment.

Reverse Logistics

Customers may return goods which are defective or excess products, etc., which are to be brought back to the warehouse.

SCM SOLUTIONS

There are so many software solutions for supply chain management. The functionalities vary from package to package. Yet, there are some common applications which are part of SCM solutions. These are:

- Customer requirement processing
- Supplier management
- Sourcing and procurement management
- Inventory management
- Warehouse management
- Modelling and forecasting environment

Leading SCM Software Vendors

SAP AG and Oracle are global leaders in supply chain management solutions. SAP holds around a quarter and Oracle one sixth of the global market share of supply chain management solutions. The features of SAP Supply Chain Management solutions are presented below.

SAP SCM

SAP SCM4 is part of its SAP Business Suite. SAP SCM provides broad functionality for enabling responsive supply networks and integrates seamlessly with both SAP and non-SAP software. The application:

- Delivers planning and execution functions that are integrated by design

- Supports best practices and provides preconfigured software for enabling collaborative business, accelerating implementation, and reducing costs
- Real-time demand and signal-based replenishment need to drive supply chains. It helps firms to balance supply and demand and run their business based on actual-versus-forecasted demand.

SAP SCM for Supply Chain Planning

- **Demand planning and forecasting** - Forecast and plan anticipated demand for products or product characteristics. Use state-of-the-art forecasting algorithms for product life-cycle planning and trade promotion planning.
- **Safety stock planning** - Assign optimal safety stock and target stock levels in all inventories in the supply network. Meet desired customer service levels while maintaining a minimum amount of safety stock.
- **Supply network planning** - Integrate purchasing, manufacturing, distribution, and transportation plans into an overall supply picture – so the user can simulate and implement comprehensive tactical planning and sourcing decisions based on a single, globally consistent model. This can involve heuristics and capacity planning, optimization, and multilevel supply and demand matching.
- **Distribution planning** - Determine the best short-term strategy to allocate available supply to meet demand and to replenish stocking locations. To achieve this, planners can determine which demands can be fulfilled by existing supply elements.
- **Supply network collaboration** - Work with partners across supply network. Using collaboration features that improve visibility into supply and demand, the firm and its partners can reduce inventory buffers, increase the velocity of raw materials and finished goods through the pipeline, improve customer service, and increase revenues.

SAP SCM and Service Parts Planning

- **Parts demand planning** - Improve the accuracy of forecasts through better modelling of demand quantities, events, and their respective deviations. The firm can select sophisticated forecast models and optimize model parameters to improve forecasting for slow-moving parts or for parts with irregular demand patterns. Through aggregated forecast-parameter profile maintenance, data maintenance becomes more efficient.
- **Parts inventory planning** - Reduce inventory levels and achieve retail service levels by providing more precise demand modelling. The inventory can be optimally distributed within the multi-echelon supply chain to ensure high service levels while keeping inventory levels at a minimum.
- **Parts supply planning** - Reduce inventory in the supply chain by improving supplier alignment, increasing automation, and developing accurate supply plans. Operational cost can be reduced through efficient purchasing practices.
- **Parts distribution planning** - Set up stock transfers for parts within a service parts network to reduce stock-out situations and operational costs.
- **Parts monitoring** - Work with suppliers and customers to exchange information and handle alerts collaboratively.

SAP Supply Chain Execution

SAP Supply Chain Management (SAP SCM) delivers supply chain execution excellence and best-of-breed functionality by integrating sales order management, transportation, and warehouse processes, and by linking to back-end financials, manufacturing, and purchasing. Its features and functions include:

- **Materials Management -** By sharing information about inventory and procurement orders, SAP SCM ensures that the materials required for manufacturing are in the right place at the right time. Plan-driven procurement, inventory management, and invoicing close the feedback loop between demand and supply - and improve fill rates and customer satisfaction through increased replenishment speed, delivery confirmation, and invoice accuracy.

- **Manufacturing Execution -** SAP SCM supports all production processes, including engineer-to-order, configure-to-order, make-to-order, and make-to-stock. It also generates optimised production schedules that take into account real-time material and capacity constraints. By integrating manufacturing with other supply chain processes, SAP SCM enables a rapid, flexible approach to responding to engineering changes and customer requirements.

- **Order Promising -** Based on the global available-to-promise (ATP) capability, order promising receives queries from order management or CRM systems, and determines when a product is available across a fulfilment network or can be built. It also shows how much the product will cost, and how long it will take to deliver. Order promising is the critical link between order management/CRM systems and supply chain planning systems, providing a window into product availability.

- **Transportation Management -** Drawing from more than 20 years of experience in transportation orchestration, SAP SCM can help to plan, consolidate, and optimize inbound and outbound shipments – while considering real-world constraints, costs, and penalties. The firm can also streamline and automate transportation tendering, execution, tracking, and settlement processes and to ensure international trade and hazardous material handling compliance in transportation processes.

- **Warehouse Management -** Warehouse management reconciles open purchase orders with incoming shipments, supports a put-away system that remembers where goods are stored, and optimises employee picking assignments. Warehouse management also supports warehousing tasks such as labelling, kitting, and deferred handling.

SAP SCM and Supply Chain Visibility Design and Analytics

SAP SCM supports supply chain visibility design and analytics with features and functions that enable supply chain design and analytics processes, including:

- **Strategic supply chain design -** With visibility across the entire supply chain network, planners and key decision makers can perform strategic and tactical business planning. They can test scenarios to determine how the supply chain network can address changes in the market, the business, or customer demand.

- **Supply chain analytics -** SAP SCM enables the management to define, select, and monitor Key Performance Indicators (KPIs) to get an integrated, comprehensive view of performance across the supply chain. The firm can also use predefined KPIs based on the supply chain operations reference (SCOR) model to monitor sourcing, planning, production, distribution, and returns processes.

Conclusion

Supply chain is a collaborative approach by suppliers, producers and distributors to facing competition in the marketplace by synchronising their activities in tune with customer requirements. It calls for a new management philosophy and work culture as its success depends on inter-organisational integration of processes and strategic cooperation in delivering superior customer experience. A number of firms come together without surrendering their ownership rights to form a loose but functioning entity to provide customer with more comfort and focused service. Software solutions are deployed to automate or improve most of the supply chain processes.

QUESTIONS

1. What is supply chain? What are its drivers?
2. What are the common functionalities offered in SCM solutions?
3. How does Supply Chain Management improve enterprise performance?
4. What are the key supply chain processes? How are they supported by IT solutions?
5. Explain the major software solutions available for supply chain management.
6. Explain the main features of SAP SCM Software.

REFERENCES

1. Mentzer, J.T., *et. al.*, *Supply Chain Management*, Response Books, New Delhi 2001, p. 5.
2. Chopra, Sunil and Meindl, Peter, Supply Chain Management, Pearson Education, New Delhi 2005, p. 52.
3. Mentzer, J.T., *et. al.*, *Supply Chain Management*, Response Books, New Delhi 2001.
4. www.sap.com/solutions/business-suite/index.epx

Case 10.1: Asian Paints Limited

Set up in 1942 in Mumbai, Asian Paints Limited (APL) has grown over the past seven decades into the largest paint company in India today. It is twice as big as any other paint company in India. It operates in 22 countries in five regions such as South Asia, Southeast Asia, Middle East, Caribbean region and South Pacific. It has 23 paint manufacturing facilities in the world and markets its products in over 65 countries. Besides APL , the group operates around the world through its subsidiaries such as Berger International Limited, Apco Coatings, SCIB Paints and Taubmans.

APL aims to become one of the top five decorative coatings companies world-wide by leveraging its expertise in the higher growth emerging markets. Simultaneously, the company intends to build long term value in the Industrial coatings business through alliances with established global partners.

Customer focus

Right from the very beginning, APL has fostered a customer-centric approach to business. A simple but unbeatable concept of "going where the customer is" drives all its retail strategies.In the early 1990s, for the first time in the paint industry, APL offered the consumer over 150 shades. The concept was extended to the dealer shops through Colour World in the mid-90s, where APL began offering over 1,000 shades. The introduction of Colour World provided a new direction for the paint industry into the age of retailing by providing the consumer a service interface. With only a limited set of bases and colourants, manufactured and transported throughout the supply chain, APL provided a choice of innumerable shades to the customer through a technology of tinting at the last retail store. The APL Helpline introduced a few years ago is a toll free service where consumers call and ask queries related to painting. The company has now extended this service to APL Home Solutions, which offers painting services in addition to the paint. This service is available in 10 cities viz., Hyderabad, Bengaluru, Kolkata, Delhi, Chennai, Ahmedabad, Mumbai, Pune, Coimbatore and Kochi.

The company entered into a new foray of prediction of colour trends in India. Intensive research is carried out with interior designers, architects and the fashion community to arrive at trend movements in colour each year. The study being done for the second year is termed Colour NEXT 2006, which is a collection of 15 shades predicted to be the trendiest and most happening colours in decor space in 2006. This study has helped consumers get an insight into the latest trends in colour. This exercise has also gone a long way in helping various industries decide their colour combinations for a range of products ranging from furnishings, floorings to home accessories.

Another important area was the offer of painting solutions for children with the launch of Kids World. A foray into Kids' World marks yet another milestone wherein the company offers painting designs for Kids Rooms as well as Kids Corners. For the first time, an attempt has been made to invite the customer to get into a Do-It-Yourself mode with these designs. Royale Play is another innovative concept introduced by the company. It is a collection of innovative and ready-to-use special effect finishes for interior walls, comprising a range of special effects. And each of these effects are available in a shade palette that is fitting for that effect in interesting colour combinations. The revolutionary product gives wall paint a whole new usage. Now, along with colour, customres can give their walls dimension, texture and life.

IT Infrastructure

Information technology plays a key role in enabling the company to grow and generate profits. APL is the only company in India to have integrated Supply Chain Management (SCM) Solution from i2 Technologies, and Enterprise Resource Planning (ERP) solution from SAP. With these IT tools firmly in place and with the backing of an extensive communication platform, the company an internally enabled enterprise. The road ahead is to integrate all stakeholders including suppliers, employees and customers and create an extended enterprise.

APL has launched a supplier portal that includes an automated digital document exchange facility that will improve the efficiency and effectiveness of interaction with suppliers. An employee portal has also been set up. Customer Relations Management (CRM) tools are being used in APL Helpline and Home Solutions initiatives.

The successful deployment of ERP, CRM, Business Intelligence and Portal software from leading solution providers and integrated SCM systems has helped improve efficiency in the business as well as increase the transparency and accuracy of information across the company. In order to affect 24x7 availability of IT infrastructure, it is setting up a disaster recovery site in South India.

To match the pace of growth in international business, it is focusing on improving transaction systems and messaging platforms. Implementing of a portal platform for improved collaboration and sharing of information across all geographies is already underway.

Supply Chain Initiative

Designing and implementing APL's complex, 5-layer supply chain was a big challenge. While designing a supply chain and IT-enabling it, the emphasis should be on how the firm can gain competitive advantage from it. APL decided to make quick and reliable delivery for its fast-moving paints products through an integrated supply chain its competitive advantage. This competitive advantage also included an extensive and motivated sales force. APL owns three layers of the supply chain –the paint factories, the regional distribution centres and the sales depots. The final layer – the dealers (hardware stores and the like) were not fully IT-enabled as yet, because of various reasons: the prohibitive cost of IT-enabling 18000+ dealers; space constraints in most dealer stores; and low immediate value from point-of-sales data for a product with predictable demand.

Certain other areas, like trans-shipment, were found to be difficult to implement in practice in APL. The IT initiative for supply chain management actually began at APL in 1997-98. It developed an in-house SCM solution and a long-term relationship with the consultants Booz-Allen & Hamilton. But this solution was too difficult to scale. Indeed, several attempts were made by independent entrepreneurs to 'optimize' APL's supply chain, to no avail. Certain key decisions were taken at this stage, including: deciding that it would be best to go for state-of-the-art IT infrastructure despite having a commanding market share of the Indian market; zeroing in on i2 Technologies' as its implementation partner, etc. APL implemented the IT system in three layers: the Execution layer at the lowest level; the Transaction layer in the middle (consisting of SAP R/3 ERP); and the Decision Support layer at the top, which included i2's SCM modules like Demand Planner, Master Planner, Production Scheduler, etc.

APL has harnessed the powers of the state-of-the-art supply chain system using cutting edge technology to integrate all its plants, regional distribution centres, outside processing centres and branches in India. The APL paints plants in India, two chemical plants, 18 processing centres, 350 raw material and intermediate goods suppliers, 140 packing material vendors, 6 regional distribution centres and 72 depots are integrated. The supply chain runs through a wide spectrum of functions right from materials planning to procurement to primary distribution. It has played a pivotal role in improving operational efficiencies and creating agile procurement, production and delivery systems. It has also enhanced the flexibility of operations, lowered output time and reduced delivery costs, while improving customer-servicing levels and profitability. The Supply Chain Management is backed by IT efforts that help the company in demand forecasting, deriving optimal plant, depot and Stock Keeping Unit combinations, streamlining vendor relationships, reducing procurement costs and scheduling production processes for individual factories.

Questions:

1. What are the difficulties of implementing an in-house developed SCM solution in a company like APL?
2. Why APL did not include retailer in its integrated supply chain?
3. What are the benefits that APL derived from SCM implementation?

(*Source:* Wikipedia and published interviews of Mr. Malekar, General Manager, Materials for APL).

Electronic Commerce

11 CHAPTER

INTRODUCTION

The Internet has transformed itself into a communications and commerce medium. This change offers phenomenal opportunities to individuals and business firms. The World Wide Web and e-mail are the two most popular services on the Internet. New forms of communications like blogging, instant messaging and social networking have emerged recently. Thousands of websites are added every day. They provide content or services for the Internet users. E-commerce is growing globally though there are security and legal issues to it.

The Internet has integrated fragmented markets into a global marketplace. The most important advantage of the Internet to business firms is that it allows reaching customers at very low cost wherever they are. Similarly, the location of the firm is irrelevant, as physical access to customers is not so much important. Once a firm sets up a website, it gets a global presence. A number of Web-related services are also emerging such as website design, hosting and maintenance, Web advertising, payment processing and web security. A host of shopping services are available on the Net today. These include airlines booking, hotel booking, railway reservation, online and Internet banking, electronic fund transfer, e-auction, online securities trading and so on.

Electronic commerce is the process of searching, choosing, buying and selling of product or service on the electronic network[1]. It uses computer and communication networks for promoting products, selling, delivery, and collection and customer service. The traditional electronic commerce used electronic data interchange (EDI) technology over private networks. The marriage of the Internet with electronic commerce, often described as 'open electronic commerce' or Internet commerce, represents the cutting edge in business today[2].

Reliable telecom infrastructure, availability of electric power and access to hardware, software and servers are the basic requirements for e-commerce. Access to telecommunications at low prices can enhance the capacity of firms and individuals to participate in e-commerce.

E-commerce is defined as the symbolic integration of communications, data management and security capabilities to allow business applications within different organisations to automatically exchange information related to the sale of goods and services. The World Trade Organisation identified six main instruments of e-commerce such as telephone, fax, television, electronic payment and money transfer systems, electronic data interchange (EDI) and the Internet.

In e-commerce, the parties to a transaction interact electronically. They may be separated by long distances physically, yet the electronic network bring them together not only to complete a transaction but also to get after-sales support. E-commerce is not just doing transactions over the Internet; it aims at a few other things as well like[3]:

- Web enabling an organisation's core business processes so that it can facilitate better customer interaction, handling customer enquiries, receiving customer orders and payments online.
- Improving customer service capabilities by allowing customers by providing Internet access to its database containing customer interest information.
- Use the web to gather customer need information and, thus, to reducing cycle time by responding to customer needs quickly. It enables the firm in coming out with new products to meet the identified customer needs and making available new product information to customers.
- Raising productivity of all activities in the organisation by improving the flow of information in the organisation.

E-COMMERCE AND E-BUSINESS

Though these terms are used interchangeably, yet there are differences between them. E-business is larger than ecommerce. When business transactions are done and payments made electronically over computer networks, it is e-commerce. There is much more to e-business than selling products and getting payment. First, there are a number of enabling factors like a business model, conducive business environment and organisational culture, website, flow traffic to the website, e-catalogs, payment processing, security, logistics, customer service and support, etc. Thus, e-commerce plus factors like the above taken together is e-business.

Electronic Commerce Business Models

A business model is a set of planned business activities that generate revenue for a firm from an identified marketplace. A business plan is drawn up when a business idea is incubated into reality. The business model deals with value proposition, revenue model, marketspace, competitive environment, competitive advantage, market strategy, organisation development and management team. Based on the parties involved in electronic transactions, the e-commerce can be classified into the following types.

- Business-to-Business (B2B)
- Business-to-Consumer (B2C)
- Consumer-to-Consumer (C2C)

Business-to-Business E-commerce: This is done between business firms. For example, electronic transactions between a manufacturing firm and its supplier firms are B2B transactions. This segment is the largest and the fastest growing one in electronic commerce. Here firms use the electronic network for purchasing products, consulting services and paying for them.

Business-to-Consumer E-Commerce: Consumers check electronic catalogs to learn about products and compare prices of products sold. They purchase products at the firm's website and may pay electronic cash or through other means like credit card.

Consumer-to-Consumer E-Commerce: Some sites offer consumers to deal directly with each other. Auction sites are examples. At these auction sites, consumers can buy and sell products.

Electronic Commerce is useful to both producers and consumers as it helps them overcome the traditional barriers of distance from markets and lack of information about market opportunities. Producers and traders no longer need to maintain physical establishments requiring large capital outlays. Virtual shops and contact points on the Internet may enable storage close to the production site and distribution can be made directly to the consumer. Increased advertising possibilities worldwide may help small and medium industries and businesses that traditionally find it difficult to reach the customer abroad. E-commerce may also enable such firms to eliminate middlemen while trying to sell their products abroad[4].

ELECTRONIC DATA INTERCHANGE (EDI)

EDI is the technology involved in the inter-organisational exchange of documents in standardised electronic formats between computer applications. The purpose of EDI is to reduce the cost of communicating structured information between business firms. It also automates data capture and data entry. Thus, it saves time and money and at the same time improves accuracy by automating recording of transaction data.

Key Aspects of EDI

- Use of an electronic network for transmission of structured information, that is, a private or public network.
- Structured messages based on standards
- Relatively fast delivery of electronic documents between the sender and receiver, and,
- Direct communication between computer applications.

EDI Components

Exchange of EDI messages requires some components. They are EDI standards, EDI software and communication networks.

EDI Standards: The exchange of message should be independent of software or hardware on either side. So for application to application communication of specific messages certain standards have to be commonly followed by the systems on either side. EDI standards lay down the syntax and semantics of the data being exchanged.

EDI Software: EDI software translates firm specific information format to the structured EDI format and communicates that message.

Communication Networks: EDI messages are exchanged over communication networks. For e-commerce, suppliers, customers and other trading partners have to be connected to one another.

Advantages of EDI

- It reduces the flow of paper communication between the participating firms
- It reduces the time and cost of transaction processing by automatic capturing and processing of transactions.
- It improves accuracy of information and reduces errors due to human negligence.
- Increases productivity
- Reduces inventory

Disadvantages of EDI

- Requires high initial investment
- Standard formats have to be used for transactions and hence it limits flexibility
- It requires standardising programs and procedures.

Open EDI, that uses the Internet in place of private network, is becoming more popular. Business firms can send documents over the Internet in two forms: FTP or e-mail. Open EDI is a more cost effective solution for e-commerce transactions. Additionally, it offers universal connectivity and hence the network reach does not limit the scope for e-commerce transactions.

Online Payment Systems

Credit cards have become the most common form of payment for e-commerce. Debit cards are also used to make online payments. But, it is less popular than credit cards. The merchants arrange enough security at e-commerce sites. Digital certificate and public key infrastructure are required to secure credit card and debit card transactions.

But, people are still afraid of using credit card or debit card for online transactions. A Smartcard is another option for payment. It has an 8-bit microprocessor that can transfer cash electronically to the merchant's device. Visa smartcard can transfer credit from bank account to the smartcard.

There are also other forms of payment for e-commerce like e-vallet, digicash, etc. The most popular online payment systems are:

- Credit card
- Debit card
- Smartcard, and,
- Various forms of electronic money like digicash

The payment may also be made by demand draft or cheque or by value payable post. In such cases, delivery will happen once payment reaches the seller except in value payable post where product is handed over on making payment.

Products for E-Commerce

Some products are particularly suitable for electronic commerce on the Net. These products are highly information-rich and can be delivered over the Net. These include:

- financial services,
- education and training,
- healthcare services,
- entertainment, and,
- tourism services like hotel and transport booking.

The Internet commerce has opened up a global electronic marketplace. It permits customers to locate more information relevant to their shopping decisions. They have better control over the buying process. The persuasiveness and interactive capability of the Net has added new dimensions to electronic commerce. The opportunities and threats it opens up are enormous.

BUSINESS OPPORTUNITIES OPENED UP BY THE INTERNET

The Internet has opened up new opportunities for business. They include the following:

Opportunities for new alliances, take-overs, mergers and acquisitions: Enterprises selling goods on the Net will need to work out ways with third party logistics companies for handling physical distribution. Individual enterprises cannot have their own distribution system to reach anywhere on the globe. Hence they need to form alliances or business partnerships or relationships with carriers and logistics companies for order fulfilment and physical distribution.

Virtual storefront: The opportunity to set up virtual storefront as a supplement to physical storefront is a great opportunity for customers to do business interactively on the Net.

Low cost of communication: Opportunities for cutting cost of communication by as much as 80% of doing business as e-mail is fast becoming the dominant form of business communication.

E-malls and private networks: Opportunities for setting up e-malls and private networks on the Internet for single point shopping which can attract more customers.

Credit card business: Credit card companies to grow rapidly as cards are being used increasingly for Internet commerce.

Innovative digital products: Opportunities for new and innovative products like digital cash, digital certificates, insurance products for covering Internet commerce related risks, etc.

Advantage to small enterprises: The Internet commerce is growing rapidly globally. A large number of companies, mostly small businesses, are exploiting the new technology to their advantage.

THREATS FROM INTERNET-BASED ELECTRONIC COMMERCE

The following are some of the threats from the Internet commerce.

Global competition: The Internet is a great leveller and size of enterprises does not influence the Internet-based business. Any enterprise, which is on the Web, gets a global presence. Firms in the same industry anywhere on the globe become its competitors and vice versa.

Legal Issues: Internet commerce opens the Pandora's box. A whole lot of legal issues with no precedence or legislation addressing them are likely to be thrown up by it. To be successful, it requires universal laws on Internet commerce related aspects and agreement among nations to comply with them voluntarily. Laws are required to deal with spam, domain name contentions, digital contracts, etc.

Security Issues: The security issues are on top of the agenda of Internet commerce. The chance of electronic fraud is very high and firms are wary of this enormous risk. Until security and confidentiality of transactions and information are ensured, the pace of growth of Internet commerce is likely to be slow.

Voluntary nature of the Internet and role of Governments: Nobody controls the Internet as such. But the Government in any country controls trade in its jurisdiction. Since Internet commerce compresses time and space into a "here and now" phenomenon, no government can effectively control trade any more. The government policies and statutes in individual countries are going to be tested from an international perspective. Transactions will be done in countries, which do not levy any tax on sales or income. Many countries will be losing in this game. Therefore, individual countries will try to protect their own interests by new restrictions and legislation, which might interfere with the voluntarism of the Net.

Tax avoidance: The transaction can be done anywhere in the world and hence the buyer and seller will be interested in doing it in countries, which do not levy any tax on Internet commerce.

Threat to existing retail organisations: The Internet commerce needs a new set of intermediaries for order fulfilment and shipping, payment processing, etc. The service of traditional retail organisations is not of any use in Internet commerce.

E-COMMERCE ACTIVITIES

Business firms use the Internet platform for communication and commerce. The e-commerce activities can be discussed as follows.

Direct marketing and selling: Business firms set up websites for direct marketing and selling. Direct selling was one of the earliest forms of e-commerce. For example, Amazon.com, Barnes and Noble and Dell computers engaged in direct selling. Gradually firms moved on to more complex operations on the Web.

Value chain integration: E-commerce does not tolerate any kind of delay. Delay in inventory tracking and management can cripple the business. E-commerce firms use EDI for exchanging transaction data among them so that transactions are automatically processed. Thus, suppliers, customers and service providers will use open EDI for integrating their transaction processing systems leading to more efficient operations.

Corporate purchasing: Internet provides opportunities for business firms to reduce cost of purchasing. Suppliers keep their electronic catalogs updated. Comparative price information is also available. Ordering can be electronically done to reduce the laborious paper work in purchasing. Officers can approve purchase orders electronically. The firm can enforce purchasing policies, provide greater services to customers and suppliers.

Financial and information services:

A wide range of financial services are offered on the Internet. They include:

- Online banking
- Online billing
- Online securities transactions, and,
- Secure information distribution

MOBILE COMMERCE

Mobile commerce is a part of e-commerce and differs from the latter in the use of mobile infrastructure for communication in place of telecommunication network. It enables a user to conduct buying or selling transactions while on the move through mobile devices like mobile phone or personal digital assistant (PDA) or WAP enabled smart phone. M-commerce includes only transactions with a monetary value and it excludes short message services (SMS) messages between users of mobile services. One condition essential for the success of mobile commerce is large user base of mobile phones and other hand-held devices like personal digital assistants. Adequate security for mobile transactions is another condition for its adoption in a big way.

Meaning

The terms 'mobile' and 'wireless', though appear to be the same, have significant differences. Mobile means portability of work. It enables users to do tasks away from office. That is, it refers to user mobility. Wireless means network connectivity without physical cables. It enables devices to be connected to a network without cables for communication. This refers to device mobility. Hence, the term 'wireless' is used with regards to devices.

Mobile phones can be used for communications and also for commerce. For example, a person books airlines ticket with his mobile phone. Another person uses his mobile phone to transfer money from his bank account to another's.

M-commerce includes purchase of products and services in addition to payment transactions like paying telephone bill over a mobile network. For m-commerce, users must have access to mobile infrastructure such as mobile phone, personal digital assistants (PDA), wireless application protocol or laptop computer connected to a mobile phone for wireless network access. It requires some amount of interactivity.

Characteristics of M-Commerce

The typical characteristics of mobile commerce are as follows:

Any time any where transaction capability: A mobile user can use the mobile infrastructure on a 24/7 basis (that is 24 hours a day, seven days a week). It is also possible to access the Web from remote places covered by mobile infrastructure.

Use of hand-held mobile devices: For conducting mobile commerce, users must have hand held devices like mobile phone or PDA. Commerce through laptop computer is not considered mobile commerce.

Stringent mobile security: Adequate security is put in place on the mobile infrastructure for mobile commerce transactions. Still there are plenty of risks.

Extended reach: Through mobile and wireless channels, business firms can reach existing and new customers for marketing their products and services.

Advantages

- M-commerce helps in maintaining competitive edge. The business firm is perceived to be technology savvy and hence, the firm and its products enjoy superior quality image.
- It ensures that customers can always access the products and services of the business
- It helps in building personal relationship with customers on a one-to-one basis.
- It increases sales and customer retention. Firms can send tailored messages to select mobile customers to promote products and to keep in touch with them.

Disadvantages

- A host of technologies are being deployed in mobile communications. With ever changing technology scenario, it is rather difficult for business firms to make an assessment about the potential gains from investment in such technologies.
- Firms, in their zeal to promote products and services for sale, may invade privacy of individuals.

- Currently, the coverage of mobile communications is not adequate in most countries. Hence, it may limit reach of firms to mobile coverage areas only, mostly cities and towns, for mobile commerce.
- It is difficult to send too much information at a time, as the client side display screen (mostly mobile handset screen) is too small.
- Despite improved security for mobile commerce, still security risk is high. This may discourage business from expanding mobile commerce activities.

Mobile Commerce Infrastructure

Wireless networks and mobile communication devices are the core technologies for mobile commerce. Its messages are displayed on small screens on the client side and hence it requires special applications and technologies different from traditional Internet and e-commerce technologies. With growing mobile communications and third generation mobile devices that can transfer data quickly, many of the technology problems in mobile e-commerce are getting resolved.

The platform for m-commerce is created by five services such as messaging services, web access services, voice activated services, location based services and digital content services.[5]

Messaging services: Short messaging service (SMS) is a popular communication service. It helps business firms in communicating with the customers on an anytime anywhere basis. Customer-interest information is sent through SMS. They can read it on the small screen of their mobile phones.

Web access services: Customers must be able to access the Web from their mobile devices. So, web service providers are required to provide them access to the web.

Voice activated services: Voice enabled services increase market reach of business firms.

Location based services: The users of mobile devices may travel from place to place. The mobile devices are tracked by the mobile infrastructure. The location information of mobile device user can be used for business purposes. It is useful for marketing some products or services like air tickets, taxi services, health care, hotel rooms, tourist destinations, books, etc.

Digital content services: The saying 'Content is king' is true in m-commerce too. Digital content can attract customers to websites.

Requirments for M-commerce

The essential components for m-commerce are[6]

Client software: The mobile or PDA needs a browser for m-commerce activity. M-commerce may require large data transfer and display capability on the client side. Mobile devices need to be equipped with Web-ready micro-browsers for m-commerce.

Client service set up: Users have to enter a set of parameters to set up a WAP connection every time the users want to access a service.

Network: Global System for Mobile communications (GSM) network is the conduit for passing content between content servers and the mobile devices. The wireless gateway converts the content into compressed binary format for transport to WAP enabled devices.

Corporate servers: Corporate servers store enterprise specific information for the mobile customers to access through the mobile network.

Security for mobile commerce: Mobile commerce infrastructure is exposed to still more risks than plain e-commerce. M-commerce requires adequate end-to-end security covering authentication, confidentiality and integrity of communications between customers and business firms.

M-Commerce Business Applications

M-commerce is steadily growing. It is its convenience that endears it to customers. More technologies are fast evolving to take most Internet services to the mobile. M-commerce opens more opportunities for online business. Some of them are:

Mobile marketing: Business firms can use the mobile infrastructure in advertising their products and services. Since mobile users can be tracked easily and the information can be had from cell phone companies for a fee, customised and context relevant advertisements can be sent to users of mobile devices.

Mobile banking: Wireless banking makes banking accessible on an anytime, anywhere basis. Customers can check their balances, pay their bills and transfer funds easily without moving physically an inch from their office or home.

Wireless security trading: Wireless security trading can take business to more people and accessible more. Trading firms can send personal messages to clients on their mobile devices for security delivery or payment.

Wireless ticketing and booking: Customers can check flight information, seat availability and book airline tickets from wherever they are.

Mobile Content: Through the mobile devices people always on the move can access digital content through networks or Web.

Mobile Entertainment: This is one of the fastest growing applications of the wireless uses. Music, cinema, video games, etc., on the web are accessed through mobile devices. The mobile entertainment enables people to use the spare time or waiting time effectively.

Mobile information services: The mobile infrastructure enables firms to offer Information services such as delivery of financial news, sports news, flight information and traffic updates to a mobile service users.

Retail business: Customers can place for retail orders on-the-fly. Delivery information can be checked and payment made through mobile devices.

Cellular Telecommunication Systems

Mobile commerce is made possible by the cellular telecommunication technologies. Some of the popular cellular telecommunication services are as follows:

GSM: GSM permits integration of voice and data services and internetworking with existing networks. It provides high quality digital voice transmission.

GPRS (General Packet Radio Services): GPRS enables mobile devices to send and receive data over IP networks at speeds of fixed line phones. With GPRS, mobile phones can be used to surf the Web, use e-mail and download digital content.

Blue tooth: Blue tooth enables computers, mobile phones and other hand held devices to communicate without physical connections between them. These devices will have a tiny blue tooth chip. This chip contains a radio transceiver to connect with other devices. Blue tooth enabled devices can be set up to automatically exchange data between them.

WLAN: Wireless Local Area Network uses radio frequency technology for data transmission. It has transceiver devices at fixed locations (called access points) that connect the wireless LAN with wired networks. Wireless LANs are highly flexible as more devices can be added without any disturbance to the existing devices.

Advantages of E-commerce

E-commerce has some advantages compared to traditional commerce. Some of the major advantages are as follows:

Economy: E-commerce is economical as it requires no investment. What it needs is a storefront and tie up for other services with business partners and suppliers.

Low transaction cost: E-commerce transactions are done electronically over networks and cost of transaction is very low compared to the cost of transaction in a physical store.

Online customer service and support: E-commerce saves a lot of time for customers. They can place orders quickly after checking details of products and services and verifying price, quality, etc. The delivery is mostly made through specialised logistics firms. Hence, they get home delivery of the product, if so desired. The website offers customer support and service in terms of product use, technical information and online support for trouble shooting, etc.

High degree of customisation: The product or service can be customised. Products, particularly of assembled products like cars, computers, etc., are produced as per customer order.

Price Comparison: It is possible for customers to compare prices of competing offerings and make an informed choice of products and services. There are websites which provide information to compare products, quality, price, etc.

E-commerce Security: E-commerce sites should have adequate security infrastructure built into the websites and processes. Measures like Secure Sockets Layer ensures reasonable security by encrypting the data exchanged between the customer and the website. The data so collected should also be stored with adequate security to maintain confidentiality.

Confidentiality of transaction data: With adequate security, confidentiality of transaction is maintained. E-commerce sites ensure high security for the transactions. Personal and credit card data is encrypted to prevent its misuse.

Comfort for customers: E-commerce provides high level of comfort and convenience for customers. They can do online buying and selling from their homes or offices.

Limitations of E-commerce

E-commerce is beneficial to the business firms and their customers and channel partners. It is expected to grow faster as people's trust and comfort level are rising with the Internet and WWW. Even then, there are some concerns which have not been adequately addressed.

Security risks: Despite the advances in security systems for ecommerce, there is no mitigation in the risk that an ecommerce customer is exposed to while doing transactions online.

Online frauds: The party to the transaction may not be known to the buyers in most cases. It is possible that the seller and buyer are in different countries. If the seller cheats, the buyer will have to suffer the loss. Legal process may be very expensive and the money involved may not be much to justify legal action.

Legal issues: Contract enforceability, taxation and copy right violations are some of the legal issues for e-commerce participants like e-merchants, manufacturers, vendors and shoppers. Legal issues relate to frauds, misleading advertising, misrepresentation, and violation of trademarks, trade names and copyrights. Resolution of cyber jurisdiction issues is also not settled among countries.

Competition and vulnerability: Competition becomes global with ecommerce. Any business has to be globally competitive to survive in e-commerce. If cost is more for the same quality product, the cost difference of a domestic firm should not exceed the extra logistics cost for a foreign firm in delivering products to a customer. In addition, the firm will need to match the competitors in customer service and technical support.

System scalability: Sometimes, the architecture of e-commerce infrastructure may not have considered the business growth actually achieved by a firm. If scalability is an issue, it affects growth of e-commerce.

Cost of winning customers: Winning a customer in cyberspace is not easy. It is also not cheap. Having won a customer, there is no guarantee of his staying with the firm as a customer in future. Sometimes, the cost of winning a group of customers may be more than the gains from them.

Some products are not suitable for e-commerce: Certain products like furniture are not bought online. Similarly, shopping is a social experience. The e-commerce sites fail in meeting that need of shoppers.

Conclusion

The phenomenal growth of the Internet since the early 1990s caught the imagination of the business community and the Internet, which was till then a defence and scientific community network, was transformed into a global marketplace in a few years' time. The Internet with its global reach and communication capabilities has revolutionised communication and commerce in the last few decades. E-commerce has been growing over the Internet. Many of the e-commerce issues have been addressed with appropriate legislation in most countries and the availability of security systems like encryption and digital certificates.

Rapid advances in mobile and wireless technologies hold great hopes for commerce on wireless networks. It is the features like simplicity, any time access and personalisation that make mobile commerce acceptable to most users in the fast-paced life. Technologies are fast evolving and getting deployed to exploit the potential that mobile infrastructure offers for commerce.

QUESTIONS

1. What is e-commerce? What are its enabling factors?
2. Describe the different e-commerce business models.
3. What are the advantages and disadvantages of e-commerce?
4. What is EDI? What are its components?
5. What is mobile commerce? How is it different from e-commerce?
6. What are the applications of m-commerce?
7. Describe the components of mobile infrastructure for m-commerce.
8. Describe the characteristics of m-commerce.
9. Describe the advantages and disadvantages of m-commerce.

REFERENCES

1. Confederation of Indian Industry, Internet in India: Its Current Status, Development and Business Opportunities, May, 1996.

2. Mougayar, W., *Opening Digital Markets*, Mc-Graw-Hill, New York, 1998, p. 8.

3. Ganesh Natarajan, *"Making E-Commerce Work"*, Business India, September 21-October 4, 1998, p. 111.

4. Note circulated by the WTO Secretariat, on the seminar on "Potential for Electronic Commerce for Businesses in Developing Countries" and "Infrastructure and Regulatory Issues at the Government Level" held on 19 February, 1999.

5. Raina, Kapil and Harsh, Anurag, *m-Commerce Security*, Tata McGraw-Hill Publishing Company, New Delhi 2002, pp. 16-17.

6. *Ibid* p. 32.

Case 11.1: 'E-KRISHI'

Introduction

The Government of Kerala set up state-wide IT infrastructure as part of its e-governnce programme startèd with a mass IT literacy programme in 2000. The first project under the e-governance programme was Akshaya Project. Over 2000 entrepreneurs set up IT training centres called Akshaya Centres throughouf the state to deliver services. Akshaya project has created broad band network across the state. It forms a base for providing value-added e-services to the citizens. E-krishi is another innovative project of the state to enable the farmers of the state to exploit the potential of information and communication technologies. It was first introduced in the district of Malappuram.

The e-Krishi project was a joint initiative of the Information Technology Mission of the state with a few other organisations for enabling agriculturists to access information about agribusiness. The other major contributors include Indian Institute of Information Technology and Management, Kerala, UNDP, National Institute of Smart Government, Hyderabad and the Department of Agriculture of the state.

The vision of the project is to 'establish a connected farmers' community throughout Kerala which has access to information on market demand, price, good agricultural practices, quality agricultural inputs supported by a technology enabled robust transaction platform that facilitates offline activities'. It has put in place a web-based platform 'to meet the needs of farmers for information, communication, transaction, payment and potential integration with related services*'. The e-Krishi portal is a free site and contains information on a number of topics related to agriculture including agricultural prices and trends.

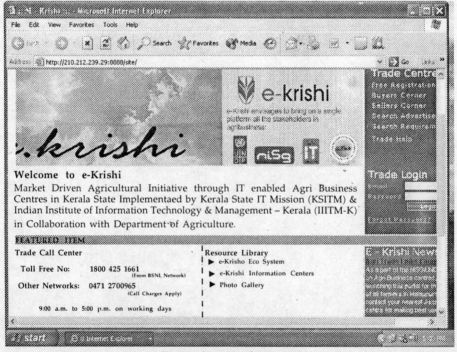

Fig. 11.3: e-Krishi Portal

After about four years of launching Akshaya project in the district of Malappuram, the number of e-Kendras has come down from 615 to 279 in 2008. Of them, about 140 Akshaya centres were re-designated as e-Krishi centres under the e-krishi project. These centres are provided with books, CDs and other materials on agriculture. A portal has been set up for agriculturists to enable them to access information and trade their produces. A toll free trade call centre is set up to answer queries of farmers. A number of farmer communities have been set up to organise farmers and identify and solve their problems. About 79 of such farmer communities have already been formed in the state.

Items Dealt with for E-Krishi

Farmers have to register with the portal for transactions. The registered farmers can offer their produces for sale through e-Krishi portal. Produces like coconut, paddy, vegetables, rubber, banana, honey, areca nut, mussels, pepper, rice, oilseeds, tubers, fish, etc., are offered for sale. The portal contains information about each farmer and what quantity he can sell of each item.

e-Krishi centres are owned by private entrepreneurs. They have invested on an average a little over US$ 5,000 (INR 250,000). Each centre has four to six computers with broad band connectivity. In addition to web resources, each e-Krishi centre has CD library, e-Krishi library and e-payment facility.

They offer e-Krishi services to farmers and traders. Yet their main source of income till now is from training programmes and DTP services. E-Vidya (that is, e-education) and e-payment facility are the other services offered by most of the e-Krishi centres.

e-Krishi centre runs campaigns for popularising the e-Krishi initiative among farmer community. They also provide data maintenance, directory listing, training and content development services.

Revenue Model

e-Krishi project has a different revenue model. The farmers have to register with one of the e-Krishi centres for which they have to pay a fee. E-Krishi entrepreneurs also continued to provide other services as e-Krishi did not ensure them adequate revenue. The sources of revenue to the e-Krishi entrepreneurs are:

- **Training income:** Each e-Krishi centre offers training programmes in information technology. Fees are collected for training depending on type and length of training.
- **Service charges:** e-Krishi centres also provide other services like e-payment facility for which they get a fee for remittances.
- **Farmer registration charges:** e-Centres charge a fee of US$ 0.20 (INR 10) per farmer for posting farmer related data at the e-Krishi portal.

E-entrepreneurs have fanned out in rural areas of Malappuram district, to begin with and are working closely with farmers in improving their agriculture practices. They have formed farmer clubs called bhoomi clubs (bhoomi means land) and are discussing ways exploiting the information content and transaction platform of e-Krishi web portal. The project has generated a new awakening among farmers and rural people about the possibilities of ICT based entrepreneurship for rural development. Most farmers have started using information from e-Krishi project's portal. But, e-transactions are very limited.

Conclusion

e-Krishi is certainly a brave and intelligent application of ICT for rural development. The project generated a lot of interest and expectations from all quarters. It succeeded in setting up a connected community of farmers. But it has to go a long way in enabling the farmers to exploit the information available at the e-Krishi portal. The Public Private Partnership model is quite appropriate but for the private entrepreneurs it does not generate enough revenue. This constitutes a serious challenge to the project's survival in the medium term. The project has necessitated the coming together of aggressive ICT entrepreneurs and conservative agri-entrepreneurs to jointly plan agricultural processes and marketing. This will result in desirable changes in agriculture and rural development in the future.

Questions:

1. Is the revenue model for e-Krishi business profitable for e-Krishi entrepreneurs?
2. What are the enabling factors for state-wide launch of such a big project?
3. What kinds of services can be offered profitably under e-Krishi project?

Exhibit 1

e-Krishi Project - Services Envisaged

(1) Buyer Information

Name, Address, Location Contact, Tel, Turnover/Stocking yard area

Crops dealt , Supply chain below (relationship), Partners (Relationship), Agriculture Produce Collection points: Inspection point, pick up point.

(2) Seller Information

Name, Address, Contact, Tel, Acreage/nos cultivated/harvest by month/qtr, Crops dealt, Preferred Delivery point

(3) Market prices

Updated Price by product/by market

(4) Buy & Sell Transaction Platform

Sell/buy offer - Transaction

Item/Type/Qty/Quality (photo upload)/Delivery point -> Seller/Buyer

Buyer gets Panchayat/block/district level aggregation

Buyer's bids giving Price and Validity date/Seek inspection date &venue/Pick up date and venue

Seller refer market prices & confirm/replies buyers advice

Close transaction offline, keep open until close

Expire by date as set date

(5) Requests for Soil testing /Visit Scheduling of mobile units

Farmers Id, Sample No., Date, Plot Id

Sample Report -collection point/Date, Link

Vehicle#, Date Location Id Date Time From time To Officer-in-charge

(6) Requests for seeds/plantlets

Farmers Id, Request Id, Date, Plot Id, Soil Test Report Id, Crop, Seed choice/Plantlet choice, Qty, Required by date, collection point, advances paid.

Distribution – activity

(7) Request for clarification of technical doubts/ experts help

Farmer Id, Plot ID, Crop id, Issue-Category, Issue Title, Issue description-format

(8) Applications to various schemes: Credits, subsidies

Farmer ID, Required docs, Office ID, Application -format

Office ID, Officer, Workflow

(9) Information dissemination

News server

(10) Contents bank

Best practices, Crop, Category, Archived Helpdesk Queries.

(11) IT enabled Citizen Interface for access to Government Schemes

(12) Value Added Services

Handholding , Good Agricultural Practices: preparation, planting, maintenance, harvest, post harvest, Extension officer visit, Q&A, Expert guidance, Clinic facility, Harvest time care

Plant protection Mechanisms, Pesticides, Application guidelines w.r.t. age of plant/nature of attack, Pesticide Sellers

Fertilizers, Application guidelines w.r.t. age of plant/nature of deficiency and requirement regarding certification (JAS, EUREPGAP), Fertilizer Sellers, Options I have for organic manure.

Agricultural equipment, Own or lease?, Collective ownership and scheduling, Who is leasing?

Schedule plucking/harvest, which warehouse and When? Self assessment of quality of my produce, Grading centres and certification, Documentation I need to maintain/submit while selling, Prices, Buyers, Decision support whether to hold goods or to sell now.

Sales contract, Venue/time/date of delivery, Logistics support, Payment

Loan, Insurance, Other support, Advance contract with buyers, Credit for goods purchased, services availed Grants, Subsidies.

First steps... What should I do in farming area? (Info tips)

Agri Labour Bank, Vocational training for agricultural labour: equipments/methodologies/ pruning

List of Farmers agreeable for Contractual obligation, Draft Contracts, Contract Management

*(http://210.212.236.212/akshaya/ekrishi.html)

(*Source:* e-Krishi Website, published sources and interviews with project coordinator and Akshaya entrepreneurs).

12 CHAPTER

Role of Computers in MIS

INTRODUCTION

Business is the major area of application of computer worldwide. Computer is basically a tool. But it is a versatile tool. It was originally used in business firms as a data processing device. Later its use got extended to every conceivable area of business management. Computer can facilitate any business process in addition to information storage and communication. Computer has gradually become an essential and integral part of organisation's basic infrastructure.

Management information system is a way of gathering and processing data for storage and communication of information in organisations. Every organisation has its information system; large or small depending upon the size of the organisation and the role assigned to MIS. Computers are linked together into a network in most organisations to provide required information gathering and sharing capabilities. Computer network is an integral part of organisational MIS. It can be used for transaction processing, office automation, process automation, communication within the organisation, communication with its trading partners and customers, decision support at higher levels of management and for electronic commerce.

ROLE OF COMPUTERS IN MIS SUBSYSTEMS

To analyse the role of computers in MIS, let us first look at computers' role in the basic subsystems of MIS.

Computers in TPS

Transaction processing is a basic activity in organisations. It is a major source of data for any kind of organisation. The transaction data, like sales data, is captured at source and is stored in organisational database. This forms the basic data for information generation for planning and control in organisations.

Since transaction processing is a routine activity, organisations find it efficient and profitable to automate this activity. Automated transaction processing receives transaction requests, processes them, and records the transactions. The transaction processing generates transaction documents like sales invoices and updates related databases.

Computer-based transaction processing exploits the potential of computers for speeding up business processes and provides quick response to customers, improves transaction efficiency and makes control more effective by enabling real time control.

Computers in IRS

Business reports present information about a business phenomenon like sales of a product for a month, plant efficiency for a period, efficiency of fund use, etc.

The kinds of reports generated by IRS are periodic and *ad hoc* report, status report and action report. They are prepared for a period such as a week, a month, etc. Periodic reports are designed to meet certain identified information needs of users. The content of such report depends on the user and the use. For instance, a report on plant utilisation will be of interest to production supervisor, production manager, general manager and the CEO of the company. The content of the report will vary from user to user depending on what each one uses it for. The general manager may want it to plan introduction of new products, production manager may want the information to improve the plant utilisation by increasing production of the same products or to control plant idling due to power shortage, equipment failure, labour shortage, etc. Hence, the reports have to be customised to meet the needs of each user.

Most reports are based on data generated from within the organisation. Some reports are based on data gathered from outside the organisation and some need data from both these sources. For example, reports for the lower level management is based on internal data mostly, and those for the top level management are based on external data mostly.

Computers in DSS

DSS provides the decision makers with a facility to interactively generate information about semi-structured and unstructured decision situations. It contains database, model base and user interface. It uses computer's processing capability and user friendly interface to make this interaction easy and fruitful for users. Without computers, DSS cannot provide the decision support that the user may want.

Computers in ESS

ESS is a DSS developed exclusively for the executives of a company. This contains specially designed database, models and user-friendly interface. It gives computer-based analytical capability to the user in exploring problems and designing and testing solutions to complex managerial problems.

Computers in ES

Expert system is an extension of artificial intelligence. It uses complex logic to solve problems. It stores knowledge and a large number of rules. It provides interactive facility for users to explore solutions to problems in the domain. Computers are essential for this.

Role of Computers in Functional Information System

Let us now look at the role played by computers in functional information systems like production, marketing, personnel and finance information systems.

PRODUCTION INFORMATION SYSTEM

Production function is engaged in transformation activity. It converts raw materials into useful products. Computer-use in production function ranges from product planning to process control. Computer software like Computer Aided Design/Computer Aided Manufacturing contributes to more efficient product development, reduced cycle time, and more efficient production processes.

The decisions in production function can be divided into three: planning, implementation and control.

Production Planning	Implementation	Control
Operations	Procurement	
Capacity	Job design	Inventory control
Location	Setting operational Standards	Cost control
Layout	Work measurement	Maintenance
Forecasting		Feedback
Scheduling		

Production function needs information support for all its activities, particularly in production planning, production control and materials management. Role of computers in production function can be looked at from the angles of inventory management, product design, production planning and production control.

Inventory Management

The purpose of inventory management is twofold:

- avoiding excess stocking and under stocking , and,
- minimising cost of carrying inventory.

Inventory for a manufacturing firm has three components: raw materials inventory, work-in-process inventory and finished goods inventory.

Computers are used in inventory management to provide real time information about current inventory levels and other control information to minimise the cost of inventory.

Computer-aided Design

The R&D department uses computer aided design (CAD) software to design new products and their components. This helps the firm in cutting design time and improving the design. The software also generates a bill of materials containing quantities and specifications of all the raw materials required for a product.

Computer Integrated Manufacturing

Manufacturing process in an information intensive activity. Computer is used to integrate the chain of activities starting from design to marketing. The engineering design of a product must be communicated to the manufacturing, raw materials must be ordered, availability of raw materials in inventory must be checked before placing purchase orders, scheduling of materials and labour, scheduling of production runs, accumulation of costs, etc., are information intensive. With a centralised database, computers can integrate this process. Computer integrated manufacturing uses the database to integrate the entire manufacturing process from engineering, to scheduling, to cost accounting and to marketing of the product.

Production Scheduling

Production scheduling aims at reducing the overall processing time to speed up turnover of work and to minimise the stocking of strategic components so that they are produced as and when they are needed in the assembly. Production scheduling has to increase or decrease the rate of output for parts and assemblies to conform to the master schedule.

Production Control

Production control ensures that facilities and personnel are economically used and cost and processing time objectives are met. It requires information on production plans, material specifications and requirements, master load schedule, actual output, forecasts of market demand, etc.

Quality Control

The computer is widely used in production and quality control for planning of production, production control, inventory management and waste control. Computers are used in automated process control systems. They monitor and control a large number of variables and report on a real-time basis for production and quality control.

Use of Computers in Vam Organic Chemicals Ltd.

Vam Organic Chemicals Limited[1] is the flagship company of the Bhartia group in Utter Pradesh. The company is the manufacturer of Vamicol brand of adhesive. It has 1,200 workers and has spent ₹ 15 million on computerisation since 1990. Despite manifold increase in sales turnover form ₹ 300 million in 1980s to ₹ 2,500 million in 1995 and branches in seven different locations in the country, it is carrying on business with the accounting staff without affecting quality of service. Vam Organic has a local area network with 120 terminals. There is a minicomputer for back-end processing and three stand-alone systems. Each branch is provided with one dozen or more microcomputers connected to LAN server. The go-downs in some of these branches have stand-alone PCs for record keeping. Data communications between branches and head office is possible using leased lines on CMC's Indonet network facility. Its factory is divided into three process plants and each plant has a microprocessor-based real-time operation control at the computer control room (CCR). The CCR monitors and controls process parameters like pressure, temperature, and floor control.

Computers are used in process control of boilers, where in on an instrumentation panel the parameters are fed in daily for the desired power output as per the projected requirements. The factory also has a Macintosh machine with CAD/CAM (Computer-Aided-Design/Computer-Aided-Manufacturing) software that helps in designing. Information technology has helped Vam Organic in not only easing the flow but also in reducing wastage of both material and time. Preparing monthly profit and loss account, which used to take a week earlier, now takes less than three hours.

Sources of Data for Production IS

Transaction processing data: Internal production transactions are captured and stored in corporate databases using computers on shop floor. The production data includes data on raw materials consumed, labour used, quantity of production, energy used, machine time used, wastage of materials, and idle time of men and machines.

Marketing data: The marketing plans are a useful source of data for production planning. The marketing plans decide the level of capacity utilisation of plant, addition to production capacity, product mix decisions, etc.

Inventory data: Timely availability of raw materials and other components is essential for normal functioning of production function. The inventory system supplies data on raw material availability. It helps the production function in production scheduling, ordering for supplies, etc.

Supplier data: The production function needs information about the suppliers of various raw materials and components, though this is strictly a function of purchasing department. This information is useful for the production function in adjusting the production process, etc.

Personnel data: The production function depends on the personnel department for workers and supervisors. If there is need to step up production, it needs to get information about the availability of workers with requisite skills. The personnel data provides this support.

External sources: The personnel function collects data about production technologies, labour availability, raw materials and their prices, etc., from the environment.

MARKETING INFORMATION SYSTEM

The marketing function identifies consumer needs and develops products based on such profitable market needs. It matches the product offering with the consumer needs and ensures ready buyers for the products of the company. Marketing is a critical activity for business firms and this function is a major user of information system facilities. Some of the application areas where computers are used in marketing are as follows.

Order Processing System

Computerised order processing system captures sales orders from customers and processes the orders for further action on them. It checks the inventory availability, pending or unfilled orders, production details, customer's credit limit, etc., before accepting the customer order. The approved orders are then passed on to the shipping department for assembling the order and to delivery department. Computerised sales order processing generates control report daily on orders processed, details of back orders, orders that could not be approved, etc.

Sales Management System

Computerised sales management system uses the data from sales order processing system to generate various sales related reports. This system supports accounts management, direct marketing, sales forecasting and sales presentations.

Logistics Management

The physical distribution is a major activity of marketing function. It uses computer based OR models to find optimum location of warehouses, shipment routes, quantity to be transported and stocked, etc. In addition to this, many companies like Hindustan Unilever Limited, Maruti Suzuki Limited, etc., have linked up suppliers and channel partners to their networked systems. This helps them in greater coordination with the suppliers and distribution facilitators.

Consumer Research

Computerised transaction processing systems capture huge quantity of data about customers and their buying patterns, etc. It is used to generate vital information about consumer behaviour. Sophisticated technologies such as data warehousing and data mining have been developed to capture and store such voluminous data and generate useful information for managerial decisions.

Sales Forecasting

Computer based mathematical and operations research models are used to forecast sales and marketing expenses.

Sources of Marketing Information

Transaction data: The transaction data includes data about marketing activities such as sales data and sales expenses data. It also records sales by product, customer, sales territory, salesman, etc. Such detailed data permits analysing the sales data in a variety of ways to measure efficiency of the marketing function in a company.

Marketing research data: This includes data about consumer, product, promotion, prices, packaging, distribution agents, etc. This data originates outside the company and is a rich source of information for the marketing function.

Corporate strategy and corporate plans: Corporate strategy and plans based on detailed analysis of the company's capabilities and environmental factors. They are formulated to achieve certain corporate objectives. These documents are useful sources of marketing information.

Marketing research agencies: Marketing research agencies like ORG-MARG regularly collect data about markets and make such database available to companies at a fee. This source of data is useful for marketing and corporate strategy planning. They also conduct market surveys for client companies for a fee.

Other Sources of Information for Marketing IS

- Sales invoices and other source documents
- Salesperson's customer call reports
- Salesperson's debriefing by marketing managers
- Customer account files
- Cost accounting system
- Sales forecasts, and,
- Sales history files

FINANCE INFORMATION SYSTEM

Computers are extensively used in finance function. The finance function is responsible for planning fund requirements, rising of funds economically and helping the management in deploying them profitably.

The specific tasks of finance function include:

- Recording and maintaining records of financial transactions
- Preparation of income statements, position statements and other reports for control

- Financial planning
- Cash management
- Credit management
- Security floatation
- Custody of funds and securities
- Budgeting and budgetary control
- Inventory control
- Tax management
- Internal audit
- Project appraisal
- Interpretation of control data.

The above activities can be grouped into funds management, record keeping and reporting, control function and auditory function.

Financial Decisions

Financial decisions are required to achieve goals of finance function. They fall into the following four categories.

- Financial requirement decision
- Investment decision
- Financing decision
- Dividend decision

Sources of Financial Data

The sources of financial data may be classified into internal and external based on the domain of its origin.

The internal sources include the following:

- **Transaction data.** Transaction processing generates huge amount data. It is the most importance source of data for financial applications.

- **Forecasting data.** Financial planning requires forecasting of business activities in terms of sales revenues, costs and profits. The forecasts are another source of financial data.

- **Corporate plans and programmes.** The corporate plans contain data about business growth and revenue projections. The finance strategy formulated to support corporate strategy is a rich source of financial information.

The external sources of financial data include the following:

- RBI publications
- Central and state Government publications
- Stock markets
- Annual reports of companies

- Database service firms like Centre for Monitoring Indian Economy
- Market research firms like ORG-MARG, and,
- Banks.

Let us now take a look at some of the application areas in finance function to know the role of computers in finance.

Accounts Receivable System

Computerised accounts receivable system generates bills for goods shipped to customers, maintains records of customers and generates information to assist in collection of accounts. For example, with computerised systems for monitoring accounts a bank can instantly know the loan defaulters by just running a query. The people resource can be used to collect the dues from the defaulters rather than wasting their time in locating such defaulters by physically checking their accounts in a manual system. The timely monitoring of accounts improves fund use and profitability of banks.

Accounts Payable System

Computerised accounts payable system keeps records of suppliers and the amounts due to them. The system tracks purchases of materials from suppliers, generates cheques to be issued to them and provides information for effective supplier management.

General Ledger

The computerised general ledger maintains financial accounts of a firm. This system generates financial statements like budgets, income statements, funds flow statement, balance sheet, etc.

Accounting has always been a top priority area for computer applications in any commercial organisation that implemented computer-based systems. It facilitates preparation of financial statements almost anytime with very high degree of accuracy. It also facilitates analysis of financial data, projection of financial figures and preparation of periodic reports such as cash flow and fund flow statements.

Forecasting

Computer facilitates financial forecasting to a large extent. Models are developed to forecast the effect of price changes, volume changes, etc., and to project cost and revenue estimates.

Financial Reporting

Report generation is another application area of computers in accounting. Report formats are pre-designed and stored in computers. The user can invoke the type of report needed and the computer generates it automatically.

Preparation of Financial Statements

Computerised financial accounting system generates financial statements for any period. These statements include Funds Flow statement, Cash Flow statement, Profit and Loss Account and Balance Sheet. They can be prepared any time.

Investment Management

Computers are used in investment analysis. Packages are available for fundamental analysis, technical analysis and portfolio management. Computer networks are used for online trading of securities. Trading in securities on leading stock exchanges in the country, such as National Stock Exchange (NSE) and Bombay Stock Exchange (BSE) is done on nation-wide networks. Scrip-less trading has been introduced in a phased manner. Depository firms like National Securities Depository Services Limited and Central Depository Services Limited have been started to facilitate scrip-less trading. These exchanges also offer facilities for Internet trading in securities.

PERSONNEL INFORMATION SYSTEM

This is a staff function that supports activities of the company. It is responsible for identifying the right people for the right job in the company and retain them with a view to ensure adequate availability of people for the smooth functioning of the business. Look us now look at some application areas in personnel function where computer is used.

Payroll Processing: Computerised payroll processing system keeps employee records, calculates salaries and wages, prints cheques and generates various information reports for managers and government agencies.

Performance Evaluation: Computer facilitates carrying out performance evaluation more objectively and regularly. It uses the corporate database about employees to evaluate their performance. The information is used in deciding compensation and promotion.

Manpower Planning: Computerised business planning models can be used to forecast manpower requirements. It can identify the number of people required and the kind of skills required in them.

HRD Information: This system maintains data about employees. The name, address, qualification, skills, language proficiency, training courses attended, etc. The information from this system is used in promotion, compensation and designing programmes for employee training and development.

Conclusion

Computer is a versatile tool. Its application is limited only by human imagination. It is used in all aspects of management these days. Its role in MIS is central. It is the use of computer that makes information systems more efficient and effective in meeting challenging needs of modern business management. Computer is used in every functional area. Its role is increasing in organisations that employ sophisticated production technologies and online marketing activities. The enterprise wide information system is an effective solution developed for organisation-wide sharing of information and communication. The computer networks now make possible things which were unimaginable a few decades ago. Computer is a basic infrastructure for any organisation now and the level of computer use in organisation is an index of its development and professionalism.

QUESTIONS

1. What is the role of computers in TPS?
2. What is the role of computers in IRS?
3. What role do computer play in functional information systems?
4. "Computer use in MIS is critical for survival of business firms". Do you agree?
5. Discuss the role of computers in Production function.
6. Discuss how computers can assist finance function.
7. Illustrate the use of computers for marketing.
8. What is enterprise information system?
9. "IT is a basic infrastructure for organisations". Comment.

REFERENCE

1. *Computers Today*, December 1995.

Case 12.1: AF Software

AF Software is a software company set up in 2003 in Kerala. The company offers business process management services and web portal solutions. The company specialises in web and enterprise portal development in addition to providing airlines solutions, CRM solutions, Human Capital management solutions and GIS. The company has customers in many countries and a significant presence in the Middle East. The company faces a number of issues as its internal processes are not integrated properly. They include inability to consolidate data from finance, marketing and sales, production and HR

A vendor offers a solution to its internal process management. The software, Netsuite, has features like:

- advanced financials
- revenue recognition
- renewals management
- advanced billing
- pricing management
- revenue management, and,
- complete financials

In addition to the above, the package is GAAP compliant, able to consolidate sales and costs in multiple currencies, giving 360° view of customers, real-time visibility, etc.

The management is considering two options:

(a) Buy and install NetSuite, or,

(b) Develop and implement a software solution for itself by the internal IT staff.

Questions:

1. Discuss the pros and cons of both the options and give your opinion on what the management should do?

2. What are the advantages and disadvantages of in-house development of the software?

13 CHAPTER

Planning for MIS

INTRODUCTION

Information system is not only expensive to build but also difficult to design and implement. Developing an information system master plan, therefore, is a crucial activity necessary for success in systems development. Information system plan forces managers and systems personnel to foresee future requirements, technologies and information resources available. This foresight helps in designing information systems that can match future requirements. It also saves wastage of time and money on unnecessary hardware and software.

Planning is important in information system development as the information system is to be developed for the entire organisation that usually involves a long period of time and large amount of money and other resources. The system is to be used by a large number of varied users for different applications. Implementing an application without proper planning often results in user dissatisfaction and disuse. Hence, a thorough plan for information system is a precondition for successful implementation of information systems in organisations.

The information system plan should be based on the organisation's business plan. The business plan identifies the goals, objectives and priorities for the organisation. That is, the strategic planning, tactical planning and the operational planning detail the above and guide the organisation towards the goals set. The strategic plan sets the direction for the organisation. It lays down the mission, goals, objectives, strategies and policies for the organisation. Strategic planning has a long-term time perspective and it is the responsibility of the top management to develop and maintain corporate strategic plan.

The purpose of IS plan is to provide advance planning and budgeting for the organisation in tune with the firm's overall goals and strategies. This will minimise unplanned expenses, reduce system downtime and improve the efficiency of the entire firm.

IS planning is an integral part of business planning. It takes into account the existing resources as well as those that will be available over a period of time, including hardware, software, data and people, for deployment. It also forecasts the requirements across functions and management levels in the organisation. The plan tries to find an optimum match between resources and requirements to maximise the benefits to the organisation.

Tactical plan specifies how the organisation is going to achieve the goals set by the strategic plan. Tactical planning is the responsibility of middle level managers. It involves setting objectives, formulation of budgets, schedules and procedures. Its time span corresponds to roughly a year. The operational planning is done at the lower level of management. Its time span is very short like a few days or few weeks or at the most a few months. This plan deals with day-to-day activities like production scheduling for the next day, material procurement, sales planning for the next week, etc.

In fact information system planning should be an integral part of business planning. Information system planning is that part of business planning concerned with deploying the firm's information system resources, including people, hardware, and software[2].

The information system planning has three components: strategic information system planning, tactical information system planning and operational information system planning[3].

STRATEGIC INFORMATION SYSTEM PLANNING

The strategic information system plan lays down broad framework for the information system in the firm. It formulates policies, objectives and strategies for providing information services to help the organisation achieve its goals and objectives. It identifies information system projects to be implemented over a period of time to support the business functions and the resources to be raised to implement the projects. It also gives broad guidelines about the priority of projects to be taken up for implementation. For example, a decision to move into e-commerce platform is a strategic one and the firm will develop a business strategy to achieve the business goals. Information technology in modern times has become a basic infrastructure for business firms. Since knowledge is recognised as a strategic resource, planning for information systems has become all the more important.

Aligning IS Planning and the Business Planning

A firm's IS plan should reflect and complement its business plan and budgeting process. IS plan identifies the decision points, methods, and strategies from the business plan. It aims to develop appropriate capabilities to ensure that the organisation's information systems will be able to support the business needs in the plan period.

Strategic Information Systems planning refers to the activities associated with setting objectives for IS, developing a long-term plan for achieving them, and implementing the IS plan.

A firm's business strategy is the approach a firm follows in pursuing its goals in a given market. Coordinating IS planning with business planning enables a firm to identify and seize opportunities in its markets, position itself effectively against its competitors and efficient use of resources. This integration necessitates the IS to gather information pertinent to making strategic decisions and supporting the process of business strategy implementation. Such an IS that dovetails with its business planning can give the firm a competitive advantage over its rivals.

The IS plan should be reviewed and updated periodically as and when organisational goals, strategies, services, and products change. This updating is necessary to maintain the fit between IS capability and the business requirements.

A firm's external environment has a major influence on its performance. The strategic IS planning process identifies the business strategies at functional level, business level and corporate level and develops plans to match the information needs and support for each. Achieving a fit between MIS planning and corporate strategy would create synergy through the coordination of different functions, leading to superior performance.

Aligning IS goals and organisational goals is a major task in strategic IS planning. Once this matching is done, the IS plan needs to identify the business processes where IS can assist a firm in implementing its business plans. This alignment process requires the firm to consider the following factors to provide a setting for this integration:

- Identifying and analysing the impact of information technology on business in future.
- The methods of leveraging information technology to support business processes
- Specifying the role of higher-level management in leveraging information technology capabilities for business processes
- Developing an organisation for information system function in the firm
- Setting up appropriate criteria to evaluate information system investments
- Developing procedures and systems to protect IS resources

The goals of IS plan should include:

- Minimising the cost of information processing,
- Developing the flexibility to provide different classes of information, and,
- The capability to provide specialised analysis and information.

Major Considerations in Strategic Planning for IS

Strategic planning for information system should consider the impact of IT on organisation strategy, structure and systems before the plan is worked out. IT can influence the strategy and structure of organisations. Hence, corporate strategy planning must analyse the potential of IT to create strategic business opportunities and competitive advantage. Similarly, strategic IS plan must look into the corporate strategy and functional strategies to support them with information resources and capabilities. Some of the major considerations in developing a strategic IS plan is discussed below.

Information Technology Choice

Choice of specific information technologies is a major factor. The technologies chosen must support optimally the current business strategy initiatives or help in shaping new business strategy initiatives. The technological options such as centralised or decentralised processing, electronic imaging, process control systems, local vs. wide area networks, data warehousing and data mining, electronic customer relationship management, expert systems and robotics are to be evaluated in terms of their fit with the business strategies to be implemented.

Synergy between Business Strategy and IT Strategy

Linking information system to business goals is the heart of IT strategy. The information technology strategy formulated must support business or corporate strategy. The factors to be considered in this respect are system reliability, acceptable cost-performance levels, interconnectivity and flexibility.

Information Technology Administration

Information technology advances are very rapid. Keeping the technology current is a Herculean task in systems administration. The firm can think of using mechanisms like joint ventures or strategic alliances or joint research for developing new information technology capabilities with Information technology vendors.

For proper planning of information system infrastructure, the Information Systems plan must address the following:

Information System Architecture

System development takes a fairly long period of time. The development may proceed in big or small chunks. Advances in information technology, business strategy, environmental changes, etc., happen all along. Proper development of information system for a firm requires a broad information system architecture. The system architecture specifies portfolio of applications, configuration of hardware, software, communication, and the database technologies.

Information System Processes

Every business process involves three flows: the physical flow of input and output, flow of costs and information flow. The information system must identify the information flow needs to support the physical flow of input and output through the organisation. It must define work processes essential for the operations of the information system infrastructure such as systems development, maintenance, and monitoring and control systems.

Information System Skills

Skills are needed to manage any resource. Information is a resource. Information system infrastructure needs to be managed properly to derive value from such investments. The firm must plan for acquisition, training, and development of the knowledge and capabilities of the individuals required to effectively manage and operate the firm's information system infrastructure.

TACTICAL INFORMATION SYSTEM PLANNING

The tactical plans are medium period plans developed to achieve the strategic plan goals. They focus on raising and utilising of resources efficiently. The tactical IS planning component deals with evaluation and ranking of projects, identifying and allocating resources for project implementation.

An IS plan for the next one year typically contains budgets and schedules for acquisition or development of software, hardware, network, and related products or services. In addition, the IS plan establishes a methodology for evaluation of major MIS purchases or outsourcing of information services.

The IS plan may also specify the methods for handling procurement, software piracy, training, security, and system misuse or abuse.

OPERATIONAL INFORMATION SYSTEM PLANNING

The operational plans are short period plans. The operational information system planning deals with preparation of operating budgets, systems development and maintenance activities. These plans set targets, benchmarks and criteria for evaluation of performance and control.

APPROACHES TO INFORMATION SYSTEM PLANNING

It is useful to have a framework or methodology to develop a firm's information system infrastructure. Many approaches have been developed in the past for information system planning. Some of the important approaches are discussed below[4].

- Stages of growth model
- Critical success factors

- Business systems planning
- Investment strategy analysis
- The scenario approach to planning, and,
- The architecture building approach.

1. Stages of growth model

The stages of growth model is explained in more detail in chapter one. The model analyses the progress of systems development and use in organisations in six stages. In stage one, called Initiation state, computers are introduced into the organisation and people experiment with them. Some early successes generate more interest in the new technology.

In stage two, called contagion, computer use proliferates in the organisation. The number of users and applications multiply and costs rise rapidly. In stage three, called control stage, costs of computer systems grow rapidly and senior managers bring EDP function under strict cost control. EDP budgets are formulated and closely scrutinised. In stage four, called Integration, MIS function gets centralised. The centralisation of MIS function results in data and systems integration. Stage five called data administration stage ushers in information resource management. During this stage information gets recognised as an organisational resource and information resource management gains in importance. In stage six called maturity stage, information is recognised as a strategic resource and the organisation develops an information systems strategy to support corporate strategy. The information systems manager becomes Chief Information Officer (CIO).

This historic model is useful as an analytical framework. The information system managers can draw insight into the stage a user group, department or division is in and to develop appropriate information system strategy. This insight will help them in planning the firm's information system infrastructure.

2. Critical Success Factors

This framework looks at individual managers and their information needs. This analysis helps in identifying information needs and designing systems to meet information needs effectively. The model lists key areas or critical success factors for each executive. Critical success factors are areas of the job where things must be done well so that the firm can flourish. This approach identifies a few areas, usually fewer than ten, as critical success factors. If performance in these key result areas is good, the organisation performs better. Critical success factors are not objectives. They are key drivers or means to achieve those objectives. The sources of critical success factors are industry, the firm, the environment and temporal organisational factors such as areas normally ignored, but needs current attention.

The critical factor method can be used to list the corporate goals and objectives. These goals and objectives are then used to find out which factors are critical for achieving them. For example, for supermarket, location is very important. In addition to good location, the critical success factors for its performance are product mix, balanced inventory, service, sales promotion and price[5].

3. Business Systems Planning (BSP)

IBM developed and popularised this approach. This approach is based on the philosophy that information resource is a corporate resource. Hence, it should be managed in such a way that it maximises the value creation. The purpose of Business Systems Planning is to develop an information system infrastructure that can support all the firm's business processes. It seeks to find out data needs of each business process and to develop an information framework based on the data needs. BSP approach claims that the framework so developed remains stable enough to develop future information systems.

The steps in BSP study are:

1. **Gaining commitment from management.** Preparing for the study. The preparations include creating study schedule, preparing list of executives to be interviewed, gathering reference material, etc.

2. **Starting the study.** The objectives of the study and study schedule are reviewed at the initial meeting.

3. **Defining business processes.** The study team identifies all the activities critical for the success of the firm such as new product development, production, marketing and quality improvement programmes.

4. **Defining business data.** The approach classifies data into data classes such as customers, vendors, parts, machines, etc.

5. **Defining information architecture.** The architecture presents relationship among data classes, processes, and information systems.

6. **Analysing current systems support.** The team studies information system support to business processes and marks processes that do not get any formal support, processes that get some support, redundant processes, etc.

7. **Interviewing executives.** The team now starts interviewing of top executives of the firm. The purpose of this interview is to discover the business assumptions and the data classes created so far, to determine the information needs of these executives and their problems and priorities.

8. **Defining findings and conclusions.** The study team summaries the huge amount of data collected and presents an information infrastructure design for the firm.

9. **Determining architecture priorities.** The team recommends priority for development of applications and a set of criteria for evaluation of information system projects.

10. **Reviewing information resource management.** The team now studies the information system management policies of the firm and recommends appropriate changes.

11. **Developing recommendations and an action plan.** The team produces final list of recommendation and an action plan for implementing the recommendations.

12. **Reporting results.** The study team now submits its findings and recommendations to the study sponsor.

13. **Overview of follow-up activities.** The BSP manual emphasises the need to follow up implementation of the recommendations.

5. Investment Strategy Analysis

This framework is based on traditional techniques of portfolio planning and investment strategies. The portfolios describe the allocation of IS resources to various IS applications.

Users represent the different classes of users for whom the IS resources are allocated. The information system investment varies from firm to firm. One firm might use information technology as a strategic tool and another might view it as just an overhead item. Depending on this assumption, the portfolio of applications developed will be different from firm to firm.

6. **Scenario Approach to Planning**

Scenarios are created to analyse the effects of certain changes on business. Several scenarios are developed and the most likely scenario is selected for system planning.

Elements of Scenario to be considered are:

- Business environment
- Government and society
- People changes
- Financial considerations

The scenario selected is used as the basis for developing information systems for the firm.

7. **Architecture building approach**

The IS architecture provides a blue print for information technology infrastructure in a firm. IS architecture integrates the business strategy and the IS strategy. It details how a firm's data processing systems, telecommunication networks and data are integrated. It answers questions like: what data is to be collected? Where it is to be collected? How it is to be stored? How the data is to be transmitted? What applications use the data and how these applications are integrated into the overall system?

The information system architecture is developed to meet the following three requirements in organisations:

- **Support the information flows in the firm:** Any organisation is a network of information flows. The systems architecture must facilitate the information flows in the form of reports, statements, transaction-oriented information flows such as online reservation and online banking, formal communication like e-mail and voicemail and document retrieval.

- **Facilitate communication between people:** The architecture may mean different things to different people involved in systems such as programmers, designers and users. The systems architecture details the objectives, data models, processes, etc. This facilitates common understanding and communication between the groups.

- **Enable the management to rethink business strategies:** The information technology advances are bringing into the realm of reality things which were dreams a few decades back. It makes possible designing organisation structures with IT infrastructure to operate business better, faster and more economically. The systems architecture provides a framework for integrating technologies with business processes.

The systems architecture provides a framework for integrating IT capabilities with the business processes. The system architecture development is very complex, as it has to blend a variety of information systems and technology into a coherent support structure.

CHALLENGES IN INFORMATION SYSTEM PLANNING

IS planning is involves lot of uncertainty about business growth, user requirements, technology etc. Some of the challenges faced in IS planning are as follows.

Foreseeing the Future

It is very difficult to foresee the advances and innovations in information technology area and assessing business opportunities arising out of them. New uses and improvements of these technologies call for keeping the plan flexible and extendable.

Difficulty in Communications between Users and Systems Personnel

The systems personnel often speak technical language that the users cannot understand. The systems personnel are also enamoured of new technologies and their potential. They do not properly consider how best the technology can be adapted to meet the specific user requirements. This often stands in the way of proper communication between users and systems personnel.

Ensuring fit between Business Strategy and IS Strategy

Every organisation is structured into divisions, functions and teams, etc., for effective functioning. These organisational subunits develop different policies and practices to suit their requirements. It is very difficult to design systems to support these variations and ensuring consistency across divisions and departments.

Difficulty in Developing Complex Systems

Large information systems are very complex and often take long years to fully implement. Most of the information system projects overshoot the time and budget limits. Yet, many of them fail in meeting the objectives. It is very difficult to design such complex information system projects.

Difficulty in Maintaining IS Performance

Even if the system is designed and implemented as planned, there will be a lot of snags and problems that affect the system's performance. The users may gradually develop dissatisfaction with the services and products of information system. The IS plan needs to anticipate such causes and provide for appropriate changes to maintain satisfactory performance.

PRINCIPLES OF *IS* PLANNING

IS planning is basically an intellectual exercise. Implementation is a major task. Successful IS plan implementation requires taking care of certain concerns and ensuring commitment to such plans. Some of the principles of information system planning that can ensure successful implementation of IS plans are briefly discussed below[6]:

Support to the Business Strategy

The purpose of information system is to provide support to the achievement of the firm's goals. Hence the IS plan should derive its goals and objectives from the business goals and objectives[7].

Commitment of Top Management

For the success of information system implementation and use in organisations, it should get unstinted support from the top management. This also ensures adequate resource allocation to information system projects.

Evaluate Technology as a Part of a Larger System

Organisation is a system with many parts, technology is just one of them. Whenever new technology is considered, its impact on organisation must be considered properly. For example, installing new software will not bring in the desired benefit if people are not given enough training in the use of that software. Similarly new hardware may not improve performance without replacing the old software.

Consider the Life Cycle Costs of Technology

The cost of information system is not just the cost of hardware and software. It also includes the cost of networking, cost of training people, cost of maintaining the systems and providing support to users. Hence, IS planning should take into account the life cycle cost of technology, and not just one-time acquisition cost only.

Design Systems that are Easy to Maintain

Easy maintainability is a major factor to be considered in information system design. The information system must be properly documented to support maintenance. The documentation must also be updated with every change in information system.

Impact of Technology on People

Even the best of the technology will fail if people do not accept it in organisations. Acceptance of system change will be more forthcoming if people involvement and participation in system changes are ensured.

Control and Support for Technical Systems

Systems will degrade if their maintenance is not properly taken care of. Hence, IS planning must also address issues of maintenance of the information systems and control over technical systems.

Conclusion

Information system planning is a tedious but necessary activity. There is a big challenge of foreseeing future and planning for adapting the information system to be in a fit with the organisation in the future. Assessing information needs and capabilities required in advance avoids wasteful investment of money and other resources. A proper IS architecture must be developed for the organisation keeping in mind future direction of technology and the IS support the business may need in the future. Aligning IS strategy with business strategy is another major concern for IS planning. Both act on each other and influence in shaping each other. IT has its impact on the strategy and structure of organisations. Similarly, the corporate strategy adopted and structure have their influence on IT use in the organisation. A properly aligned IS strategy can facilitate easy implementation of business strategy.

QUESTIONS

1. What is the need for planning information system development in organisations?
2. What are the factors to be considered in strategic planning of information systems?
3. Explain the different levels of information system planning and the activities to be planned at those levels.
4. What is information system architecture? What is its use?
5. What are the challenges to IS planning? How can they be managed?
6. What are the principles of IS planning that can ensure successful IS implementation?
7. Discuss the need for aligning IS strategy with business strategy and how to achieve it?

8. Discuss the approaches to IS planning that can provide a conceptual framework for IS planning in organisations.

9. How does Business System Planning help IS planning?

REFERENCES

1. Barbara C. McNurlin and Ralph H. Sprague Jr., *Information Systems Management in Practice*, Prentice Hall International, London, 1989, p. 89.

2. Steven Alter, *Information Systems*, Addison Wesley Longman (Singapore) Pte. Ltd., Delhi, 2000, p. 283.

3. James A. Brien, *Management Information Systems*, Galgotia Publications, New Delhi, 1996, p. 504.

4. Barbara C. McNurlin and Ralph H. Sprague Jr., *Information Systems Management in Practice*, Prentice Hall International, London, 1989, p. 95.

5. Jerome Kanter, *Managing with Information*, Prentice Hall of India, New Delhi, 1996, pp. 41-42.

6. Steven Alter, *Information Systems*, Addison Wesley Longman (Singapore) Pte. Ltd., Delhi, 2000, p. 386.

7. Cerpa, Narciso and Verner, June M., Case Study: *The Effect of IS Maturity on Information System Strategic Planning"*, Information & Management, Volume 34, 1998, pp. 199-208.

Case 13.1: GI Limited

GI Limited, Calicut is a unit of a large private sector Indian company . It has two divisions: Pulp and Fibre. The company has 3,500 regular employees and about 1,500 casual workers. The EDP department has five employees under a deputy manager. Computerisation started in the late 1980s in the company. The applications developed include payroll, purchase, inventory, sales and central excise. The system development is user-driven at GIL. If a user or user group requests for an application, the EDP department makes a quick study of the requirements and develops an application. Since EDP Department has only a few employees, they develop applications but do not care to develop the documentation of such applications. The Deputy Manager, EDP Department says "Documentation is a laborious and time consuming activity. The EDP department has absolutely no time for documentation as requirement study, development and maintenance of the applications have to be done by the Department. The department has already developed a large number of applications; about 1,500 of them over the last several years. The Department produces about 650 reports periodically in a year for management".

IT Resources

GIL has two local area networks one each for Pulp division and Fibre division. The networks have 58 personal computers and two servers each. The network cables were laid several years ago. The hardware maintenance is outsourced at a cost of ₹ 3,00,000 a year. Most applications are developed internally. Nearly 80% of transaction processing has been computerised.

The volume of transactions has increased over the years. The network servers hang too often. The system takes unduly long time to process reports. There are also problems in entering transactions. For example, the purchase of metal nuts is recorded in kilogram but issues are made in number of nuts. The issue pricing cannot be done automatically. The stock position is also difficult to be determined any time. Users need a lot more flexibility to enter data such as advance payment to suppliers. If advance payment is made, the amount of advance must appear in the payment advice form. But it does not offer this kind of flexibility for users.

Exhibit 1

Designation, qualification and experience of EDP Staff

Sl. No.	Designation	Qualification	Year joined	Previous Experience
1	Deputy Manager	B.Com., PGDCA	1990	2 years
2	Systems Analyst	B.Sc., DCA	1998	15 years
3	Asst. Programmer 1	B.Sc., DCA	1996	1 year
4	Asst. Programmer 2	B.Sc., (Computer Science)	1994	Nil
5	Jr. Programmer	B.Sc., DCA	1996	1 year
6	Method Analyst	B.Com.	1977	10 years

The EDP department has suggested increasing capacity of the system and replacing the network cables with fibre optic cable.

Questions:

1. What are the problems with the EDP department and how do you address those problems?
2. Can the problems be solved by replacing the old network cables with fibre optic cables? If it cannot, suggest how they can be addressed?

■ ■ ■

14 CHAPTER

Systems Development

INTRODUCTION

Systems development involves conceiving an information system project, implementing and maintaining it to the users' satisfaction. Information systems projects are initiated by requests from managers or users in organisations. Information system personnel may also suggest projects. The information system (IS) applications are designed to solve business problems and facilitate information flows that are necessary to effect transactions. Information system projects are evaluated as portfolios of such applications. Each application portfolio generally consists of a group of IS projects. The request from a user or manager triggers the systems development activity in the organisation.

Systems analysis suggests possible alternative systems like centralised, decentralised, client/sever systems, etc., and documents them. Similarly, a cost/benefit analysis is also part of systems analysis.

Reasons for IS project requests:

- To solve a problem
- To make use of an opportunity
- To comply with a requirement or directive, or,
- To effect broad improvement in business processes.

SYSTEMS DEVELOPMENT METHODOLOGIES

The effectiveness of information systems project depends on three factors[1]: the people, the problem and the process. People management is a crucial factor for software project management. It calls for people with varied and multiple skills. The people involved in IS project management are senior managers, project managers, practitioners, customers and end-users. People must be organised into effective teams and their activities must be coordinated. They must be motivated to do high quality software development work.

A project team is constituted for each IS project. Team leader is responsible for motivating the technical people, organising the software processes and encouraging innovation within the constraints identified.

The problem identification and definition is another factor. A requirements study is to be carried out to determine the objectives, scope and constraints of IS project. It is followed by the development of alternative solutions and selection of the best approach to solve the problem. This phase identifies the functionality to be delivered and the software process that can provide the functionality.

There are many models for system development. Some of the popular models are (described) below.

(i) Systems Development Life Cycle Model

The systems development life cycle model has a well-defined iterative process. It involves a few phases. The development follows the phases fairly exactly. The process never ends theoretically as the cycle gets repeated; that is, on completion of one cycle the next cycle starts with preliminary investigation.

In this approach, the systems design activities such as preliminary investigation, requirement analysis, systems design, systems acquisition and systems implementation are carried out in strict sequence.

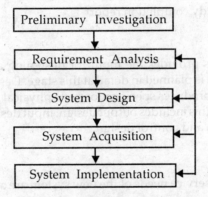

Fig. 14.1: Systems Development Life Cycle

The traditional system development life cycle stages are to be gone through serially and in strict sequence. Systems development life cycle is made up of the following stages:

Preliminary Investigation

It is an investigation into the problem and comes up with options for the management to consider for the proposed system change. The preliminary investigation examines the request for system change in detail to know precisely the requirements. A set of feasibility studies is used to ascertain the viability of the project. This includes technical feasibility, economic feasibility, operational feasibility and schedule feasibility. The report is submitted to the management for consideration and action.

The steps include:

  a. Conducting preliminary analysis.
  b. Determination of objectives, scope and constraints of the proposed system
  c. Developing alternative solutions
  d. Estimate cost and benefits of each such alternative
  e. Submit a preliminary report with recommendations

Requirement Analysis

If the management permits the system development to continue after studying the preliminary investigation report, new system requirements are analysed in detail. After the analysis, the results are presented in requirement report to the management. Requirement is any feature that is to be included in the new system.

This process starts with defining scope of system analysis and identifying users of the current system. Analysts carry out a study of current user requirements and deficiencies of the current system in meeting them. It describes the new system and the benefits it provides to the users. It also produces a requirement definition document.

Steps include:

a.   Gather data employing tools like document walk-through, interviews, questionnaires, observation etc.

b.   Analyse the data using CASE tools, data flow diagrams, system flowcharts, decision tables.

c.   Prepare a system study completion report

Systems Design

The requirement analysis provides the input for designing a new system to meet the user requirements. The new system is planned in detail at this stage. Design translates the requirements into ways of meeting them. It produces specifications of a physical system that is expected to meet the requirements. Specifically, this includes output design, input design, procedure design, database design, documentation design and control design.

Systems Acquisition

Hardware, software and service needs of the new system are ascertained and vendors chosen for acquisition.

This includes:

a.   Develop or acquire software

b.   Acquire hardware, and,

c.   Test the system

Systems Implementation

The system is finally tested and put into operation. Implementation comprises all the activities involved in putting the system together physically and getting the people adopt the new system. This requires training for people and conversion of data and procedures to be in agreement with the new system.

Steps include:

a.   Train the operators and users

b.   Convert to the new system

c.   Develop final documentation

Systems Maintenance

The system may need modifications or updating due to changes in requirements. If the changes are minor, they are incorporated into the system. If the changes are major, they start another cycle of system development.

Steps include:

- Perform system audit to see whether the new system implemented is as it should be
- Perform evaluation of system performance against a set of criteria.

(ii) Prototyping Model

A small version of the system is designed and is made available to users for experimentation. This original system is developed based on customer specification of general requirements. Detailed study of input, processing or output requirements is not carried out to save time or due to uncertainty about the study approach. The users work with this quickly and inexpensively made prototype and suggest modifications to the prototype. Such modifications are incorporated into the prototype after consideration of its feasibility. This process continues until a satisfactory system is evolved and the final version of the system is implemented for use.

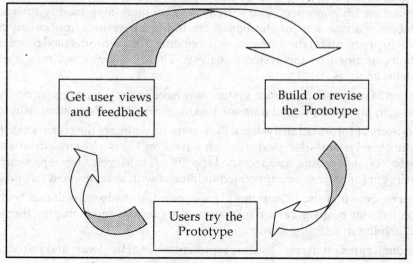

Fig. 14.2: The Prototyping Approach

The prototype is a working system developed to test the behaviour of the new system. The prototype generates output from input of data fed to it and this output is evaluated to know possible enhancements to the prototype. Ideally the prototype serves as a tool for determining requirements. The revised model, after all modifications are carried out, becomes the final system or the knowledge so generated is used to design and inplement a new information system in the organisation.

Steps in Prototyping

The steps in prototyping are:

a. Identify a set of known information requirements
b. Develop a working prototype

c. Make it available for use and note changes and enhancements made to it

d. Revise the prototype in the light of the experience gained about the system requirements, and,

e. Repeat these steps until a satisfactorily working system is developed.

(ii) End-user Development

End users who are provided with microcomputers and related facilities can develop their own application systems. These end-users may follow system development life cycle approach or prototyping approach for developing the systems.

PEOPLE INVOLVED IN SYSTEMS DEVELOPMENT

1. **System analysts:** These are professional systems personnel who work with the users to analyse existing systems and design new ones. They determine the information requirements, data capture and storage and the software and hardware requirements of the organisations. The systems analysts are programmers often with experience and training in specialised areas like accounting, finance, engineering and marketing.

2. **Programmers:** The programmers fall into two categories: Systems programmers and application programmers. The system programmers may modify operating systems, database management or develop some utility programs. Application programmers develop programs for meeting user requirements. They write detailed programs to process data as specified by the systems analysts. These programmers may also function as systems analysts.

3. **System Managers:** Information system may have several managers such as programming manager, input-output and data entry manager, and database administrator.

4. **End-users of Information Systems:** End-users are people of the organisation for whom the information system is designed to serve information. Users may range from workers, clerical employees, supervisors, managers and specialists at all levels. User representatives, such as a manager for an area, are appointed to interact with systems analysts and designers.

5. **System Consultants:** In systems development, outside consultants with specialised expertise may be given certain roles such as organising and managing the system project and helping in selecting hardware.

6. **Vendor Representatives:** These are representatives of hardware and software companies. They offer advice to clients on hardware and software features.

7. **Managers of the Organisation:** The managers provide leadership, motivate users to co-operate and facilitate systems development by allocating necessary resources.

8. **Internal Auditors:** Internal auditors work with the systems analysts to ensure that the new system will meet control requirements. They may also function as members of audit team after implementing the system to check its effectiveness.

TOOLS FOR SYSTEMS DEVELOPMENT

Many tools have been developed to assist the systems development efforts. These tools can be classified into three groups such as analysis tools, design tools and development tools[3].

Analysis Tools

Systems analysts use these tools for detailed system documentation and requirements determination. These tools include data collection tools, charting tools and dictionary tools.

Data collection tools. These tools describe current system and procedures. They help in identifying requirements.

Charting tools. These tools assist in representing the system and procedures graphically. The specific tools used include context diagrams, data flow diagrams, structure charts, etc.

Dictionary tools. These tools assist in documenting data names, data stores and aliases.

Design Tools

The system designers use these tools to formulate the features of a new system based on the requirements identified by systems analysts.

Specification tools. These tools specify the features to be included in an application. The specifications cover input, output, process and control aspects.

Layout tools. They help in formatting screen display, reports, input forms and output, etc.

Development Tools

These tools help in converting specifications into real applications.

Software engineering tools. They help in formulating software designs and in documenting the design.

Code generators. They produce source code and applications from functional specifications.

Testing tools. These tools help in evaluating a system or part of it against system specifications.

MODELS FOR SOFTWARE DEVELOPMENT

The software process consists of three stages: definition, development and maintenance. The models for software process are[2]:

- Linear sequential model or life cycle model or waterfall model
- Prototyping model
- RAD model
- Evolutionary software process models
- Incremental model
- Spiral model
- Component assembly model
- Concurrent development model
- Formal methods model
- Fourth generation techniques model

The linear sequential model and prototyping model have been discussed in the beginning of this chapter. The remaining methods are discussed briefly in the following section.

Rapid Application Development Model

It is a linear software development model, but it emphasises quick development and implementation. It uses a component based construction approach to software development. Once the requirements are identified, a development team quickly develops a complete application system to meet those requirements.

Evolutionary software process models

These processes are iterative. Newer versions of the software incorporate more features and facilities and over a period of time reach a more complete form. These models include incremental model, spiral model, component assembly model and concurrent development model.

(a) **The Incremental Model:** It combines elements of the linear sequential model and the prototyping model. This model develops a core product initially to meet basic requirements. Many additional features have to be added to it. The core product is made available to users. Based on the evaluation of the core product, a plan is drawn up for the next increment. It builds the features demanded by users to the core product. This iteration is continued until the complete product is delivered.

(b) **Spiral model:** This combines features of prototyping model and linear sequential model.
•   It employs the iterative process of refining the software as in prototyping model with the predictable and controlled development of the linear development model. The spiral model involves six tasks: customer communication, planning, engineering, construction and release, customer evaluation, and, customer communication. The planning stage determines objectives, alternatives and constraints of the system. Risk analysis activity includes identification of alternatives and the risks involved in each of them. Engineering activity builds the next level of the software product. Customer evaluation provides the feedback on how effective is the software in meeting the customer needs.

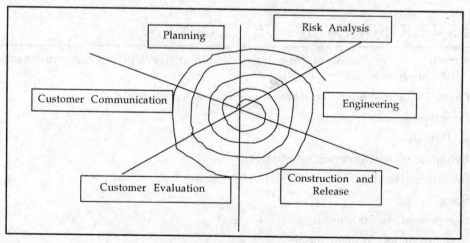

Fig. 14.3: The Spiral model

(c) **The component assembly model:** This model uses object technologies for building software systems. Each pre-packaged software component (often called classes) encapsulates its data and code. These reusable components are combined into applications based on identified requirements. This model employs the iterative process for developing more evolved software.

(d) **The concurrent development model:** The concurrent process model recognises the fact that any time activities will be in various stages of completion (states) in every task area like none, under development, awaiting changes, under revision, under review, baselined, done etc. This model gives a picture of current state of a software project. It defines a network of activities. Event in one activity area triggers changes in the state of other activities.

The Formal Methods Model

This model involves a set of activities that generate a mathematical specification of software. Ambiguity, incompleteness and inconsistency in the software can be detected and corrected using a mathematical analysis.

Fourth Generation Techniques

The fourth generation technologies include tools like nonprocedural languages for database query, report generation, data manipulation. They also include high-level graphic capability, spreadsheet capability etc.

This model starts with identification of user requirements. After identification of requirements, an operational prototype is developed and implemented for use. For small applications, this model is very effective. Time is not wasted on cumbersome procedures. Development of large applications using fourth generation techniques poses the same problems as with any other model of software development.

Conclusion

Systems development has the difficult task of identifying requirements, many of them are to arise in the future and not articulated by user community, and designing and implementing systems that should satisfy user needs in terms of support to managerial processes, business processes and information processes. There is need for a proper methodology that can force the people involved in systems development to follow certain identified and documented method for designing, developing and implementing information systems.

QUESTIONS

1. What is systems development? What are the stages in systems development?
2. What are the approaches to systems development?
3. What is system life cycle approach to system development?
4. What are the tools used in systems development?
5. What is end-user development? What are the advantages and disadvantages of this approach?
6. Discuss the type of people involved and their role in system development.
7. Discuss the process of prototyping approach to system development and its advantages.
8. Explain the software process models and how they assist developing robust software.

REFERENCES

1. Pressman, Roger S., *Software Engineering*, McGraw-Hill International, Singapore, 1997, p. 58.
2. *Ibid*, p. 68.
3. Senn, James A., *Analysis and Design of Information Systems*, Mc-Graw Hill Publishing Co., Singapore, pp. 10-41.
4. O'Brien, James. A., Management Information Systems, Galgotia Publication Private Limited, New Delhi, 1996, pp. 95-96.
5. (O'Brien,) *Ibid*, p. 96.
6. Senn, James A., *Analysis and Design of Information Systems*, Mc-Graw Hill Publishing Co., Singapore, p. 10.
7. Parker, Charles S., *Management Information Systems*, McGraw Hill Publishing Company, Singapore, 1989, pp. 581-82.

Case 14.1: CBS at The Federal Bank Limited

Introduction

The Federal Bank Limited was incorporated in 1931. With 745 branches, over 700 ATMs and five million plus customers all over the country in 2011, it is the largest old generation private sector bank in India. It has been growing organically and inorganically and believes in delivering world class service to its customers. For that in 1996 the bank formulated an Information Technology Strategic Plan 2000 for automating its branches in a phased programme. It developed bank automation software in-house in 1997 called "Fedsoft" in collaboration with Datanet Corporation, Bangalore. The bank set up its first ATM in Mumbai in the same year. It also set up its website "www.federal-bank.com" that enabled customers to know about its products and services. It set up a financial subsidiary, Federal Bank Financial Services Limited, in 1997. In the year 2000 Federal Bank started Internet banking and in 2001 mobile banking. In the year 2003 the bank launched 'Anywhere Anytime Banking' for its customers in over 300 interconnected branches and by 2004 all the branches were interconnected. The bank introduced e-pay services in the same year.

Early IT Initiatives

The bank introduced several innovative financial services like Fed Flexi deposit scheme, Internet banking service with Fednet, e-pay, e-shopping payment gateway, mobile alerts and mobile banking service, express remittance facility from abroad, RTGS facility at all branches, loans to IPO investors etc. The bank has the distinction of being the first among the old private sector banks to launch these services in India.

In its IT initiative to computerise all branches and interconnect them, one of the challenges faced by the bank was to make a choice between its own award winning bank automation software 'FedSoft' and core banking software packages from other companies. The bank had lined up several plans for aggressive growth and the management team was not sure of FedSoft's capability to match the business growth and the delivery of superior customer experience planned for the future. Hence, it decided to implement a new generation core banking solution. The management wanted the software solution to support existing and new products, provide superior customer comfort, ability to interface with several other delivery channels like ATM, Internet banking, mobile banking, etc.

Federal Bank drew up a set of criteria for the selection of the CBS package and a team of experts was identified to advise the bank on package selection. A thorough selection process was carried out which short listed three packages for final selection. The experts carried out next phase evaluation, vertical and horizontal evaluation process. The team mapped the capabilities of each solution package against the business requirements and finally 'Finacle' from Infosys Technologies Limited was recommended for implementation. It chose a centralised architecture with Oracle RDBMS as its back-end. The bank had identified 36 channels for service delivery. Integration of these channels was an important task in implementation.

Implementation of Finacle

The FedSoft replacement started with rigorous testing of the new core banking solution software with a large number of test cases. Data centre and disaster recovery site were set up in different seismic zones. Federal Bank started roll out of the new software in a phased manner in April 2007 with 16 branches in the pilot implementation project. It threw up a big challenge for the bank. The staff had to unlearn FedSoft and relearn Finacle. The change was not easy and it needed a great amount of motivation for staff to migrate to the new environment without much discomfort to customers. The bank took six months to complete the implementation. The seamless integration was achieved without affecting service to the customers during the transition period. Most of the FedSoft legacy system was integrated with Finacle Messaging Service and an interface was developed internally for communications between FedSoft and Finacle. All the channels were integrated with this interface.

Finacle is one of the most user-friendly core banking solution software packages. It is very fast and highly scalable. Besides, it has powerful built-in CRM engine. Its superior multi-channel delivery capability makes it one of the finest bank automation software packages. Finacle has an inbuilt integrated financial and accounting management system that caters to multicurrency and hierarchical bank structures comprising hundreds of branches and profit centres. The integrated General Ledger supports real-time online updating of transactions. The transaction manager provides the facility to auto generate batch and online transactions while processing large volume of transactions, complete with validations and defined checks.

Finacle has sophisticated security management at application, database and user levels with in-built checks and role-based access. Integrated, secure and scalable reporting infrastructure to meet various reporting needs is yet another feature of the package. Its track record of 100% successful implementation across the globe was another advantage of the package for banks.

Features of Finacle

Core Banking: Finacle core banking solution is comprehensive and integrated. The modular business solution handles strategic and day-to-day or core processes of banks

E-Banking: Finacle consumer e-banking solution is proven Internet and mobile banking solution for retail banking customers

CRM: Finacle CRM solution is a modular, multilingual, web-based customer-centric application that enables banks to leverage ready-to-deploy CRM functionality

Treasury: Finacle treasury solution is an integrated yet modular front, middle and back office solution built on best-of-breed open technology platforms, providing high scalability and flexibility.

Mobile solutions: Finacle mobile solutions have two parts – mobile payments and mobile banking solutions.

Alerts: This feature empowers banks with the capability to alert end-users about events recorded by the bank's business systems.

Benefits to the Bank

Finacle helped the Federal Bank to centralise control over operations. The service is available 24/7 with 99% uptime for its five million plus customers. Realignment of industry practices has been achieved as part of Finacle implementation. It lowered support and maintenance costs. Interest rate changes, daily exchange rates, etc., are centrally administered. Most back office jobs like account opening, issue of cheque books, customer letters, clearing, etc., are centralised at a central processing centre. MIS reports are now generated centrally as and when needed. They were earlier prepared at branches. Data warehousing and data mining initiative helps the bank in asset liability management, monitoring compliance with regulatory requirement, etc. CRM module helps the bank in segmenting customers and designing products for each segment or group of segments.

Conclusion

Federal Bank was one of the pioneers in implementing information technology solutions for banking in the country. The bank's own solution was very user-friendly package. Still the management was not confident of its capability to scale up to meet the bank's future growth. So, the

CBS software from Infosys was implemented in all the branches and the bank rolled out customer-friendly financial products and services. The bank's growth after the Finacle implementation has been impressive.

Exhibit 1

Vision and Mission of Federal Bank Limited*

Vision:

- Become the dominant "numero uno" bank in Kerala and a leading player in target markets.
- Be the 'trusted' partner of choice for target (SME, Retail, NRI) customers.
- Be a customer-centric organisation setting the benchmarks for service.
- Offer innovative yet simple products supported by the state-of-the art technology.
- Have a dynamic and energised workforce with a strong sense of belonging.
- Deliver top tier financial performance and superior value to stakeholders.
- Be a role model for corporate governance and social responsibility.

Mission:

Devote balanced attention to the interests and expectations of stakeholders, and in particular:

- **Shareholders:** Achieve a consistent annual post-tax return of at least 20% on net worth.
- **Employees:** Develop in every employee a high degree of pride and loyalty in serving the Bank.
- **Customers:** Meet and even exceed expectations of target customers by delivering appropriate products and services, employing, as far as feasible, the single-window and 24-hour-seven-day-week concepts, leveraging strengthened branch infrastructure, ATMs, and other alternative distribution channels, cross-selling a range of products and services to meet customer needs varying over time, and ensuring the highest standards of service at all times.

Pursue excellence in various facets of banking

Adopt best industry practices

- Develop, adopt, and review a well-conceived business plan for achieving realistic targets of growth, profitability, and market share over the medium term.
- Operate within a well-defined, diversified, risk profile and adopt prudent risk-management norms and processes and effective control practices.
- Employ and leverage appropriate modern information technology to: enhance the quality, speed, and accuracy of product/service delivery; provide 'anytime-anywhere' banking facility; strengthen management information and control systems and processes; improve productivity; and reduce costs.
- Increase awareness of the "Federal Bank" brand among targeted customer groups through cost-effective marketing.
- Adopt a robust corporate governance code emphasising a high degree of professionalism of the Board and the management, and accountability and disclosure to shareholders.

- Decentralise decision making with accountability for decisions made, and assign cascading profit responsibilities to middle and junior management.
- Develop a conducive and transparent work environment that fosters staff commitment, competence, initiative, innovation, teamwork and service-orientation.

Questions:

1. Why did the bank decide to drop FedSoft in favour of Finacle? Could it have been better to modify and update FedSoft to meet future growth requirement?
2. What was the reason for Fed Bank's implementation of Finacle?
3. What procedure was adopted by Federal Bank to implement the CBS?
4. What were the major challenges to implementing a CBS like Finacle?
5. Why did the bank choose a phased implementation of the CBS software?
6. How did the bank benefit from the Finacle implementation?

Source: www.federal-bank.com

Courtesy: Mr. Mohandas C. P., General Manager, The Federal Bank Ltd.

15 CHAPTER

Systems Analysis

INTRODUCTION

Systems analysis is an orderly and systematic process of identifying and solving problems. A system is made up of interrelated and interacting component parts. Analysis is the process of dividing 'a whole' into parts to examine them in detail. Such examination enables understanding the nature, functions and relationship of the parts within the system. Information system development comprises mainly three major activities: systems analysis, systems design and systems implementation. Before a system is designed or modified, it is required to see how the existing system is functioning. It is done by systems analysis. Systems analysis gives a set of inputs and design ideas for the next activity, that is, systems design.

Systems analysis is a formal enquiry into a problem to help a decision maker to identify a better decision or better course of action than that he would have made without it. It is required to handle problem situations that are complex and involve uncertainty of high order about alternatives and their outcomes. It identifies objectives, constraints, alternative solutions to the problems and the consequences of each such alternative considered in terms of costs, benefits and risks. It presents the findings to the decision-maker to enable him to make a better choice of the course of action.

The systems analysis is one of the crucial stages in systems development life cycle and serves as a basis for designing and installing a system. It is carried out to acquire a thorough understanding of all important business aspects under consideration, and to identify the user requirements in the proposed system. The emphasis is on investigation and questioning to learn how the system is currently operating. The analyst will gather information about equipment, personnel demands, operating conditions and limitations of the present system.

Systems analysis is a detailed study of[1]:

- information needs of the organisation and its end users
- the activities, resources, and products of any present information systems, and,
- the information system capabilities required to meet the information needs of users.

The final product of systems analysis is a set of requirements and design ideas for the proposed system. The functional requirements so analysed are presented in the form of systems requirements report. The system requirements become the needs to be met by systems design that follows systems analysis.

James A .O'Brien[2] conceptualises the activities involved in systems analysis as follows:

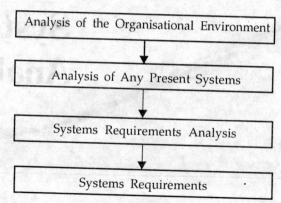

Fig. 15.1: Major Activities in Systems Analysis

In the first stage, the information needs of the organisation, its subsystems and environmental systems are analysed. In the second step, the resources, products and activities of any existing information systems are studied. In the systems requirements analysis, the information system capabilities required to meet the information needs identified earlier are analysed. The above steps lead to the specifications of systems requirements such as input requirements (sources of input and format) output requirements (output formats, frequencies and volume), processing requirements (processing operations), storage requirements (size of database), and control requirements (accuracy, security and integrity).

Systems analysis is the process of analysing a system with the potential goal of improving or modifying it. Analysing is the process of breaking down problems into smaller elements for study and, ultimately, solving a problem or systems improvement.

James A. Senn defines systems analysis[3] as "the process of gathering and interpreting facts, diagnosing problems, and using the information to recommend improvements to the system". A system study precedes the systems analysis, as a lot of facts have to be accumulated for systems analysis.

Reasons for initiating Systems Analysis

Systems analysis is in general an orderly and systematic process of identifying and solving problems. Systems are generally complex entities. Complex systems are difficult to study at the total system level. Analysis is the process of dividing a whole into its parts to examine them in detail. Such examination enables understanding the nature, functions and relationship of the parts within the system. Systems analysis is not an end in itself; it is carried out to meet certain objectives, which arise in any of the following contexts:

1. **Problem solving.** Understanding a problem in a proper perspective necessitates a system study.

2. **New requirement.** System changes are required when a new law or a new accounting practice or a new management practice has to be introduced. Systems analysis is carried out to study the kind of changes required, the feasibility of implementing changes, etc.

3. **Implement a new idea or technology.** It is done to study the likely impact of a new idea or technology on the organisation and how to implement it with as little disturbance as possible.

4. **Broad systems improvement.** Sometimes systems analysis is initiated to study how the existing system can be improved.

In the process of understanding the existing system, the systems analyst also identifies the strengths and weaknesses of the existing system in meeting the user's requirements. Users at different levels of an organisation have different information requirements for decision making. Information is required for monitoring and control decisions, planning decisions and policy formulations.

STRUCTURED SYSTEMS ANALYSIS

Structured approach to systems analysis divides the analysis work into modules. Systems analysis and design is undertaken as project. The project team breaks and divides the work into suitable modules and assigns them to small groups. These components are briefly explained below.

i.   **System Study Proposal.** The project team draws up a plan of the system study activities. The objectives of system study are mentioned in this proposal.

ii. **System Survey.** The objective of system survey is to have an overview of the present system and its working. It makes an assessment of the present system and documents it in sufficient detail.

iii. **Problem specification.** In this stage, the problem is properly identified and is defined. Location of the exact problem is a difficult process. The analysts will have to probe deeper to identify it.

iv. **System study proposal review.** After the specification of the problem in full, the original systems study proposal is revised. This revised proposal details the remaining system study activities and outlines probable activities of systems design stage.

v.   **Systems analysis.** When the system survey focuses on the old system, the systems analysis focuses on the features of the new system that is going to be designed. The objectives of the new system and how they are to be accomplished are the issues involved here.

vi. **System requirement specification report.** This is the final stage in systems analysis phase. This report spells out the requirements of the proposed system. They may cover such aspects as the hardware and software requirements, personnel requirements, system reliability requirements, formats and frequency of reports, error tolerance rates and special security needs for sensitive data.

Structure of System Study Proposal

The system study proposal may have a structure like the following:

a. Introduction
    - Purpose of the report
    - Details of the project request
    - Scope of the report
    - Structure of the report
b. Tools and techniques used
    - Solution generated
    - Feasibility analysis (cost-benefit)

c. Information systems requirements
d. Alternative solutions and feasibility analysis
e. Recommendations
    Appendices

SYSTEMS ANALYSIS TOOLS AND TECHNIQUES

Systems analysts employ a number of tools and techniques for carrying out systems analysis. Some of them are:

- interviewing the people in the organisation
- flow charting of the system and processes
- organisation charts to study organisational relationships and information flows
- operating manuals for standard operating procedures of the present system
- job descriptions of various positions to know who makes what decision and the consequent information needs
- questionnaires to elicit views of key persons on system requirements and problems
- document walk-throughs to know the processing of files at various workstations
- direct observation of the system in operation
- logic description with decision trees and decision tables
- work measurement at various workstations to know the processing efficiency, and
- examination of other systems to study their operations which are similar to the system under study.

Feasibility Studies

Systems analysis involves detailed feasibility analysis of the possible IT solutions to business problems. Further action on system development work hinges on the management decision on the feasibility report. The report addresses different concerns of the management and presents the expert opinion in the following format:

Technical feasibility. It is an examination of the solution in terms of its technical details. The core of the analysis involves key questions like: whether the solution is technically practical and whether the people have the technical expertise to design and build this solution.

Economic feasibility. It examines whether the solution is cost-effective. It takes into account the cost of the project and the benefit from the project to the client organisation.

Operational feasibility. It analyses the capacity of the solution to meet the users' requirements and how much the users will accept the changes in the users' work environment.

Schedule feasibility. It analyses whether the solution can be designed and implemented within an acceptable time.

Risk feasibility. It examines the level of risk attached to the project in terms of the probability of a successful implementation using the technology and approach suggested.

SYSTEM ANALYSTS

These are professional systems personnel who work with the users to analyse existing systems. They determine the information requirements, data capture and storage and the software and hardware requirements of the organisation. The systems analysts are programmers often with experience and training in specialised areas like accounting, finance, engineering and marketing.

Work of systems analysts depends on the role assigned to them. The role of a system analyst may be viewed as that of a consultant, and a change agent. The systems analyst is a person with technical competence acquired over a long period as a part of system development personnel. He understands both business and computing. With vast and varied experience, he is in a position to offer expert advice to the client organisations on possible configuration of system components and implementation options. It enables the client organisation to choose the right type of hardware and software solutions and implementation methods.

Systems analyst also plays the role of a change agent. As part of systems analysis, he conceives ideas for effective design of alternative solutions to the business issues. He diagnoses the ills of the client organisation and suggests solutions to them. He apprises the client organisation on the extent of change needed and how it can be smoothly introduced. Such changes help the client organisation to achieve competitive advantage.

Based on the extent of system development work assigned to him in specific projects, his responsibilities are[4]:

i. **Systems analysis only.** Systems analysts are not involved in systems design. They are asked to study the system to gather relevant facts about the system and analyse the study facts to suggest possible design approaches.

ii. **Systems analysis and design.** Analysts are given an additional responsibility of designing systems in addition to systems study.

iii. **Systems analysis, design and programming.** They conduct systems investigation, develop design specifications and software to implement the design. This job gives the analysts an important role throughout the systems development work.

Qualities of a Systems Analyst

The job of a systems analyst is a high-skilled one. He needs to have through knowledge about the entire system design, development and implementation activities. He must have a system orientation. That is, he should keep in mind the large picture of the organisation, that is, system thinking, when he suggests changes in any part of the organisation. The solution suggested should actually work and produce desired change. For that, he should have some qualities and skills. These are:

- Knowledge of business processes of client organisations
- Expert knowledge of information and communication technologies
- Programming experience
- Problem-solving skills
- Good communication skills
- Good interpersonal skills
- Concern for ethics and values

Object Oriented Systems Analysis

Object oriented systems analysis is a different approach to systems development. It is closely related to object oriented programming (OOPs). OOPs is based on some fundamental concepts like objects, classes, messages, encapsulation, inheritance and polymorphism. The Coad and Yourdon approach to object oriented analysis uses a five layered model. The five layers are class and object layer, structure layer, service layers, attribute layer and subject layer. Techniques of discovering objects are the same as for identifying processes and data entities for non-object based systems analysis. The reader may use a book on object oriented programming to understand these concepts and techniques as they are out of the scope of this book.

Conclusion

Systems analysis is a systematic approach to ascertain whether a process can be improved with better procedures and methods. Systems analysis and systems design are the two major activities in systems development. Systems analysis is a time consuming but unavoidable process in systems development. It identifies and documents system requirments which form the basis for system design and implementation.

QUESTIONS

1. What is systems analysis? Why is it initiated?
2. What is structured systems analysis? What are the steps in it?
3. What are the tools and techniques used in systems analysis?
4. Describe the nature of work of systems analyst.
5. "System analysis is a critical process in systems development criticise."

REFERENCES

1. O'Brien, James. A., *Management Information Systems*, Galgotia Publication Private Limited, New Delhi, 1996, pp. 95-96.
2. *Ibid*, p. 96.
3. Senn, James A., *Analysis and Design of Information Systems*, Mc-Graw Hill Publishing Co., Singapor,. p 10.
4. *Ibid*, p. 12.

Case 15.1: Life Insurance Corporation of India

The life insurance business is in for a major change with the entry of foreign and domestic private firms into the industry that was until recently a monopoly of LIC of India. LIC, the state owned monopoly, set up in 1956 by nationalising insurance business in India, has grown into a very large insurer with an asset base of over ₹ 1,60,000 crore in the year 2000. It had 11.5 crore policy holders, 8.5 lakh agents and 2048 branches all over the country. It also has entered mutual fund and housing loan business.

Insurance Regulatory Authority has been set up to regulate the insurance business in India. Insurers like Allianz, Standard Life and Prudential have entered the industry. More are waiting to set up business in the insurance industry in the country.

LIC is gearing up to face the competition. Much before the privatisation of insurance business, LIC started preparing for it. It went on a restructuring exercise in the mid-1980s that resulted in decentralising the business. Branches have been given powers to sell policies and settle claims.

G.N.Bajpai, Chairman LIC says, "We will be ahead of competition. ... There are three areas of concern at the LIC – technology, human resource and customer care". To provide better service to customers, it has already computerised branches and networked them locally. This has improved quality of service particularly claims settlement. The outstanding claims are down by 2.74% from 3.47% in 1995 (it was 14.27% in 1980). LIC has also set up a Metro Area Network (MAN) to offer better service to its customers. About 26% of its customers are expected to benefit from the MAN.

On technology front it is planning to put in place a country-wide network to provide the best of service to its customers. The objective is to acquire the capability required to serve its customers walking into any of its branches in the country to transact any kind of insurance business.

Retaining the insurance agents and actuaries is yet another concern for LIC. 30% of its agents bring in 80% of its business. India has only 150 qualified actuaries out of the 40,000 qualified actuaries worldwide. Actuaries are professionals who design insurance products. The IRDA insists that insurance firms operating in India can employ only Indian actuaries. Hence, with more private firms entering the industry, there will be poaching of LIC's efficient insurance agents and professional actuaries.

Providing care to customers is another vexation at LIC. As a monopoly, LIC until recently was not much oriented to customer needs. It now has to address issues of delivering quality service and ensuring reasonable return to policyholders.

Questions:

1. Discuss how IT can help LIC in meeting its concerns.
2. Analyse the feasibility of LIC setting up a nation-wide network to do insurance business and offer customer service.
3. What kind of solution should LIC implement? A custom-built software or an ERP kind of package sourced from leading vendors like SAP AG?

16
CHAPTER

Systems Design

INTRODUCTION

The systems design is a creative process that is guided by the broad objectives of the organisation. Achievement of the organisational objectives requires structuring of many subsystems into a hierarchy, where each subsystem is designed to provide the output for the next higher subsystem. That is, each subsystem's objective directly helps in achieving the objective of the higher subsystem in the hierarchy.

Systems design work begins after systems analysis is completed. Systems analysis lists user requirements. Now it is the task of systems designer to identify data requirements and data sources. The systems design may be divided into conceptual design and physical design.

Data flow analysis helps in designing a logical organisation of data into computer files. For example, an inventory file will contain many inventory records each record carrying the necessary information of an item like its name, description, unit of measurement, quantity on hand, value, etc. Structured systems design tools such as Data Flow Diagram (DFD) and data dictionary facilitate this analysis.

Data processing analysis helps in conceptualising the processing logic. Structured systems design tools such as decision tables, decision trees and structured English facilitate this analysis by clearly displaying and documenting the processing logic for each processing step identified in a DFD. These steps force the analyst to identify all possible conditions and decisions, and represent them in a tabular form (decision table), in a tree form (decision tree) or in structured English language (Structured English).

Thus, logical design provides an estimate of the processing requirements. The physical design looks at the physical hardware of the system to meet the processing requirements. Upgrading the existing hardware and acquiring new computers to meet the processing requirements are also planned at this stage. Subsequently file organisation details are worked out and appropriate file organisation methods established for processing and storing data.

The design process starts with output for end-users. The end-users may need information products at regular intervals. The output points to the input required and the procedure for processing the data into information products.

OUTPUT DESIGN

The purpose of information systems is to minimise uncertainty in decision-making by providing information about the problem and its solutions so that the decision makers can be more confident about the decision outcomes. Information is made available in the form of reports, screen displays etc. The report formats are designed after considering the information needs, frequency and nature of use by each user group. Such formats are pre-designed and frozen so that the users can invoke a particular application to generate the report as and when they want it.

The outputs from processing are either communicated to the users directly or stored temporarily in the form of reports, etc. The outputs are normally defined during the logical design of the system. It identifies user or user groups and defines the output formats, content, frequency, media, response time etc.

INPUT DESIGN

Input design requires very careful attention. The quality of output depends on the quality of input to the system. Adequacy of input is another important aspect. Accuracy and adequacy of data has to be ensured through proper input design and validation procedures.

Input Stages

The input process consists some or all of the following activities:

- Data capturing and recording at source
- Data transcription (transfer of data to an input form)
- Data control (checking the accuracy of data)
- Data validation (checking the data as it enters the system)
- Data editing (correcting the errors in the data).

Input types

The logical input design identifies the source of data. It needs to be explicitly stated in this stage. The source of data may be:

- External like sales orders, purchase invoices, etc.
- Internal like bill of material, purchase order, etc.
- Interactive like the data entered by user during the interaction with the application.

The designers must also identify the impact of the data on the system. Output of one system may form inputs to other systems.

The input data may be manually captured and entered. It may also be automatically captured through automated transaction processing such as automated order processing or EDI messages.

PROCEDURE DESIGN

Procedures are to guide the programmers, operators and users of information systems. Some procedures concern the programming like documentation procedures that tell the programmers how to document software they have coded and tested. Some others concern operators, like how to prepare and enter input into the system; some may concern the users like how to interact with the system and how to interpret certain results.

Various tools are used to specify the procedures. Some of these tools like flowcharts, data flow diagrams, decision trees, decision tables, data dictionary, and pseudo code have been discussed in Chapter 17.

FILE DESIGN

Physical data forms the basis of any information processing activity. The data must be captured, structured and stored in databases to facilitate retrieval and use in organisations. Data is stored in files. Hence, file design is a crucial activity in system development.

Computer Files

The primary memory of a computer is limited and hence programs and data are deleted from primary memory once their use is over. These programs and data are organised into files for permanent storage on secondary storage devices for reuse. These files are structured in a particular way depending upon the type of access required and the media on which they are stored. If the data requires quick access, it is stored on disks and if it requires only serial processing the data is usually stored on tape.

Each file is given a name for its identity. The name generally consists of two parts: the first is a single-word name and the second, a three-letter extension name to indicate the type of file. For instance .COB, .PRG, etc., for program files and .DBF, .DAT, etc., for data files. For example, in stock.dat, stock is the first part of the file name and .dat is the extension.

A file holds records of logically similar data. Each record consists of a set of fields for data. Each field holds data of defined nature like date field holds only dates, name field holds only names, etc. The computer files are organised on physical storage devices like magnetic tape, disk and CD-ROM.

File Structure

A file is a collection of related records. A record is made up of a number of fields to hold data items. Each field is made up of a number of storage spaces. Each storage space can hold a byte of data. A collection of logically related files forms a database. It usually contains a number of files holding data, which can be accessed by many users.

Roll No.	Name	Sex	Address
7 bytes	30 bytes	1 byte	50 bytes
9501101	ARATHI GOPIKA	F	2/3422, SK STREET, CALICUT
9501105	BIJOY ARAVIND	M	AISWARYA, MG ROAD, TRICHUR
9501112	ROSHINI JOHN	F	R-VILLA, K-PALAYAM, BANGALORE
9501240	BIMAL KISHAN	M	ARATHI, NEW STREET, CHENNAI
9501267	ARUN GOKUL	F	'NIRMAL', NEW STREET, KANNUR
....			
....			

Roll no, name, sex and address are the field names. Each field reserves some spaces for storage of respective data. For example, Roll No. has 7 bytes storage space, Name has 30 bytes storage and so on. Roll No filed holds data items 9501101, 9501105 and 9501112 as roll numbers of students. ARATHI GOPIKA, BIJOY ARAVIND, etc., are data items in the name field. Each line of fields relates to an entity: student. Attributes of the student-entity such as roll no, sex and address become the field names. Data fields hold the basic elements of data in them. All attributes of an entity taken together form a record. When such related records are put together, that collection is called a file or table. Record design can be logical or physical. Logical design represents the logical relationship among the data items in the field. The physical record design means the way data items are physically stored on some media like disk and tape.

File Organisation

The file organisation means the way the records are written up in a file and depends on:

(i) File activity,

(ii) Volatility of information, and

(iii) Storage device

File activity means the properties of records processed in one run. If only a few records are accessed in a single run, activity is low. If the file activity is low, it can be stored on disk device for efficient file processing. On the other hand, if a good number of records are accessed in any given time, the file activity is high and such files can be stored on tapes so that processing is more efficient and less costly.

File volatility means the proportion of record changes. If records are changed very frequently, the volatility is very high. For high volatility files such as seat reservation files in a transport firm, disk medium is more efficient and offers a finite access.

Storage medium also influences the file organisation. If only magnetic tapes are available, then files are organised in sequential organisation. On the other hand magnetic disks offer more flexibility as they support both sequential access and direct access.

Other considerations in file organisation are:

(i) Response time (direct access for quick response)

(ii) Cost of storage medium

(iii) Volume of storage, and,

(iv) Security of data

Methods of File Organisation

The following are the popular file organisation methods.

(1) Serial file organisation

(2) Sequential organisation

(3) Indexed sequential organisation

(4) Direct file organisation

1. Serial file organisation: The records in a serial file are stored randomly and are generally appended at the end of a file as the data originates. The logical order of records with respect to a key field does not bear any relation to the order of physical storage of such records in the file. It is also referred to as non-keyed sequential file.

2. Sequential file organisation: This file can be created on a magnetic tape or disk. Each record is written up on the tape or disk one by one logically ordered on one or more key fields. For example, ordering can be in the ascending order of roll no in case of a student file. The records are stored in a sorted order. If new records are added or existing records are deleted, the file has to be re-sorted in case of disk file. If the file is stored on a magnetic tape, another new file has to be created to update the existing file with the changes to be effected since creation or last update of the file. This is done to maintain the proper sequence of the records in the file. The advantages of sequential file are simple organisation and ease in accessing records sequentially.

To minimise the cost of update, the new records are bunched in a transaction file and the master file (that is the original file which is relatively permanent) is updated in a single run leading to the creation of a new master file. This file update is called grand father-father-son update, as there will be three files any time.

3. Indexed-sequential file organisation: An index is a combination of key and storage address of records. This file organisation creates an index file in addition to the data file created. The index file holds pairs of key and storage address of records in the data file. The index file helps in randomly locating records in the data file as the physical storage location of the record is obtained from the index file. This file organisation supports both sequential access and random access of records in the file.

4. Direct file organisation: These files are created on disks or CD-ROMs. In direct file organisation a hashing technique is used to generate storage address of records in the file. There are quite a number of ways of converting a key (such as roll no for a student file, and product-code for an inventory file) to a numeric value. The keys may be numeric, alphabetic or alphanumeric. In the case of alphabetic and alphanumeric keys, numeric key value has to be generated. Direct mapping is done by performing some arithmetic manipulation of the key value, called hashing. The hashing function, $h(k)$, generates a value for each key, which is used as an address for storage location. Direct file supports direct access of files and minimises the access time of records. The records need not be sorted before storage as in an indexed-sequential file.

Modes of File Access

The computer file can be accessed in three modes: sequential, random and dynamic.

1. Sequential Access: This means that for accessing a record sequentially, the file has to be read from the beginning, that is, record 1, record 2, and so on until the required record is reached. The access time of a single record depends on the position of the record in the file. That is, if it is the first record in the file, it takes much less time to access than a record that is at the end of the file.

2. Random Access: This method takes the same time for accessing the record in the file wherever the record is physically located in the file. The storage location of the record is obtained by converting the key value of the record into its numeric location address by hash function. Then the record is located directly.

3. Dynamic Access: This mode combines both sequential and random modes of access. At times, it may be required to start sequential access from a given record only. For example, a file holds 2000 records and records 1220 to 1250 are required to be accessed. In this case, it is better to locate the record number 1220 randomly and access the remaining records in sequential mode.

File updating

Updating of files means making the file current by incorporating changes to the records held in the file or adding new records to it. If data is very large or is likely to change occasionally, such data is held in a master file. Master files are relatively permanent and are used for referring to the data there in when required. Data, which arises out of day-to-day transactions, changes very often and it is, therefore, temporarily stored in a transaction file.

The master files have to be made current by incorporating changes in data to the master files. This process is called file updating. There are three ways in which these changes are effected: addition of a record to master file, deletion of a record from, and modification of a record held in, master file.

Methods of Updating Sequential file

Sequential files can be updated in two ways: direct updating and grandfather-father-son updating.

Direct updating

In case of direct update, the data is processed on line and files are updated directly, that is no back up files are maintained. The direct update keeps all files updated and enables real-time response. It saves disk space, as transaction files are not opened for temporary storage of data. But it is very difficult to recreate a file if it is corrupted or deleted accidentally. Deletion of records is also not possible. For direct updating, the data must be stored in random access files. Examples of random access storage devices are magnetic disks, magnetic drums and CD-ROMs.

Grand Father-Father-Son update

In this method two files are used as input files and they result in the creation of a new updated master file. The two input files are the master file requiring updating and the Transaction file containing the transaction data of the period. Both the files are to be sorted in the same order on the same key before updating starts.

Updating Process

Both the master file and transaction file are read

(1) The keys are then compared

(2) If the master file key is less than the transaction file key, no change is required. The record is copied to the new master file.

(3) If the master file key is equal to Transaction file key, then the record is to be either deleted or modified.

(4) If the master file key is greater than transaction file key, then it means that the transaction file record is new and is therefore to be copied to the new master file.

(5) Three generations of files are maintained always. Hence, the name Grandfather-father-son update.

Indexed File Updating

Indexed file has random access capability. Indexed files allow direct updating. Whenever any change in data takes place, the particular record is randomly accessed and updated. The disadvantage of direct updating is that no back up files are maintained and it may be difficult to undo changes effected.

Indexed file or Indexed sequential file organisation keeps, in addition to data files, an index or table which lists the address of records on disk (namely, track and sector number) according to the contents of the key field. The key chosen must be able to identify a record uniquely. Any record in the file can be read at any time. Updating is easier in case of indexed files as only those records requiring modification need only be read and modified. Indexed file is highly suitable where quick response is required; for example, airline reservation or railway reservation requires direct updating.

DATABASE DESIGN

Database is a huge repository of data. It is the heart of any information system. Its design is important for a good information system as only a robustly designed database can store huge amount of data, permit easy update and enable quick retrieval of data in any way the user wants.

Database System

A database is a set of logically connected data files that have common access methods between them. It stores transaction data. It does not contain any input or output data. The input data may cause a change to operational data but is not part of the database. Similarly, the output data means the reports or query responses from the system. The input data and output data are transient and they are not stored in the database. The word 'data bank' is sometimes used to mean a collection of databases.

The database system gives centralised control over the database resources. The advantages of centralised control over the data are[5]:

- Redundancy can be reduced,
- Inconsistency can be avoided,
- The data can be shared,
- Standards can be enforced,
- Security restrictions can be applied, and,
- Integrity can be maintained.

The concept of IRM calls for treating information as an organisational resource. In traditional file management system, applications owned their own data and it was not shared with other applications. Each application defined its data, created its file structure and stored the data conveniently to be accessed by its application program. Thus, applications like payroll, inventory management, etc., owned their own data. Several applications stored the same data in many files. This caused a lot of duplication in data storage and the consequent data inconsistency, as the related files were not updated simultaneously. Often application programs had to be modified to use data files of other applications.

Database is a centrally controlled, integrated collection of logically organised data. The central control ensures data sharing among applications and enforces database security procedures. The data items in the database are logically related and this helps in integration of database.

Advantages of Database Systems

The database system approach has the following advantages

- **Data independence:** The data is logically designed into databases and it is independent of applications. Since the data is program-independent, any application can use it without any modification to the code.
- **Data shareability:** Database permits simultaneous multiple access to the database. Thus, multiple users can share the same data.

- **Data integrity:** Access to the database is controlled by the database management system. The system authorises personnel for entering, editing and deleting data. It also authorises people to access data for various data processing activities. Since the database stores one data item only in one place and updates it with fresh transaction data automatically, there is little chance of inconsistency in the database.

- **Data availability:** The database is centrally controlled and access to data is permitted through an authorisation scheme. The data resources are therefore available to the users in the organisation subject to the authorisation procedure.

- **Data evolvability:** The database is flexible and can store huge quantity of data. It can evolve as the number of applications and queries increases to meet their data requirements.

Components of Database System

The common database components are database files, DBMS, host language interface, natural language interface, report generator, etc. These are briefly mentioned below.

Database files: The database files store the transaction data.

DBMS: It is a set of programs that manages the database. It performs a number of tasks like controlling access to the database, making security checks, etc.

Host language interface system: This system interacts with application programs and interprets their data requests that are issued in high-level language.

Natural language interface: DBMS needs to process queries and data requests issued to it in natural languages called English-like language. The natural language interface performs interpreting the queries and requests in natural language. It also facilitates managerial interaction with the database for decision support applications.

Application programs: The application programs request for data from the database. The data independence permits the applications to use the data for a variety of purposes.

Data Dictionary: The data dictionary contains schema of the database. It defines each data item in the database, lists its structure, source, person authorised to modify it, etc.

Report generator: The system generates output for users in the form of query response or reports. It might also produce documents like invoice and process ad-hoc queries and special report requests.

Users of Database Systems

There are three broad classes of users for organisational database systems. They are:

(1) Application programmers who write application programs that manipulate the data in the database.

(2) End-users who access the database by invoking application programs or through a structured query language, and,

(3) Database Administrator who is responsible for planning, designing, creating and maintaining the database.

DATABASE MANAGEMENT SYSTEM (DBMS)

DBMS is a set of system programs that manages the entire database. It controls access to files. It updates files and retrieves data from the files on request by applications for processing. DBMS maintains database by adding, deleting and modifying records in database. It permits multiple users to access the same files simultaneously. It acts as an interface between the application programs and the data in the database. If the user wants a piece of data from the database, the DBMS processes the request, locates the data in the database and displays it for the user. In traditional file management system, the user needs to specify both the data and its storage location. DBMS requires storing the database on direct access storage devices.

DBMS is general-purpose system software. It works in conjunction with the operating systems to create, process, store, retrieve, control and manage data. Its tasks include defining, constructing, and manipulating database for applications. Defining database involves specifying data types, data structures, storage constraints, etc. Constructing database means storing the data on storage medium under the control of the DBMS. Database manipulation includes merging databases, generating reports, processing queries, etc.

The three main components of a DBMS are data definition language, data manipulation language, and data dictionary.

Data Definition Language

The contents of database are created using the data definition language. It defines relationships between different data elements and serves as an interface for application programs that use the data.

Database Manipulation Language

Data is processed and updated using a language called data manipulation language. It allows a user to query database and receive summary or customised reports. The data manipulation language is usually integrated with other programming languages, many of which are 3GLs or 4GLs.

Each database package has its own query language with unique rules and instruction formats. Hence, there is no universal query language. Query language is used to access the data for report generation, query processing and other data processing activities.

Structured Query Language (SQL) is a non-procedural language that deals with data, data integrity, data manipulation, data access, data retrieval, data query and data security. Most DBMS packages use some version of SQL whose primary purpose is to allow users to query a database and generate *ad hoc* reports that provide customised information.

Data Dictionary

Data dictionary is an electronic document that contains data definition and data use for every data type in the database. It describes the data and its characteristics such as its location, size and type. It identifies its origin, use, ownership and methods of accessing and security of data. DBMS uses data dictionary to store all details of data such as data definition, data storage, data use and access privileges.

DATABASE ADMINISTRATOR (DBA)

Organisations that implement database systems constitute a function called database administration to supervise the organisational database resources. Database administrator supervises the database administration function. The job of database administrator is to plan, design, create, modify and maintain the database of the organisation with special emphasis on security and data integrity. He is not much concerned with the details of the application programs that access the database for data. He maintains the schema and data dictionary. Any change in the form of data item, its creation, etc., can only be done by the database administrator.

The specific responsibilities of DBA include:

- Guiding the initial design of the database, and later developing and extending it to meet growing organisational requirements.
- Establishing the database and monitoring the use of it.
- Deciding on the content of the database. He has to see that the relevant data is collected and stored in the database.
- Establishing and monitoring database control and security policies and procedures.
- Servicing database users by educating and training them in the use of the database.

Disadvantages of Database

The following are some of the disadvantages of database:

Higher data processing costs: The database system causes higher data processing costs. This is due to the strict and elaborate procedure for data access, updating and processing.

Increased hardware and software costs: It requires more direct access memory capacity, greater communication capability (including communication software), and additional processing power. This increases the hardware and software costs.

Data insecurity and integrity: Most of the security and integrity problems are related to the fact that many users have access rights to the database. Elaborate security systems are implemented to protect the database and to prevent unauthorised access.

Insufficient database expertise: Database technology is complex. Most organisations do not have enough personnel with necessary expertise to implement and manage database systems.

Database Architecture: The purpose of database is to facilitate huge storage and quick retrieval of data from the database. There are three basic ways of organising data in a database. They are hierarchical, network and relational structures.

Hierarchical Structure: The relationships between records form a hierarchy. The records or aggregates of data are logically conceived to be stored at different levels of hierarchy. The structure looks like a tree with branches turned upside down. The relation between entities is structured in such a way as to link it with only one data item at the higher level. In a hierarchical database, the relationship between records is one of parent-child. One record can be linked to only one record at the higher level. Data stored in a lower level node (child record) can be accessed only through the higher-level node (parent record).

Network Structure: This structure can represent more complex logical relationships. This structure permits multiple relations between data items. One entity can be linked up to any number of other types of entities. That is, it allows many-to-many relationships among records. Any data element can be related to any number of other data elements.

Relational Structure: Relational structure is the most recent of these three structures. All data elements stored in the database are conceived to be stored in tables. Different data tables are linked up using common type of data item in different tables. The table is called a relation; the columns of the table are called domains and the rows are called tuples. A tuple contains values of data items called data elements of an entity.

Analytical Database: It stores static read-only data in databases for archival and analysis.

Operational Database: This kind of database allows users to modify the archived data. It is used in real time systems.

Object Oriented Database: It can handle new types of data including graphics, photographs, audio and video. It can store data from different media sources and formats.

DESIGN DOCUMENTATION

Documentation is a dirty job, but is very essential for proper maintenance of the system. The design documentation includes design document, user manual and operations manual.

The design document contains detailed description of the physical design of the system. It may be in the form of reports and documents. Specifically it includes the following:

- A brief description of the system
- Design objectives
- Design constraints
- List of programs
- List of input files
- List of data files
- List of reports or other output forms
- Manual procedures
- Program specification
- Input/output specification
- System test conditions, etc.

The user manual is intended to be used by the system users. It normally contains:

- An overview of the system
- Input forms and instructions to fill in them
- Output formats and instructions on interpreting the output
- Anticipated exceptions to be handled by the users
- The role of users in the department or organisation.

The operations manual is for the use of computer operators. It details the operation of the system. It contains a scheme of execution of programs, an overview of the system from the operators' point of view and guidelines for ensuring security, privacy and integrity of data.

Conclusion

Design is the logical conversion of the requirements into ways of building physical system to meet system objectives. Design is an iterative process and it produces a blue print of the physical system to be implemented. It develops formats for output and input. It also develops details of building database and procedures to operate the system and use the output from it.

QUESTIONS

1. What is system design? Who does the work of system design?
2. What are the differences between logical and physical designs?
3. What is input design? What is its importance?
4. What is design documentation? What are the contents of such documentation?
5. "Design is a creative process of generating a blue print for system implementation." Comment.

REFERENCES

1. O'Brien, James. A., *Management Information Systems,* Galgotia Publication Private Limited, New Delhi, 1996, pp. 95-96.
2. *Ibid,* p. 96.
3. Senn, James A., *Analysis and Design of Information Systems,* Mc-Graw Hill Publishing Co., Singapore, p. 10.
4. Parker, Charles S., *Management Information Systems,* McGraw Hill Publishing Company, Singapore, 1989, pp. 581-82.
5. Date, C.J., *An Introduction to Database Systems,* Vol. 1., Narosa Publishing House, New Delhi, 1996, pp. 11-12.

Case 16.1: Leave Management System

Mr. Vijayakrishnan, General Manager, HR of MC Enterprises Limited (MCEL) is worried about the employees of the company taking too many days of leave than is allowed by its HR policy. Some of the leave goes unreported from departments very frequently. Hence, the payroll computation does not deduct wages of excess leave or leave without pay. MCEL implemented software solutions about five years ago. It considered a few ERP solutions initially. But, since its in-house developed software was meeting the requirement and the employees were comfortable with it, the management decided not to go for ERP. On the request of Mr. Vijaykrishnan, Mr. Sudip Sohan, Managing Director gave permission for developing an application for computerising leave management.

GM, HR met the Head, Systems Department, and wanted an application to be developed and implemented in a month. He told him about the procedure for leave sanctioning. The employees are entitled to take 10 days of casual leave in a year and 10 days of half-pay leave for every completed year of service. Year for leave calculation is calendar year. The casual leave if not availed cannot be carried forward to the next year. The half-pay leave can be accumulated and availed at any time after getting sanction. The leave is to be sanctioned by the department head. If an employee takes more than the eligible leave, the wages equivalent to the excess leave availed is to be deducted from the salary of the month in which excess leave is taken. For deduction, gross salary is to be taken into account.

The IT department presented a leave management system to the HR department for its comments. As part of its design a few forms were designed. They are given below. MCEL maintains a master database on employees as part of its HR solutions already implemented. Tables will be designed for leave management. These forms will be connected to the databases to update the relevant tables.

The login form is to be used by each employee for applying for leave. Leave management system will display the following form for login.

(a) **Login form:** After logging in, leave sanction form is to be used for getting the leave sanctioned. The employee will fill out the leave sanction form and submit it to the leave sanctioning authority.

```
┌─────────────────────────────────────────────┐
│              LOGIN  FORM                      │
├─────────────────────────────────────────────┤
│                                               │
│    USER ID        ┌──────────────────────┐   │
│                   └──────────────────────┘   │
│    PASSWORD       ┌──────────────────────┐   │
│                   └──────────────────────┘   │
│                                               │
│   ┌──────────┐          ┌──────────────┐     │
│   │    OK    │          │    Cancel    │     │
│   └──────────┘          └──────────────┘     │
└─────────────────────────────────────────────┘
```

(b) **Leave sanction form:** The holiday list will be entered by the HR staff. This will be done once every year or as when holiday is sanctioned for a department.

```
                    LEAVE SANCTION FORM

        Staff Code          [                    ]

        Name                [                    ]

        Leave type          [                  ]

        Reason for leave    [                    ]


            From  [          ]      To  [          ]

          ( Clear )      ( Submit )       ( Close )
```

(c) **Holiday list**

```
                    HOLIDAY LIST FORM

            Date          [                ]

            Description   [                ]

        ( Add )    ( Clear )    ( View )    ( Close )
```

Questions:

1. Discuss whether the above forms are enough to capture the input data required for leave management?

2. Is the data enough to sanction leave? If more data is needed, what additional data will be needed for leave sanctioning?

3. Can you suggest an alternate design of forms for input and output?

17 CHAPTER

Program Development

INTRODUCTION

Computer-based problem solving requires coding of a sequence of operations leading to a solution. The problem is analysed and the logic for solving the problem is developed. The program design is represented by means of flowcharts, pseudo code, structured English, etc., and checked before being coded in a programming language. When code is written up, it is checked for errors (independent inspection). Usually the program is written in a high level language and the language compiler detects syntax errors. The program is modified and compiled again and again until it is free from syntax errors. When the source code is free of syntax errors, it is due for test runs. These test runs help in detecting logical errors. Similarly presentation to, and discussion of the program logic with, the other programmers (called structured walk through) leads to detection of logical errors and correction (called debugging of code).

Computer-based solutions are developed following a systems approach. It takes a total view of the system as a whole and how the system modification or system change is to be introduced with as little disturbance and waste as possible. The systems approach views it as having different stages in its life cycle.

Algorithm

Computer-based problem solving should proceed systematically. There should be a step-by-step progression towards the solution. The small steps or operations to be performed are arranged in their natural order or sequence. This sequence of instructions for solving a problem is called algorithm. That is, the algorithm represents the logic of processing. Thus, algorithm is a sequence of precise and unambiguous instructions for solving a problem in a finite number of operations. If these operations are sequentially carried out, it results in the desired output.

Developing an algorithm requires a high degree of ingenuity. It specifies a sequence of operations in order to achieve a goal. The sequence of instructions to be called algorithm should possess the following characteristics:

(i) Each and every instruction should be precise and unambiguous.

(ii) Each operation must be capable of being performed in a finite time.

(iii) No operation shall be repeated infinitely that prevents termination of the algorithm.

(iv) The algorithm should lead to the solution of the problem.

The following is an example of algorithm to find the total number of male and female employees in an organisation.

Step 1:   Initialise the Total-Males and Total-Females as zero

Step 2:   Open the Employee file for input

Step 3:   Start at the first record

Step 4:   Read the record

Step 5:   Check the sex field whether it is 'M' or 'F'

Step 6:   If the sex is 'M' add 1 to Total-Males

Step 7:   If the sex is 'F' add 1 to Total-Females

Step 8:   IF file-end is not reached, go to Step 4

Step 9:   Print Total-Males and Total-Females

Step 10: Stop

TECHNIQUES FOR PROGRAM DEVELOPMENT

Program development is a laborious task requiring a great lot of brain and skill. A lot of tools and techniques have been developed to aid the designing and programming work. Some of the techniques employed for greater efficiency in program development are:

- Modular programming,
- Structured programming, and,
- Top down and bottom up designing.

MODULAR PROGRAMMING

An effective approach to program development is to break sown a large problem into a series of smaller and more understandable tasks. Modular programming employs systems approach to programming. Large problem is divided into less complex sub-problems. The sub-problem is further divided into small manageable problems. This refinement process is carried out until the original problem, which is too complex, can be directly solved. Thus, when all the modules or sub-programs written to solve sub-problems are integrated, it gives a master program that solves the original problem.

The concept of modular programming is that all programs should consist of a number of modules with little interaction between them. Each module is made up of a group of instructions. Each module should be performing one identifiable function largely independent of other modules so that modification can be done easily without affecting other modules.

Complex programs are difficult to design, code, test and debug. To simplify the entire program development work, modular programming divides the large programs into a number of small and simple modules. Since the modules are so designed that they are independent of other modules, they can be coded, tested and debugged by small groups of programmers separately. This approach to programming is called modular programming. Initially general modules are designed, coded and tested. These modules are than used by other modules. Modular programming facilitates easy coding, testing and debugging of large and complex programs. It also helps in allotting program development work among a number of programmers.

Thus, the programmer may first develop a main program that is used to outline the major segments that are needed to solve a problem. The main program specifies the order in which each subordinate module in the program will be processed. The programming analysis stage continues until every module has been reduced to the point that the programmer is confident that a solution can be worked out at that level. All the modules required for the main problem is integrated with the main or control program and as and when required each module is invoked to perform the task it is designed to carry out. An instruction in the control program, such as CALL PROCEDURE NAME, sends control to the module and loads those instructions into memory and performs the specified task. After that the module if not required for processing immediately is removed from memory by giving a command like CANCEL PROCEDURE NAME. The control then is passed to the next module depending upon the sequence of processing tasks. Thus, the modular program design nests programs within programs, each module or subroutine forming a small program.

Advantages of Modular Programming

(i)   Complex programs become manageable and simple when modular design is employed for programming.

(ii) Program development is faster as programmers are simultaneously working upon the modules independently.

(iii) Programming efficiency improves as a number of standard modules developed into a library of modules can be used in the programs, obviating the need for coding of such modules every time such routine is required to be part of a program.

(iv) Modular design helps in fast debugging as the errors can be localised into the respective module and corrected there itself.

(v)   Modular structure always carries more user-friendly features and the users can use it effectively.

STRUCTURED PROGRAMMING

Large programs are difficult to understand. Hence complex programs are written using three logic structures: sequence, selection and iteration. A sequence construct is a set of instructions serially performed without any looping. A selection construct involves branching within but the branches join before the exit point. An iteration construct contains loops in it but has only one exit point. If these constructs are used in conjunction with other principles such as minimum coupling, maximum binding and single entry and single exit, the result is structured program.

Structured programming employs standard tools and program constructs. The structured programming contains three standard control structures.

(i)   sequence,

(ii) selection, and

(iii) iteration.

Thus, programming using these standard constructs is called structured programming. Modular design and structured programming make program development more understandable and quicker. The sub problems or program segments are distributed among a few programmers who write the codes for the sub problems distributed to them. All of the programmers use standard methods for coding. Coding and debugging are facilitated as the program is properly segmented and errors can be localised. Each module, which performs a given task after debugging, is integrated with other modules to form a full program. Programming work is faster and programmer productivity is higher than unstructured programming.

Advantages of Structured Programming

- takes less time for programming
- program is divided into functional modules; each module performs one simple function and is easy to understand,
- each module can be coded and debugged independently,
- programming work can be shared by a number of programmers, each working independently of others,
- errors can be localised as the errors in one module can be located and corrected before being integrated.

Disadvantages

- Code duplications and subroutines slowdown execution resulting in lower execution efficiency.
- Several layers of modules in hierarchy can complicate logic and debugging.

Basic Programming Structures

The basic programming structures include sequence, selection and iteration.

(i) **Sequence:** The normal flow of control is in the natural order, that is, from top to bottom, from left to right unless there is an intervening control structure (example a loop) that changes the flow of control. Thus, the first instruction in the program is executed first, and then control passes to the next instruction in that sequence.

(ii) **Selection:** Here a decision is required and the flow of control depends on the selection.

Selection constructs:

(a) If ... then
   If condition
   then
   statement
   If condition
   then
   statement(s)

(b) If ...then... else
   If conditions
   then
   statement (i)
   else
   statement(s)

(c) If...else...if
   If condition(1)

statement(1)

else

if condition(2)

statement (2)

else

if condition (3)

statement (3).

(iii) **Iteration:** This construct allows repeated execution of a set of codes without repeating codes in the program. It saves the trouble of writing the same codes again and again in the program.

Loop Properties

1. Do... while
   - Loop exit is pre-tested
   - Loop exit when loop condition evaluates false

   While condition
   - loop may be skipped

   do

   statements

   enddo.
   - loop exit is post tested
2. Repeat....until
   - loop exit when loop condition evaluates true

   Repeat ...
   - must be executed at least once.

   Until condition.
3. For...next
   - loop exit after a specific number of iterations

   for i in range 1 to N
   - loop exit when loop counter exceeds the end-value

   do

   statements

   end do.
   - loop is pre-tested
   - loop may be skipped

Example:

For i in range 1 to 5

    accept name;

    display name;

    enddo.

These three iteration constructs or loop constructs execute the statements given within the loop until certain condition is satisfied. Loop represents a reversal in the program flow.

Loop Components

A loop has four components, such as:

(i) **loop initialisation:** It is the preparation required before entering a loop: setting accumulators and counters.

(ii) **loop body:** This represents the main process of the loop.

   (iii)   **loop modification:** Values calculated in the loop body are rolled into accumulators, and

   (iv)   **loop exit:** A condition to check for exiting the loop.

Top-Down and Bottom-Up Design

In top-down approach, system design starts at the system level. The first step is to develop a control program that outlines and controls subprograms. The entire system work is divided into a number of subtasks. Each subtask is performed by a subprogram. The main control program is then tested for logical correctness. Undefined subtasks are represented temporarily by stubs (dummy subprograms). The stub is defined and replaced by subprograms. Each such subprogram is tested and debugged and integrated with other higher level programs. Top-down design uses modular programming. Structured programming can also be used with top-down approach to program development.

In bottom-up approach to development, programs are developed first for specific tasks and they are integrated into a complete system. This approach can be employed where the precise processing steps are well defined at the task level. The subprograms are integrated after all subprograms are developed.

DATA FLOW DIAGRAM (DFD)

DFD is a graphical representation of the flow of data. It presents the logical data flow in terms of its source, processing and storage in a sink. The process may require some data stored elsewhere other than that originating from the source. Similarly the process may require intermediate data store which is required for subsequent processing.

DFD uses the following conventions.

- an open rectangular box to denote a file or data store.
- a circle to depict a process. Processes are numbered in the order of processing.
- an arrow to denote the direction of flow of data.
- a rectangular box to represent external entities that are outside the system.

A DFD models a system and gives an overview of the system as to what data flows into the system, how it is processed and how the output data flows. It depicts the flow of data from an external entity into a process which transforms the data into output and transfers it to the other processes or entities or files. Data from files may also flow into the process as input. The DFDs are structured in such a way that it can be expanded into a number of DFDs that give finer details of the processing and other operations within the system.

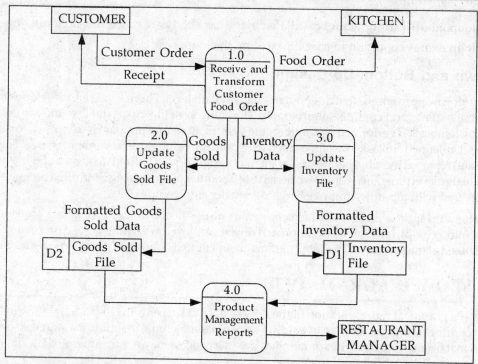

Fig. 17.1: Data Flow Diagram of Ordering System for a Restaurant

DATA DICTIONARY

Any computerised system will have a large number of data types and large volume of data to be stored and accessed. Details about these data types, data store, etc., are stored in a data dictionary for reference. A single data item may be referred to by different names. Each data type must have a unique name and other users should know aliases if they are used. For example, inventory code may be labelled as I-code, inv-code, invent-code, inventory-code, etc. The data dictionary helps in avoiding redundancy in data storage. It provides a complete documentation of all elements of DFD namely data items, data flows and data stores.

Data Type: data item/data store/data flow.

Data Name: name of data item/data store/data flow.

Data aliases: alternate names used for convenience by multiple users.

Data Description: a short description of data, explained in simple terms.

Data Characteristics: characteristics of each data type such as numeric or alphanumeric, and width.

A data store is characterised by its composition (set of data terms) organisation (sequential, indexed, random), etc. A data flow is characterised by its origin, destination, etc.

DECISION TABLE

A decision table is similar to a flowchart in construction and use. It shows conditions and actions in a simplified and orderly manner. By presenting logical alternatives under various operating conditions, it enables a decision-maker to think through a problem and present its solution in compact notation. It permits a computer problem to be divided into logical segments that provide multilevel structure in the problem analysis. At the highest level, decision tables can be used for an overall system by referring to lower level tables, resulting in a modular approach. The purpose of a decision table is to assemble and present complex decision logic in such a way as to facilitate easy understanding of its meaning. This can be used independently of, or as complementary to, the flowcharts.

Example: A company classifies its customers into class I, class II, class III categories based on the amount due and duration for which the amount was due. Class I if the period is less than one month, class II if a customer owes ₹ 25,000 for a period not less than two months and if he owes less than ₹ 25,000 for more than three months, other customers are categorised as class III.

	Amount	Less than ₹ 25,000	Y	Y	Y	Y	N	N	N	N
		Less than one month	Y				Y			
Condition		1-2 months		Y				Y		
	Period	2-3 months			Y				Y	
		More than 3 months				Y				Y
		One	X	X						
Action	Class	Two			X	X	X			
		Three						X	X	X

Fig. 17.2: Decision Table

Once a decision table is prepared, it is easy to code the decision logic into program. Logical errors can be checked before the program is fully developed.

Steps in Constructing a Decision Table

- Define the problem to be solved
- Identify the conditions to be checked in the problem
- Identify the corresponding actions to be taken with each condition or combination of conditions, and,
- Tabulate the conditions and actions

DECISION TREE

Decision tree is another way of representing program logic especially when the number of alternatives is too many. Combinations of conditions are represented along the branches of a decision tree. The outcome of each combination of conditions is given at the end of the final branch.

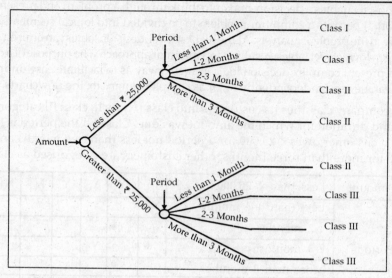

Fig. 17.3: Decision Tree of Bank's Customer Classification

Pseudo Code

Pseudo code is another analysis tool that helps in developing and checking program logic. 'Pseudo' means false or imitation and 'code' means program instructions. It describes the program logic using English language and certain programming language control words such as if ...then. It is in fact a description of logic independent of any programming language. It lists in plain English language the sequence of operations necessary to solve a problem. Sentences are generally written line by line, each line for one sentence, with proper indentation. For Pseudo code rules of syntax are not strict. The purpose is to allow easy readability and proper documentation. Pseudo code is not language oriented and uses plain English for detailing the sequence. The lines are properly intended for ease in reading and understanding the sequence of operations. Iteration constructs (repeat...until and Do while…Enddo statements), and selection constructs (if.. then..else and if.. else if.. statements) are also used in detailing the processing.

Differences between Pseudo Code and Flowcharts

Pseudo code is self-explanatory since it is in plain English. It does not require separate documentation. It uses a structure similar to that of basic program. Whereas flowcharts tend to extend in all directions and their paths of instructions do not conform to the final basic code.

Advantages of Pseudo code over Flowchart

- Less cumbersome and time consuming,
- Easier to modify,
- Easier to code directly from Pseudo code, and
- Easily readable and understandable due to the use of proper indentation and program structures.

Procedure for computer-based problem solving

Computer-based problem solving proceeds systematically from problem to solution. The steps in computer-based problem solving can be identified as follows:

(i)   Define the problem and understand it thoroughly.

(ii) Draw up a list of variables that are needed to solve the problem.

(iii) Design the layout of output format.

(iv) Select the programming technique that is able to solve the problem.

(v)   Code, test and debug the program.

(vi) Use data validation procedure to guard against processing of wrong data.

Example 1: Write a pseudo code for accepting two numbers as input and to display the larger number.

```
DISPLAY "ENTER ANY TWO NUMBERS";
ACCEPT NUM-1, NUM-2;
IF NUM-1 > NUM-2
THEN
DISPLAY " THE LARGER NUMBER IS", NUM-1;
ELSE
DISPLAY " THE LARGER NUMBER IS", NUM-2;
ENDIF.
```

Example 2: Write a pseudo code to find the sum of first N natural numbers and display the sum after accepting N from the user.

```
DISPLAY " ENTER A NUMBER TO FIND SUM OF N NUMBERS";
ACCEPT N;
SUM = 0;
FOR I IN RANGE 1 TO N
DO
SUM = SUM + I;
ENDDO;
DISPLAY " THE SUM OF", N, "NUMBERS IS", SUM.
```

Example 3: Write a pseudo code for the following. A wholesaler offers a trade discount of 3% on orders up to 5,000 units and 5% on orders exceeding 5,000 units. Accept product code, quantity and rate as input and display product code, quantity, gross amount, trade discount and net amount as output.

```
DISPLAY "ENTER PRODUCT-CODE, QUANTITY, RATE";
ACCEPT PROD-CODE, PROD-QTY, PROD-RATE;
IF PROD-QTY <= 5000
THEN
DISCOUNT-RATE = 0.03;
```

ELSE

DISCOUNT-RATE = 0.05;

GROSS-AMOUNT = PROD-QTY * PROD-RATE;

TRADE-DISCOUNT = GROSS-AMOUNT * DISCOUNT-RATE;

NET-AMOUNT = GROSS-AMOUNT- TRADE-DISCOUNT;

DISPLAY PROD-CODE, PROD-QTY, GROSS-AMOUNT, TRADE-DISCOUNT, NET-AMOUNT.

Characteristics of a Good Programmer

A good programmer should have the following characteristics:

(a) **Technical skills.** He should have adequate knowledge of programming languages and practices.

(b) **Communication skills.** He should have good communication skills as he has to interact with analysts, designers and users.

(c) **Patience and self-discipline.** Program logic development follows a step-by-step approach to solution. The programmer should thoroughly check the program logic several times to find better ways of solving it.

(d) **Balanced personality.** A good programmer should acknowledge his weaknesses and deficiencies and should welcome constructive criticism from other analysts, designers, programmers and users.

Characteristics of a Good Program

A good computer program should have the following characteristics.

1. It should be correct. It should give the correct result in terms of the algorithm being exercised.

2. It should be reliable. That is, it should function properly for a long time.

3. It should not break down when running, that is, it should be robust.

4. It should be efficient in development.

5. It should be efficient in execution.

6. It should be easy to use.

7. It should be maintainable.

8. It should be testable.

9. It should be portable.

10. It should be unique. That is, in any situation it should give one and only one result.

FLOWCHARTING

Program flowchart is a tool that aids program development. Before writing a program, it is usual to draw program flowchart to arrive at the correct program logic. A flowchart is a diagrammatic representation of program logic. Program logic refers to the order in which the computer executes the statements in a program. It illustrates the sequence of operations to be performed to arrive at a solution. The operations are placed in boxes and arrows connect the boxes in the order of execution. A structured flowchart is, thus, a diagram that depicts an algorithm. Flowcharting is the process of representing system's processes and sequences of operations through charts.

The flowcharts simplify the reasoning process and present the sequence of steps to the solution. Construction of flowchart is a valuable exercise in arriving at the right logical solution of a problem. Flowcharts are widely used to facilitate better understanding of methods, processes or systems. The construction of flowcharts is in conformity with human tendency to read from left to right and top to bottom. A deviation from this natural flow is allowed if it improves the presentation.

Kinds of Flowcharts

There are several types of flowcharts .The flowcharts most often used in structured programming are (a) System flowchart and (b) Program flowchart.

(a) System Flowchart: The system flowchart defines the broad processing in the organisation showing the origin of data, file structure, processing to be performed, output to be generated and necessity of any off-line operation. System analysts use it to describe the data flow and operations for a data processing cycle. It depicts the flow of data through all parts of a system with a minimum of detail. Generally it shows the entry of input into the system, how the input is processed and how it is passed out in the form of output.

(b) Program Flowchart: Programmers normally use it to represent pictorially the sequence of operations to solve a problem. It is used to check the program logic and perfect it. It plans the program structure and serves the purpose of documentation of a program.

Advantages of Flowcharts

They are mostly used to help the programmers in developing the program logic and also to serve as documentation for a completed program. It also has several other advantages.

1. It is a convenient method of communication
2. It indicates very clearly just what is being done.
3. It is a key to correct programming
4. It is an important tool in planning and designing a new system
5. It avoids many inconveniences that may arise in future and serves the purpose of documentation for a system
6. It provides an overview of the system and also indicates the relationship between the various steps.
7. It facilitates trouble shooting.
8. It promotes logical accuracy.
9. It makes sure that no logical path is left incomplete without any action being taken.

Program Flowchart Symbols

(a) **Terminal symbol:** This is used to indicate the beginning or ending of a program.
(b) **Input/Output Symbol:** I/O symbol is used to denote inputs into, or output from, the process.
(c) **Process symbol:** This represents some processing of data. There is one entry into the process box and one exit out of it.
(d) **Decision symbol:** This shows a decision situation. There is one entry into the box and two or three exits out of it. But good programming restricts exits to two.
(e) **Sub-routine Symbol:** This denotes that a separate module is designed to handle a task. It helps in simplifying a complex program by giving an overall idea of the program logic.

(f) **Flow line symbol:** This shows the direction of flow of program. This symbol connects all other symbols.

(g) **Connector symbol:** This is used to avoid loops criss-crossing each other on a program chart.

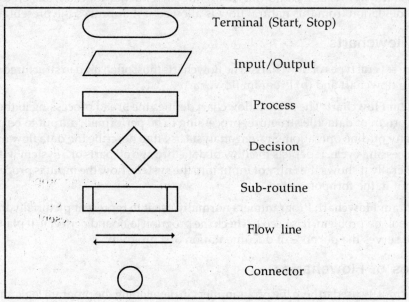

Terminal (Start, Stop)

Input/Output

Process

Decision

Sub-routine

Flow line

Connector

Fig. 17.4: Flowchart Symbols

Flowcharting: Examples.

1. Draw a flowchart to find and print the largest of three distinct numbers X, Y and Z.

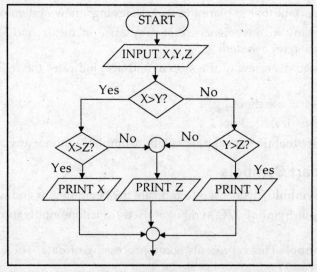

Fig. 17.5: Flowchart to find the Largest of Three Numbers

2. Draw a flowchart to print each 2-digit even number and its square.
   (Hint: Two digit even numbers: 10, 12, 14 ... 98).

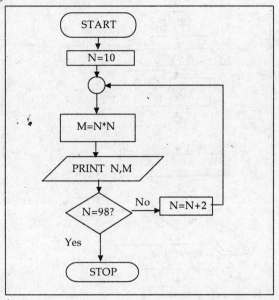

Fig. 17.6: Flowchart to Print each Two-digit Even Number and its Square

3. Draw a flowchart to print factorial of N numbers.

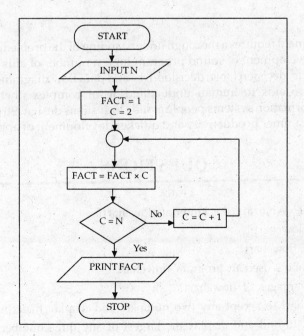

Fig. 17.7: Flowchart to Print Factorial of N

4. Draw a flowchart to add N terms of the series: S = 1 + 4 + 9 + 16 + ... and display the sum.

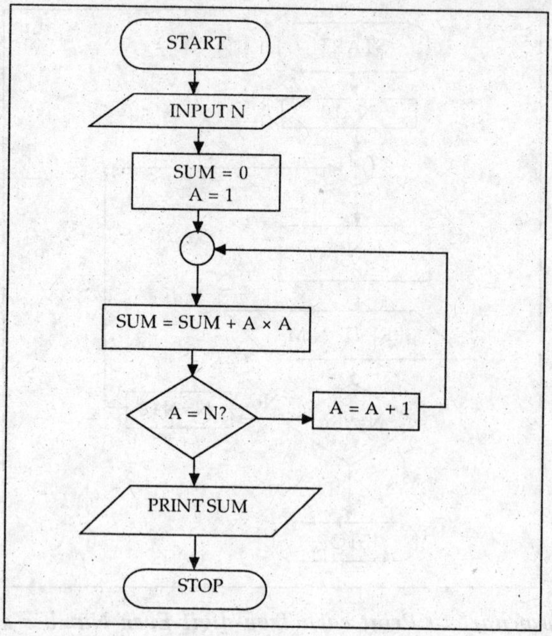

Fig. 17.8: Flowchart to Add and Display N Terms of the series S=1+4+9....

Conclusion

Program development requires a thorough understanding of the problem to be solved. For better understanding and development of sound program logic a number of aids have been developed. Flowcharts, pseudo code, decision table, decision-tree and data flow diagrams facilitate the problem solving. Flowcharts are aids to human understanding of complex phenomena and they are frequently used by information systems people as aids in systems design. Structured programming helps improving programmer productivity and quicker development of applications.

QUESTIONS

1. What is flowchart? What are the kinds of flowchart?
2. What is system flowchart?
3. What is program flowchart?
4. What are the symbols used in program flowchart?
5. What are the advantages of flowchart?
6. Draw up a flowchart to accept any two numbers and display their product.
7. Draw a flowchart to find and display the largest of any three numbers.
8. Draw a flow chart to find and print the sum of the series 1,5,9,...,n.
9. "Flowcharting is a programming aid". Justify the statement.

10. What is structured programming? What are the programming constructs used in structured programming?
11. Explain any two iteration constructs.
12. What is DFD?
13. What is DD? What is its role in systems development?
14. What is decision tree?
15. What is pseudo code? How is it different from program flowchart?
16. What are the characteristics of a good programmer?
17. What are the characteristics of good program?

Case 17.1: BANK ONE

Bank One is a leading private sector bank with around a million customers and national wide branch network in India. Banking industry in the country has changed substantially in the past 15 years. Competition among the banks has heightened and customers are offered differentiated services and superior service delivery through multiple channels. Bank One is considering a change in its customer management policy. It has decided to adopt a customer integration and loyalty programme whereby customers are to be treated differently based on a few criteria. The customers will be divided into four categories: A, B C and D. Category A customers will get the most favourable treatment in all services of the bank, category B will get less but more than Category C, and Category C more than Category D which gets the least preference. The criteria for categorisation are fixed as follows:

Category A – More than 15 years as customer of Bank One and annual value of transaction in the last full year exceeding ₹ 10,00,000 or, more than 10 years as a customer and value of annual transactions more than ₹ 20,00,000.

Category B – More than 10 years being a customer and ₹ 10,00,000 in transaction value or not less than 5 years of service and ₹ 15,00,000 in annual transaction value

Category C– More than 5 years being a customer of the bank and value of transaction more than ₹ 5,00,000 or More than 3 years of service and annual transaction value more than ₹ 10,00,000.

Category D – When none of the above criteria is met.

Questions:

1. Discuss whether the above logic is complete for categorisation of customers.
2. If a customer has defaulted in payment of a substantial amount, should it affect the categorisation for preferred customer treatment? If so, how will you modify the criteria to accommodate this factor?
3. How do you represent this logic so as to convey it easily to the programmers for coding?
4. Draw a program flow chart showing the categorisation.
5. Draw a decision table to show all the conditions and actions.
6. Also draw decision tree to represent the entire decision logic including default factor.

18
CHAPTER

Systems Implementation

INTRODUCTION

Systems implementation follows systems design. In this phase, the systems designed in detail at the design phase are actually installed by acquiring the hardware, software, etc., and replacing the existing system with the new system. Systems implementation is the process of carrying out the operational plans developed as part of information system planning. Implementation is a major activity in systems development. Even well conceived and designed projects fail due to poor implementation. Implementation includes all the activities required to replace the old system by the new system. The new system may be a modified form of the old system or a totally new system like a fully automated system developed to replace a manual system in use in the firm. In both the cases implementation is very important. Any lapse in implementation will impact on the system's acceptance and performance. The implementation process involves acquisition of IS resources, testing, documentation, installation and conversion activities. Implementation of information system is basically a change management process. Any alteration of existing system or introduction of a new system has a strong behavioural and organisational impact. It disturbs the existing power structure in the organisation and hence it is likely to start a wave of power struggles between the losers and winners of power. Strong leadership intervention is needed to oversee successful project implementation.

STEPS IN SYSTEMS IMPLEMENTATION

Implementation of IS project starts after system planning is completed and adequate resources are identified for its implementation. Usually project management team with technical and administrative experience is constituted to oversee the project implementation. The steps in the systems implementation are:

1. **Hiring and Training of Personnel:** For successful use of new systems, extensive training to people already in the firm and those freshly hired is essential. The people who are associated with the new system as operators or users must be clear about their roles and responsibilities. This training in various aspects of the new system is required for all the people in the firm who will be associated with the new system as input providers, operators, users of output or systems managers. Operators are responsible for keeping the equipment running and providing support services. They need to be trained to handle

equipment and maintenance. Similarly the data entry people must also be given adequate training in data entry methods and procedures. The users must be trained in equipment use and troubleshooting. They must also be trained in data handling activities and equipment maintenance.

2. **Program Development:** Program development may be done by hired software professionals or by in-house software professionals. Large firms usually develop their own software and they employ software professionals for such work. Program design stage specifies program development tasks. The programs have to be designed in detail using programming aids, coded programs have to be checked and rechecked until they are error free and functioning satisfactorily. Documentation of all programs developed is the next step. Program documentation contains flowcharts, source listings, instructions to data entry personnel and users of output from the program, etc.

3. **Site preparation:** Site preparation includes activities like electrical wiring, humidity controls, air-conditioning and space allocation. The site must be prepared before the equipment arrives at the site. Large computer systems require controlled environment such as air-conditioning, and dirt and humidity control. The system engineers or consultants prepare detailed specifications for site preparation.

4. **Acquisition and installation of hardware:** The next step is to acquire and install the equipment required for the system. Computers vary in size and capacity. Each manufacturer has many models to choose from. The first decision in hardware acquisition is determining the system capacity. Relevant features to be considered includes processor speed, size of random access memory, number of input, output and communication ports, auxiliary storage units that can be attached, system support and utility software provided, etc.

5. **Software Acquisition:** If the firm does not develop software in-house or if it decides to partly out-source software requirements, the required software that is specified in systems analysis phase is to be acquired from software vendors.

6. **File conversion:** In case of a totally new system, the new system might need restructuring of old data files. In that case, the data in the existing files has to be converted into new format. The conversion can be done manually by re-entering data into new files or through software that can convert existing files into new formats. This activity is the most time consuming one among conversion activities.

7. **Documentation:** Detailed documentation of the system is essential for maintaining the system and training personnel in using the system. It would also be useful in trouble shooting system problems.

8. **System Conversion:** The next step is conversion. It is the process of changing from the old system to the new system. There are four methods for replacing the old system with the new one. The appropriate method depends on the conversion situation.

   (i) **Direct cut-over:** In the direct cut-over method, the new system replaces the existing system entirely. This cut-over may be done overnight or over the weekend. This method is good when the new system is expected to work satisfactorily.

   (ii) **Parallel running and conversion:** In the parallel operation method, both the old and new systems run in parallel. They are operated simultaneously for some time to ensure that the new system is error-free and reliable. Once the new system is found working satisfactorily, the old system is discontinued. This is the safest method for conversion. But the disadvantage of this method is the extra cost of running both the systems till the new system is found reliable. The new system may not also get a fair trial if both the systems are running in the firm.

(iii) **Phased cut-over:** This method is used when it is not possible to implement the new system throughout the firm. In the phased cut-over method, separate modules are developed, tested and implemented at different times. When all the modules are developed and implemented, the new system replaces the old system fully.

(iv) **Pilot approach:** In the pilot method, the system is developed and implemented in a small part of the firm. The problems and errors are corrected as they arise. Once the new system is found functioning properly, the system is implemented in all the other parts of the firm. For example, a working model of the system may be implemented in a department. Changes are made to the system based on feedback from the users in the department. Over a period of time the system stabilises as most of the errors are located and corrected. When the system is found complete and stable, it is implemented throughout the firm.

A conversion plan is prepared to implement the new system. The plan specifically includes the following activities[1]:

* List all files to be converted
* Identification of data required to build new files during conversion
* List of all the new documents and procedures to be used during conversion
* Developing control procedures to be used during conversion
* Assigning responsibility for each activity, and,
* Verifying conversion schedules.

Acceptance of the System

After installing the system, the system has to be checked for errors and other malfunctioning. If the system functions reliably, the system is accepted formally.

Post Audit

When the new system is implemented and has been working satisfactorily for a reasonable period of time, a post audit of the system is due. It is carried out to ensure that the new system meets the requirements. It also looks into the possibility of improving the system. An audit team checks whether the system was developed and implemented in the time agreed upon and whether the system functions satisfactorily. This post implementation audit also provides information for maintenance requirements.

System Maintenance

System would need minor modifications to ensure that it continues to meet the requirements. It is the task of system maintenance to make such minor modifications to the system. If the system requires major modifications, then it would necessitate starting all over again with the systems investigation.

MANAGING SYSTEM IMPLEMENTATION: FACTORS FOR SUCCESSFUL IMPLEMENTATION

Though it is not possible to anticipate every implementation problem, proper planning of implementation can increase the chance of successful implementation of information system projects[2].

1. **Involving users in project implementation:** Successful project implementation calls for user involvement in implementation. The users can be selected as project leaders or active project team members. They can also be put on steering committee for the project or as supervisors for training the personnel, etc.

2. **Setting up a cohesive project management group for implementation:** Projects implementation is complex task. It requires technical knowledge, technical skills and human skills of a high order. The project leader must be technically competent to understand the various technical, human and managerial dimensions of the project. The team members must also have project management experience in addition to relationship orientation and technical qualifications required for the project implementation. The team must be formed in such a way that the team members possess different skills and competence which when put together can match the skills and capabilities that the project management needs.

3. **Using project management tools like PERT, CPM, etc., to estimate time, budget and other resources for project planning:** Project management tools like Program Evaluation and Review Technique (PERT), Critical Path Method (CPM) and Gantt Chart can be used in estimating the budget, time and other technical resources required for the project.

4. **Use of formal control tools to monitor project implementation:** Control tools for monitoring project implementation help in controlling the implementation process. Actual work done must be periodically compared with the schedules, plans and budgets to minimise slippages, waste of resources, etc. Gantt chart, status reports, reports detailing deviation from plans, etc., are useful tools in controlling the project cost and implementation time.

5. **Overcoming user resistance:** IS project implementation is an exercise in change management. Any major change in organisation disturbs or alters the current power and politics situation in organisations. Hence the implementation plan must take care of efforts at thwarting project implementation. The user resistance must be anticipated and the organisation must be prepared for change before the project implementation starts. Top management has a special responsibility for successful implementation of projects.

CAUSES OF IMPLEMENTATION FAILURE

Many IS projects fail for various reasons. Most IS projects have overshot the original budgets substantially. Many projects could not be implemented within the time planned. The causes for failure vary from project to project. Yet, some of the common causes for implementation failures have been identified. They are briefly mentioned below.

1. **Low user involvement in project implementation:** Involvement of users in IS project planning and implementation is a critical factor in systems acceptance. If the users are not involved in the project, absence of user involvement may impede the acceptance of the system by users, leading to its failure.

2. **Lack of commitment from top management for the project:** If managers at various levels of management do not support the project, the chance of its success is remote. The management support is needed for resource allocation. In the absence of management support, the project gets neglected.

3. **Complexity of project:** Complex projects have poor structure and are difficult to manage. Large projects also carry high risk of failure. It is very difficult to properly estimate the time, budget etc. required for such projects. The project team may lack the required expertise to manage such large and complex projects.

4. **Poor management of project implementation process:** Projects very often fail for want of proper management of the implementation process. In the absence of proper planning of implementation, the projects may be abandoned after heavy cost overruns, time slippages and technical shortfalls.

PROJECT MANAGEMENT

Project management is a function of operational planning, implementation and control.[3] The project management concept views each major IS application development as a project.

Information system projects must be carefully conceived and planned to meet user requirements and other organisational goals. Small projects are relatively easy to manage and implement. Large projects are very complex and risky. They need proper planning for success in implementation. Project management activities range from initial implementation planning to implementation control. It calls for administrative, human and technical skills. Normally, a single individual will not possess all the required skills in the degree required. Hence, a project management team is constituted for managing implementation of IS projects. The project team is headed by a project leader. The project leader is entrusted with wide powers to control resources for its implementation.

Project Management Activities

The activities of project management can be seen under the following heads.

1. **Identifying the project tasks:** First step is to identify the tasks in implementing the IS project on hand.

2. **Sequence planning:** The tasks identified need to be properly sequenced after studying their interrelationships. For sequencing the tasks properly, time estimates for each task must be obtained. PERT or CPM may be used in planning the sequence of these tasks.

3. **Budgeting:** Budgeting is the process of estimating cost, resources and other performance indicators required of project implementation and control.

4. **Project execution:** The project team oversees the project implementation. It procures the resources needed for the project and assigns responsibilities to project team members for various tasks planned.

5. **Reporting and controlling:** For controlling the project timely reports showing the use of resources, stage of completion of project, time taken for each task, etc., must be reported to the project team. Appropriate action must be taken to ensure compliance with the plan of implementation.

Conclusion

Development of IS applications is taken up as projects. Project teams are formed to implement each IS project. The project leader is given wide powers to command the resources required for its implementation. Implementation of IS project is a difficult task. Successful implementation needs commitment of top management, involvement of user groups in implementation and effective control over the project implementation process among others. Systems implementation is basically a change management process. Resistance to change is quite natural in organisations. The top management needs to prepare the organisation for accepting the change before the systems implementation process starts.

QUESTIONS

1. What do you mean by "project management"? What are the tasks involved in it?
2. Why do you need project management tools for IS implementation?
3. Explain the steps in systems implementation.
4. What is system conversion? What are the methods of system conversion?
5. What are the tasks in managing systems implementation?
6. How can a project be successfully implemented?
7. What are the causes for project implementation failure?
8. "IS systems implementation is basically a change management process". Comment.
9. Identify the systems management activities and how they are to be planned for successful implementation of IS projects.

REFERENCES

1. James A Senn, *Analysis and Design of Information Systems,* McGraw Hill Publishing Company, New York, 1989, p. 751.
2. Kenneth C. Laudon and Jane P. Laudon, *Management Information Systems,* Prentice Hall of India, New Delhi, 1999, p. 539.
3. James A. O'Brien, *Management Information Systems,* Galgotia Publications, New Delhi, 1996, p. 527.

Case 18.1: IT at University of Calicut

The University of Calicut is acclaimed for its information technology use in delivering services to students and teachers of the University and its affiliated colleges. It is getting requests from other Universities in the State of Kerala for software solutions and guidance for designing and implementing IT systems. The University's web portal is visited by a few thousand people everyday for information, applying for programmes of study, registration for examination, downloading of admit cards etc. Yet the University has to go a long way on its road to implementing an integrated and reliable network and Wi-MAX enabling the Campus.

Examination Department — Work Process

The examination department conducts thousands of examinations a year (15,000 exams to be precise). The process starts with an application from students to register for examinations. Then, the examination department prepares list of candidates, makes out admit cards (hall tickers) and despatches the admit cards to colleges for distribution to student applicants. Verification of applications is a time consuming activity. Admit cards are issued only after the verification of eligibility. University now gets question papers set and printed. They are packed with utmost secrecy. Before the exam dates, the question paper packets and answer papers should reach the colleges. Then, the students write the examinations they applied for. The colleges send answer papers in bundles to the University after the examinations or are collected by university staff from each college. The Exam department gets the papers valued. The examiners give the mark lists to the Controller of Examinations. The marks are now entered in a tabulation register. Board of examiners convene a meeting and approve the result with or without moderation. The exam department gives effect to the moderation decision, if any, and finalises the results. After that, the mark lists are made out and sent to the colleges for distribution to students.

History of Computerisation

The more than two decade old history of computerisation at the University can be divided into two parts: First IT Initiative and Second IT Initiative.

First IT Initiative

The University of Calicut launched its first computerisation initiative in 1987. It hired a state public sector enterprise, Kerala State Electronics Corporation (Keltron), to computerise the examination department. It was asked to computerise the data entry and printing of mark sheets. People from Keltron brought their hardware and software, and started their work. They entered marks of thousands of students and took printouts of mark sheets. But they were full of mistakes and had to be abandoned. The project failed because employees did not cooperate with the people brought in from outside.

The employee unions were up in arms to fight this as they feared job losses and also found an opportunity in it to build unions. Strikes and protest marches were òrganised. As the employees continued to put pressure on the university against it and the resistance was unabated, the University gave up its first initiative on computerisation.

Second IT Initiative

Later, the University invited a team from National Institute of Technology, Calicut (the then Regional Engineering College) for computerisation. It did a system study at the exam process and put a proposal for computerisation of the whole Exam Department. The amount was too much for the university. Yet, the team was given the project. After a year, as nothing happened, the project was cancelled. It was decided to engage a team of internal experts to do the job and to take up project by project, so that large scale changes are not involved. A systems manager, who had joined the University service a few years ago, was given the charge. He was given a few employees for it and he set about his task of computerisation. The first project was computerising provident fund section. Hardware was bought, software installed, databases created and tested. The project got finally implemented. Two regular employees were posted for the work in PF section. Every employee could know his or her PF credit. It was difficult to know the amount of PF credit of an employee before as the PF records were not updated regularly. Later, salary section was computerised. These two were appreciated by every employee. The amount of salary of each employee was credited to the bank account of the employee. Salary section gives a soft copy of the salary statement to the bank (State Bank of Travancore (SBT)) and the bank uses it to update accounts of employees. On the first of every month employees could get their salary credited to their accounts month after month. SBT set up an ATM on the campus to avoid crowding of employees at the branch office. Later, one more ATM was set up on the campus. Earlier, it took nearly 30-45 minutes to cash a salary cheque. An employee had to walk to the SBT branch office, deposit the cheque and withdraw money. Now, the employee is not going to the bank. He goes to any of the ATMs to withdraw money. SBT started Internet banking and mobile banking later. Money could now be withdrawn through ATMs or transferred electronically to other accounts.

New work culture

There is significant amount of change in the behaviour of employees now. They are willing to be part of the computerisation initiative. Those who opposed computerisation and ensured its failure earlier are now requesting for more applications and training in computer use. Computerisation of exam department was taken up. It was housed in separate building with a network of large number of computers, and skilled operators were hired on a temporary basis to supplement the efforts of regular employees. Soon, the university started data entry of exams, printing of mark lists, online registration for admission and examination, downloading of admit cards (hall tickets), etc. University's web portal was developed and it was used to share information with the employees, students and the public. Most of the teaching departments set up their local area networks and got linked up with the administration, library, etc., into a network on the campus with fibre optic connections between them. The university took up another initiative to create a Wi-Fi campus. Initially, it is used to share Inflibnet resources (UGC initiative) available with the central library on the campus with the teaching departments. The researchers and students in the teaching departments could access research journals online from their departments without going to the central library.

After nearly 25 years of its first computerisation initiative, the University is ahead of any other university of its kind in the state in using information technology for service delivery. Its services are being sought by other affiliating universities in the state in their effort to computerise operations. But, still the University has more projects on hand to complete the computerisation and create a truly networked and Wi-MAX-enabled campus.

Questions:

1. What systems development approach was used by the university originally? Was there a change in its approach later?
2. Why did the employees hate computerisation originally and later, support it and ask for more?
3. What are the difficulties of a piece-meal approach to systems development?
4. What difficulties may be faced by the University in future in its effort to integrate all teaching and research departments with the exam department and administration department?

Note: Inflibnet: Information and Library Network (INFLIBNET) Centre is an Autonomous Inter-University Centre (IUC) of University Grants Commission (UGC) involved in creating infrastructure for sharing of library and information resources and services among Academic and Research Institutions. INFLIBNET works collaboratively with Indian university libraries to shape the future of the academic libraries in the evolving information environment. (http://www.inflibnet.ac.in/)

19 CHAPTER

Social and Legal Aspects of Computerisation

INTRODUCTION

Computer is perhaps the most wonderful and versatile tool ever invented by man. Networking has added to its capabilities manifold. The Internet is another amazing invention. Yet, computer is not an unmixed blessing. It has its negative impacts on individuals, organisations, society and for the whole world. Any new technology solves a few existing problems and may create new problems for the society. Computer in that sense is not an exception. Its deployment in homes and offices has given rise to many ethical, social and security problems. Information resources are quite valuable for individuals and organisations. They are exposed to risks. Hence, it is in the interest of every one to design and implement proper control over information resources.

Ethical and Social Issues Relating to Information Technology

Ethics refers to the principles of right and wrong that the society accepts over a period of time. These are used in judging behaviour of every member of the society. Since information technology and information systems cause massive changes in social and organisational spheres, they also give rise to some social and ethical issues. For example, in organisations introduction of information technology changes power structure. Some people lose power due to loss of control over data and information. Similarly, the technology is misused for committing fraud, intruding into privacy of individuals, and business spying. Protecting intellectual property rights (IPR) in digital economy is very difficult. Violation of such intellectual property rights gives rise to new issues in protecting intellectual property rights.

MORAL DIMENSIONS OF INFORMATION TECHNOLOGY USE

Information technology use in homes and offices causes some moral dilemma to any society. At individual level, people are helpless in countering it. Collectively, it is possible to contain issues like privacy intrusion and IPR violation.

Privacy and Freedom in an Information Society

Privacy refers to the right of individuals to keep personal information to themselves. Personal information like one's health problems, income sources, spending habits, and leisure activities may be of interest to some firms as they use it for business planning. Some firms may gather such personal information and sell it to other firms.

Individuals want to be left alone at home and workplace without being subjected to any surveillance. Employers may intercept emails and other communication by employees. The security systems of organizations often involve surveillance or interference that violates the privacy of individual employees.

Internet and Privacy of Individuals

The Internet–based new technologies pose serious challenges to individual privacy. Every Internet user is tracked without he or she being aware of it. Software like cookies tracks the visitors to websites and their surfing behaviour. The data is used for market research by business firms.

'Cookies' are pieces of special software that are stored on the hard disk of the user's computer when he or she visits a site. The users might feel they are not watched by anyone, but it is not true. The cookies gather vital information about the user's surfing habits, online buying habits, etc. When they visit the same site next time the cookie passes information about the users. Cookies, thus, track the Internet users.

Spamming is another serious challenge that every Internet user faces and the threat is growing rapidly. The practice of sending unsolicited emails is called spamming.

Intellectual Property Rights (IPRs)

IPRs cover any tangible or intangible properties of human mind. These properties are subject to misuse. Hence, legislation is required to protect them. The protection is in the form of trademarks, copyrights, and patents. These are means to prevent misuse of trademarks etc. by others. Copyright protects one's intellectual property from being copied by others without permission of the author. Patent grants a legal right to an inventor for exclusive use of invention until its protection period expires.

In a networked environment it is very difficult to ensure protection for intellectual property. On the Web any digitised content can be accessed and distributed without the author's permission or knowledge. For example, the illegal copying and distribution of MP3 music files and movies over the Web is a major challenge to music and film industries worldwide. Similarly, it is very easy to download any publication from the Internet and it can be copied in any other work.

Software piracy is another major threat in the networked world. It is the unauthorised distribution or use of software. Software firms lose their revenue because of software piracy and do not get enough return for the effort involved in software development. Similarly, images, movies and sounds downloaded from the Internet can be modified beyond recognition using scanners and multimedia equipment. This leaves little remedy to the original copyright holder.

SOCIAL ISSUES

The current intellectual property laws are not adequate to meet the challenges of information age. Copying and distribution of music, software piracy etc. affects further development of technology.

Quality of Data and Poor System Performance

Software bugs and errors, hardware failures, poor input data quality, etc., affect the system performance. Large software packages contain millions of lines of code and the package cannot be expected to be free of any bug or defect. If people expect the software to be infallible, who is to be blamed for that: the software company or the operator or the user? Similarly, poor quality of input data causes business system failure.

Pornography

Certain adult material is freely distributed on the Internet though the user hates it. Children are exposed to such obscene stuff on the Internet. This is a big problem for parents. For example, sex is the most sought after material on the Internet. Similarly, employees in many firms use their valuable time and office facility for searching for sex material and viewing them at work.

Health Risk

The computer keyboard is a cause for the occupational disease called repetitive stress injury. Eyestrain, techno-stress caused by computer use, etc., are some health risks which the users are exposed to.

COMPUTER CRIMES

Computer crime is any illegal act or offence in cyberspace which causes loss or inconvenience to others. They include theft of hardware and software as well as wilful destruction of data, etc. They are illegal acts against computers or telecommunication facilities using computers or telecommunications. They include:

- Theft of hardware
- Theft of software
- Misuse of office computer for personal use
- Stealing and misusing password to access databases and sites without right to access them
- Intercepting and misusing credit card information
- Theft of corporate information
- Hacking of systems and sites — hackers gain unauthorised access to computers and telecommunication facility for the fun of it
- Cracking of systems — crackers gain unauthorised access to systems and cause destruction to them. They may steal information, destroy data, pirate software or deny service.
- Spamming

Spam is unwanted email. It is unsolicited and the user is in no way connected to it. He does not want to read it. Usually they are sent as bulk mails that clog the inbox of hundreds of users. Spam senders seek to sell goods online or propagate religion or con the user into a fraudulent transaction etc. It is a nuisance for users. Internet Service Providers offer spam filters that stop spam emails. Spam filter software installed on a computer identifies spam mails and sends them to junk mail box.

- **Spoofing**
- **Phishing**

IMPACT OF COMPUTERS ON INDIVIDUALS, ORGANIZATIONS AND SOCIETY

Computers have their effect on individuals, organisations and society. The impact in terms of benefits and harmful effects are discussed in the following section.

Computers and Individuals

Computer is a tool for enhancing human capability. It can perform intellectual (for example, decision-making) as well as physical tasks (cheque sorting). It is highly versatile and its use is limited only by human imagination.

(a) Benefits to Individuals

Professionals like doctors, engineers, teachers, legal practitioners and accountants are benefited in many ways. Specialised applications for these professionals help increase their efficiency. For example, a doctor can be at his home and treat his patient online, perform surgery through the help of robots at a distant hospital etc. A teacher can help thousands of students use his materials and lecture classes through computer networks. An engineer can develop designs for buildings easily and quickly. Legal practitioners use computers for preparing their briefs. They are also immensely helped by the database of court verdicts in preparing their briefs.

Consumers get better and quicker service at service counters like at railway stations (booking on any train from any of the booking counters, cancelling tickets from any booking counter, etc.,) and bank counters or through Internet banking, etc.

Digital library, interactive online classrooms, multimedia presentations, online examinations etc. have revolutionised learning process for students.

Farmers can plan crops based on cropping pattern in other regions and countries so that the crop they produce fetches better prices.

Fishermen use computer-based information on weather and fish movement for increasing their catch.

(b) Harmful Effects

Computer is not an unmixed blessing. It produces some harmful effects for the individual. Some of these are meantioned below.

Security of Data

Computers increase efficiency. It increases the leisure time available for people. It makes people lazy by doing things much quicker and more efficiently. They depend less and less on their brainpower. Too much dependence on computer over a long period may lead to loss of memory and mental skills.

Computer skill has become an essential qualification for many jobs. Hence, every job seeker is forced to acquire computer skill even though one might have an inherent dislike for it.

Loss of importance at work place is fallout of the computerisation. As computer steals away the individual roles at work places, the employees might feel insignificant and helpless. It will add to their stress and frustration.

The individuals will be exposed to some health hazards like radiation, etc. Frequent and continuous use of computer exposes the individual to certain health problems due to radiation and also due to faulty sitting and working postures.

Computers and Organisations

Organizations that use computer are benefited in a number of ways. It is used in every area of business, from data entry to strategic decision-making.

Benefits of Computer Use to Organisations

- Computer is extensively used in business organisations in the following areas.
- Computers in online transaction processing
- Computers in decision-making
- Computers in planning and forecasting
- Computers in control-financial and inventory control
- Process automation
- Computers in market research
- Computers in communication
- Computers in e-commerce
- Computers in supply chain management and customer relationship management

Harmful Effects to Organisations

- Poor return on investment in IT infrastructure
- With rapid changes in information technology, the skill set required for using information technology changes drastically. This causes frustration to people involved in information technology and the organisation's management.
- Threat of unemployment and consequent insecurity of staff will affect their morale and motivation.
- The organisation might become overstaffed. Introduction of computers into routine activities in the organisation automates many activities or replaces many jobs.
- Introduction of computers and networks disturbs the power structure in the organisation. Some people lose their power, some gain power. Power and politics in organisations change and jockeying for regaining power aggravates the organisational environment. Computerisation leads to loss of power for some people who were the custodians of information till computers were introduced. Once, computer networks are put in place, information becomes an organisational resource and freely available to every user. Those who lost their hold over information (a source of power for them) will try to regain the power through other means which leads to more organisational problems.
- Security risk and frauds may increase. Electronic frauds are difficult to detect unless there are systems to detect them in time and plug them.
- Too much transparency makes the organisation vulnerable to competitive attacks. In a network environment, information is shared freely. The information may be misused or it may be used by competing firms against the organisation.
- System failure may bring entire operation to a halt. Any computer system is susceptible to failure. Computerised systems run the risk of system failure and the consequent disruption of normal routines.
- System malfunctioning is yet another problem. The system may malfunction due to operator error, data errors, software bugs or hardware problems.

Computer and the Society

Technology impacts on the social sphere in many ways. It has both positive and negative consequences. Technological pursuits have the objective of raising quality of human life. But they often interfere with the nature and create imbalances.

Benefits to the Society

More effective use of technology. Computer is used in every technological pursuit. It also improves efficiency of use of technology.

Better and cheaper communication. It offers the most convenient and cheapest form of communication, that is, e-mail. Computer is central to any communication technology these days. Telecommunication has computer at its heart. Internet-based communication has revolutionised communication in the recent years.

Prevention of loss of lives due to timely prediction of natural catastrophes like flood, earthquake, drought, etc.

Advances in Medicine

Computers are used in hospitals for a variety of purposes such as patient registration, patient appointment, diagnosis, online medicare, patient billing and hospital administration. Medical databases and medical expert systems are available to assist physicians in diagnosis and treatment. Medical databases give information on diseases and their treatment, medical expert systems help in diagnosis and treatment. Computers are widely used in pathological tests as well.

Apollo Heartline, an online medicare of Apollo Hospitals, Delhi, ensures critical care to heart patients over telephone. Telephones at the hospital are connected to a computer with special hardware and software boards. When a patient experiences chest pain, he can telephone into the hospital. Three probes attached to the patient's body monitor his heartbeat and rate and relay these data signals over the telephone lines to the hospital. Doctors can advice the patient on the treatment needed.

Weather Forecasting

Computer is used in weather forecasting. Weather prediction requires continuous measurements and monitoring of a large number of parameters such as temperature, humidity, type of clouds, wind speeds and pressure from many different places through remote sensing satellites etc. The volume of data is enormous and it requires simultaneous capturing and analysis of data. Very powerful computers, usually supercomputers, are employed in weather prediction applications.

Public Service Becomes More Effective

Police, military service, public governance etc. are facilitated by information technology in a big way.

Military and Police

The computer was originally developed for military applications and it is widely used for such applications like simulated testing of nuclear devices, fighter pilot training, launching, tracking and intercepting of missiles, and military communications.

The Police use it for storing information about criminals and in crime detection. For example, cops use e-mail to receive information about crimes and criminals. They store fingerprints, photographs and other details of criminals. This database is helpful in investigations as they can match the photographs, etc., with the description of criminals given by the complainants. In most countries, the police force is setting up special units with computer professionals to track and fight computer-related crimes that are on the rise.

Education

Computer has made learning easier through multimedia and interactive education software. In fact, interactive learning, multimedia training, etc., have revolutionised education. Computers have made 'virtual varsity' possible and it has become a reality. Institutes in India too have started offering educational programmes over the Internet.

Electronic commerce

The companies can go global very easily in a networked world. They can sell goods and services on the Internet.

Electronic governance

Governance is made easier through the use of computers. It helps in communication between the public and the bureaucracy. Information about government rules and regulations are available at state sites, facility for online filing of applications for various state services, etc., are facilities offered to the members of public.

Harmful effects to Society

The computing technology has its negative impact on society in the form of unemployment, excessive radiation levels particularly in wireless environment, health hazards due to growing laziness and lack of physical exercise, etc.

Unemployment: In countries with large populations like India, computerisation leads to unemployment. For example, the new generation banks use less staff and limited number of branch offices for banking. They are growing rapidly and are extending banking services through networked banking, Internet banking and Automated Teller Machines. Though computerisation creates new jobs in countries like ours, the growth in new jobs is not adequate to provide gainful employment to the teaming millions who join labour pool every year.

Division in society due to new knowledge and skills: Computer literacy has become very essential these days. It requires little bit of proficiency in English language. But for a vast majority of people, it is a luxury and cannot afford to learn English language and computer use. But some State Governments have started a computer literacy mission to reach the computer skill to as much of the population as possible.

Fraud increases: Electronic fraud is on the rise globally. Security and surveillance systems fail in detecting frauds. Billions of dollars worth assets are exposed to this threat on the Internet.

Security risk: Computers in strategic areas like defence subject the society to disaster due to machine errors.

Health Hazards: Technology makes life easy. Information technology makes them lazy. Children get addicted to video games, young employees in BPO firms spend hours on end in front of computers virtually staring at the screen. These young people are deprived of enough physical activity affecting their health and physical fitness adversely.

Social networks and moral issues: Social network sites like Orkut, Facebook, etc., are a craze with the Internet users. People waste their precious time chatting or messaging with netizens in other parts of the world. It is becoming too much of a passion as to affect their regular social life.

Legal Dimensions of Computerisation: Computers and the Internet were not there when most of the legislation was enacted. For instance, many of the pieces of legislation in the country are over a century old. Indian Evidence Act 1872, Indian Contract Act 1872, Indian Telegraph Act 1885, Banker's Books of Evidence Act 1891, General Clauses Act 1897, etc., are examples. There is need for comprehensive legislation to take care of legal issues arising out of the use of computer and the Internet for business and e-governance. The Information Technology Act 2000 is a bold step in this direction. The Act addresses most of the concerns of information technology users. There are also a few other important pieces of Indian and International legislation involved in cyberspace related crimes. These include legislation relating to copyright, patent and design, Intellectual Property Rights, etc.

The Information Technology Act, 2000

The Information Technology Act 2000 ushers in a new electronic era in India. The Act puts in place a legal framework for electronic commerce and electronic governance. It provides for authentication of electronic records, use of digital signatures and security systems etc. Amendments to related legislation is also planned to give effect to the provisions in the new legislation. Henceforth records can be maintained in electronic form and digital signatures are valid. The Act lays down measures to tackle electronic crimes, tampering of electronic records etc.

The Act gives wide powers to police officers and other investigating agencies. Officers may enter into any public place, search and arrest any person, without a warrant, if they are suspected to have committed or about to commit any offence under the Act. The Act proposes amendment to related legislation to give effect to the provisions in the Information Technology Act 2000. The amendments are to be made to the Bankers Book Evidence Act 1891, Reserve Bank of India Act, 1934, Indian Evidence Act 1872, Indian Contract Act 1872, Indian Penal Code 1860, etc.

The bare act is given in the appendix. Details of the Act can be had there.

MAJOR SECURITY THREATS

A threat is a potential cause of an untoward incident that leads to some harm to system or organisations. Risk is the combination of the event and its consequence (ISO 17799:2005). Security threat may be either due to natural disasters like flood, earthquake, etc., or due to human error. The human error may be malicious or inadvertent. Either way the consequence can be disastrous. Particularly serious is the malicious action that often causes security problems. The security issues include loss of data, corruption of data, alteration or mutilation of data, etc. It may concern the integrity of data, secrecy of data and security of data. The security aspect covers the accidental or deliberate actions leading to loss of data. Threat in the digital world is posed by criminals, hackers, terrorists, spies and spammers.

The mainframe based centralised computing has given way to distributed computing with desktop and laptop computers. Similarly mobile computing is on the rise. They raise the risk of exposure to malicious attacks. Most business firms have e-commerce sites and hence they are exposed to increased risks on the Internet. Similarly, as part of e-governance programme, most state departments have online connectivity to databases and other information resources. The hacking sites update hacking tools and they are proliferating. Access to such hacking tools freely encourages more to hack websites and cause damage to systems. Consequences of such threats if materialise are financial loss to individuals and organisations, disruption of business activity, damage to corporate image, violation of privacy, etc. With new technologies like Instant Messaging, the threat takes new forms. Managing security threats is, therefore, a huge challenge for system administrators in organisations.

Information security

'Information security is the preservation of the confidentiality, integrity and availability of information: in addition, other properties, such as authenticity, accountability, non-repudiation and reliability can also be involved' (ISO 17799:2005). Business these days gathers and processes huge amount of data routinely. Ensuring security of such data resources is a herculean task to organisations. Since most business firms have digital connectivity with the world outside, their data resources are exposed globally to such information threats.

The major security threats to information resources are:

- Intrusion or hacking
- Viruses and worms
- Spoofing
- Sniffing
- Phishing
- Denial of Service

Hacking: Hacking is gaining access to a computer system without the knowledge of the owner or administrator of the system. It is perpetrated by hackers. There are two types of hackers — ethical and unethical. One group is harmless and the other is wilful criminals who cause damage or destruction to information resources and systems. Hackers may steal information or modify information at websites. They mostly target e-commerce sites. They spend a lot of time watching the site, its weakness, holes in operating systems, etc., and takeover the target site. Hidden fields in html forms, poor implementation of shopping carts, buffer overflow forms, etc., are used by them to gain access to the systems. Organisations are required to conduct vulnerability tests to identify possible hacking threats and take measures to stall them.

Viruses and Worms: Viruses and worms are programs that interfere with the working of computers. They cause systems to malfunction. More details on viruses and worms are given elsewhere in this chapter.

Trojan Horse: These were programs originally used for system administration. They enabled system administrators to gain control of remote workstations. The program has two parts — one part runs as server on remote workstations and the other as client on administrator's systems. The program can be sent as e-mail attachment. Hackers use these programs to gain control of target workstations and they may steal private information on target system.

Spoofing: Spoofing is deceiving computer users. Spoofing has different forms like IP spoofing, DNS spoofing and ARP spoofing. In IP Spoofing, the source address of the IP packet originating from a hacker's system hides its IP address and shows that of a legitimate source. Firewalls may fail to detect the intrusion with IP spoofing. But, with appropriate configuration of firewalls, it is possible to detect these intrusions. In DNS spoofing, the visitor is directed to a different website, often to hacker's website, and takes personal data and credit card information, etc., illegally through web forms. In Address Resolution Protocol (ARP) spoofing, the hacker gets legitimate access to a network by sending a message from his machine to the ARP claiming that it is the legitimate computer.

Sniffing: Sniffing was originally a technique to solve network problems. It is seeing all packets passing through the network. Hackers use it to scan login name and passwords. It can be avoided by encrypting data before sending it across the networks. Encryption makes sniffing difficult.

Phishing: Phishing is online theft of personal identity. The miscreants send spam e-mails requesting for log in and password, credit card details, bank account numbers, etc. The spam mail will have links to genuine looking websites and once the user is directed to the website, he is asked for updating his personal information. It may be misused to commit frauds online. The victim's bank balance may be transferred or credit card number may be used to purchase things or pay for services online, etc.

Denial of Service: The objective of this attack is to prevent a website from functioning. Hackers do not mount such attacks from their machines. Instead, they install programs like zombies on some intermediate computers and use them to remotely run these programs. When the targeted system gets too many messages from a large number of intermediate level computers in the network, it breaks down because of overload. The legitimate users may not get access to the website under denial of service attack.

Risk Management

Proper management of risk from security threats needs a process for risk management in organisations. The organisation should have a team of trained persons to manage information security risks. The process should identify potential risks, assess impact of such risks and take measures to manage them. As part of management, certain risks are eliminated, certain risks reduced and certain risks transferred to others, say, to insurance companies.

For risk management, there should be appropriate controls which may fall into four categories: preventive control, deterrent control, detective control and corrective control.

SECURITY MEASURES

Organisations need to put in place certain safeguards for protecting their computer and information resources against unauthorized access, disasters and systems failure. The first step in managing security threats is to make computer users aware about the possible threats and precautions to be taken. For example, most banks with Internet or mobile banking facility frequently send information to customers over mobile phone to inform them about security threats. Internet banking site also gives information about security threats and how to ward off such threats. Security has to be designed into the system at the time of system architecture planning and development. It should also take into account the following:

- Security responsibilities
- Security metrics for reporting
- Common security controls
- Security testing and assessment techniques
- Secure design, architecture and coding practices
- Certification and accreditation process

The system administrators and users must be trained in detecting and handling vulnerabilities of systems. The other security measures have to be arranged in rings like physical level, data level and software level.

Physical Level

The measures to be taken to ensure physical security of the system include:

- Control access to systems and deny access to unauthorised people.
- Maintaining systems under dust free environment under controlled temperature.
- Ensure continuous power supply by installing UPS and back up facilities.
- Have facilities to prevent fire and fight it if it happens.
- Prevent rodents, pests, etc., from entering the computer rooms.

Data Level

The steps to be taken to improve data security include:

- Ensure fool-proof transaction acceptance for online or interactive transaction processing systems
- Prevent loss, tapping, etc., during data transmission.
- Keep the relevant old master file and transaction file so that it is possible to reconstruct the current master file anytime if it is tampered or destroyed by fire, flood, earthquake, etc.
- Take proper care of archived data. Sometimes data is kept archived for months without reading the tapes, etc. Later, it may become unreadable or irretrievable. It is a good practice to read the data from tapes, etc., once every few months.
- Conduct proper audit of hardware every year.
- Keep track of software changes so that there will not be software version conflict, etc.
- Never use pirated software, particularly application software, which is most vulnerable to attacks.
- Have planned monitoring of access to systems to detect unauthorised access and prevent them.

Software Level

These measures include firewall, passwords, data encryption, and antivirus software.

Firewall: Firewall is a combination of software and hardware that prevents hackers and others from infiltrating a computer or internal network from an outside network. It is simply a barrier between two networks. One of the networks is internal, that is trusted, and the other is external to the organisation. The external network is not trusted. Firewalls are designed to protect an organisation's network, its data and systems. Firewalls check incoming and outgoing packets of data and block or let them flow according to a set of rules defined by the administrator.

Firewalls are particularly important in the Internet environment. The firewall in the following illustration may automatically allow or deny access to the web server based on the set of rules coded into it.

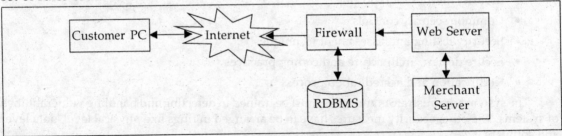

Fig. 19.1: Use of Firewall for Security

Antivirus Software: Antivirus software must be installed on systems to avoid virus attacks. The antivirus software scans the system memory and hard disks, and cleans data and programs if viruses are present.

Password: Password, as the name indicates, is a set of characters that form a string of certain length. Each user of a system or network is given a login name and a password for identifying him or her to the system. The password is used in controlling access to information resources.

Each user is identified by the login name and password. When the user turns on the machine, the system asks for typing in his or her login name and password. If the login and password are right, the system permits access to the information resources that the user is authorised to access. If the login or password or both are wrong, the user is denied access to it. Thus, the password-based access control protects information resources by preventing unauthorised access.

Encryption: It is the altering of data so that it is not usable unless the changes are undone, that is, de-encrypted. It is particularly useful when sensitive data is transmitted over a public network. Encryption is used to prevent unauthorised access to any message sent over telecommunication networks. It involves scrambling of data at the sender's end, transmitting scrambled data over the communication line and unscrambling the data at the recipient's end. Public key pair is used to encrypt and decrypt the message. The sender encrypts the message with the public key of the recipient. Only the recipient's private key can decrypt the encrypted message.

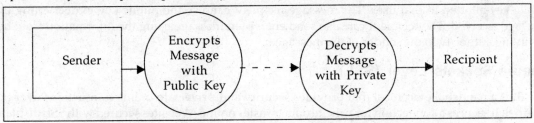

Fig. 19.2: Use of Public Key and Private Key for Sending Message

Digital Signature: Electronic documents sent over public networks may be intercepted and tampered. Digital signature is an electronic identifier that uses cryptography technology to ensure its reliability. It uses a digest function (hashing algorithm) to summarise the content of an electronic message. The digest function reduces the message into more manageable chunk of data. It may be reduced into a few lines by hashing. It is called the message digest. The message digest is then encrypted with the private key of the sender. The result is digital signature. The sender's software appends this digital signature to the document. Now all the hashed data is signed.

The recipient's software decrypts the signature changing it back into message digest. If it works, it means the document is signed by the sender as only he has its corresponding private key. The recipient uses his private key to decrypt electronic message. The recipient's software hashes the document data into a message digest. If the two digest results match, then the message has not been tampered. Thus, digital signature ensures security of data sent over public communication networks and also authenticates the source of the message.

Digital signature is generally used when financial transactions are involved and when forgery or tampering has to be blocked like confidential information is being sent across public networks. Digital signature uses asymmetric cryptography.

The digital signature to be effective, the following points have to be taken care of:

- Secure algorithm
- The algorithm should be implemented well
- The public key owner should be verifiable
- The private key should be kept confidential, and,
- The signature protocol should be carried out properly.

Digital Certificate

It is still possible, even after digital signature is applied to a message, that a person other than the recipient interprets the message on its way and manages to access the message. He may modify the message or create a new message as if it were created by the original sender. This is possible as generating a digital signature mimicking that of another is not impossible.

Digital certificate is used to validate the identity of the message sender to the recipient. It is used to protect the identity of the users and to provide security for electronic transactions. A trusted third party, called certifying authority, provides the authentication. The certifying authority verifies the identity of the digital certificate user and provides information about the identity of the user and the public key allotted to that user. The message recipient can use the public key in decrypting the message received. The recipient can also send encrypted message using the information from the certifying authority to the sender of the message.

Secure Sockets Layer (SSL)

It is a handshake protocol that provides security and privacy to online transactions over the Internet. It secures a connection for private data transfer online. Websites secured with SSL displays a padlock in the browser's URL. E-commerce websites protects their sites with SSL, and sometimes with Extended Validation Certificate (EV SSL certificate), to provide confidentiality of credit card payment made and personal data submitted at the site.

Disaster recovery plans

These are methods of restoring information processing operations that were disrupted or halted by destruction or accident. It is required to restart operations quickly after any disruption in its normal operations.

VIRUSES AND WORMS

Computer virus is a hostile program that generally replicates itself and infests other files. These malicious programs are developed by computer hackers and disgruntled programmers. They are usually written in assembly language or high-level language like 'C'. Some of these may be harmless as they display some message or play a tune. But most of the viruses are highly harmful to computer systems. The harm done to the computer system depends on the type of virus and frequency of its strike. Viruses are quite common in DOS and Windows an environments. They normally spread through floppy diskettes carrying pirated software. With microcomputers joining the Internet, the spread of virus is swift and wide through this global network.

A worm is a program that copies itself repetitively into computer memory or disk drives until the memory or disk space is exhausted. It can cause the computer to stop functioning as it runs out of memory to load and run applications. Worm is an autonomous agent capable of propagating itself without the help of other programs. Most worms disrupt services and create problems for system management. Some worms scan passwords and other sensitive information and pass them to the attacker. Some worms can install viruses that can cause destruction of data or damage to systems.

Origin of Computer Virus

John Von Neumann first suggested the concept of self-replicating programs in 1950. A few of the programmers at AT&T started working on self-replicating programs as a game. The game involved writing code to destroy other's code in the computer memory and the one who has maximum number of lines of code wins the game. The game was kept a secret and was never released for the public. Later, Ken Thomson, co-author of UNIX encouraged programmers to write programs like the one at AT&T. Early viruses were developed by hackers to enter other's systems.

These viruses spread through the diskettes and the network. If a computer is infected with virus, any file copied from that computer on to a floppy disk carries copies of the virus as well. When that file is copied on to another computer the virus also gets copied to that computer. In a networked world virus travels at lightning speed. It spreads through email messages or infected web sites when the content from that site is downloaded without virus checking.

Types of Viruses

There are thousands of viruses and several thousand variations of these viruses. These viruses can be classified into boot sector viruses, file viruses and multipartite viruses.

Boot Sector Virus: This virus affects the boot sector of the affected computer. It resides in the boot sector and is difficult to remove. When the computer is turned on, it copies itself into the memory and infects other files.

File Virus: This virus attaches itself to executable files. When the executable file is activated, the virus also gets activated. Once activated, it infects other files.

Multipartite Virus: This virus affects both boot sector and files and is more dangerous than the other two types. Stealth virus is a type of multipartite virus that is deadly and difficult to locate.

Macro Virus: Macro virus is another type of virus that infects MS Word and MS Excel documents. Macros are miniature programs written to save time in doing repetitive tasks. The virus attaches itself to the macro program and becomes active when the macro is invoked.

Some of the commonly found computer viruses are:

Stone Marijuana Virus: This affects boot sector of floppy diskettes and the master boot record containing partition table on hard disks. It displays a message "Your PC is stoned".

The Vienna-648 Virus: This infects files with size larger than 10 bytes. It usually infects '.com' files and increases infected file size by 648 bytes.

Joshy: This virus is of Indian origin and affects boot sector of floppy diskettes and master boot record of hard disks. It becomes active on the 5th of January every year and the computer system hangs when the virus is active. If the message "Happy Birthday Joshy" is typed, the system starts functioning normally.

Dark Avenger Virus: It infects files with size larger than 1800 bytes and is very difficult to remove. It affects '.com' and '.exe' files. It increases the size of infected files by 1800 bytes, reduces RAM by 4 KB and displays the message "Eddie Lives Somewhere in Time".

Stealth Viruses: Stealth viruses are hard to detect and are very dangerous. They include 512A, Holocaust, V-2000 Whale, Murphy and Michael Angelo. The Michael Angelo virus wipes out data on hard disk on Friday the 6th of March, the birthday of the artist, Michael Angelo.

Flush Virus: It is a memory-resident virus that infects '.com' and '.exe' files.

Jerusalem Virus: It affects '.exe' and '.com' files. It increases the size of '.exe' files by 1808 bytes and that of '.com' files by 1813 bytes.

Perfume: It infects '.com' file and increases its size by 765 bytes. It shoots a question and if the number 4711 (the name of a German perfume) is typed, it functions normally.

Bomb: It can take the form of Trojan horse and can harm like a virus or a worm. Its signature is either a time trigger or a logic trigger that activates it. Time trigger activates the bomb when a data is passed. The bomb prevents the infected program from functioning.

Bacteria: These are relatively harmless programs, but they replicate themselves exponentially. They eventually take up all the processor capacity, memory and disk space. Users cannot access the system thereafter.

Trap Door: A trap door is a secret entry point into a program that allows the hacker to gain access to the network, etc., without going through the usual security procedures.

Cookies

A cookie is a piece of software sent by a web server that is installed on a user computer. It is a tiny program file which stores the browsing behaviour of the user. Every time the user visits the site the cookie communicates with the web server. The cookie thus helps the web server in tracking the user preferences etc. The web server stores the information from the cookie about a person's viewing habits, etc. It uses this information to customise information to the user. The web server may update the cookie as and when needed. The customer may not know about this kind of information exchange between the cookie and the web server. The information stored at the web server may be shared with other web servers. This might lead to the user getting unsolicited e-mails, etc. This actually violates the privacy of user.

Detection of Viruses

Disk Scanners: Disk scanners, like UTScan, can be used to check the hard disk or floppy diskettes for viruses and display the result of scanning.

Boot Monitors and File Monitors: They give an alarm to users if a virus attempts at infecting boot sector or '.com' and '.exe' files.

Removal of Viruses

Anti-virus software is available for removing known viruses. After locating a virus, the anti-virus software is run to remove the virus from the affected files and the boot sector. For example, UTScan has a scanning program, (Scan.exe) to scan the disk for viruses and a cleaning program (Clean.exe) to remove them. Other packages of anti-virus software include Nashot, VirScan, Red Alert and Norton Anti-virus.

Computer Forensics

Computer crimes are getting reported frequently and are being taken to courts for compensation etc. Service of experts in computer crime tracking is being used for crime detection. If a crime is committed, it leaves some evidences somewhere. The crime like sending a scandalous e-mail tarnishing the image of a celebrity may damage the person's fame. If he files a petition, the police will mount an investigation to find out the origin of the e-mail. Forensic experts help the police in digging up such information to present the evidence in a court of law.

Computer forensics is defined as the collection, authentication, preservation and examination of electronic information for presentation in court[2].

Conclusion

Computer is a versatile tool that is used in all walks of human life and its application is growing day by day. It benefits individuals, organisations and the society. It has some negative effects that impact on individuals, organisations and the society badly.

Information technology throws up serious security risks that are difficult to be plugged. Viruses, hacking and electronic frauds raise the risk of operating in the virtual world. Computer security, data integrity and confidentiality are key concerns for organisations. Encryption, firewalls, digital signature, etc., are some techniques to address the major security threats. Yet, the threats take more challenging forms to thwart all security plans of companies and state organs worldwide. Hence, effective legislation is essential to support healthy practices in cyberspace. In addition, it calls for a powerful authority to oversee cyber activities to ensure safe and secure electronic transactions.

QUESTIONS

1. What are the social and moral issues of increasing use of information technology?
2. What are the impacts of computer use on individuals, organisations and society?
3. What is computer crime? How does it happen?
4. What is hacking? How does it affect security of information systems?
5. What are the security measures that can prevent misuse of IT resources?
6. What is virus? What are the types of virus?
7. What is password? How can it protect information resources?
8. What is digital certificate? Who issues it?
9. What is firewall? How does it protect information resources?
10. What are the legal issues in the use of information technology resources?
11. What are the security threats to information resources? How can they be guarded against?

REFERENCES

1. http://commin.nic.in/doc
2. Haag, Stephen *et. al., Management Information Systems for the Information Age*, Tata McGraw Hill, New Delhi, 2003, p. 424.

Case 19.1: E-GOVERNANCE IN THE STATE OF KERALA

The State's Department of IT initiated a number of IT projects in the recent past to move towards e-governance paradigm. They include an integrated services centre called FRIENDS (Fast Reliable Instant Efficient Network for Disbursement of Services) with a view to enable a smooth and transparent C2G (Customer to Government) interface. These centres accept all utility bills, taxes and fees pertaining to the participating departments and offer quality services to the citizens. FRIENDS has been launched in all the 14 district headquarters in the State.

Package for Effective Administration of Registration Laws (PEARL) is a project being implemented in 14 Sub Registrar Offices of the State covering all the 14 districts of the state. PEARL intends to replace the existing registration system by a system of online processing. Thus, every sub-registrar office would have a LAN with adequate terminals for customer servicing. This project is jointly implemented by the Department of IT and the Registration Department with the technical assistance and guidance from National Informatics Centre.

IT policy of the State of Kerala addresses three key issues in IT dissemination to masses: bringing the benefits of information technology to the households (access), providing ample Information base in local language relevant to citizens' lives (content) and providing sufficient understanding of the world of information technology and how it can touch their lives (skill sets).

The Akshaya Project

Project Akshaya aims to 'Bridge the Digital Divide' by enabling tens of thousands of ordinary state citizens to access relevant information in the local language over the Internet. Akshaya will develop a comprehensive digital network. In the first phase, the project will impart e-literacy to at least one member each from 6.4 million families in the state.

The IT Department expects Akshaya to reduce significantly the divide between "information haves" and "information have-nots" and to help in reaching the benefits of IT to the common man. The project, envisages to be implemented in three years' time, is expected to:

- set up a network of 6,000 information centres in the state
- create about 50,000 employment opportunities, and,
- generate investment opportunities to the tune of ₹ 5 billion.

The e-literacy campaign is the foundation on which the state seeks to bridge the digital divide. The underlying objective of the campaign is to remove the "fear of the unknown" that common people have about technology in general and computers in particular.

Akshaya Project is implemented in two phases: Akshaya and AkshayaNext. The first phase, Akshaya, will impart the required e-literacy to the common people and the second phase will launch full shaft of e-governance services. As a pilot project, Akshaya was implemented in the Malappuram District of Kerala.

In the second phase of the project, the state plans to create state-wide IT network infrastructure based on wireless technology. The Akshaya entrepreneurs are to meet part of the capital cost of setting up this infrastructure and pay for its use. Malappuram district will move on to Phase II soon. The initial cost of setting up the wireless infrastructure is to be shared by the entrepreneurs and the state in the ratio of 50:50. In addition, each entrepreneur is to pay monthly rent of around ₹ 1,000 for using the infrastructure. The work contract for setting up a high bandwidth wireless infrastructure in the district has been given to an IT firm.

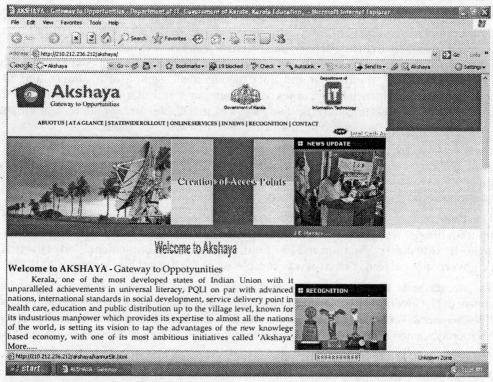

Business Model for Akshaya Centres

Akshaya centres will be the delivery end of the e-governance programme of the state. They will offer training, communication facilities, information services, e-transaction facilities and e-governance services. The entire project will be implemented through the participation of the three-tier *panchayati raj* institutions. District Panchayat will be the overall coordinator. Committees are proposed at State, District, Block, Panchayat/Municipality, and Ward levels for the implementation and monitoring of the project.

Once the people are introduced to the immense possibilities of ICT in Phase I, the next phase, AkshayaNext, envisages making facilities available to the people for exploiting the technology for everyday use. The focus here is to ensure a viable, sustainable service delivery mechanism for the citizens of the state through Akshaya centres.

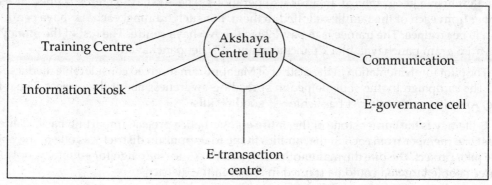

Fig. 19.3: Business Model of Akshaya Next

The Akshaya centre will be having necessary equipment and facilities like computers, fax, printers, telephones, broad-band Internet connection, etc., and software so as to cater to the information and communication requirements of the local citizens. The services to be launched during the second phase include Internet telephony, browsing and chatting, home delivery of entertainment through broad-band connectivity, digitisation and data management, selling of insurance and financial products, franchises of financial companies, etc., assembling and marketing computers under the brand name 'Akshaya', ticketing and hospitality services, market research, multimedia, animation and designing centres, health kiosks and telemedicine, and, marketing of goods.

These services are not tested and are not uniformly needed across the state. Depending upon the potential of each area, the Akshaya entrepreneurs will have to launch new services. Hence, each entrepreneur has to do market research to find out what the market needs. The viability of the centre depends on launching of profitable products and services.

The President of India inaugurated 'Akshaya Project' on the 18th of November 2002. Malappuram district was chosen for the initial pilot implementation. The district is unique with a large minority (Muslim) population and low political rivalry. The implementation of the first phase of the e-governance project, Akshaya, was completed in the district by December 2003.

The Kerala State IT Mission is the autonomous nodal IT implementation agency for the Department of IT, Government of Kerala that provides managerial support to the Department's various initiatives. Science & Technology Entrepreneurship Development Board (STED) which is a project set up by National Science & Technology Entrepreneurship Development Board, Government of India.

The Centre for Development of Imaging Technology (C-DIT) is an autonomous centre under the Government of Kerala, established in 1988. For the Akshaya project, C-DIT has developed and supplied IT literacy CD with customised software like Chithravidya, Ganithavidya and Aksharavidya. The entire programme is implemented with the active participation of the existing *panchayati raj* institutions. The private entrepreneurs invest money in their Akshaya ventures which are the delivery nodes of the project. Centre for Development of Advanced Computing (C-DAC) is another public sector body involved in the Akshaya project.

Entrepreneurial selection, training and support are provided by the IT Mission and local self governing bodies meet the cost of training. The private entrepreneurs bear the business risk and deliver the services to the masses. This public-private participation in project implementation is unique in Kerala.

Each Akshaya centre was allotted, on average, 1,000 households. Thus, each Akshaya centre had an exclusive geographical area for its operations. The Akshaya centres trained at least one member from each of the families allotted to them. For such training, each Akshaya centre was to get ₹ 140 per trainee. The trainee is to pay ₹ 20 to the Akshaya centre. The rest of the money (₹ 120) came from gram panchayat, block panchayat and district panchayat.

The pilot implementation in the district of Malappuram received considerable media space and time. The campaign by the state helped in spreading awareness about the project. The e-literacy drive, Akshaya, in the district has achieved good results.

E-literacy is the corner stone of the entire e-governance project. Imparting basic IT literacy to at least one member from each of the families in the Malappuram district was one of the objectives of the pilot project. Despite the mammoth effort and the state campaign for e-literacy, only two out of three people targeted could be trained in IT use in the district.

The average investment required for an Akshaya centre was around ₹ 200,000. Most of the Akshaya entrepreneurs borrowed money from financial institutions for investment. In the first phase of the project just completed, each centre was certain about their revenues and expenditures to a large extent. But the next phase is quite uncertain. The entrepreneurs need to introduce services demanded by customers in their markets. Estimating the revenue and cost is much more difficult in the second phase, AkshayaNext.

In the second phase, additional capital investment and revenue expenditure are involved in the form of meeting cost of broadband wireless network and monthly rent for using broadband connectivity. The Akshaya entrepreneurs have established strong emotional bondage with the public based on mutuality and trust. The project name has become a strong and trusted brand. The Akshaya entrepreneurs have recognised its potential and are marketing goods under the brand in some pockets now.

The Akshaya project was initiated by Government of Kerala to bridge the digital gap between the 'information haves' and 'information have-nots'. The first experimental phase of Akshaya project has been implemented in the district of Malappuram in Kerala. Based on the experience gained in implementing the pilot project, the state is planning to rollout the project in the remaining 13 districts of the state. This study found the first phase of the project to be reasonably successful. Yet, it failed in meeting the target set by the project managers by a third. Though the claim is 90% of the people have been made e-literate, the entrepreneurs put it at around 67%. The brand 'Akshaya' is strong and has the potential to generate enough business for a significant number of the Akshaya entrepreneurs in phase two of the project. Trust, mutuality and state patronage were the corner stones on which the Akshaya network was built. If the state withdraws its support to the project, a large number of Akshaya centres may be closed down. This would certainly affect the reach and delivery capability of the network.

Exhibit 1

Factors for E-governance Effectiveness

- E-literacy and change in attitude of user community
- Administrative reforms and changes in the attitude of government servants
- Building IT infrastructure
- Setting up Information Interfaces for public access
- Ensuring adequate budgetary support to e-governance initiatives
- Cyber laws and security.

Questions:

1. What are the benefits of E-governance programme for the common people of a state?
2. How was Akshaya, the pilot Project's implemented in Malappuram district of Kerala?
3. What kinds of services are offered through the Akshaya Project? Can the IT infrastructure meet the future needs of the customers?
4. What are the factors to be taken into account when such a massive project is implemented in a state?

20 CHAPTER

Computer Networking

INTRODUCTION

With standardised hardware and easy-to-use software, microcomputer provides user-friendly environment. It meets the computing requirements of most users. But, the need for interaction with other computer users and with other computer systems for exchange of data, etc., has increased over the years. Computer networks are increasingly meeting this need. Computer networking is the process of interconnecting two or more computers so that the users can communicate with each other, share resources and overcome other limitations of stand-alone systems. The network can be established with a variety of combinations of computers such as a network of only microcomputers, microcomputers and one or more minicomputers and a set of microcomputers connected to a mainframe computer. The computers in a typical network are autonomous in the sense that they have processing capability independent of the network.

Advantages of Networking

Computer networks open up opportunities for real-time communications and commerce. Besides that, it permits individuals and organisations to collaborate. The main advantages of networking are:

(i) **Resource sharing:** Network enables sharing of expensive resources such as processor, storage space and peripherals like modern, fax, and laser printer.

(ii) **Sharing of Data:** The network permits concurrent access to the same data by many users on the network. Thus corporate databases are shared by users in many areas like sales department, production centre, inventory department, etc.

(iii) **Sharing of Software:** Any user in a network can load and use the software installed on any of the computer or fileserver in the network.

(iv) **Communication between Users:** The Network users can communicate between them. E-mail facility can also be used for communication.

(v) **Decentralised Data Processing:** In a network, the data processing can be decentralised by enabling local offices to capture and store data, and generate information to meet most of their requirements at local level itself.

TYPES OF NETWORK

The networks can be classified into three: local area network (LAN), metropolitan area network (MAN) and wide area network (WAN). They are explained in the following sections.

WIDE AREA NETWORK (WAN)

WAN is made up of a number of autonomous computers distributed over a wide geographical area. WANs were originally developed in the late 1960s to enable communication between computer centres and sharing of hardware, software and other communication facilities. WAN can be implemented using private or public networks. In a private network an organisation takes on lease telephone lines to connect such sites into a network. It is also possible to connect computers in different locations using microwave or satellite transmission. Public networks are installed by the Government owned telecommunication agencies. WAN spans large geographic distances. It is also called long-haul network. WAN is usually operated at lower speeds than MAN and involves delay.

Most organisations use private networks for communication. Society for Worldwide Interbank Financial Transactions (SWIFT), a non-profit organisation of banks, owns a private network. The network exchanges financial transactions between the participating financial institutions, about 3000 in number in over 60 countries. The terminals of these participating banks are hooked with SWIFT's access centres. The network offers data communication service 24 hours a day, 7 days a week.

METROPOLITAN AREA NETWORK (MAN)

Metropolitan area network covers a wider area than a local area network. Usually MAN covers a large metropolitan city and is a scaled down version of wide area network. It operates at high speeds over distances sufficient for a metropolitan area.

LOCAL AREA NETWORK (LAN)

A LAN is a system of interconnected microcomputers, sharing common resources like disks, printers, etc. It links a number of computers (workstations) together to allow many people to use the same software and data files. Each user in such a multi-user environment accesses the resources through his microcomputer workstation. The network operating system integrates all the network components and makes operations smooth and transparent. LAN works in restricted geographical area such as within a large building or offices within a few kilometres.

The LAN is an interconnection of computers that need to communicate with each other in a limited geographical area. The network may have other sharable devices attached such as fax, laser printers and copiers. The network includes a central facility with huge storage capacity. The processing may be centralised or decentralised depending upon the requirements of the organisation.

LAN Topology

The design of network requires selection of a particular topology and architecture for the interconnection of network components. Topology refers to the way the computers are physically connected into the network. The network architecture includes the specifications of the components that can be connected to the network. IBM's Systems Network Architecture (SNA) is an example of vendor developed network architecture. Such network architecture specifies network components such as terminals, workstations, printers, cluster controllers, host computer and communication controllers.

There are a number of network topologies. Of them ring, star and bus are popular.

Star Topology: In star network the nodes are connected to a central computer called the host computer. The nodes cannot communicate directly. Each node can communicate with the host computer. The host computer takes the message and routes it to the other node or nodes.

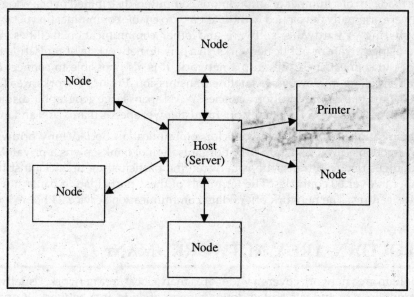

Fig. 20.1: Star Network

In a star network centralisation of control over the network resources is easy. It is also possible to network minicomputer or mainframe with other microcomputers and dumb terminals. It eliminates single point failure of a common wire. If one of the host computers fails, it does not usually affect the others in the network. But the hub becomes a central point of failure in a ring network. If the host computer breaks down, the entire network breaks down.

Ring Topology: In a ring network the computers can communicate directly with each other and also with the central computer. The nodes are connected to a line that is closed like a loop. The ring network is more reliable than star network. Even if the central computer in the network fails, the other computers can continue to communicate with each other.

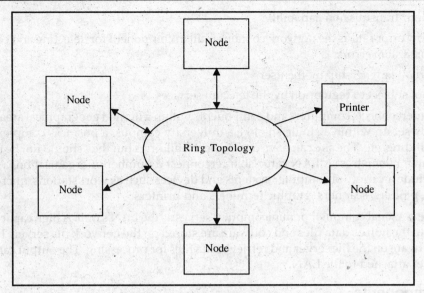

Fig. 20.2: Ring Network

Bus Topology: A bus network configures computers to a single non-looping channel. The computers connected to the network share the same bus or communications channel. Bus wiring is easy and needs much less wiring for small segments.

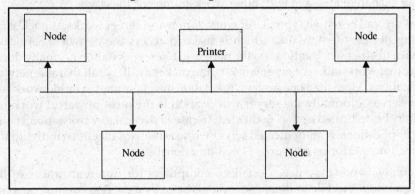

Fig. 20.3: Bus Network

Old Ethernet bus wiring is prone to cable failure. If the bus wiring connection is broken at any point, the entire network fails.

In most cases, instead of a single topology, a combination of topologies may be used for greater flexibility and reliability.

Features of LAN

The features of LAN include the following:

- limited geographical area say within a few kilometres
- Common communication link for sharing information, software and peripheral devices without regard to proximity of user to such resources on the network.

- High transmission capability.
- Low error rate as the network contains built in component for detecting and compensating for system errors.
- Private ownership by the user.
- Not subject to regulation by the telecom services.

LAN interconnects computers and components within a limited geographical area. Such LANs are normally set up within a single site like a university campus, a business complex, a hospital, an office-building, etc. The site can have one or more buildings but they should not be too far away, say less than 5 kilometres. A LAN can also interconnect a number of organisations. The network can also include a variety of computer systems and devices such as workstations, microcomputers, file servers, plotters, scanners, graphic terminals and printers.

A large personal computer or minicomputer serves as the LAN's hub. A high capacity hard disk is attached to the hub as data files and software are stored on the network file server. The users can load the software on the file server and retrieve data files for processing. The output can be directed to the printer attached to the LAN.

LAN Components

The components of LAN are file server, workstation, network operating system, LAN cable, active and passive hubs, etc.

(a) Workstation: It is a single-user microcomputer with powerful processor and communication facilities. It can exchange message with other workstations or fileserver.

Workstations can be of two types: User workstation and server workstation. User workstation is a microcomputer on the network, which is used to access the network. Service workstation performs service to other workstations on the network. User workstation normally does not process requests from other workstations. Server workstation makes available all sharable network resources to other workstations. More than one server workstation may be added to the network such as printer server and fileserver. Normally the server workstation is the most powerful workstation. Server workstation may be dedicated or non-dedicated. In case of dedicated workstation, it is not available for other user applications. Non-dedicated server workstation doubles as an individual workstation and at the same time performs network-related functions.

(b) Servers: Network may use specialised computers for different processes like database services, print services, etc. File or database server is actually a process running on a computer that provides the clients access to database on that computer. The term is loosely applied to mean computer that runs file server software. In this sense, it is a powerful computer with special software to serve files to other workstations on the network. The files, which may be program files or data files, are simultaneously shared by a number of workstations. Similarly, a print server takes care of all print jobs issued by clients on a network.

(c) Gateway: The gateway assists in communicating between LANs. A workstation may be dedicated to serve as gateway. This is required particularly when two networks with different technologies have to communicate with each other. Gateway may also be used to connect LAN with a mainframe computer.

(d) Network Interface Unit: The network interface is a printed circuit board installed in the microcomputer. It may be called network card, network adapter or network interface unit. It connects the workstations functionally and physically with the network.

(e) Active Hub: Hub is an electronic device to which multiple computers are attached usually using twisted pair cables. Active hub is a powered distribution point with active devices that drive distant nodes up to one kilometre away. It can connect up to eight nodes on the network. The maximum distance carried by an active hub is about 2,000 ft.

(f) Passive Hub: This hub is a distribution point that does not use power or active devices in a network to connect up to four nodes within a short distance. The maximum distance covered by a passive hub is nearly 300 ft.

(g) LAN Cable: LAN requires superior cable capable of transferring data at high speed. Coaxial cables or fibre optic cables may be used for networking computers.

(h) Network Operating System (NOS): The NOS integrates all the network components. The NOS facilitates file and print serving along with other functions like communications and e-mail between workstations. In most LANs the NOS exists along with the computer's operating system. The computer's operating system processes the system requests first and processes them if they can be done with the workstation resources. If it is not a local request, meaning that the network resources have to be used, the request is transferred to NOS for carrying out. Thus, the NOS is responsible for controlling access to data, storage space and sharing of other peripheral resources.

(i) Application Software: Another component of LAN is application software. It has to be ensured that the application software works in the multi-user environment.

(j) Middleware: Networks these days are very complex with different types of hardware, software and different types of networking, for example client/server computing, etc. Middleware is a set of programs that controls the communication between server and clients. It takes care of data conversion and coordination.

(k) Protocols: Data transmission between devices requires protocol. Protocols are sets of rules and procedures to control the data transmission between computers and other devices. They are common technical guidelines for communication between devices. They specify the order in which signals will be transferred, the signal for completion of transfer, etc. Only Devices using the same protocol can communicate directly. Both the sending and receiving devices must use the same protocol for effecting communication. For communication between devices using different protocols requires intermediate interpretation device or software.

The protocol performs the following functions.

- Set up a link with the other device in the communication.
- Identify the component to other components in the communication (sending device's channel ID).
- Send and interpret the data
- Provide a continuous feedback on data transmission like data is not being received and understood.
- Request for retransmission of garbled data.
- Engage recovery procedure when error occurs.
- Provide an acceptable way of terminating transmission so that all devices have completed the process.

The protocol is embedded in communications software designed to use a particular protocol. The user need not bother about the protocol as the components involved in the communication perform the protocol matching. The data communication protocols are of two main types:

asynchronous and synchronous. The synchronous protocol permits continuous data transmission. The devices in communication must be synchronised with the other. The transmission is governed by a time interval and not by start-stop bits. For example, clock, in the modern, sets the time interval.

Integrated Services Digital Network (ISDN)

ISDN is a generic name for any form of network that connects users with service firms such as banks, investment companies, airlines, cinema theatres, etc., using a digital network. The users can be homes, educational institutions, business firms, etc. One important feature of this network is its ability to connect a wide variety of users and services to the network using the X.25 interface protocol. Telephone companies offer digital network service.

APPROCHES TO NETWORKING

A network can be configured in different ways. Processing can be centralised or distributed. It is also possible to combine these two approaches. The major approaches to network are discussed below.

Centralised Computing

Centralised computing uses a large computer, for example a mainframe computer, for performing all data processing. A large number of terminals are connected to the mainframe. All the software and databases are stored on the central computer. Certain applications require this kind of network architecture. For instance, online securities trading requires all transaction processing to be done with a centralised facility.

Distributed Computing

A distributed system interconnects computer locations with facilities to capture and process data, stores data and sends information to other computer locations called nodes. Large organisations interconnect their computer systems at different offices and plants into network. With the Internet technologies, connecting offices across the globe into a single network is possible at very low costs.

Data processing in such a network can be distributed. This allows offices, plants, etc., to collect, store and process data as they occur and use the information locally. The information relevant to other offices and headquarters is transferred to the computer location at the headquarters. The computer facility at the headquarters can be easily accessed from multiple nodes on the network. Thus, the local offices are able to capture and process operating data in their own way and at the same time head quarters receives all information it needs from such local offices.

By permitting data transfer and processing at other sites, the distributed system permits load sharing between nodes. It also permits sharing of software. It is possible to run software on remote location and the results can be downloaded at the accessing node.

The distributed system lowers data communication costs by storing data close to the users. But the system is likely to have inconsistent data if the same is kept in multiple locations.

Client/Server Computing

A client/server system is a distributed system with a server and one or more clients. The server is a powerful computer, usually a mainframe or a minicomputer. The clients are usually small computers: PCs or workstations. The server and the clients are interconnected using a network, normally a LAN. The server and the clients share tasks and processes. The server stores common programs and data used by several user systems. The clients request the server for data and programs. The server processes the requests and makes available the requested data and programs.

Client-server architecture enables the roles and responsibilities of a computer system to be distributed among a number of independent computers on a network. It also permits one or more computers on the network to be removed or replaced without other computers being affected by it.

In addition to the hardware, the Client/Server computing requires special software at front-end (client side) and back-end (server side). The friend-end software provides user interface, facilitates data manipulation and handles communication with server. The back-end software takes care of data acquisition and integrity, transaction management and data recovery in the event of system failure.

The client system usually manages the user interface portion of the application, validates the data entered and despatches requests to the server programs. The server machine fulfils the client request. It retrieves data, updates it and manages data integrity. It despatches responses to the service request from client machines.

Client/Server environment is different from a LAN environment. In a LAN environment the host transfers, on request, the entire program file or data file to the workstation for processing. This requires a lot of data traffic between the server and the workstations. In Client/Server environment the server processes the request and transfers the data or program requested by the client; it does not transfer the entire file. This reduces the data traffic on the network.

Network Computing

Network computing combines the advantages of centralised computing and distributed processing. It uses thin clients which are personal computers with much less power. They do not store data or programs. Programs and data are stored on centralised computers.

Per-to-Peer Networking

Peer-to-peer networking is an alternative to Client/Server for networking. In a peer-to-peer network, each workstation can communicate with any other workstation on the network without going through any specialised computer. It is useful when workstations can do their tasks independently and they do not need much data sharing with others on the network.

MODEM

The ordinary telephone lines transmit data in analog form. Computers are digital devices and use digital signals for data processing. Modems are used to connect digital computers with telephone lines. Modem at the originating computer modulates the digital signals and at the receiving computer demodulates analog signals. It converts digital signals into analog signals for transmission over telephone lines. At the other end of the channel, the modern converts the analog signals back into digital signals.

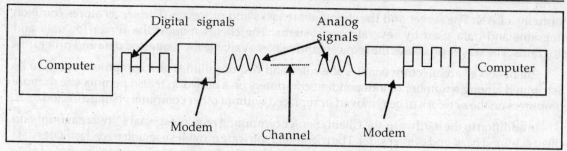

Fig. 20.4: Modem and its Working

Types of Modem

Internal modems: These are built on cards and these cards are fixed into a slot on the motherboard of the computer.

External modems: They are plugged into RS 232 or RS 232 C connectors.

Acoustic coupler modems: These are not direct modems; they require telephone handset as intermediary equipment.

Modems come in different speeds like 9.6 kbps, 33.6 kbps, etc. The modem speed should at least be equal to the bandwidth of the communication channel that sets the maximum size of data that can be sent at a time. If the modem speed is less than the bandwidth, modem will become a bottleneck in communication as it slows down the rate of data transfer.

ELECTRONIC COMMUNICATIONS

Technology has revolutionised communications in the recent times. Satellite infrastructure opened up new opportunities for communication in the 1960s. Information technology has significantly altered the ways of communications in the recent past. The Internet was a path breaking invention that changed commerce and communications beyond recognition. Wireless technology is now making waves by taking communications to remote and inaccessible locations. Thus, introduction of satellites, computers, mobile phones and blue tooth technology into communications represent some of the landmark events in the evolution of communications in the last few decades.

Satellite Communication

1960s marked the beginning of the space and satellite communications era. In 1962, the American telecommunications company, AT&T, launched the world's first commercial satellite, Telstar. Since then a large number of satellites were sent into space to facilitate telecommunications.

The satellite communication system consists of two main components: the satellite (the space segment) and the receiving stations (earth segment). The satellite consists of fuel system, the satellite and telemetry controls and the transponder. The transponder consists of a receiving antenna, broadband receiver and a frequency converter. The antenna picks up signals from the ground station. The broadband receiver is an input multiplexer and the frequency multiplexer is used to reroute the received signals through a high-powered amplifier for downlink. The ground station sends to, and receives signals from, the satellite segment.

The satellite reflects signals sent to it from earth stations. In case of a telecommunications satellite, the primary function is to receive signals sent from an earth station and send them down to another earth station that is located at a considerable distance from the first earth station.

Satellite data transmission systems use microwave systems. The microwave station broadcasts signals to the satellite, which retransmits the signals to another microwave station on earth. It is also possible for one satellite to receive the signals and retransmit them to another satellite to be sent to another microwave station on earth, beyond the range of the first satellite. Satellite data transmission is most economical and is particularly useful when microwave stations are separated by long distance or by ocean, etc. The use of satellite systems today includes traditional telephone communications, television broadcast services, cellular communications, marine communications, global positioning services and defence observation.

Modern communication is mostly real-time or close to real-time and it is heavily technology depended. Some of these are discussed below.

Electronic Communication

Electronic communication systems are one of the major application areas of office automation technology. Electronic communications cover a variety of electronic communication services such as electronic mail, voice mail and facsimile. The systems transmit and distribute text, voice and image data in electronic form over telecommunication networks. Electronic communication reduces the volume of paper communication in the form of memos, letters, circulars, reports and documents. It is much cheaper and quicker than traditional forms of communication.

E-Mail

Electronic mail (E-mail) is a communication facility to send documents over a network to the intended recipient(s). E-mail is the most commonly available service on any network. It is also one of the least expensive communication network services. This communication system requires the sender and the receiver of the message to have access to a network for communication. This can be done in three ways. The first is to set up a private network linking the workstations involved in communication. The second is to subscribe to an e-mail service provider who maintains the network. The third is to have the Internet connectivity.

The e-mail communication is incredibly simple. A person with a PC and a modem to connect to the network can communicate with the others so connected to the network. The message can be prepared and sent instantly. The other person finds the e-mail when he checks his mailbox and may reply to the message in the same way. The message sent is private and other unintended persons cannot read it.

Each user of e-mail service has a user ID serving as e-mail address and a password to access e-mail box. First thing to do is to get online using modem and communication software. The user needs to have access to an email service provider. It may be an Internet Service Provider. But most non-business users register with a web based e-mail service like Yahoo or Gmail. On registering with such e-mail service each user is allotted a pair of e-mail-id and password and a mailbox to store e-mail messages. The e-mail system requires the user to login every time with the e-mail-id and the password allotted to him or her to access the mailbox.

The mailbox is simply a file into which the e-mail system stores electronic documents. All incoming e-mail messages are stored in the mailbox of the particular user. The user can check his or her mailbox for messages any time convenient to him or her. If the mailbox, usually the inbox, has a message from his contacts, the user opens it and reads it. He can also reply to it by typing his message and clicking 'Send' button. The user can also prepare his message in the form of a document using a word processor and save it on the disk. The saved document can be attached to the e-mail to be sent to a contact. Sending fresh message to any contact requires to type in his or her e-mail address (e-mail-id such as mohan22@hotmail.com) of the recipient and the subject (such as 'Contract renewal') before clicking 'Send' button.

Through e-mail, documents are prepared and sent electronically. The recipient need not be present at the other end to send the message. The message gets stored in the electronic mailbox of the addressee. The recipient can open the mailbox whenever he is free and he can read or print the message.

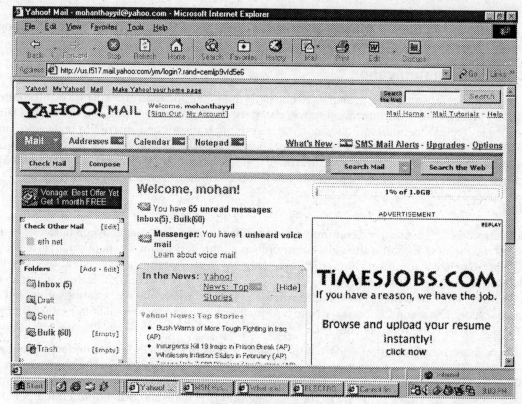

Fig. 20.5: Mailbox

E-mail is a document communication facility. To ensure that the recipient also understands the emotions as well, a set of special symbols is used to convey some non-verbal signals. A few of such symbols are given below.

Symbol Emotion

:- Humour

:) Smile

:(Frown

:/) Not funny

p- Private

:* Kiss

(: - (Very sad

E-mail is the transmission of information electronically from terminal to terminal. The basic facilities in e-mail include message creation, message transfer and post delivery service. The e-mail service may be traditional mainframe based or minicomputer based or LAN based system with PCs to access from.

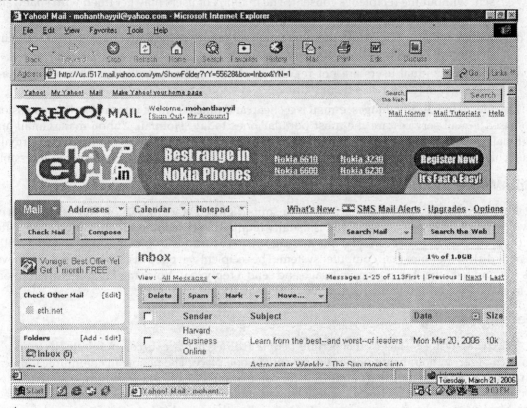

Fig. 20.6: Messages in the E-mail Inbox

Advantages of E-mail

(i) Messages can be prepared and sent any time convenient for the sender.

(ii) Message can be received at the convenience of the recipient.

(iii) The transmission takes place instantly and the message gets stored in the mailbox of the recipient.

(iv) The system can confirm delivery of message.

(v) Copies of message can be sent to multiple recipients,

(vi) It reduces paper work.

(vii) User can be alerted through SMS (short messaging service) over mobile phone about the arrival of an email message from a contact.

Disadvantages

(i)   All e-mail users must subscribe to e-mail service. They must also have access to the Internet through their own computer, modem and telephone or through an Internet cafe.

(ii) Poor telecommunication affects the quality of message transmitted.

(iii) Spamming is an irritant to e-mail users. Spamming is unsolicited commercial e-mail. It is sent without the recipient's consent. The mailbox of users may get filled with spam, and messages from one's usual contacts may not be stored for want of storage space.

(iv) If there is disruption in telecommunications or failure of computer hardware or software, the user may not be able to access his mailbox.

(v)   Most individual users are not regular in checking their mailboxes. Hence, important messages may not reach them in time.

Despite all the disadvantages, e-mail is a cheap and quick form of information transmission. Web-based e-mail services are the most popular ones today. Hotmail, Yahoo mail, Gmail and Rediffmail, are very popular among Indian Internet users. These web based e-mail services normally do not charge for e-mail service. They can be used from any location where Internet is accessible.

Voice Mail

E-mail exchanges text data. Voice mail transmits digitised voice messages. The sender dials up the voice mail service organisation and is usually required to type in his identification code. After identity is checked, the user can send this message in voice form. The voice message is stored on the magnetic disk of the voice mail computer system. The recipient can open his voice mailbox whenever he is free and hear the stored voice message and send a reply to it. Voice mail requires microphone and speakers in addition to the requirements for e-mail.

Teleconferencing

Teleconferencing is a facility that permits people in different places to communicate electronically with each other without being physically present at one place. The people in communication can be in different offices in the same building, in the same country or anywhere on the globe. The people at different locations are connected with a television link that enables them to see and hear each other. More advanced systems use computer network with the facility to transmit audio and motion video for teleconferencing.

Video Conferencing

Video conferencing is a facility to interact with people without all of them being physically present at one place. Each participant in the conference may be in different places but electronically they interact with each other. This requires real time transmission of communications between the places where the participants are stationed. Companies engage in video conferencing to monitor progress of projects, review of major assignments, etc. This avoids travel and saves a lot of time for each executive involved in the video conferencing. But, video conferencing requires specially equipped studios for each participant to join in the conference. Alternatively, video conferencing can be done with a PC, video camera and broadband Internet connectivity.

Communication for Collaboration

Many tasks these days are organised into team assignments. The members of the team may belong to distant places. People working in teams, but geographically dispersed, will have to keep in touch with other members of the team on a regular basis. Such teams are called virtual teams. The virtual team members need to collaborate with other members for completion of the joint task. For example, a software development project may involve team members from many countries. They will work on the software project from their respective offices in their countries. But, they will have to communicate with each other regularly without travelling from their offices. Collaboration tools allow people in different geographic locations to effectively communicate, in real-time, with each other. Collaboration tools include online whiteboards, email, web-based file and document sharing, discussion groups and bulletin boards, chat and instant messaging, etc.

Online Whiteboards

Whiteboard allows multiple users to view a shared screen over the Internet. Any of the team members can draw or mark or annotate an image on the shared screen. Other members can view instantaneously the changes made to the screen. Teams can, thus, use the whiteboard to quickly share ideas and information without using email or fax. Audio conferencing can also be combined with whiteboards for enhancing communications.

E-mail for Collaboration

E-mail is an effective tool for collaboration. Each member of the collaborating team sends e-mail message to others in the team. The information about the e-mail can be passed to the other members through mobile phone alerts. The other members may respond to the e-mail. Files can also be attached to the messages.

Web-based File and Document Sharing

The web-based file sharing applications allow members of the collaborating team to exchange files and documents. The members can download from or upload files to any website.

Discussion Groups and Bulletin Boards

Bulletin boards over the Internet allow members of a team to post information to other group members. They read the information and give their comment about it. This facilitates exchange of information among project team members.

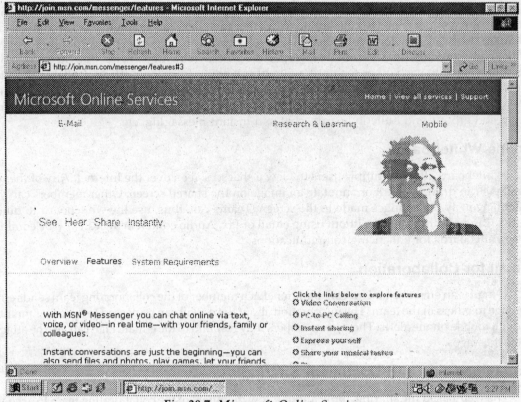

Fig. 20.7: Microsoft Online Services

Chat and Instant Messaging

Chat and Instant Messaging tools allow real-time communication of information. The team members can chat without using email or telephone. Multiple members can join chat sessions. Popular portals like Yahoo.com and MSN.com have chat and instant messaging facilities.

GroupWare

GroupWare is commonly understood as any application that is networked and allows users to share data. It is defined as specialised computer aids that are designed for the use of collaborative work groups. It includes both group processes and the software that supports collaboration between workgroups in organisations. A complete GroupWare infrastructure has three dimensions: communication (exchanging mail, etc.), collaboration (sharing information and building shared understanding) and co-ordination (delegating tasks, sequential sign-offs, etc.)

GroupWare software systems include Lotus Notes (It is essentially a messaging system. It also supports an application development environment and a document database), Collabra Share (It is a PC based document sharing system that looks a lot like Windows file manager), and NCSA Collage (It is a GroupWare system for interactive analysis of scientific data) among others.

The application sharing can be group aware or group unaware. In a group aware application, a group of users simultaneously interact with one or more program executions, the result of which they can all see. Such applications accept inputs from multiple sources. The group aware programs may run in two alternative ways: First, it may run on a single machine accepting inputs from multiple sources and the second, it may run with a copy of the application on each machine in the GroupWare environment with only relevant commands sent to a site.

Sketchpads or Whiteboards are an important Group aware application. The system provides the users with a shared whiteboard for different users to write or draw in different colour. A user can use his area on the board for drawing or writing which the other users can see simultaneously. Examples of such systems are ShowMe Whiteboard, NCSA Collage and XTV.

Group unaware applications do not allow multiple users to be active at a time.

Conclusion

Networks are an essential part of modern information systems and their importance is fast growing. Communication networks link computer facilities across offices and plants. This makes possible quicker and more economic forms of communication, sharing of processing tasks, sharing of expensive hardware and software resources etc. They also open up new dimensions for business competition. Internet, Intranets and extranets have opened up great opportunities for all forms of communication.

Modern communication tools include mobile devices, email, teleconferencing, video conferencing, instant messaging, Internet based document sharing, etc. These modes of communications are not only cost effective; but also rich and highly convenient. The use of multimedia in communications makes it more attractive and lively. Today, with the Internet spanning across the globe, it is a connected world we are living in. The current communications technologies enable people to stay connected anywhere, anytime.

QUESTIONS

1. What is communication network? What are the types of network?
2. What is LAN? What are the components of LAN?
3. What is electronic communication? What are the types of electronic communication?
4. What is LAN topology? Explain the popular LAN topologies.
5. Explain the meaning and purpose of communication protocols.
6. What is e-mail? What are the advantages of e-mail?
7. What is teleconferencing?
8. Describe the process of sending and receiving e-mail communication.
9. What is collaboration? What are the tools for collaboration?

Case 20.1: NSE: Technology Driven Stock Exchange

The National Stock Exchange of India Limited was set up 1992 with a mandate from the Government of India to establish a stock exchange to enable automated trading of debt/capital market instruments throughout India. By virtue of its mandate, NSE was required to be of national character enabling its members to be located anywhere in the country. In the long run this will result in the creation of a single unified national market linking all regions of our country even with small clusters of investor population. NSE was recognized as a stock exchange in 1993 and it started security trading operations in Debt market in June 1994, and equity market in Nov., 1994. NSE started derivative trading in Index Futures in June 2000 and Index Options in 2001. Internet trading was also introduced in 2000. NSE became the largest stock exchange in India in 1995 and it is one of the largest stock exchanges in the world today.

NSE India was instrumental in bringing about revolutionary changes in Indian capital market and financial sector. It set up the first Indian electronic clearing corporation in 1995, (NSCCL) depository (NSDL) in 1996, etc. It introduced currency futures in 2008 and Interest Rate Futures in August 2009.

Automated Trading System

NSE's approach towards the organisation of trading is based on two ideas: the use of automated order-matching, and the use of satellite communication technology to allow full access to the nationwide market from locations all over the country. The NSE IT set-up is the largest by any company in India. It uses satellite communication technology to energise participation from around 320 cities spread all over the country. In the recent past, capacity enhancement measures were taken up in regard to the trading systems so as to effectively meet the requirements of increased users and associated trading loads. With upgradation of trading hardware, NSE can handle up to 6 million trades per day in Capital Market segment. In order to capitalise on in-house expertise in technology, NSE set up a separate company, NSE.IT, in October 1999. This is expected to provide a platform for taking up new IT assignments both within and outside India and attaining global exposure.

NEAT is a state-of-the-art client server based application. At the server end, all trading information is stored in an in-memory database to achieve minimum response time and maximum system availability for users. The trading server software runs on a fault tolerant STRATUS main frame computer while the client software runs under Windows on PCs.

The telecommunications network uses X.25 protocol and is the backbone of the automated trading system. Each trading member trades on the NSE with other members through a PC located in the trading member's office, anywhere in India. The trading members on the various market segments such as CM/F&O, WDM are linked to the central computer at the NSE through dedicated 64Kbps leased lines and VSAT terminals. The Exchange uses powerful RISC -based UNIX servers, procured from Digital and HP for the back office processing. The latest software platforms like ORACLE 7 RDBMS, GUPTA - SQL/ORACLE FORMS 4.5 Front - Ends, etc., have been used for the Exchange applications. The Exchange currently manages its data centre operations, system and database administration, design and development of in-house systems and design and implementation of telecommunication solutions.

NSE is one of the largest interactive VSAT-based stock exchanges in the world. Today it supports more than 3000 VSATs. The NSE- network is the largest private wide area network in the country and the first extended C- Band VSAT network in the world. Currently more than 9000 users are trading on the real time-online NSE application. There are over 15 large computer systems which include non-stop fault-tolerant computers and high end UNIX servers, operational under one roof to support the NSE applications. This coupled with the nation wide VSAT network makes NSE the country's largest Information Technology user.

In an ongoing effort to improve NSE's infrastructure, a corporate network has been implemented, connecting all the offices at Mumbai, Delhi, Kolkata and Chennai. This corporate network enables speedy inter-office communications and data and voice connectivity between offices.

In keeping with the current trend, NSE has gone online on the Internet. Apart from having a 2mbps link to VSNL and own domain for internal browsing and e-mail purposes, it has set up its own Website. Currently, NSE is displaying its live stock quotes on the website (www.nseindia.com) which are updated online.

NSE's VSAT network has several advance features:

- A network availability in excess of 99.9%.
- A uniform response time of less than 2 seconds for members situated across the country, made possible by a unique time and frequency satellite access scheme that facilitates efficient use of satellite bandwidth.
- Remote communications equipment — VSATs — to be used at the member locations, were made affordable to the members by shifting all the design complexities to the hub location and keeping the VSATs simple and economical.
- Extremely high security provision by built-in measures against jamming, interference and illegal access.
- Expandability of the exchange, allowed for by design of the central hub in a modular fashion.
- Network partitioning, allowing money market and capital market operations to function independently by the use of advanced network management features.
- Ability to handle high peak-loads through the use of data flow control techniques.

Business applications supported by NSE's VSAT network are:

- Equity Market
- Wholesale Debt Market
- Clearing and Settlement System
- National Security Depository System
- Reports/Circulars/Messages downloads, etc.

Overview of NSE's IT Set-up

NSE trading system software named NEAT (National Exchange for Automated Trading) is a state-of-the-art client server application. At the server end, all trading information is stored in an in-memory database to achieve minimum response time and maximum system availability for users. The trading server software runs on a fault tolerant STRATUS main frame computer while, the client software runs under Windows on PCs.

NEAT is a fully automated screen-based trading system which adopts the principle of an order driven market and allows trading members to trade from their offices through a communication network. The telecommunications network is the backbone of the automated trading system. Each trading member trades on NSE with other members through a computer located at the trading member's office, anywhere in India. The computers of a few trading members are linked to the central computer at NSE through dedicated high speed (64 Kbps) lines. These leased lines are multiplexed using dedicated 2 Mbs, optical fibre links.

The Exchange uses powerful RISC-based Digital and HP UNIX servers, for the back office processing. These systems are clustered and connected on HOT-STANDBY mode for high availability. The latest software platforms like ORACLE 7/SQL SERVER, RDBMS, GUPTA-SQL/ORACLE FORMS 4.5 Front-Ends, are used for the exchange applications. The 20 large computer systems in NSEIL include non stop fault tolerant computers and high end UNIX servers, connected through UTP LAN having over 800 PC nodes and a large number of NT and SUN Unix servers, all operational to support NSE applications. This coupled with the nation wide VSAT network makes NSE the country's largest Information Technology user.

National clearing and settlement system has been implemented to support nationwide clearing operations from four regions. NSE has developed in-house an Online Position Monitoring System as a part of its surveillance system. The system provides an online real-time information on trade by trade member's position. The system generates alerts at 3 levels: First warning is displayed on the member's trading workstation on reaching a level of 80% of his position limit. The Second warning is displayed on reaching 90% level and if the member still continues to build the position further, his trading workstation is automatically disconnected by the system on reaching 100% position limit. NSE is the only exchange in the world having such system. Additionally, the website provides a number of dynamic interactive applications; such as personal portfolio management.

NSE implemented an Enterprise-wide Data Warehouse system to facilitate its own data management analysis and strengthen decision support systems. This Data Warehouse would provide the information infrastructure which will enable NSE to adapt to its dynamic business environment. Unlike a normal On Line Transaction Processing (OLTP) system, a Data Warehouse will house clean, static, unified data pool, taking periodically data feeds from multiple operational systems which will provide On-Line Analytical Processing (OLAP) capability and will act as a vital Decision Support System.

The Exchange runs a help desk for 12 hours on each working day. This has been successful in addressing member problems quickly. Problems have ranged from how to start the computer to complex requirements for regulations. Most problems are addressed immediately and very few problems are carried over beyond a day. The Exchange has installed an Interactive Voice Response (IVR) system to automate the Help Desk operation. Additionally, it provides facilities like fax on-demand, voice mail, audio text information etc. For critical problems, on-site service is also offered by NSE.

The Exchange has been electronically delivering to all members daily reports regarding trades, obligatic... etc. This allows to have a direct interface to their computerised back office systems. The Exchange has a computerised 'Bulletin Board Services' (BBS) for distributing information electronically to its members and newsvendors.

Questions:

1. BSE was set up in 1875 and NSE in 1992. How could NSE beat BSE so easily?
2. How did the information technology infrastructure help NSE India in reaching out nationwide?
3. What benefits NSE India had because of its lead in information technology use?
4. How did NSE India influence Indian financial sector? What effects its innovations in securities market had on the financial services industry?
5. NSE India has dominant position in securities market in India. In derivative segment, NSE has a virtual monopoly in India and in cash segment its market share is above 60%. What do you attribute this achievement of NIS India to?

21
CHAPTER

The Internet

INTRODUCTION

The Internet is indeed one of the most marvellous inventions in the history of human beings. It is actually a giant global network of networks. The word 'Internet' was coined by combining 'interconnection' and 'network'. The Internet is, in fact, an amorphous collection of networks and millions of computers across the globe. It all started with the Advanced Research Project Network (ARPANET) set up by the Defence Department of the United States. It wanted to create a large computer network for military communication with no controlling centre. ARPANET was used primarily by research institutions until the mid-1980s when its use was widened. By 1990 the network came to be known as Internet and since then its growth has been phenomenal.

The Internet has changed the entire communication and business paradigm. Though its growth was limited in the first two decades from the early seventies, it grew astronomically in the 1990s. It is sweeping the entire world by its sheer reach and ease of use. Millions of host computers and users form the global Internet community opening opportunities unheard of before. The Internet technology has changed the way people communicated, and the way companies did business, the way they distributed products, the way they collected payments and the way they served customers, Certainly, the Internet has caused a paradigm shift and has a long-term impact on society in general and the business in particular. The business was cautious in its approach to the Internet in the early1990s. But by the second half of 1990s, the Internet technology and its potential were integrated with the overall business strategy of most business firms.

The Internet is made up of three kinds of networks[1].

- High speed backbone networks such as the supercomputers at San Diego, Cornell, Pittsburgh and Illinois
- Mid-level networks such as those at universities and companies, and,
- Small networks connected to the Internet such as individual LANs, and computers at companies and other organisations.

The computers, whether networked or not, having Internet connectivity vary widely in hardware and software resources. The interconnection of these networks and computers resulted into a gigantic network, which uses common communication protocol – Transmission Control Protocol/Internet Protocol (TCP/IP). Every form of communication, like telephone, radio and print, reshaped itself to migrate to the Internet. So, the new forms of communication like voice over Internet protocol, chatting, blogging, instant messaging, and social networking are increasingly becoming popular on the Internet.

HISTORY OF THE INTERNET

In the aftermath of the launch of Sputnik by the USSR, the US Defence Department set up Advanced Research Projects Agency (ARPA), later renamed as Defence Advanced Research Projects Agency (DARPA), to establish superiority in military technology. ARPA sponsored a study on computer networking for communication that cannot be disrupted by the destruction of a few installations in enemy action. The first ARPANET was formed by networking four computers at universities of California Los Angeles, Stanford Research Institute, University of Utah and University of California, Santa Barbara in 1969.

One of the goals of the ARPANET was research on distributed computer systems as the US military wanted to develop a failure tolerant computer network for communication. The purpose was to have a communication infrastructure without a central system so that even if a part of the system breaks down or is destroyed by enemy action, rest of the communication system should not be disturbed. A large number of universities and research institutions joined the network by connecting their computers to ARPANET in the early 1970s.

The TCP/IP protocols were developed in the mid 1970s by Vinton Cerf of Stanford University and Robert Kahn of BBN (between 1973 and 1978) and since 1983 they became the standard protocols for network communication. In the same year the US government spun off MILNET from ARPANET. By 1984, over 1,000 hosts formed part of the Internet.

Meanwhile the Xerox Corporation developed Ethernet technology for networking computers and around this time TCP/IP protocols were built into the UNIX operating systems. TCP/IP over Ethernet became a common way for workstations to connect to one another[2]. PCs with add-on Ethernet cards and TCP/IP software made them to talk to UNIX systems. By the middle of 1980s, TCP/IP protocols were used for LANs and WANs and this period marked the beginning of a period of explosive growth of the Internet.

Internet Protocols Suite

There are a large number of Internet related protocols. Some of the important Internet protocols are TCP/IP, HTTP, HTML, SMTP and FTP. Of them the two most popular protocols are TCP and IP.

TCP/IP: The Transmission Control Protocol/Internet Protocol and related protocols are the basic Internet technology which has paved the way for fast growth in Internet use. TCP/IP is a collection of protocols developed in the mid 1970s to facilitate communication over a packet-switched network with dissimilar computers. This set of protocols permits any computer to communicate with any other computer regardless of the platform. TCP is a transport layer related protocol. It breaks a large message into a number of small packets or datagrams. Each packet is assigned a sequence number, source address and destination address in addition to error control information. The packets are reassembled at the other end in the order of the sequence number to recreate the full message. Internet Protocol is a network-layer protocol and is a very important protocol. It enables internetworking. It contains some addressing and control information for routing of messages, among others. It gives the physical address of the computer on the Net. Every computer forming the network has a unique IP address and it helps in routing the message on its way to its destination. In simple words, IP takes care of transporting the packet to destination.

HTML: The Hyper Text Markup Language defines how text, images and sound are delivered to users. HTML is basically a tag language. The tags help in inserting files, images, voice, forms, etc., into documents. It is used to create static web pages or documents for web publishing.

```
<!doctype html>
<html>
<head>
<title>Hi</title>
</head>
<body>
<p>Hi Everyone</p>
</body>
</html>
```

(The text between <html> and </html> describes the web page, and the text between <body> and </body> is the visible page content except for the markup text '<title>Hi</title>' -which is the browser tab title.)

HTTP: The Hyper Text Transfer Protocol decides how HTML documents are to be served via the Internet. It works on the client/server principle. It allows client computers to connect with web servers or other computers and request for service: HTTP request specifies the kind of service the client needs and tells the server what action is to be taken.

SMTP: Simple Mail Transfer Protocol enables the basic text based message communication between users.

Other support protocols include Telnet, File Transfer Protocol, Common Gateway Interface, etc.

Administration of the Internet

Internet is not controlled by anybody. National Science Foundation, being instrumental for the creation of Internet has greater influence on Internet's use. It is responsible for maintaining the Internet backbone which is a series of cables connecting hardware pieces for high speed data communication. Yet, some international bodies like Internet Engineering Task Force (IETF), Internet Resource Task Force (IRTF) and Internet Architecture Board (IAB) share responsibility for certain technical aspects of Internet like maintaining protocols, etc.

The ultimate authority on technical matters concerning the Internet rests with the Internet Society. It monitors the growth of the Net and deals with the social, political and technical issues of the use of the Internet.

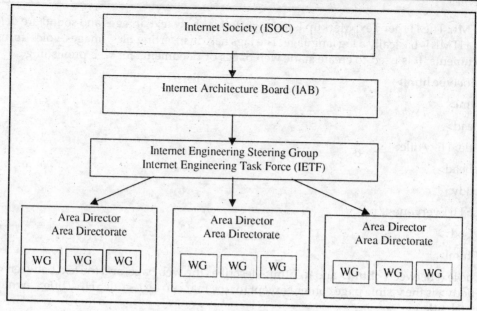

Fig 21.1: Internet Governance hierarchy

(*Source:* Adapted from Ravi Kalkota and Andrew B. Whinston, *Frontiers of E-Commerce*, Addison-Wesley, New Delhi, 1999, p 121.)

Growth of the Internet

The setting up in the mid 1980s of the National Science Foundation Network (NSFNET) by connecting five supercomputers and providing access to these supercomputer data centres was a landmark event in the history of the Internet. The growth in the number of Internet hosts is phenomenal since the middle of 1980s. Table 21.1 lists landmark events in the history of the Internet. The Internet is the result of collaborative research among defence department, research institutions and universities. The landmark events in the history of the Internet are given in Table 21.1.

Table 21.1: Landmarks in the History of the Internet

Year	Event
1957	ARPA was formed
1969	ARPANET was commissioned for research into computer networking
1971	E-mail and e-mail utility became available
1973	First international connections to ARPANET. University College of London and Royal Radar Establishment, Norway.
1974	Telnet
1975	Operational management of the Internet transferred to DCA (DISA).
1979	USENET; ARPA established the Internet Configuration Control Board (ICCB).
1982	TCP/IP suite declared as standard of Department of Defence.
1983	MILNET separated from ARPANET.
1984	Domain Name System introduced; number of hosts exceeds 1,000.
1985	Domain name registration system introduced

1986	NSFNET was established; IETF and IRTF came into existence under the IAB.
1988	Internet Relay Chat developed.
1989	Number of hosts exceeds 1,00,000.
1990	ARPANET ceases to exist; Dial up Internet connections by ISPs
1991	WAIS, Gopher and World Wide Web
1992	Internet Society is chartered; Number of hosts breaks 1,000,000 Veronica released
1993	Business and media take note of the Internet; Mosaic takes the Internet by storm. WWW proliferates, grew by 341,634% a year; Gopher grew by 997%.
1994	ARPANET/Internet celebrates 25th anniversary; shopping malls on the Internet.
1995	NSFNET reverts back to research network. Main US back bone traffic re-routed through interconnected network providers. Search engines developed.
1996	Government restrictions on the Internet use around the world.

Source: http://www.Isoc.org/zakon/Internet/History/HIT.htmal

Services Available on the Internet

The following are the services available on the Internet.

- World Wide Web
- Electronic Mail
- News groups
- FTP
- Telnet
- Internet Relay Chat

The services are briefly detailed in the following section.

WORLD WIDE WEB (WWW)

One of the ways of accessing information on the Internet is through the World Wide Web (WWW or the Web in short). The Web had its origin in 1989 at the European Centre for Particle Physics (CERN), Geneva. It was the brainchild of Tim Berners-Lee. Berners-Lee conceived it as a way of publishing hyperlinked scientific documents over the Internet. The concept allows users to follow ideas from one document to another irrespective of where the documents are stored. The links connect documents on one computer to documents on the same computer or other computers in the same location or in distant locations. The concept was extremely useful in collating data present in scattered locations.

Meanwhile IBM was working on a concept similar to the one Berners-Lee was working on and that was later standardised by the International Organisation for Standardisation (ISO) as the Hypertext Markup Language (HTML). This language identifies each element in a document like heading, addresses, paragraphs, body text, etc., with mark up code or tags.

The Web is basically a bunch of resources linked together with the hypertext pointers that allows users to move from one resource to another on the Net. Each clickable item that connects the user to more information is a link. All these links put together is called the Web. The Internet uses client/server technology. Any computer on the Internet that uses Hyper Text Transport Protocol is called a server and the computer that requests to it for a service is called a client. The client computer runs browser software for requesting, receiving and presenting information to users.

The Web was restricted mostly to scientific community until the arrival of Web browsers. The Web caught the imagination of business and common user communities once the web browsers became available. The business firms started putting up websites to provide information about the firm and its products, etc., to users.

A Uniform Resource Locator (URL) that gives the type of data available and its address identifies each Web site. The URLs are usually in the form http://www.microsoft.com where the term http refers to HyperText Transfer Protocol, the Web's native format. The graphical Web browsers like Netscape and Internet Explorer give the Web a real touch of class.

E-MAIL: E-mail is the earliest and the most popular Internet tool. It began with developers exchanging notes over the ARPANET in the early 1970s. E-mail systems were later developed for mainframe platforms and local area networks. E-mail service providers sprang up offering value added services. This service is the most widely used on the Internet today and the communication is quicker and more convenient than any other form of communication. It is reliable and identifies the sender of the message. It works similar to the paper mail but everything is electronic here. It works on a store and forward model. The sender can send message at his convenience. Delivery occurs immediately if the path to the destination is clear. It is stored in the inbox of the recipient. The recipient can open the mailbox and read it at his convenience. Most e-mail packages have utilities to reply to the message, forward the message to others, to store addresses, to send a message to multiple destinations etc.

An Internet e-mail has two parts: the message header and the message body. The header information is structured into fields like as From, TO, CC, Subject, Date, etc. The body holds the content as unstructured text.

At the e-mail originating and destination points, e-mail programs called user agents help the users in typing, editing, addressing, or viewing messages. The e-mail package in turn depends on one or more message transfer agents (again programs) to move the mail across networks from the source to its destination. These message transfer agents co-operate in transporting the message over the Internet to deliver it to the addressees.

When a user composes and sends a message over the Internet, an email server on the access provider's network wraps up the message in an electronic envelope with onward and return addresses and sends it out. The sender's computer may not have direct connection with the recipient computer. So, the message hops from network to network and is finally relayed to the ultimate destination. At each stop, the message is temporarily stored on the intermediate computers and the best way to route the message is figured out. The network gateway at the receiving end assembles the message for storing in the mailbox of the recipient.

Emails can carry attachments now. Any type content and any number of file attachment is possible now. But, web-based e-mail service providers, like Yahoo and Hotmail, usually limit the number of attachments and the size of such attached files. Emails carried only text content earlier. It was a major limitation. File attachment is a solution to the earlier text only limitation of the email content.

Emailing Process: The e-mail sender composes message using a mail software, called client. He may attach text, audio, video or other files also to the message

- TCP divides the message into packets and adds packet handling information
- Packets are sent to mail server of the sender's ISP or internal network

The e-mail address follows certain rules and it has four parts: user, @, provider and domain. Thus, in mohanthyyil@yahoo.com, mohanthayyil is the user, yahoo is the provider and .com is the domain. Yet, modern email addresses vary from this old email address format.

The ISP mail server converts the domain name of the recipient's mail address into IP address

The Internet routers read the IP address on each packet and relay it to the destination by the most efficient path.

The packets may travel along different routes and reach the destination mail server.

The desination mail server assembles the packets in their original order and stores the message in the recipient's mailbox.

The recipient access the mailbox and the client software dispays the message on opening the message.

As they are becoming more and more popular, the risk is also growing. Spamming, spoofing, e-mail worms and email bombing (sending too many messages to target address to make it unusable) are growing concerns for e-mail users. There is possibility of email privacy being compromised at times. It is because the e-mail message is unencrypted and it has to be exchanged between many intermediary servers and the ISPs store the messages on their mail servers and retain them there for months. The header information can identify the message sender, recipient and the type of content.

E-mail fatigue or email bankruptcy is a term coined to describe the state of an email service user who falls behind in checking his messages and answering them. It may happen when he gets too many e-mails to read resulting in over load or when most of them do not have any relevance for him.

TELNET

Telnet is a remote login facility. It allows a user with a microcomputer or a terminal to get connected to a powerful host far away and use its processing capacity. The user's PC becomes a terminal of the host telnetted to and can do processing on the Net. It makes the user believe that the computer he is currently working on is directly connected to the host computer or the server he is telnetted to. The low Internet charges have made telnet a cheap alternative for computing. Telnet requires opening account on host systems by the users.

FILE TRANSFER PROTOCOL (FTP)

FTP is part of TCP/IP protocol suite. It works on client/server principle. It is used to transfer files between computers. Such file transfer access on FTP servers requires the user to have accounts with host computers on the Net. But there are hundreds of anonymous ftp servers from which the user can download files without opening accounts. These anonymous ftp sites accept 'anonymous' as login ID and by convention the user's e-mail address is entered as password.

INTERNET RELAY CHAT (IRC)

IRC is a facility for fascinating discussions. It is basically a chat program that allows several users spread all over the globe to chat simultaneously. All the people using IRC are split up into channels representing common topics.

USENET

Usenet is a worldwide discussion medium. It is also referred to as Network News or Netnews. Millions of users read Usenet articles daily and post their views. It is more like a huge bulletin board service with hundreds of message areas or news groups. The news groups in the Usenet are organised hierarchically with categories, groups and subgroups. For example, the 'sci' category includes several subgroups such as Mathematics and Physics. The Physics subgroup again has a number of subgroups.

Examples of Usenet News Groups

alt.bbs.internet	Link of Internet accessible bulletin boards
alt.Internet.access.wanted	Internet access options by location
comp.os.ms-windows.misc	Microsoft Windows
sci.space.news	NASA and other space news
soc.culture.indian	Culture of India.

CORE FEATURES OF THE INTERNET

The Internet has a set of charactreistics that gave it the potential to deliver extra value for the business. Some of these are:

Simplicity of Use: The Web browser software is comparatively easy to learn and simple to use. It can operate on a wide range of operating system platforms and can access any mainstream application like SAP and Oracle. The flexibility of the Web combined with the simplicity of the browser software has resulted in reduced staff training costs, lower development costs and an increase in the range of users who can have access to the organisation.

Breadth of Access: The Internet is a global network like the telephone network. Its access is not conditioned by geographic boundaries. Unlike the telephone network, the cost involved in global connection is not related to the distance involved. No other communication medium has had access to such a large audience and range of people which increases the ability to leverage the value of information to a scale that has never before been possible.

Synergy with other Media: Apart from using the existing telecommunication technology, it supports or complements other media. Internet services have demonstrated a high degree of synergy with other media as can be seen from the following examples:

- Book, magazine and newspaper publishers have used the Web to supplement and extend their written products.
- Publishers of CD-ROMs have used the Web to maintain the currency of the information they can deliver. Microsoft's encyclopaedia CD-ROM, Encarta, allows seamless interface to information accessed from the company's Web site.
- Publishers of software and games now deliver their products directly over the Internet.
- Entertainment companies regularly provide over the Internet extracts of their films and music recordings to promote the real products.

Low relative cost: The costs involved in conducting a process using Internet technology are less than those involving other methods. The Internet access requires telephone line for most individual users. The pricing of telephone service is one which is independent of distance. The charge for the usage of telecommunication line is based on local charge rate irrespective of what is sent over the line or how distant the recipient is.

Extension of existing IT resources: Resource sharing was underlying rationale for the development of the Internet. It allows the IT resources to be shared by multiple users in organisations and also with others related to the organisation such as trading partners.

Flexibility of Communications: The Web browsers greatly extend the ways in which individuals can communicate. They support text, voice and multimedia formats and can provide immediate access to shared information. These facilities are available for intra-company communications as well as those between individuals in separate organisations.

Security: Security has been a major issue in Internet as any security breach can cause financial loss, leak of sensitive information, etc. Standards for secure electronic transactions have been developed and reasonable security is in place now for all kinds of transactions.

Speed and Availability: The transmission speed is very low and it takes a bit too long for downloading files. However, compared to other means of communication, it is indeed fast. It also provides a wide range of communications services that are inexpensive and relatively easy to access for millions of users through a standard set of protocols.

Social networking medium: The Internet has become a new way of social interaction. Social networking sites like Facebook, Twitter and MySpace are very popular among Net users globally. These sites offer great many features to users like publishing document and personal album, connecting with friends, relatives, school mates, real-time chatting, messaging, etc. YouTube is another great website which allows users to upload, and also view, videos. The site has hundreds of videos on various subjects for users to view free of cost. It attracts users in large numbers to the Internet.

INTERNET BACKBONES

These are like the spines of the Internet that connect the individual and organisational links of the Internet. It is made up of telephone circuits that connect the routers together. All users of the network share the circuit. Internet Service Providers (ISPs) hire telephone lines from telephone companies and maintain large network backbones. These backbones vary in their bandwidth. Small network backbones have the bandwidth in kilobits per second (14.4 KBPS to 56 KBPS) whereas large network backbones have bandwidth in many megabits (1.544 MBPS or more). Since the Internet is a network of networks, the transmitted data can take different routes through different network backbones on its way to its destination. The speed of transmission, therefore, depends on the path chosen to its destination. If a network backbone is congested, the data transmission along that path will be delayed.

Packet Switching

The Internet uses the same packet switching technology that the telephone and satellite carriers employ for data transmission. The computers in the network are connected physically with cables or through satellite channels or with wireless technology. The computers on the network serve as conduit for data traffic. Messages are broken into small packets. Each packet has source address, destination address and a serial number. Each node that receives the packet routes it to another node closer to its destination. They retain packets addressed to them and pass on those addressed to other computers on the Net. On receipt of the data packets, the receiving computer assembles the packets in the right sequence and recreates the original file and stores it at appropriate locations.

The Internet and the Web

The Internet and the Web are not identical. Internet is a global system for data communications with huge hardware and software infrastructure backing it. It provides connectivity among computers worldwide. The World Wide Web is one of the services available on the Internet. The Web is a collection of documents and other resources linked together by hypertext and identified by URLs.

Accessing the Internet

The Internet can be accessed in many ways. For home users, dial-up, cable broadband, landline broadband, Wi-Fi, satellite and 3G or 4G cell phones are means of access to the Net. Internet Cafes and Wi-Fi Cafes provide access to individual users at a charge. Public place access points are available at hotels, airports, railway stations, bus stations etc. at a cost or free. They are used for diverse purposes like ticket booking, email communications, online banking and e-payment etc. Cell phones can connect to the Net via cellular phone network, and it truly makes the Internet mobile.

Domain Name

Domain name (often reduced to domains) gives unique identity to a website. It is an identification label that defines a realm of administrative autonomy to the registrant (domain owner) on the internet. Individual Internet host computers use domain names to identify hosts. The domain name serves another important objective. It provides easily recognisable and memorisable names to numerically addressed Internet resources which are hard to remember. A domain name may have multiple IP addresses if the site needs to build redundancy as it might attract large traffic. Domain name must comply with the rules and procedures of the Domain Name System (DNS). The domain name has to be registered with any of the registrars. Domain name assignment is controlled by Internet Corporation for Assigned Names and Numbers (ICANN) which is headquartered in California, United States. ICANN manages the top-level development and architecture of the Internet domain name space and authorises registrars to grant domain names to individuals and organisations for a fee.

Registration does not give any legal ownership to the registrant but an exclusive right to use the registered domain name for a certain period of time. The registration has to be renewed for continued use after the expiry of the period of last registration.

Major Domains

.com
.edu
.org
.gov
.mil
.int
Country domains
.in for India
.uk for the United Kingdom

Sting up a Website

The Web is growing rapidly. Every day thousands of websites are being added. It is not business firms and other organisations that are setting up and maintaining websites but also individuals of all kinds. The websites also vary widely in content, looks and interactivity. Thus, there are family websites, blogging websites, business websites, and information websites. Yet, the basic steps in setting up a website are more or less the same. The first step is actually planning the website. What kind of website is needed? Based on the purpose, the design, hosting etc. vary. Once, the website planning is over, the following steps have to be gone through.

Steps in Setting up a Website

The basic steps in setting up a website are domain name selection and registration, choosing a web host, designing website and uploading website.

Selecting a Domain Name

Before registering a name it must be ensured that others do not use the same name. This is to avoid any legal issues later. The names are allotted on a first-come-first-served basis. Checking the proposed name at search engines is a sure way of ensuring that others do not use the same name. There are websites like www.internic.net, where domain name availability can be checked. A list of domain names may be created first. Then, try the domain names one by one, most preferred first, then next and so on.

The name is to be registered with the appropriate domain name registrars. A fee has to be paid for this. The domain name has to be renewed on expiry by paying renewal fee. The major domains are .com, .org, .edu. .info, etc. Business firms use .com domain. Thus, National Stock Exchange of India Limited got the domain name www.nse-india.com. It advertises the domain name to attract people to the site. Customers just type the domain name to access the NSE's site. The domain name is important as it can play a part in attracting the right kind of traffic to the site. The domain name should be as short and simple as possible so that it is memorable. It also should not violate trademarks of other firms.

Registration of the Domain Name

If the proposed domain name is not in use, the next step is to register the name. For registering the name, the proposed name, server address etc. must be submitted to the domain name registrar along with the registration fee.

Choosing a Web Host

Web hosting services include providing, managing and maintaining software, hardware, content integrity, security, and reliable high-speed internet connection. Internet Service Providers offer hosting services for a fee. This fee is usually for a specific period and has to be renewed paying necessary fee. The ISP allocates storage space on its server for the website. The storage space required depends on the content the site should have. The storage space can be hired on a rental basis. There are quite a large number of web hosts. It is important to choose the right web host for hosting the website. Personal websites may prefer free web hosting as not much traffic is expected. The web host may add advertisement at such free sites. For an e-commerce website, the web host has to be very carefully chosen. It should have enough bandwidth to give fast access to the site and support the traffic expected. It should also have acceptable uptime, reliability and customer support.

Website Design

Website design is very important to attract and retain customers. The website may have three types of pages such as home page, intermediate page, and content page. The home page is the first page a user visits at a website. The intermediate pages are one level down. They can be accessed from the home page. Each intermediate page usually has a link back to the home page. The content pages hold details and are usually accessible from intermediate pages. The content page may also include link back to the home page and to other relevant resources. Web publishing as the name indicates is the publishing of anything on the Web. A web publication consists of a home page and many other pages linked to the home page.

There are many web page design tools. Web pages are designed using any of the web design software packages like Microsoft FrontPage, Dreamweaver from Macromedia, WordPress, and Fusion from netobjects.

Uploading of Web Pages

The web pages and associated files are to be stored in a directory on the web server. If the server is remote, FTP package is used to copy web page files onto the remote web hosting server.

Promotion of the Website

Now the site is up and running. The registered domain name can be used to access the site. But, the site may not be known to the target audience. So, it requires certain amount of promotion to get the right kind of traffic to the website. Submission of the website to leading search engines like Google, Yahoo and Bingbot may help in getting the website listed in search results. Online and offline advertisement may also be considered to bring more awareness among customers.

An e-commerce website needs a lot more capabilities like catalogue, shopping cart, payment processing, security, insurance, tie up with logistics firms, etc.

Advantages of Website to Business Firms

Global presence and reach: With a website, a business firm gets global presence. It can give detailed information to existing and potential customers about its products and services. It can also take orders online if it is e-commerce enabled. Customers from any country can contact the firm for products or services.

Global customer base: A business firm with a website can attract customers from anywhere. Dell is an online computer vendor. Customers from all over the globe place orders with Dell at its website. Hence, Dell reaches customers everywhere very quickly.

Low cost: The website enables a firm to communicate with the customers and do business with them at comparatively low cost.

Effective Public Relations: The firm can publish information about its purpose, core values, ethical way of doing business and corporate social responsibility projects. It helps the firm in improving its corporate image.

Brand building and product promotion: Website is a rich source of information to customers and the general public. Rich content and innovative advertisement help a firm in getting more traffic to the site and bring awareness about its brand of products and services. With links and banner advertisement at popular search engines, the site can attract a steady flow of customers.

24/7 availability of service: The website offers service any time anywhere. Customers can access the website and get service. For example, a customer of an HP DeskJet Printer might experience a problem with its software. He can download a copy of the software from HP's website anytime. There is also a lot of trouble shooting help at the site.

Interactivity: The website allows two-way communications. Interactive web pages take input from the customer and give him what information he is searching for. Some sites will also have chat facility for the visitor to interact with a contact person.

Customised products and services: It is possible to customise products and services to each customer's needs. This is particularly so for products like software, books, music, personal computers and accessories, etc.

Test marketing of products and services: Website offers opportunities to test products and get feedback from customers about products and services.

UNIFORM RESOURCE LOCATOR (URL)

URL is the global address of a document or other resources on the web or the Internet. URL consists of four parts: protocol, host name, folder name and file name. Protocol is the first element in the URL and it identifies the service that specifies which protocol is to be used like http, ftp, etc. The host name indicates the server that stores the html document. The protocol identifier and the hostname are separated by a colon and two forward slashes. The folder name gives name of the folder that holds the document on the server. The file name is the name of the html document that contains text, image etc.

SEARCHING

The Internet is often described as a massive jungle where it is impossible without appropriate tools to find the information one is searching for. Navigations tools were developed to help a user to access the required information on the Net. The navigation tools enable burrowing through the disorganised and fast growing Web for information. The Net has grown too large and lacks centralised control. With rapid growth in the number of hosts and services offered, it became a necessity to have some tools to locate the hosts and the services. Navigational tools have been developed since 1990s to help the surfers in locating the services on the Internet. Early navigational tools developed includes Archie, Veronica, NetLink, and Wide Area Information Servers (WAIS).

BROWSING OR NET SURFING

The Internet is a huge jungle of information. The user needs to search for information. Browsing is the process of seeking information on the Web with the help of browser software. The Web is a huge collection of hypertext documents. The hypertext facilitates moving from documents to documents quickly. When user clicks on a hypertext in a document, the browser opens up another window and displays the new document retrieved from the same computer or a different computer usually far away.

Web Browsers

The Web gained popularity only after web browsers became available. A Web browser is a program that allows a user to easily retrieve and present information resources available on the Web.

The browser follows the link in the hypertext document, which was made possible by the HTML. URL of the information resource has a uniform resource identifier (URI). URI identifies the resource like a document, a video, a music file or software etc. The resource hyperlinks to other resources. Each such link contains a URI. When the user clicks the link, the browser decodes the URI and uses the address to retrieve the resource and presents it to the user.

Though browsers are used to access World Wide Web, yet it can also access resources stored on web servers in private networks. It does not require a user to login from remote location to get information from a web server. Most web browsers can display text, images, audio, video and XML files. Most web browsers allow multiple resources to be opened in separate windows.

The user interface of most web browsers provides the following:

- An address bar to enter URI of the information resource to be retrieved and displayed
- A search bar to give input to the search engine to locate resources
- A home button to return to the home page from anywhere in the document or resource
- A refresh button to reload the current resource
- Back and forward buttons to go back to previous page and forward
- A status bar to display the current state of retrieval of resource
- A stop button to cancel retrieval of the resource

Mosaic: The first Web browser, named Mosaic, was developed by Marc Andreessen at the National Centre for Supercomputing Applications, University of Illinois. It was released in June 1993. Soon a number of other browsers became available for browsing the Web. Mosaic could perform searches across many Internet services. Mosaic versions became available for various platforms such as MS Windows, Macintosh and X window system under UNIX. Mosaic allowed images and videos to be downloaded and viewed. The mosaic and WWW server enable delivery of multimedia documents. With the arrival of Netscape and Internet Explorer as more user-friendly browsers, Mosaic is little used now.

Netscape: One Web browser that became hugely popular was the Netscape Navigator. This was again developed by Marc Andreessen, the founder of Netscape Communications Corp. It not only allowed browsing through hyperlinked documents but also supported use of other services available on the Net such as ftp, telnet and Gopher. Later versions of Netscape Navigator (Version 2.0) also supported Sun Microsystems Inc.'s Java programming language. In addition to English, the Netscape browser is available in German, Japanese and French languages.

Netscape Communicator is the latest suite of client-side software tools for the Internet on the Web from the Netscape Communications Corp. The suite contains email, groupware and browser programs. It provides a complete set of tools needed for communicating, sharing and accessing data on the Internet and Intranets.

The Netscape Communicator consists of the Navigator 4.0 (browser), an e-mail application (Messenger), a groupware application (Collabra), a scheduling program (Calendar), an HTML editor (Composer) and a program that facilitates audio and data conferencing (Conference).

Internet Explorer: Internet Explorer (IE) is one of the most popular Web browsers today. It is available only on Windows platform. The IE was bundled with MS Windows 95 and later integrated with Windows 98. Microsoft dominates the web browser market now with its Internet Explorer installed on more PCs than anyother.

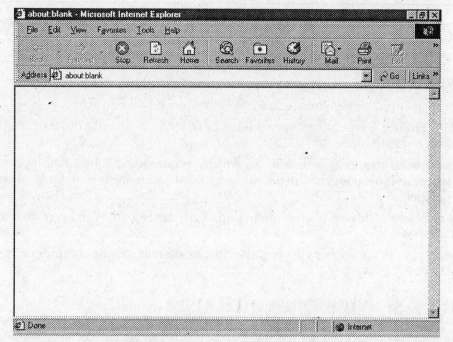

Fig. 21.2: *Microsoft Internet Explorer when invoked*

Internet Explorer makes it easier to get the most from the World Wide Web, whether one is searching for new information or browsing favorite Web sites. And built-in IntelliSense technology can save time by completing routine Web tasks, such as automatically completing Web addresses and forms for users, and automatically detecting network and connection status.

Features of Internet Explorer is as follows[9]:

- When you start typing a frequently used Web address in the Address bar, a list of similar addresses appears that you can choose from. And if a Web-page address is wrong, Internet Explorer can search for similar addresses to try to find a match.

- Search for Web sites by clicking the Search button on the toolbar. Then in the Search bar, type a word or phrase that describes what you're looking for. When your search results appear, you can view the individual Web pages without losing your list of search results.

- You can also search directly from the Address bar. Just type common names or words, and Internet Explorer can automatically take you to the site that most likely matches what you are searching for, and list other likely sites as well.

- Go to other Web pages similar to the one you are viewing, without even doing a search. Just use the Show Related Sites feature.

- Once you are on a Web page, Internet Explorer can help you complete entries in any kind of Web-based form. Start typing, and a list of similar entries appears that you can choose from.

- Browse through a list of Web pages you recently visited by clicking the History button on the toolbar. In addition, you can rearrange or search the History list.

- Listen to broadcast and Internet-only radio stations while you browse. Choose from a wide variety of music and talk radio stations, and add them to your Favourites list. The radio toolbar is available in Internet Explorer when you install Windows Media Player.

Other Web Browsers

There are many other web browsers. Some of these are mentioned below.

Mozilla Firefox: Firefox is an open source browser from Mozilla Foundation started by Netscape Inc., in 1998.

Opera: Opera is another browser software which was introduced in 1996. It has only minuscule customer share and is not popular with the Net users. But it is growing in popularity among mobile web browser users.

Chrome: Google Chrome is growing in popularity among the Web users, mostly among Apple Mac users.

Safari: Safari is a web browser popular among users of Apple computers. It was first introduced in 2003.

INTERNET SERVICE PROVIDER (ISP)

ISP is an organisation that connects users to the Net. To access the Net, users have to keep an account with an Internet Service Provider. On registration with an ISP, each user gets a login name and a password. The user can access the Net with any means like telephone, mobile phone, cable or wireless depending upon the choices offered by the ISP.

Types of ISP: There are different types of ISP like access ISPs, hosting ISPs and transit ISPs. They are complementary in their activities.

Access ISPs: These Internet Service Providers connect the users' computer to the Internet. They have to create and maintain infrastructure to provide access to users. The users may be individuals and organisations. Organisations may include small, medium and large business firms. They differ in their requirements. Hence, these ISPs offer different options to customers like dial-up connection, broadband connection, cable connection, satellite connection, ISDN connection etc. Home users usually go for dial-up connection, broadband connection, cable connection, Digital Subscriber Line (DSL) or Wi-Fi. Business users with large broadband requirement may choose DSL, leased line connection, Ethernet technologies or satellite connection.

Hosting ISPs: These ISPs maintain web servers and fast access connectivity. They lease server space for others for web hosting and providing email and FTP services. They may also offer cloud computing services.

Transit ISPs: These ISPs maintain network backbones and telecommunication lines to connect hosting ISPs with access ISPs. The ISPs together create and maintain the Internet backbones. They have their networks which connect the networks with others forming the Internet. Each higher level ISP will have more network reach and connections to the higher networks. The ISPs pay to other ISPs for granting access to upstream networks.

ISPs in India: ISPs started functioning in India in the early 1990s. ERNet and NICNet were the first ISPs in India. Software Technology Parks of India was also allowed to provide Internet access but within restricted areas. But the entry of VSNL in 1995 was a turning point. It launched Gateway Internet Access Service for public Internet access. After that, VSNL became a virtual monopoly ISP in India. But later private ISPs were allowed and they slowly but steadily gained dominance in Indian ISP services.

There are two categories of ISPs in India: public sector and private sector. BSNL and MTNL are the two public sector ISPs and there are a large number of private ISPs. The ISPs with nation-wide operations include Airtel, Aircel, Hathaway, Idea, Reliance Communications, Sify, Spectranet, Tata DoCoMo, Tata Indicom, Tata Telecom, and Vodafone.

The Internet Service Provider Policy, 1998 categorised ISPs into three: Category A, Category B and Category C based on their area of operations.

Category	Area of Operation
A	Whole of India.
B	20 territorial Telecom Circles, four Metro Districts – Delhi; Mumbai, Kolkata or Chennai and four major Telephone Districts – Ahmedabad, Bengaluru, Hyderabad or Pune.
C	Any Secondary Switching Areas (SSA) of DOT with geographical boundaries as on 1.4.1998.

SEARCH ENGINES

Archie was the first search tool developed in 1990 to search the Internet. Gopher, Veronica, Jughead, etc., followed. But they were not good at searching the Web. In 1993, W3Catelog, primitive web search engine and a web robot were announced. WebCrawler and Lycos were released in 1994. Soon many search engines were released which included Magellan, Excite, Infoseek, Inktomi, Northern Light, AltaVista and Yahoo. Later by 2000 Google search engine shot into prominence and continues to dominate search engine space.

The Web contains hundreds of thousands of websites with content on hugely different topics. Users need search tools to get to the information they look for easily. Search engines, directories, indexes etc. help the users in their search.

Web search engines are applications designed to search and locate resources on the World Wide Web and ftp servers. Search engines use key words and phrases to search the Internet. The user types in key words into the search engine which runs a search of the resources and lists the results, page by page, called hits.

Fig. 21.3: http://www.bing.com

Web search engine has three essential features – crawling, indexing and searching. The web crawler also called spider or bot is an automated program. Bingbot, Yahoo!Slurp and PolyBot are examples of Web crawlers. The crawler starts with a list of URLs to visit. It visits every page on a website that is to be searched and reads the hypertext links there. An indexing program, also called catalog, creates an index from the pages that are read. Search program accepts the key words typed in by the user and compares the entries in the index and returns the results of the search for the user.

Search engines use web crawlers to look for content at websites and index those pages for easy and quick retrieval. Search engines store information about web pages in an index database. But, the search engine does not index all web pages at a website. When a search engine visits a website, the crawler checks the robots.txt in the root directory which tells the robot as to which pages are not to be crawled. When a user types key words into the search engine, it checks its index database and provides a list of best-matching web pages with a short summary of the resource.

Some of the popular search engines today are listed below:

Alta Vista	http://www.altavista.com
Excite	http://www.excite.com
HotBot	http://hotbot.lycos.com
Go	http://www.go.com
Google	http://www.google.com
Lycos	http://www.lycos.com
Northern Light	http://www.northernlight.com
Web Crawler	http://www.webcrawler.com

Meta Search Engines

These are search engines that search other search engines. Often they also search smaller, less well known search engines and specialised sites. Meta search engines frequently include indexes :and other search tools. Examples of meta search engines are[10];

- RedeSearch   http://www.RedeSearch.com
- BigHub   http://www.thebighub.com
- C4   http://www.C4.com
- InfoZoid   http://www.infozoid.com
- Brightgate   http://www.brightgate.com
- Ask Jeeves   http://www.askjeeves.com
- Dogpile   http://www.dogpile.com
- MetaCrawler   http://www.metacrawler.com
- All4One   http://www.all4one.com

Subject Directories

Examples for subject directories are:

About.com	http://www.about.com
Big Hub	http://www.thebighub.com
Invisible Web	http://www.invisibleweb.com
Links2Go	http://www.links2go.com
Open Directory Project	http://dmoz.org
Qango	http://www.qango.com
Yahoo	http://www.yahoo.com

Google, Yahoo and Bing are the most popular search engines now. In addition to metasearch engines, search engines, and indexes, the Internet contains a wealth of topic specific search tools and resources. A number of specialised browsers as for the blind etc. are available for using the Web resources.

Search Engine Optimisation (SEO)

Search engine optimisation is the process of improving visibility of the website or web resource in a search engine. There is a high degree of positive correlation between number of search result listing of a website and the number of visits to the website. Hence, by increasing visibility at the search engine a firm can attract more traffic to its website for marketing or e-commerce. SEO depends on the kind of searches Internet users make and what kind of content they look for. The key words searched are useful in designing content of website to get more listing of a site by the search engine. Thus, when a website updates its content to meet the popular text, video and image searches at popular search engines, it improves its web presence. The webmasters and content providers need to know what is being searched at the search engines, what key words are typed into the search engine and how the search engine indexes web content etc. to optimize the website visibility to its target audience.

Blog and Blogging

Blog is an abbreviation of weblog meaning a website that maintains a record of information. Blog has evolved from the earlier online diary. It is a website where an individual posts information regularly with an intention to allow others to read the content and comment about it. It is kind of a diary maintained by an individual or organisation with regular entries of comments, description of events etc. The blog may also carry pictures and videos for viewing. The entries are displayed in reverse chronological order.

A blog can be designed for almost anything. It is used to publish one's thoughts about public interest subjects or it can present a collection of links about relevant topics etc. Blogs are interactive and attract lots of visitors. They can post their own comments on any content of the blog. Any individual can create a blog at blogger sites. Such blogs are public by default and they can be read by anyone on the Internet. It is also possible to create private blogs. The blog should have regular postings to build a loyal group of users. It may be risky to put up personal information at the blogs. Some blogger sites like Twitter allow bloggers to share their thoughts instantaneously with friends and relatives etc. and they reach them faster than email.

Types of Blog: There are at least two types of blog: the personal blog and the corporate or institutional blog,

Personal Blog: It is an ongoing diary of an individual and is the most popular type of blog.

Corporate and Organisational Blog: Blogs used inside a business firm for improving internal communication or externally for marketing products and services are called corporate blogs or organisational blogs.

Advantage and Disadvantage of Blogs: The blogs are easy to update. It is particularly important for personal blogs where information has to be updated frequently. Another advantage is the visibility of the content. It is very quick to reach readers worldwide. One disadvantage is that one may post some content without much of a thought and may regret over the content later. But by that time, the damage would have been done.

INTRANET

The intranet is basically a communications environment created within an organisation using Internet technology. It is an internal Web site that utilises the Internet technology such as protocols for efficient internal communication. Internal corporate communication in the form of multiple copies of documents of all important internal communication costs a quite a bit of money. With Intranet, documents can be created, saved, retrieved and distributed at low cost. Such documents can be created on any device and displayed on client PCs using the Internet technology. Creating such an Intranet requires a host computer or server (with hardware platform and operating system such as UNIX or Windows NT, etc.) and Web browser software.

Intranet is a local area network that uses Internet technologies for communication within an organisation. It is not accessible for outsiders. Internet Protocol suit such as TCP/IP, SMTP, WWW, FTP and remote login are used for communications within an organisation. The internal applications are integrated with e-mail, FTP, Web server, Mail server, etc. It requires a local area network to be set up and then the network resources are integrated with the Internet technologies. Users browse the network with a web browser to access information within an organisation. The web browser becomes a simple user interface for sharing data. The Intranet need not be connected to the Internet, as it is implemented within organisations.

Intranet uses TCP/IP network and technologies besides Internet resources such as WWW, e-mail, telnet and FTP. But the network is not open to people outside the organisation. The intranet is separated from the Internet using a firewall that prohibits access to the intranet from outside the organisation.

Intranet allows electronic collaboration between people in the organisation. Groupware technologies are employed to support online brainstorming, group meetings and other collaborative work. It also facilitates videoconferencing between people in various parts of the country or world.

Intranet improves internal communication. One of its most important advantages is the quick access it provides to published documents. It is very useful when large amount of constantly changing information has to be communicated simultaneously to a large number of people within an organisation.

Intranet requires

- Network
- TCP/IP on servers and clients
- Browsers
- Hardware for hosting Internet services
- Software for hosting web services

Advantages of Intranet

- Easy availability of information
- Fast access to information
- Low cost of communication
- Organisation wide access to critical information
- Facilitates collaboration among employees in an organisation

Extranet

When an organisation extends access to its intranet resources to its business partners, like suppliers and customers, the intranet becomes an extranet. External organisations are provided access to information relevant for them.

Extranets are presently being used as[8]:

- Project management tools for companies and collaborating third parties.
- Sharing proprietary ideas with select a select group.
- Online training for resellers
- A way of using high volumes of data using Electronic Data Interchange (EDI)
- Sharing product catalogs and inventory levels exclusively with partners
- Collaborating with other companies on joint development efforts
- Providing services offered by one organisation to a group of other companies, such as an online banking application managed by one organisation on behalf of affiliated banks
- Share news of common interest exclusively with partner companies

Cloud Computing

Usually, the Internet is shown as a cloud in network diagrams. The concept of cloud computing has emerged from that. It is a kind of computing like the grid computing. But it is different from grid computing which integrates a numbers of computers to apply their processing power to solve a single problem at the same time. Cloud computing standards are yet to be standardised. Some of them like IBM' Blue Cloud is based on open source software.

It is, in plain language, the use of the Internet for simple tasks usually done with a computer. It is, in other words, the process of taking the tasks and services of a computer to the Web. The cloud needs a platform to run applications. A platform is the basic structure that runs applications. Windows, Mac OS etc. are platforms. For cloud computing, the Web is the platform.

Fig. 21.4: Cloud Computing

The word 'cloud' in the term 'cloud computing' is used as a metaphor for the Internet. It is actually a collage of many different kind of computers which are linked together to form a very large computer. IT permits everyone to store and retrieve data. The objective is to minimise investment in infrastructure. There are cloud providers for software, infrastructure and platform. The cloud customers of these services pay for the cloud providers. A stumbling block to cloud computing is the lack of interoperability of applications on the Web.

The cloud provider maintains the server and pays for the application software license and updates and the cloud customer pays for the service availed. The cloud customer does not spend on expensive servers or applications. He saves on hardware, software and operating costs like cost of energy used by the server and its air conditioners, etc.

The components of cloud computing include clients, data centre and distributed servers. The clients are devices which cloud customers use to access the cloud servers like desktop, laptop, mobile phones or PDAs. The data centre is the collection of cloud servers which host applications. The cloud servers are distributed all over to provide more options to the cloud provider to take service to cloud customers.

Conclusion

The Internet was originally designed as a medium for fault-tolerant communications using networked computers. From a small network in the US in the 1970s for military communication, the

Internet has now grown into a global network and carries all sorts of data such as business, educational, scientific and personal. The growth of the Internet since the middle of 1990s has been phenomenal and the trend is still continuing. The Web and the Web browser software have made the Net hugely popular. The business was late to take note of the potential of the Net. But later, a large number of firms took to the Internet in a big way for commerce and communications. The Internet continues to grow exponentially. Today, almost all business firms use the Internet for internal and/ or external communications, marketing and e-commerce. Social networking, entertainment

QUESTIONS

1. Trace the history of the Net and explain what factors contributed to its fast growth in the 1990s.
2. What are the core features of the Internet?
3. What do you mean by IP protocol suite? Describe each.
4. What are the popular Internet services?
5. What is WWW? Explain how it works?
6. What is intranet? What is its use?
7. What is browsing? What are the browsers available?
8. What is search engine? How does it work?
9. What is e-mail? How does it work?
10. What is website? What are the steps in setting up a website?
11. What is blogging?
12. What is the business of an ISP? Name a few national ISPs in India.
13. What is cloud computing?

REFERENCES

1. Perry, P.J., *"World Wide Web Secrets"*, Comdex Publishing, New Delhi, 1996, p. 30.
2. Wiggins, R.W., *"The Internet for Every One"*, McGraw Hill Inc., New York, 1994, p. 9.
3. Wiggins, R.W. *"The Internet for Every One"*, McGraw Hill Inc., New York, 1994, p. 291.
4. Ghosh, Shikhar, *"Making Business Sense of the Internet"*, Harvard Business Review, March-April, 1998, p. 127.
5. Shroud, Dick, *"The Internet Strategies, A Corporate Guide to Exploiting the Internet"*, Macmillan Press Ltd., London, 1998, pp. 54-55.
6. http://www.actinic.com
7. Mougayar W., *Opening Digital Markets*, Mc-Graw-Hill, New York, 1998, p. 8.
8. Online Market Research : Possibilities and Realities of Virtual Marketplace, March 1997.
9. Microsoft Internal Explorer, online help.
10. www.search.com/

22 CHAPTER

Information System Audit

INTRODUCTION

Organisations in general and business firms in particular spend huge amount of money on building enough information technology infrastructure. Information technology advances rapidly. New technologies become available much quicker than before. Business firms spend a lot of money year after year on modernising hardware and software, and updating people skills. These investments are expected to create new capabilities for business firms and organisations. There must be a feedback on what capabilities a firm has and how well it is using these capabilities. In a networked environment, security threats are also growing. Information systems cannot generate revenue for most business firms. They can only support business processes. There is a growing need to ensure that the investment on IT infrastructure yields enough returns by enabling the business operations and business processes to be carried out more efficiently.

Information system audit is a process of collecting and analysing data about an organisation's information system practices, operations and resources. The process looks at whether the organisation has enough IS assets, safety of these assets and how much the IS function supports organisation's goals.

Organisations employ a variety of IT solutions for operations, planning and control of business activities. Investment made in IT infrastructure is also growing. Projects are identified every year for further application development and implementation costing large amount of money. These investments are made with specific objectives tied to each project along with an overall goal of acquiring and retaining competitive advantage for the organisation.

Along with the growth in computerisation of business transactions and operations, the frauds and cyber crimes are also rising. It is a responsibility of executives to conduct an audit of organisation's vulnerabilities and ways of plugging them. Hacking, phishing, spamming, etc., are becoming part of e-life. The IS audit helps in assessing the preparedness of an organisation to fight these or protect its resources from the criminal intrusions and violations of privacy.

IS audit is different from financial audit. The financial audit focuses on the accounting principles followed by the firm and fairness in reporting its income, expenses, assets and liabilities of a period. In IS audit, the objective is to evaluate efficacy of firm's IS infrastructure, its vulnerabilities and shortcomings.

With growing computing power and proliferating applications, it is important to take a stock of IT resources and how they are used in an organisation. The objectives of such an exercise will include:

- The appropriateness of the IT architecture
- The adequacy of hardware and software resources
- The communication technologies and their utilisation
- The skill sets of people, shortage in any and how to acquire talent with the skill set required
- The amount of internal and external threat to the information resources and the extent of risk involved
- The controls implemented to regulate access to information
- The extent of competitive advantage, potential and actual, for the organisation based on the IT infrastructure.

IS audit's concern can be stated under three heads:

- **Availability:** It is a concern about the downtime of the computer system. Critical applications need 24 hour availability. The question whether the system will be available to meet business needs when needed, is therefore, very important in IS audit.
- **Confidentiality:** It is about the security measures and access procedures followed to protect resources and how access to data resources is controlled to ensure confidentiality of data. The potential threats and risk levels are also assessed to suggest ways of improving controls.
- **Integrity:** It is about the accuracy, reliability and timelines of information. IS auditors look at the comfortable level of accuracy and reliability of information and how much of that is met by the present systems.

THE NEED FOR *IS* AUDIT

IS function is expected to support the business processes and help in attaining the objectives of the organisation. There is a need for an independent review of IS support for the business processes. Data resources are the basis for information that is supplied in the form of reports, screen displays, query responses, etc., to users in the organisation. The data must be accurate, regularly collected, structured and stored in databases. The current procedures and policies for data access, data accuracy, security of data, etc., must be subjected to a thorough examination to identify problem areas and ways of improving the systems.

IT resources in organisations may be misused in the absence of policies and rules regarding their use. Employees may use the facilities for personal or unauthorised purposes. For example, employees using e-mail for union activities that result in hostility between managers and workers is a misuse of the facilities. Similarly, accessing sensitive information without being authorised to do it, wilful destruction of data, etc., are the kind of abuse of IT resources that must be checked. Otherwise, they may cause irreparable damage to the corporate image, work culture and ethics of the organisation. An IS audit can bring out the misuse of such resources to the attention of managers concerned for intervention.

Malicious hacking, criminal intrusions and security lapses are growing in the networked world. Organizations need to protect their information technology assets and valuable data resources against these criminal acts. They need to put in place security systems to ward off threats from internal and external sources to these assets. IS audit can suggest the design of such security systems and control procedures.

IS audit team must gauge the security vulnerabilities and the potential damage from internal and external threats. It must recommend appropriate security systems keeping in mind the objective that the solutions suggested are cost effective as well.

It calls for personal integrity as well as system integrity. Employees must understand the corporate security policies and their implications for their organization. Their commitment to security must be demonstrated in greater vigil against internal and external security threats and greater attention to details of security routine. Their neglect may cause damage to the IT infrastructure and IT assets. IS auditor helps in spreading the kind of awareness needed about such security concerns.

The security management system must support all business processes and protect critical corporate data assets. This is achieved by a broad range of security functions, ranging from the efficient administration of access rights all the way to round-the-clock monitoring of critical systems, databases, applications and networks.

Auditing is a traditional professional service started long before IT was deployed in business. But the tools and procedures of conventional audit can be applied to IS audit to ensure that the IT resources are managed properly and the data assets are secure against internal and external threats.

With automated audit tools, analysing IT security information captured in audit logs can become a daily activity, allowing issues to surface before they become big problems.

Types of IS Audit

Information System Audit can be done for different objectives. Hence, there are different types of IS audit. Some of these are mentioned below.

- **Systems Development Audit:** It is audit carried out to check whether the system under development can meet the objectives of the organisation. It is also done to ensure that the system development follows the accepted standards of system development.
- **Systems and Applications Audit:** It is carried out to verify that the systems and applications are appropriate, efficient and adequately controlled to give valid and reliable output.
- **Technological Position Audit:** This audit looks at the technological infrastructure for information systems and whether it needs upgrading.
- **IT Management Audit:** It verifies whether the IT management has developed appropriate organisational structure and procedures to ensure efficient information processing.

OBJECTIVES OF THE *IS* AUDIT

A comprehensive audit, covering all elements of the IT infrastructure including LAN, WAN, firewall, hosts, remote access system, application and business continuity procedures that will:

- Assess current practices and policies of the organisation's different IT functions.
- Identify flaws in the design, implementation, procedures, and policies related to the organisation's operating system, software, network, etc.
- Provide recommendations for each process to plug design flaws and streamline procedures, and,
- Provide recommendations, which will act as a baseline to define correct policies.

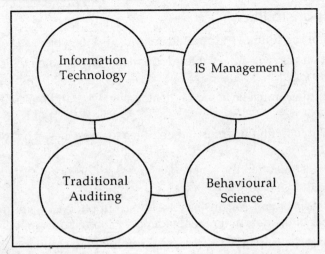

Fig. 22.1: IS Auditing and Other Related Disciplines

(*Source:* EDP Auditing, Ron Weber, McGraw-Hill International, Singapore, 1988, p.17)

Traditional Audit and IS Audit

Traditional audit is narrow as it looks at the accounting and reporting aspects only. External audit is periodic in nature. External auditors visit the organisation after the closure of the accounting year to verify accounts and statements as agents of the shareholders of the corporate entities. IS audit focuses on the state of use of IT infrastructure in the organisation and the security risks and organisational capability to respond to security challenges.

STEPS IN *IS* AUDIT

1. **Planning the audit:** Planning is the first step in IS audit. Once the audit engagement is accepted and an audit engagement letter is received from a client, an external auditor prepares for the IS audit. He must assign appropriate staff to the audit, obtain background information about the client, understand objectives and legal obligations of the client organisation etc. as part of planning IS audit. He must plan tests for checking the effectiveness of administrative, financial and application system controls.

2. **Tests of controls:** This involves testing whether the controls in operation in the organisation are reliable. The management controls are tested first and then application controls.

3. **Tests of transactions:** These tests are designed to identify errors and irregularities in transaction processing that might affect the quality of financial information. If these tests bring out substantive irregularities, the IS auditor may expand the tests of account balances and tests of overall results.

4. **Tests of Balances and Overall Results:** These are used to judge the extent of losses or misstatements in financial statements due to the failure of information system function in safeguarding the assets, maintaining data integrity, etc.

5. **Completion of audit and preparation of report:** This is the last stage of the IS Audit. The auditors must analyse the data and evidences they collected and conclude about the client organisation's systems and procedures. He must report his findings objectively. The control weaknesses, potential losses due to inadequate controls, etc., are to be stated in the report.

IS Auditor's Responsibilities

- The IS auditor (or at times the audit team) must list the objectives of IS audit.
- He must obtain relevant and reliable information from the sources identified for achieving the objectives listed.
- The audit findings must be based on detailed analysis and interpretation of the data so received.
- A report of the audit findings must be submitted to the requester on completion of the audit work.
- The report must mention the scope, objectives, period of coverage, and the nature and extent of the audit work performed.
- The audit findings and conclusions are to be supported by appropriate analysis and interpretation of the data and other evidences gathered during the audit process.
- The report must specify any restrictions on circulation, if any.
- The report must state any reservations or qualifications that the auditor has with respect to the audit.
- The report must also mention the audit steps performed and audit evidences gathered.

BENEFITS OF IS AUDIT

IS audit has become a necessity especially for organisations that use IT resources for running critical applications. The benefits that can follow from a functioning IS audit system are as follows.

Design and Fine-tune Internal Controls

An IS auditor can recommend internal control measures for effectively securing business applications and IT assets. An effective IS audit of the IT applications provides inputs to ensure that the business application of IT is consistent with all the business policies. It also enforces the policies through suitable preventive controls or highlights deviations from the policies through suitable reports.

Recommending Changes in Business Procedures to Leverage the IT Potential

An IS auditor can judge the IT capabilities of an organisation and how they are utilized presently. He can suggest changes to business procedures so that these capabilities are exploited for strategic advantage. That is, he can recommend appropriate complementary business procedures around the applications so that the benefit is maximised.

Network Security

Computer networks are exposed to security risk however well designed it was at the time of implementation. Design deficiencies and security holes creep in exposing the network resources to security risk. Periodic IS audits can detect these security lapses and design deficiencies and suggest ways of plugging them.

Efficiency of Control Systems

IT infrastructure automates controls and processes. Since an IS auditor is not tied down by any considerations of the function or department, he is ideally positioned to evaluate the controls in the information systems that replace human controls and advise about their adequacy and efficacy.

Evolving IT Security Policy

IS auditor offers suggestions to improve security policy or to improve compliance with it. Such periodic updating of security policy makes it current and meeting the needs adequately.

Awareness about IT Security

Periodic review of security policies and their implementation increases security awareness and compliance to security measures. It also motivates security officers and systems administrators to do their jobs effectively.

Efficiency of IT Investments

Information technology is a strategic resource. IS audit is concerned not just with security and controls. It evaluates strategic objectives and organizational performance, exploitation of IT potential and return on IT investments. IS auditor suggests ways for better alignment of IT and business so that the IT potential contributes to profits of the organisation.

Fraud Detection

It detects errors or frauds committed deliberately or inadvertently. If IS audit becomes a routine, it reduces chances of frauds and violations of norms in the future.

Expert Advice for Improvement

It offers an opportunity to an organisation to review its IS procedures and also processes as the audit team gives its expert view of the organisation's resources and competencies.

CONDUCT OF IS AUDIT

When external auditors are hired to audit the information system, the audit procedure employed is as follows :

Procedures to obtain an understanding of controls: The external auditors use interviews, inspections, enquiries and observations to gain an understanding of the administrative controls, financial controls, etc., existing in the organisation and their effectiveness.

Tests of controls: Inquiries, inspections and observations are used to study whether the administrative and financial controls have been designed well and how effective they are.

Substantive tests of details of transactions: These tests are designed to locate errors or irregularities in recording transactions that would affect the financial statements. Similarly, they focus on whether transactions are processed within the target time limits, etc.

Substantive tests of details of performance: These tests are designed to check whether the performance parameters set for a period are met. These may relate to the overall efficiency and effectiveness of the organisation. The IS auditors may survey the users in the organisation to study the effectiveness of the groups, divisions, etc.

Analytical review procedures: These tests are designed to identify areas that requires detailed audit. The fluctuations in data over a period are analysed and areas are identified for detailed investigation. Critical performance areas may be subjected to detailed analysis to find out bottlenecks and failures.

Conclusion

IS audit is a necessity in organisations that employ computer and computer networks for critical applications. It is carried out to know whether the IS resources are effectively and efficiently utilised to get maximum value addition. The IS audit can help create better security systems, policies and procedures to protect the IT resources and data assets. IS audit looks at the controls at work in organisation and how effective they are in achieving the objectives of the organisation. It ends with a report that details the findings about the level of efficiency and effectiveness of the client organisation's systems and procedures, shortcomings identified and losses and damages due to poor managerial and application controls.

QUESTIONS

1. What is information system audit?
2. What are the objectives of IS audit?
3. What are the benefits from IS audit?
4. What are the responsibilities of an IS auditor?
5. Describe the IS audit process.
6. Discuss the steps in IS audit.
7. Explain the IS audit procedures employed by external auditors.

REFERENCES

1. Vineet Kapoor & Associates - Indian CA, Indian CPA, Chartered Accountants.htm
2. S. Anantha Sayana, CISA, CIA, http://www.isaca.org/benfitsofis.htm
3. Ron Weber, *Information Systems Control and Audit*, Pearson Education Asia, New Delhi, 2002, p. 45.

SATYAM COMPUTER SERVICES LIMITED

Satyam Computer Services Ltd., was the fourth largest IT company in India and it had a turnover of US$2.1 billion in 2007-08. It had over 690 clients in 20 industry groups in more than 65 countries, including 185 Fortune 500 corporations. Satyam's key verticals included engineering and product development, supply chain management, business process quality, business intelligence, enterprise integration and infrastructure management. Mr.B.Ramalinga Raju, who held about 8% equity, was the Chairman of Satyam Computer Services Ltd.

In mid-December 2008, Satyam announced acquisition of two companies - Maytas Properties (100% equity) and Maytas Infrastructure (51% equity) floated by Mr.B.R.Raju's sons. They also floated 21 other companies under the Maytas name. Due to adverse reaction from institutional investors and the stock markets, the deal was withdrawn within 12 hours. Analysts and investors questioned the wisdom of the Board in approving the acquisition as it was a related party transaction. After the deal was aborted, four of the prominent independent directors resigned from the board of the company. On 7th January 2009, Raju revealed that the revenue and profit figures of Satyam had been inflated for past several years. The revelations were shocking for the country in general and the Indian IT industry in particular.

Raju and his family have been systematically spiriting out cash from Satyam. Through an elaborate and well-ramified set of procedures he inflated profits. He indulged in bogus transactions to show higher revenue. The payroll of the employees was another source of fraud. The company claimed it had 53,000 employees when it had just over 40,000 employees. The payment to the nearly 10,000 employees was faked. It went on for years.

Raju maintained thorough details of the Satyam's accounts and minutes of meetings since 2002 in different documents such as 'Insider Trading Register', 'Fakeover Registers' and 'Investment Registers'. Records of minutes of meetings were kept at the firm's office at May Fair Trade Centre on SP Road in Hyderabad, other records were maintained at a Financial Records Godown located 40 km away at Bahadurpalli. Raju stored records of accounts for the latest year (2008-09) in a computer server called 'My Home Hub'.

A web of 356 investment companies was used to allegedly divert funds from Satyam. These companies had several transactions in the form of inter corporate investments, advances and loans within and among them. One such company, with a paid up capital of ₹ 5 lakh had made an investment of ₹ 90.25 crore and received unsecured loans of ₹ 600 crore. Simultaneously, it had lent ₹ 419.63 to some other companies. Details of accounts from 2002 till January 7, 2009 were stored in two separate Internet Protocol addresses[1].

According to the Serious Frauds Investigation Office report, the falsification of accounts started in 2001 to keep the share prices high. The promoters sold much of their shareholding in Satyam over a period of time and used the proceeds to acquire land. Raju promoted 374 infrastructure firms and eight investment companies to serve his real estate ambitions.

Fake invoices and bills were created using software applications such as 'Ontime' that was used for calculating hours put in by an employee. A secret programme was allegedly planted in the source code of the official invoice management system creating a psuedo id "Super User" with the power to hide or show the invoice in the system. The cash so raised was used to purchase several thousands of acres of land across AP to ride a becoming reality market.

It presented a growing problem as facts had to be doctored to keep showing healthy profits for Satyam that was growing in size and scale. Every attempt made to eliminate the gap failed. As Raju put it, "It was like riding a tiger, not knowing how to get off without being eaten". Cashing out by selling Maytas Infrastructure and Maytas Properties to Satyam for an estimated ₹ 7,800 crore was the last straw. The attempt failed and Raju made the stunning confessions three weeks later.

Operating margin of Satyam was as low as 3% while other leading IT companies had it ranging from 20 to 30%. Satyam lost over 125 clients, including big companies like Coke and Caterpillar pulled out between December 2008 and April 2009. Its market cap sank by ₹ 10,000 crore in one day alone.

The employees experienced first a sense of undiluted anger, then a sense of betrayal— how could he do this — and the third emotion was of shame. Why did he have to do this? Raju's revenue figures, inflated to keep share prices high and keep the picture looking rosy, the financial make up was almost to the tune of 50% of the annual revenues. Employees had their own tales of woes. Banks did not give loans. Many house owners asked them to vacate or validate their rent paying capacity. Satyam employees felt extreme social pressure in their own homeland where once they were the most eligible bachelors or prosperous relatives. Employees found their financial power radically slashed; in some cases employees had to even pay for their visa fees for official visits abroad.

The irregularities in Price Waterhouse's handling of Satyam accounts were reported repeatedly to SEBI in 2001 and 2002. But SEBI failed to conduct an investigation. Similarly, an MP filed a complaint with SEBI about Satyam in 2003. The Income Tax Department unearthed several cases of illegal transfers of money by Satyam as early as 2002. Bu the concerned official was transferred and the investigation was suppressed. In 2008 SEBI also approved the acquisition of Maytas investments.

On 18th December 2008, two days after the Board met to approve the acquisition of the two real estate companies, independent director Krishna Palepu received an anonymous e-mail that laid bare the fraud. Palepu forwarded the e-mail to another independent director, Mr. Rammohan Rao who chaired the Satyam Audit Committee. Mr. Rao forwarded the e-mail to Mr. Gopalakrishnan, partner, Pricewaterhouse, the auditors of the company. Gopalakrishnan told Rao over phone that there was no fraud and it was untrue.

The central government waking up to the larger consequences of the scandal, invoked special provisions of company law to acquire control of Satyam's operations and eventually found a rescuer in the Mahindra group, which had the uphill task of putting the company back on rails.

The Transition

The months following the confession saw the nomination of six directors by the Government of India. Raju was replaced and Satyam was taken over by the Pune-based Tech Mahindra. The transition happed during the world's worst economic downturn since the great depression of the 1930's which added to the uncertainties surrounding customer loyalty, employee retention and leadership.

Change Process

The first step that Anand Mahindra, Vice Chairman of Mahindra and Mahindra group took was to address the shaken technology workers to infuse back an asset most eroded in the preceding three months - trust.The straight talking and affable Anand Mahindra reassured them by saying that "the uncertainty is over now". He spoke to thousands of employees whose careers had got tainted for no fault of theirs. The next step was to regain the lost confidence of the about to switch vendor type of customers. Mahindra created a strategic team. Team members were chosen from Tech Mahindra (TechM) , the M&M's relatively new and small IT services company. In the quick response mode, Tech Mahindra called its strategy "Reboot" to communicate the message of renewed confidence building through focus on sales, delivery excellence, cross leveraging skill sets and on customers and profits. They criss-crossed the globe to reassure their customers and showed that they cared.

Leading his team from front, Mahindra himself along with Mahindra Satyam's Chairman, Vineet Narayan, and CEO, C.P. Gurnani, systematically raised the confidence in their customers including big names like GE and Glaxo SmithKline Beecham who have since renewed their deals. "Of course there have been some concerns. And we have responded quickly and in a transparent and effective manner, which has assuaged their apprehensions" Gurnani shared in an interview with *Hindustan Times*. He further added , "The company has won 35 new customers while retaining and renewing long-term contracts with many big clients.

Questions

1. Study the corporate governance structure that existed at Satyam Computers.

2. Discuss the failure of control systems in Satyam computers? How could appropriate IT infrastructure have altered the situation?

3. Discuss how IS audit can be designed and conducted in such an environment and what kind of findings and suggestions would it bring up.

References

1. Priya Suchi, Satyam - *Yesterday and Today, Advances in Management*, Vol. 3(9), September 2010, pp. 47-49.

2. Websites

Appendix

THE INFORMATION TECHNOLOGY ACT, 2000

An Act to provide legal recognition for transactions carried out by means of electronic data interchange and other means of electronic communication, commonly referred to as "electronic commerce", which involve the use of alternatives to paper-based methods of communication and storage of information, to facilitate electronic filing of documents with the Government agencies and further to amend the Indian Penal Code, the Indian Evidence Act, 1872, the Bankers' Books Evidence Act, 1891 and the Reserve Bank of India Act, 1934 and for matters connected therewith or incidental thereto.

WHEREAS the General Assembly of the United Nations by resolution A/RES/51/162, dated the 30th January, 1997 has adopted the Model Law on Electronic Commerce adopted by the United Nations Commission on International Trade Law;

AND WHEREAS the said resolution recommends inter alia that all States give favourable consideration to the said Model Law when they enact or revise their laws, in view of the need for uniformity of the law applicable to alternatives to paper-cased methods of communication and storage of information;

AND WHEREAS it is considered necessary to give effect to the said resolution and to promote efficient delivery of Government services by means of reliable electronic records.

BE it enacted by Parliament in the Fifty-first Year of the Republic of India asfollows:

CHAPTER I

PRELIMINARY

---

1. Short title, extent, commencement and application

(1) This Act may be called the Information Technology Act, 2000.

(2) It shall extend to the whole of India and, save as otherwise provided in this Act, it applies also to any offence or contravention there under committed outside India by any person.

(3) It shall come into force on such date as the Central Government may, by notification, appoint and different dates may be appointed for different provisions of this Act and any reference in any such provision to the commencement of this Act shall be construed as a reference to the commencement of that provision.

(4) Nothing in this Act shall apply to,

(a) a negotiable instrument as defined in section 13 of the Negotiable Instruments Act, 1881;

(b) a power-of-attorney as defined in section 1A of the Powers-of-Attorney Act, 1882;

(c) a trust as defined in section 3 of the Indian Trusts Act, 1882;

(d) a will as defined in clause (h) of section 2 of the Indian Succession Act, 1925 including any other testamentary disposition by whatever name called;

(e) any contract for the sale or conveyance of immovable property or any interest in such property;

(f) any such class of documents or transactions as may be notified by the Central Government in the Official Gazette.

2. Definitions

(1) In this Act, unless the context otherwise requires, -

(a) "access" with its grammatical variations and cognate expressions means gaining entry into, instructing or communicating with the logical, arithmetical, or memory function resources of a computer, computer system or computer network;

(b) "addressee" means a person who is intended by the originator to receive the electronic record but does not include any intermediary;

(c) "adjudicating officer" means an adjudicating officer appointed under subsection (1) of section 46;

(d) "affixing digital signature" with its grammatical variations and cognate expressions means adoption of any methodology or procedure by a person for the purpose of authenticating an electronic record by means of digital signature;

(e) "appropriate Government" means as respects any matter,-

(i) Enumerated in List II of the Seventh Schedule to the Constitution;

(ii) relating to any State law enacted under List III of the Seventh Schedule to the Constitution, the State Government and in any other case, the Central Government;

(f) "asymmetric crypto system" means a system of a secure key pair consisting of a private key for creating a digital signature and a public key to verify the digital signature;

(g) "Certifying Authority" means a person who has been granted a licence to issue a Digital Signature Certificate under section 24;

(h) "certification practice statement" means a statement issued by a Certifying Authority to specify the practices that the Certifying Authority employs in issuing Digital Signature Certificates;

(i) "computer" means any electronic magnetic, optical or other high-speed data processing device or system which performs logical, arithmetic, and memory functionsby manipulations of electronic, magnetic or optical impulses, and includes all input, output, processing, storage, computer software, or communication facilities which are connected or related to the computer in a computer system or computer network;

(j) "computer network" means the interconnection of one or more computers through-

(i) the use of satellite, microwave, terrestrial line or other communication media; and

(ii) terminals or a complex consisting of two or more interconnected computers whether or not the interconnection is continuously maintained;

(k) "computer resource" means computer, computer system, computer network, data, computer database or software;

(l) "computer system" means a device or collection of devices, including input and output support devices and excluding calculators which are not programmable and capable of being used in conjunction with external files, which contain computer programmes, electronic instructions, input data and output data, that performs logic, arithmetic, data storage and retrieval, communication control and other functions;

(m) "Controller" means the Controller of Certifying Authorities appointed under sub-section (l) of section 17;

(n) "Cyber Appellate Tribunal" means the Cyber Regulations Appellate Tribunal established under sub-section (1) of section 48;

(o) "data" means a representation of information, knowledge, facts, concepts or instructions which are being prepared or have been prepared in a formalised manner, and is intended to be processed, is being processed or has been processed in a computer system or computer network, and may be in any form (including computer printouts magnetic or optical storage media, punched cards, punched tapes) or stored internally in the memory of the computer;

(p) "digital signature" means authentication of any electronic record by a subscriber by means of an electronic method or procedure in accordance with the provisions of section 3;

(q) "Digital Signature Certificate" means a Digital Signature Certificate issued under sub-section (4) of section 35;

(r) "electronic form" with reference to information means any information generated, sent, received or stored in media, magnetic, optical, computer memory, micro film, computer generated micro fiche or similar device;

(s) "Electronic Gazette" means the Official Gazette published in the electronic form;

(t) "electronic record" means data, record or data generated, image or sound stored, received or sent in an electronic form or micro film or computer generated micro fiche;

(u) "function", in relation to a computer, includes logic, control arithmetical process, deletion, storage and retrieval and communication or telecommunication from or within a computer;

(v) "information" includes data, text, images, sound, voice, codes, computer programmes, software and databases or micro film or computer generated micro fiche:

(w) "intermediary" with respect to any particular electronic message means any person who on behalf of another person receives, stores or transmits that message or provides any service with respect to that message;

(x) "key pair", in an asymmetric crypto system, means a private key and its mathematically related public key, which are so related that the public key can verify a digital signature created by the private key;

(y) "law" includes any Act of Parliament or of a State Legislature, Ordinances promulgated by the President or a Governor, as the case may be. Regulations made by the President under article 240, Bills enacted as President's Act under sub-clause (a) of clause (1) of article 357 of the Constitution and includes rules, regulations, bye-laws and orders issued or made there under;

(z) "licence" means a licence granted to a Certifying Authority under section 24;

  (za) "originator" means a person who sends, generates, stores or transmits any electronic message or causes any electronic message to be sent, generated, stored or transmitted to any other person but does not include an intermediary;

  (zb) "prescribed" means prescribed by rules made under this Act;

  (zc) "private key" means the key of a key pair used to create a digital signature;

(zd) "public key" means the key of a key pair used to verify a digital signature and listed in the Digital Signature Certificate;

(ze) "secure system" means computer hardware, software, and procedure that-

(a) are reasonably secure from unauthorised access and misuse;

(b) provide a reasonable level of reliability and correct operation;

(c) are reasonably suited to performing the intended functions; and

(d) adhere to generally accepted security procedures;

(zf) "security procedure" means the security procedure prescribed under section 16 by the Central Government;

(zg) "subscriber" means a person in whose name the Digital Signature Certificate is issued;

(zh) "verify" in relation to a digital signature, electronic record or public key, with its grammatical variations and cognate expressions means to determine whether-

(a) the initial electronic record was affixed with the digital signature by the use of private key corresponding to the public key of the subscriber;

(b) the initial electronic record is retained intact or has been altered since such electronic record was so affixed with the digital signature.

(2) Any reference in this Act to any enactment or any provision thereof shall, in relation to an area in which such enactment or such provision is not in force, be construed as a reference to the corresponding law or the relevant provision of the corresponding law, if any, in force in that area.

CHAPTER II
DIGITAL SIGNATURE

3. Authentication of electronic records.

(1) Subject to the provisions of this section any subscriber may authenticate an electronic record by affixing his digital signature.

(2) The authentication of the electronic record shall be effected by the use of asymmetric crypto system and hash function which envelope and transform the initial electronic record into another electronic record. Explanation.-For the purposes of this sub-section, "hash function" means an algorithm mapping or translation of one sequence of bits into another, generally smaller, set known as "hash result" such that an electronic record yields the same hash result every time the algorithm is executed with the same electronic record as its input making it computationally infeasible-

(a) to derive or reconstruct the original electronic record from the hash result produced by the algorithm;

(b) that two electronic records can produce the same hash result using the algorithm.

(3) Any person by the use of a public key of the subscriber can verify the electronic record.

(4) The private key and the public key are unique to the subscriber and constitute a functioning key pair.

CHAPTER III

ELECTRONIC GOVERNANCE

4. Legal recognition of electronic records.

Where any law provides that information or any other matter shall be in writing or in the typewritten or printed form, then, notwithstanding anything contained in such law, such requirement shall be deemed to have been satisfied if such information or matter is-

(a)   rendered or made available in an electronic form; and

(b)   accessible so as to be usable for a subsequent reference.

5. Legal recognition of digital signatures.

Where any law provides that information or any other matter shall be authenticated by affixing the signature or any document shall be signed or bear the signature of any person (then, notwithstanding anything contained in such law, such requirement shall be deemed to have been satisfied, if such information or matter is authenticated by means of digital signature affixed in such manner as may be prescribed by the Central Government. Explanation. For the purposes of this section, "signed", with its grammatical variations and cognate expressions, shall, with reference to a person, mean affixing of his hand written signature or any mark on any document and the expression "signature" shall be construed accordingly.

6. Use of electronic records and digital signatures in Government and its agencies.

(1)   Where any law provides for-

    (a)   the filing of any form. application or any other document with any office, authority, body or agency owned or controlled by the appropriate Government in a particular manner;

    (b)   the issue or grant of any licence, permit, sanction or approval by whatever name called in a particular manner;

    (c)   the receipt or payment of money in a particular manner, then, notwithstanding anything contained in any other law for the time being in force, such requirement shall be deemed to have been satisfied if such filing, issue, grant, receipt or payment, as the case may be, is effected by means of such electronic form as may be prescribed by the appropriate Government.

(2)   The appropriate Government may, for the purposes of sub-section (1), by rules, prescribe-

    (a)   the manner and format in which such electronic records shall be filed, created or issued;

    (b)   the manner or method of payment of any fee or charges for filing, creation or issue any electronic record under clause (a).

7. Retention of electronic records.

(1)   Where any law provides that documents, records or information shall be retained for any specific period, then, that requirement shall be deemed to have been satisfied if such documents, records or information are retained in the electronic form, if-

    (a)   the information contained therein remains accessible so as to be usable for a subsequent reference;

(b) the electronic record is retained in the format in which it was originally generated, sent or received or in a format which can be demonstrated to represent accurately the information originally generated, sent or received;

(c) the details which will facilitate the identification of the origin, destination, date and time of dispatch or receipt of such electronic record are available in the electronic record: Provided that this clause does not apply to any information which is automatically generated solely for the purpose of enabling an electronic record to be dispatched or received.

(2) Nothing in this section shall apply to any law that expressly provides for the retention of documents, records or information in the form of electronic records.

8. Publication of rule, regulation, etc., in Electronic Gazette.

Where any law provides that any rule, regulation, order, bye-law, notification or any other matter shall be published in the Official Gazette, then, such requirement shall be deemed to have been satisfied if such rule, regulation, order, bye-law, notification or any other matter is published in the Official Gazette or Electronic Gazette: Provided that where any rule, regulation, order, bye-law, notification or any other matter is published in the Official Gazette or Electronic Gazette, the date of publication shall be deemed to be the date of the Gazette which was first published in any form.

9. Sections 6,7 and 8 not to confer right to insist document should be accepted in electronic form.

Nothing contained in sections 6, 7 and 8 shall confer a right upon any person to insist that any Ministry or Department of the Central Government or the State Government or any authority or body established by or under any law or controlled or funded by the Central or State Government should accept, issue, create, retain and preserve any document in the form of electronic records or effect any monetary transaction in the electronic form.

10. Power to make rules by Central Government in respect of digital signature.

The Central Government may, for the purposes of this Act, by rules, prescribe—

(a) the type of digital signature;

(b) the manner and format in which the digital signature shall be affixed;

(c) the manner or procedure which facilitates identification of the person affixing the digital signature;

(d) control processes and procedures to ensure adequate integrity, security and confidentiality of electronic records or payments; and

(e) any other matter which is necessary to give legal effect to digital signatures.

CHAPTER IV

ATTRIBUTION, ACKNOWLEDGMENT AND DESPATCH OF ELECTRONIC RECORDS

11. Attribution of electronic records.

An electronic record shall be attributed to the originator-

(a)   if it was sent by the originator himself;

(b)   by a person who had the authority to act on behalf of the originator in respect of that electronic record; or

(c)   by an information system programmed by or on behalf of the originator to operate automatically.

12. Acknowledgment of receipt.

(1)   Where the originator has not agreed with the addressee that the acknowledgement of receipt of electronic record be given in a particular form or by a particular method, an acknowledgment may be given by-

(a)   any communication by the addressee, automated or otherwise; or

(b)   any conduct of the addressee, sufficient to indicate to the originator that the electronic record has been received.

(2)   Where the originator has stipulated that the electronic record shall be binding only on receipt of an acknowledgment of such electronic record by him, then unless acknowledgment has been so received, the electronic record shall be deemed to have been never sent by the originator.

(3)   Where the originator has not stipulated that the electronic record shall be binding only on receipt of such acknowledgment, and the acknowledgment has not been received by the originator within the time specified or agreed or, if no time has been specified or agreed to within a reasonable time, then the originator may give notice to the addressee stating that no acknowledgment has been received by him and specifying a reasonable time by which the acknowledgment must be received by him and if no acknowledgment is received within the aforesaid time limit he may after giving notice to the addressee, treat the electronic record as though it has never been sent.

13. Time and place of dispatch and receipt of electronic record.

(1)   Save as otherwise agreed to between the originator and the addressee, the dispatch of an electronic record occurs when it enters a computer resource outside the control of the originator.

(2)   Save as otherwise agreed between the originator and the addressee, the time of receipt of an electronic record shall be determined as follows, namely:

(a)   if the addressee has designated a computer resource for the purpose of receiving electronic records,-

(i)   receipt occurs at the time when the electronic, record enters the designated computer resource; or

      (ii)   if the electronic record is sent to a computer resource of the addressee that is not the designated computer resource, receipt occurs at the time when the electronic record is retrieved by the addressee;

    (b)   if the addressee has not designated a computer resource along with specified timings, if any, receipt occurs when the electronic record enters the computer resource of the addressee.

(3) Save as otherwise agreed to between the originator and the addressee, an electronic record is deemed to be dispatched at the place where the originator has his place of business, and is deemed to be received at the place where the addressee has his place of business.

(4) The provisions of sub-section (2) shall apply notwithstanding that the place where the computer resource is located may be different from the place where the electronic record is deemed to have been received under sub-section (3).

(5) For the purposes of this section, -

    (a)   if the originator or the addressee has more than one place of business, the principal place of business, shall be the place of business;

    (b)   if the originator or the addressee does not have a place of business, his usual place of residence shall be deemed to be the place of business;

    (c)   "usual place of residence", in relation to a body corporate, means the place where it is registered.

CHAPTER V

SECURE ELECTRONIC RECORDS AND SECURE DIGITAL SIGNATURES

---

14. Secure electronic record.

Where any security procedure has been applied to an electronic record at a specific point of time. then such record shall be deemed to be a secure electronic record from such point of time to the time of verification.

15. Secure digital signature.

If, by application of a security procedure agreed to by the parties concerned, it can be verified that a digital signature, at the time it was affixed, was-

    (a)   unique to the subscriber affixing it;

    (b)   capable of identifying such subscriber;

    (c)   created in a manner or using a means under the exclusive control of the subscriber and is linked to the electronic record to which it relates in such a manner that if the electronic record was altered the digital signature would be invalidated, then such digital signature shall be deemed to be a secure digital signature.

16. Security procedure.

·   The Central Government shall for the purposes of this Act prescribe the security procedure having regard to commercial circumstances prevailing at the time when the procedure was used, including-

(a)   the nature of the transaction;

(b)   the level of sophistication of the parties with reference to their technological capacity;

(c)   the volume of similar transactions engaged in by other parties;

(d)   the availability of alternatives offered to but rejected by any party;

(e)   the cost of alternative procedures; and

(f)   the procedures in general use for similar types of transactions or communications.

CHAPTER VI

REGULATION OF CERTIFYING AUTHORITIES

---

17. Appointment of Controller and other officers.

(1)   The Central Government may, by notification in the Official Gazette, appoint a Controller of Certifying Authorities for the purposes of this Act and may also by the same or subsequent notification appoint such number of Deputy Controllers and Assistant Controllers as it deems fit.

(2)   The Controller shall discharge his functions under this Act subject to the general control and directions of the Central Government.

(3)   The Deputy Controllers and Assistant Controllers shall perform the functions assigned to them by the Controller under the general superintendence and control of the Controller.

(4)   The qualifications, experience and terms and conditions of service of Controller, Deputy Controllers and Assistant Controllers shall be such as may be prescribed by the Central Government.

(5)   The Head Office and Branch Office of the office of the Controller shall be at such places as the Central Government may specify, and these may be established at such places as the Central Government may think fit.

(6)   There shall be a seal of the Office of the Controller.

18. Functions of Controller.

The Controller may perform all or any of the following functions, namely:

(a)   exercising supervision over the activities of the Certifying Authorities;

(b)   certifying public keys of the Certifying Authorities;

(c)   laying down the standards to be maintained by the Certifying Authorities;

(d)   specifying the qualifications and experience which employees of the Certifying Authorities should possess;

(e)   specifying the conditions subject to which the Certifying Authorities shall conduct their business;

(f)   specifying the contents of written, printed or visual materials and advertisements that may be distributed or used in respect of a Digital Signature Certificate and the public key;

(g)   specifying the form and content of a Digital Signature Certificate and the key,

(h)   specifying the form and manner in which accounts shall be maintained by the Certifying Authorities;

(i)   specifying the terms and conditions subject to which auditors may be appointed and the remuneration to be paid to them;

(j)   facilitating the establishment of any electronic system by a Certifying Authority either solely or jointly with other Certifying Authorities and regulation of such systems;

(k)   specifying the manner in which the Certifying Authorities shall conduct their dealings with the subscribers;

(l)   resolving any conflict of interests between the Certifying Authorities and the subscribers;

(m)   laying down the duties of the Certifying Authorities;

(n)   maintaining a database containing the disclosure record of every Certifying Authority containing such particulars as may be specified by regulations, which shall be accessible to public.

19. Recognition of foreign Certifying Authorities.

(1)   Subject to such conditions and restrictions as may be specified by regulations, the Controller may with the previous approval of the Central Government, and by notification in the Official Gazette, recognise any foreign Certifying Authority as a Certifying Authority for the purposes of this Act.

(2)   Where any Certifying Authority is recognised under sub-section (1), the Digital Signature Certificate issued by such Certifying Authority shall be valid for the purposes of this Act.

(3)   The Controller may, if he is satisfied that any Certifying Authority has contravened any of the conditions and restrictions subject to which it was granted recognition under sub-section

(4)   he may, for reasons to be recorded in writing, by notification in the Official Gazette, revoke such recognition.

20. Controller to act as repository.

(1)   The Controller shall be the repository of all Digital Signature Certificates issued under this Act.

(2)   The Controller shall-

(a)   make use of hardware, software and procedures that are secure .iJm intrusion and misuse;

(b)   observe such other standards as may be prescribed by the Central Government, to ensure that the secrecy and security of the digital signatures are assured.

(3)   The Controller shall maintain a computerised database of all public keys in such a manner that such database and the public keys are available to any member of the public.

21. Licence to issue Digital Signature Certificates.

(1)   Subject to the provisions of sub-section (2), any person may make an application, to the Controller, for a licence to issue Digital Signature Certificates.

(2)   No licence shall be issued under sub-section (1), unless the applicant fulfills such requirements with respect to qualification, expertise, manpower, financial resources and other infrastructure facilities, which are necessary to issue Digital Signature Certificates as may be prescribed by the Central Government

(3)   A licence granted under this section shall-

(a) be valid for such period as may be prescribed by the Central Government;

(b) not be transferable or heritable;

(c) be subject to such terms and conditions as may be specified by the regulations.

22. Application for licence.

(1) Every application for issue of a licence shall be in such form as may be prescribed by the Central Government.

(2) Every application for issue of a licence shall be accompanied by-

(a) a certification practice statement;

(b) a statement including the procedures with respect to identification of the applicant;

(c) payment of such fees, not exceeding twenty-five thousand rupees as may be prescribed by the Central Government;

(d) such other documents, as may be prescribed by the Central Government.

23. Renewal of licence.

An application for renewal of a licence shall be-

(a) in such form;

(b) accompanied by such fees, not exceeding five thousand rupees, as may be prescribed by the Central Government and shall be made not less than forty-five days before the date of expiry of the period of validity of the licence.

24. Procedure for grant or rejection of licence.

The Controller may, on receipt of an application under sub-section (1) of section 21, after considering the documents accompanying the application and such other factors, as he deems fit, grant the licence or reject the application:

Provided that no application shall be rejected under this section unless the applicant has been given a reasonable opportunity of presenting his case.

25. Suspension of licence.

(1) The Controller may, if he is satisfied after making such inquiry, as he may think fit, that a Certifying Authority has,-

(a) made a statement in, or in relation to, the application for the issue or renewal of the licence, which is incorrect or false in material particulars;

(b) failed to comply with the terms and conditions subject to which the licence was granted;

(c) failed to maintain the standards specified under clause (b) of sub-section (2) of section 20;

(d) contravened any provisions of this Act, rule, regulation or order made thereunder, revoke the licence:

Provided that no licence shall be revoked unless the Certifying Authority has been given a reasonable opportunity of showing cause against the proposed revocation.

(2) The Controller may, if he has reasonable cause to believe that there is any ground for revoking a licence under sub-section (1), by order suspend such licence pending the completion of any inquiry ordered by him:

Provided that no licence shall be suspended for a period exceeding ten days unless the Certifying Authority has been given a reasonable opportunity of showing cause agains the proposed suspension.

(3) No Certifying Authority whose licence has been suspended shall issue any Digital Signature Certificate during such suspension.

26. Notice of suspension or revocation of licence.

(1) Where the licence of the Certifying Authority is suspended or revoked, the Controller shall publish notice of such suspension or revocation, as the case may be, in the database maintained by him.

(2) Where one or more repositories are specified, the Controller shall publish notices of such suspension or revocation, as the case may be, in all such repositories:

Provided that the database containing the notice of such suspension or revocation, as the case may be, shall be made available through a web site which shall be accessible round the clock:

Provided further that the Controller may, if he considers necessary, publicise the contents of database in such electronic or other media, as he may consider appropriate.

27. Power to delegate.

The Controller may, in writing, authorise the Deputy Controller, Assistant Controller or any officer to exercise any of the powers of the Controller under this Chapter.

28. Power to investigate contraventions.

(1) The Controller or any officer authorised by him in this behalf shall take up for investigation any contravention of the provisions of this Act, rules or regulations made thereunder.

(2) The Controller or any officer authorised by him in this behalf shall exercise the like powers which are conferred on Income-tax authorities under Chapter XIII of the Income-tax Act, 1961 and shall exercise such powers, subject to such limitations laid down under that Act.

29. Access to computers and data.

(1) Without prejudice to the provisions of sub-section (1) of section 69, the Controller or any person authorised by him shall, if he has reasonable cause to suspect that any contravention of the provisions of this Act, rules or regulations made thereunder has been committed, have access to any computer system, any apparatus, data or any other material connected with such system, for the purpose of searching or causing a search to be made for obtaining any information or data contained in or available to such computer system.

(2) For the purposes of sub-section (1), the Controller or any person authorised by him may, by order, direct any person in-charge of, or otherwise concerned with the operation of, the computer system, data apparatus or material, to provide him with such reasonable technical and other assistance as he may consider necessary.

30. Certifying Authority to follow certain procedures.

Every Certifying Authority shall, -

(a) make use of hardware, software and procedures that are secure from intrusion and misuse;

(b) provide a reasonable level of reliability in its services which are reasonably suited to the performance of intended functions;

(c) adhere to security procedures to ensure that the secrecy and privacy of the digital signatures are assured; and

(d) observe such other standards as may be specified by regulations.

31. Certifying Authority to ensure compliance of the Act, etc.

Every Certifying Authority shall ensure that every person employed or otherwise engaged by it complies, in the course of his employment or engagement, with the provisions of this Act, rules, regulations and orders made thereunder.

32. Display of licence.

Every Certifying Authority shall display its licence at a conspicuous place of the premises in which it carries on its business.

33. Surrender of licence.

(1) Every Certifying Authority whose licence is suspended or revoked shall immediately after such suspension or revocation, surrender the licence to the Controller.

(2) Where any Certifying Authority fails to surrender a licence under sub-section (1), the person in whose favour a licence is issued, shall be guilty of an offence and shall be punished with imprisonment which may extend up to six months or a fine which may extend up to ten thousand rupees or with both.

34. Disclosure.

(1) Every Certifying Authority shall disclose in the manner specified by regulations-

(a) its Digital Signature Certificate which contains the public key corresponding to the private key used by that Certifying Authority to digitally sign another Digital Signature Certificate;

(b) any certification practice statement relevant thereto;

(c) notice of the revocation or suspension of its Certifying Authority certificate, if any; and

(d) any other fact that materially and adversely affects either the reliability of a Digital Signature Certificate, which that Authority has issued, or the Authority's ability to perform its services.

(2) Where in the opinion of the Certifying Authority any event has occurred or any situation has arisen which may materially and adversely affect the integrity of its computer system or the conditions subject to which a Digital Signature Certificate was granted, then, the Certifying Authority shall-

(a) use reasonable efforts to notify any person who is likely to be affected by that occurrence; or

(b) act in accordance with the procedure specified in its certification practice statement to deal with such event or situation.

CHAPTER VII

DIGITAL SIGNATURE CERTIFICATES

35. Certifying Authority to issue Digital Signature Certificate.

   (1) Any person may make an application to the Certifying Authority for the issue of a Digital Signature Certificate in such form as may be prescribed by the Central Government

   (2) Every such application shall be accompanied by such fee not exceeding twenty-five thousand rupees as may be prescribed by the Central Government, to be paid to the Certifying Authority:

Provided that while prescribing fees under sub-section (2) different fees may be prescribed for different classes of applicants'.

   (3) Every such application shall be accompanied by a certification practice statement or where there is no such statement, a statement containing such particulars, as may be specified by regulations.

   (4) On receipt of an application under sub-section (1), the Certifying Authority may, after consideration of the certification practice statement or the other statement under sub-section

   (5) and after making such enquiries as it may deem fit, grant the Digital Signature Certificate or for reasons to be recorded in writing, reject the application:

Provided that no Digital Signature Certificate shall be granted unless the Certifying Authority is satisfied that-

   (a) the applicant holds the private key corresponding to the public key to be listed in the Digital Signature Certificate;

   (b) the applicant holds a private key, which is capable of creating a digital signature;

   (c) the public key to be listed in the certificate can be used to verify a digital signature affixed by the private key held by the applicant:

Provided further that no application shall be rejected unless the applicant has been given a reasonable opportunity of showing cause against the proposed rejection.

36. Representations upon issuance of Digital Signature Certificate.

A Certifying Authority while issuing a Digital Signature Certificate shall certify that--

   (a) it has complied with the provisions of this Act and the rules and regulations made thereunder,

   (b) it has published the Digital Signature Certificate or otherwise made it available to such person relying on it and the subscriber has accepted it;

   (c) the subscriber holds the private key corresponding to the public key, listed in the Digital Signature Certificate;

   (d) the subscriber's public key and private key constitute a functioning key pair,

   (e) the information contained in the Digital Signature Certificate is accurate; and

   (f) it has no knowledge of any material fact, which if it had been included in the Digital Signature Certificate would adversely affect the reliability of the representations made in clauses (a) to (d).

37. Suspension of Digital Signature Certificate.

(1) Subject to the provisions of sub-section (2), the Certifying Authority which has issued a Digital Signature Certificate may suspend such Digital Signature Certificate,-

    (a) on receipt of a request to that effect from-

        (i) the subscriber listed in the Digital Signature Certificate; or

        (ii) any person duly authorised to act on behalf of that subscriber,

    (b) if it is of opinion that the Digital Signature Certificate should be suspended in public interest

(2) A Digital Signature Certificate shall not be suspended for a period exceeding fifteen days unless the subscriber has been given an opportunity of being heard in the matter.

(3) On suspension of a Digital Signature Certificate under this section, the Certifying Authority shall communicate the same to the subscriber.

38. Revocation of Digital Signature Certificate.

(1) A Certifying Authority may revoke a Digital Signature Certificate issued by it-

    (a) where the subscriber or any other person authorised by him makes a request to that effect; or

    (b) upon the death of the subscriber, or

    (c) upon the dissolution of the firm or winding up of the company where the subscriber is a firm or a company.

(2) Subject to the provisions of sub-section (3) and without prejudice to the provisions of sub-section (1), a Certifying Authority may revoke a Digital Signature Certificate which has been issued by it at any time, if it is of opinion that-

    (a) a material fact represented in the Digital Signature Certificate is false or has been concealed;

    (b) a requirement for issuance of the Digital Signature Certificate was not satisfied;

    (c) the Certifying Authority's private key or security system was compromised in a manner materially affecting the Digital Signature Certificate's reliability;

    (d) the subscriber has been declared insolvent or dead or where a subscriber is a firm or a company, which has been dissolved, wound-up or otherwise ceased to exist

(3) A Digital Signature Certificate shall not be revoked unless the subscriber has been given an opportunity of being heard in the matter.

(4) On revocation of a Digital Signature Certificate under this section, the Certifying Authority shall communicate the same to the subscriber.

39. Notice of suspension or revocation.

(1) Where a Digital Signature Certificate is suspended or revoked under section 37 or section 38, the Certifying Authority shall publish a notice of such suspension or revocation, as the case may be, in the repository specified in the Digital Signature Certificate for publication of such notice.

(2) Where one or more repositories are specified, the Certifying Authority shall publish notices of such suspension or revocation, as the case may he. in all such repositories.

┌─────────────────────────────────┐
│   **CHAPTER VIII**   │
│   │
│   **DUTIES OF SUBSCRIBERS**   │
└─────────────────────────────────┘

40. Generating key pair.

Where any Digital Signature Certificate, the public key of which corresponds to the private key of that subscriber which is to be listed in the Digital Signature Certificate has been accepted by a subscriber, then, the subscriber shall generate the key pair by applying the security procedure.

41. Acceptance of Digital Signature Certificate.

(1) A subscriber shall be deemed to have accepted a Digital Signature Certificate if he publishes or authorises the publication of a Digital Signature Certificate-

    (a) to one or more persons;

    (b) in a repository, or otherwise demonstrates his approval of the Digital Signature Certificate in any manner.

(2) By accepting a Digital Signature Certificate the subscriber certifies to all who reasonably rely on the information contained in the Digital Signature Certificate that-

    (a) the subscriber holds the private key corresponding to the public key listed in the Digital Signature Certificate and is entitled to hold the same;

    (b) all representations made by the subscriber to the Certifying Authority and all material relevant to the information contained in the Digital Signature Certificate are true;

    (c) all information in the Digital Signature Certificate that is within the knowledge of the subscriber is true.

42. Control of private key.

(1) Every subscriber shall exercise reasonable care to retain control of the private key corresponding to the public key listed in his Digital Signature Certificate and take all steps to prevent its disclosure to a person not authorised to affix the digital signature of the subscriber.

(2) If the private key corresponding to the public key listed in the Digital Signature Certificate has been compromised, then, the subscriber shall communicate the same without any delay to the Certifying Authority in such manner as may be specified by .the regulations.

Explanation.- For the removal of doubts, it is hereby declared that the subscriber shall be liable till he has informed the Certifying Authority that the private key has been compromised.

┌─────────────────────────────────┐
│   **CHAPTER IX**   │
│   │
│   **PENALTIES AND ADJUDICATION** │
└─────────────────────────────────┘

43. Penalty for damage to computer, computer system, etc.

If any person without permission of the owner or any other person who is in charge of a computer, computer system or computer network, -

    (a) accesses or secures access to such computer, computer system or computer network;

(b)   downloads, copies or extracts any data, computer database or information from such computer, computer system or computer network including information or data held or stored in any removable storage medium;

(c)   introduces or causes to be introduced any computer contaminant or computer virus into any computer, computer system or computer network;

(d)   damages or causes to be damaged any computer, computer system or computer network, data, computer database or any other programmes residing in such computer, computer system or computer network;

(e)   disrupts or causes disruption of any computer, computer system or computer network;

(f)   denies or causes the denial of access to any person authorised to access any computer, computer system or computer network by any means;

(g)   provides any assistance to any person to facilitate access to a computer, computer system or computer network in contravention of the provisions of this Act, rules or regulations made thereunder;

(h)   charges the services availed of by a person to the account of another person by tampering with or manipulating any computer, computer system, or computer network, he shall be liable to pay damages by way of compensation not exceeding one crore rupees to the person so affected.

Explanation.-For the purposes of this section,-

(i)   "computer contaminant" means any set of computer instructions that are designed-

(a)   to modify, destroy, record, transmit data or programme residing within a computer, computer system or computer network; or

(b)   by any means to usurp the normal operation of the computer, computer system, or computer network;

(ii) "computer database" means a representation of information, knowledge, facts, concepts or instructions in text, image, audio, video that are being prepared or have been prepared in a formalised manner or have been produced by a computer, computer system or computer network and are intended for use in a computer, computer system or computer network;

(iii) "computer virus" means any computer instruction, information, data or programme that destroys, damages, degrades or adversely affects the performance of a computer resource or attaches itself to another computer resource and operates when a programme, data or instruction is executed or some other event takes place in that computer resource;

(iv) "damage" means to destroy, alter, delete, add, modify or rearrange any computer resource by any means.

44. Penalty for failure to furnish information return, etc.

If any person who is required under this Act or any rules or regulations made thereunder to-

(a)   furnish any document, return or report to the Controller or the Certifying Authority fails to furnish the same, he shall be liable to a penalty not exceeding one lakh and fifty thousand rupees for each such failure;

(b)   file any return or furnish any information, books or other documents within the time specified therefor in the regulations fails to file return or furnish the same within the time specified therefor in the regulations, he shall be liable to a penalty not

(c) exceeding five thousand rupees for every day during which such failure continues;

(d) maintain books of account or records, fails to maintain the same, he shall be liable to a penalty not exceeding ten thousand rupees for every day during which the failure continues.

45. Residuary penalty.

Whoever contravenes any rules or regulations made under this Act, for the contravention of which no penalty has been separately provided, shall be liable to pay a compensation not exceeding twenty-five thousand rupees to the person affected by such contravention or a penalty not exceeding twenty-five thousand rupees.

46. Power to adjudicate.

(1) For the purpose of adjudging under this Chapter whether any person has committed a contravention of any of the provisions of this Act or of any rule, regulation, direction or order made thereunder the Central Government shall, subject to the provisions of sub-section (3), appoint any officer not below the rank of a Director to the Government of India or an equivalent officer of a State Government to be an adjudicating Officer for holding an inquiry in the manner prescribed by the Central Government.

(2) The adjudicating officer shall, after giving the person referred to in sub-section

(3) a reasonable opportunity for making representation in the matter and if, on such inquiry, he is satisfied that the person has committed the contravention, he may impose such penalty or award such compensation as he thinks fit in accordance with the provisions of that section.

(4) No person shall be appointed as an adjudicating officer unless he possesses such experience in the field of Information Technology and legal or judicial experience as may be prescribed by the Central Government.

(5) Where more than one adjudicating officers are appointed, the Central Government shall specify by order the matters and places with respect to which such officers shall exercise their jurisdiction.

(6) Every adjudicating officer shall have the powers of a civil court which are conferred oh the Cyber Appellate Tribunal under sub-section (2) of section 58, and-

(a) all proceedings before it shall be deemed to be judicial proceedings within the meaning of sections 193 and 228 of the Indian Penal Code;

(b) shall be deemed to be a civil court for the purposes of sections 345 and 346 of the Code of Criminal Procedure, 1973.

47. Factors to be taken into account by the adjudicating officer.

While adjudging the quantum of compensation under this Chapter, the adjudicating officer shall have due regard to the following factors, namely:

(a) the amount of gain of unfair advantage, wherever quantifiable, made as a result of the default;

(c) the amount of loss caused to any person as a result of the default;

CHAPTER X

THE CYBER REGULATIONS
APPELLATE TRIBUNAL

48. Establishment of Cyber Appellate Tribunal.

(1)   The Central Government shall, by notification, establish one or more appellate tribunals to be known as the Cyber Regulations Appellate Tribunal.

(2)   The Central Government shall also specify, in the notification referred to in sub-section (1), the matters and places in relation to which the Cyber Appellate Tribunal may exercise jurisdiction.

49. Composition of Cyber Appellate Tribunal.

A Cyber Appellate Tribunal shall consist of one person only (hereinafter referred to as the Residing Officer of the Cyber Appellate Tribunal) to be appointed, by notification, by the Central Government

50. Qualifications for appointment as Presiding Officer of the Cyber Appellate Tribunal.

A person shall not be qualified for appointment as the Presiding Officer of a Cyber Appellate Tribunal unless he-

(a)   is, or has been or is qualified to be, a Judge of a High Court; or

(b)   is or has been a member of the Indian Legal Service and is holding or has held a post in Grade I of that Service for at least three years.

51. Term of office

The Presiding Officer of a Cyber Appellate Tribunal shall hold office for a term of five years from the date on which he enters upon his office or until he attains the age of sixty-five years, whichever is earlier.

52. Salary, allowances and other terms and conditions of service of Presiding Officer.

The salary and allowances payable to, and the other terms and conditions of service including pension, gratuity and other retirement benefits of. the Presiding Officer of a Cyber Appellate Tribunal shall be such as may be prescribed:

Provided that neither the salary and allowances nor the other terms and conditions of service of the Presiding Officer shall be varied to his disadvantage after appointment.

53. Filling up of vacancies.

If, for reason other than temporary absence, any vacancy occurs in the office n the Presiding Officer of a Cyber Appellate Tribunal, then the Central Government shall appoint another person in accordance with the provisions of this Act to fill the vacancy and the proceedings may be continued before the Cyber Appellate Tribunal from the stage at which the vacancy is filled.

54. Resignation and removal.

(1)   The Presiding Officer of a Cyber Appellate Tribunal may, by notice in writing under his hand addressed to the Central Government, resign his office:

Provided that the said Presiding Officer shall, unless he is permitted by the Central Government to relinquish his office sooner, continue to hold office until the expiry of three months from the date of receipt of such notice or until a person duly appointed as his successor enters upon his office or until the expiry of his term of office, whichever is the earliest.

(2) The Presiding Officer of a Cyber Appellate Tribunal shall not be removed from his office except by an order by the Central Government on the ground of proved misbehaviour or incapacity after an inquiry made by a Judge of the Supreme Court in which the Presiding Officer concerned has been informed of the charges against him and given a reasonable opportunity of being heard in respect of these charges.

(3) The Central Government may, by rules, regulate the procedure for the investigation of misbehaviour or incapacity of the aforesaid Presiding Officer.

55. Orders constituting Appellate Tribunal to be final and not to invalidate its proceedings.

No order of the Central Government appointing any person as the Presiding Officer of a Cyber Appellate Tribunal shall be called in question in any manner and no act or proceeding before a Cyber Appellate Tribunal shall be called in question in any manner on the ground merely of any defect in the constitution of a Cyber Appellate Tribunal.

56. Staff of the Cyber Appellate Tribunal.

(1) The Central Government shall provide the Cyber Appellate Tribunal with such officers and employees as that Government may think fit

(2) The officers and employees of the Cyber Appellate Tribunal shall discharge their functions under general superintendence of the Presiding Officer.

(3) The salaries, allowances and other conditions of service of the officers and employees or' (e) the Cyber Appellate Tribunal shall be such as may be prescribed by the Central Government.

57. Appeal to Cyber Appellate Tribunal.

(1) Save as provided in sub-section (2), any person aggrieved by an order made by Controller or an adjudicating officer under this Act may prefer an appeal to a Cyber Appellate Tribunal having jurisdiction in the matter.

(2) No appeal shall lie to the Cyber Appellate Tribunal from an order made by an adjudicating officer with the consent of the parties.

(3) Every appeal under sub-section (1) shall be filed within a period of tony-five days from the date on which a copy of the order made by the Controller or the adjudicating officer is received by the person aggrieved and it shall be in such form and be accompanied by such fee as may be prescribed: Provided that the Cyber Appellate Tribunal may entertain an appeal after the expiry of the said period of tony-five days if it is satisfied that there was sufficient cause tor not filing it within that period.

(4) On receipt of an appeal under sub-section (1), the Cyber Appellate Tribunal may, after giving the parties to the appeal, an opportunity of being heard, pass such orders thereon as it thinks fit, confirming, modifying or setting aside the order appealed against.

(5) The Cyber Appellate Tribunal shall send a copy of every order made by it to" the parties to the appeal and to the concerned Controller or adjudicating officer.

(6) The appeal filed before the Cyber Appellate Tribunal under sub-section (1) shall be dealt with by it as expeditiously as possible and endeavour shall be made by it to dispose of the appeal finally within six months from the date of receipt of the appeal.

58. Procedure and powers of the Cyber Appellate Tribunal.

(1) The Cyber Appellate Tribunal shall not be bound by the procedure laid down by the Code of civil Procedure, 1908 but shall be guided by the principles of natural justice and, subject to the other provisions of this Act and of any rules, the Cyber Appellate Tribunal shall have powers to regulate its own procedure including the place at which it shall have its sittings.

(2) The Cyber Appellate Tribunal shall have, for the purposes of discharging its functions under this Act, the same powers as are vested in a civil court under the Code of Civil Procedure, 1908, while trying a suit, in respect of the following matters, namely:

 (a) summoning and enforcing the attendance of any person and examining him on oath;

 (b) requiring the discovery and production of documents or other electronic records;

 (c) receiving evidence on affidavits;

 (d) issuing commissions for the examination of witnesses or documents;

 (e) reviewing its decisions;

 (f) dismissing an application for default or deciding it ex pane;

 (g) any other matter which may be prescribed.

(3) Every proceeding before the Cyber Appellate Tribunal shall be deemed to be a judicial proceeding within the meaning of sections 193 and 228, and for the purposes of section 196 of the Indian Penal Code and the Cyber Appellate Tribunal shall be deemed to be a civil court for the purposes of section 195 and Chapter XXVI of the Code of Criminal Procedure, 1973.

59. Right to legal representation.

The appellant may either appear in person or authorise one or more legal practitioners or any (f) of its officers to present his or its case before the Cyber Appellate Tribunal.

60. Limitation.

The provisions of the Limitation Act, 1963, shall, as far as may be, apply to an appeal made to the Cyber Appellate Tribunal.

61. Civil court not to have jurisdiction.

No court shall have jurisdiction to entertain any suit or proceeding in respect of any matter which an adjudicating officer appointed under this Act or the Cyber Appellate Tribunal constituted under this Act is empowered by or under this Act to determine and no injunction shall be granted by any court or other authority in respect of any action taken or to be taken in pursuance of any power conferred by or under this Act.

62. Appeal to High Court.

Any person aggrieved by any decision or order of the Cyber Appellate Tribunal may file an appeal to the High Court within sixty days from the date of communication of the decision or order of the Cyber Appellate Tribunal to him on any question of fact or law arising out of such order Provided that the High Court may, if it is satisfied that the appellant was prevented by sufficient cause from filing the appeal within the said period, allow it to be filed within a further period not exceeding sixty days.

63. Compounding of contraventions.

(1) Any contravention under this Chapter may, either before or after the institution of adjudication proceedings, be compounded by the Controller or such other officer as may be specially

authorised by him in this behalf or by the adjudicating officer, as the case may be, subject to such conditions as the Controller or such other officer or the adjudicating officer may specify:

Provided that such sum shall not, in any case, exceed the maximum amount of the penalty which may be imposed under this Act for the contravention so compounded.

(2) Nothing in sub-section shall apply to a person who commits the same or similar contravention within a period of three years from the date on which the first contravention, committed by him, was compounded. Explanation.-For the purposes of this sub-section, any second or subsequent contravention committed after the expiry of a period of three years from the date on which the contravention was previously compounded shall be deemed to be a first contravention.

(3) Where any contravention has been compounded under sub-section no proceeding or further proceeding, as the case may be, shall be taken against the person guilty of such contravention in respect of the contravention so compounded.

64. Recovery of penalty

A penalty imposed under this Act, if it is not paid, shall be recovered as an arrear of land revenue and the licence or the Digital Signature Certificate, as the case may be, shall be suspended till the penalty is paid.

CHAPTER XI

OFFENCES

65. Tampering with computer source documents.

Whoever knowingly or intentionally conceals, destroys or alters or intentionally or knowingly causes another to conceal, destroy or alter any computer source code used for a computer, computer programme, computer system or computer network, when the computer source code is required to be kept or maintained by law for the time being in force, shall be punishable with imprisonment up to three years, or with fine which may extend up to two lakh rupees, or with both. Explanation.-For the purposes of this section, "computer source code" means the listing of programmes, computer commands, design and layout and programme analysis of computer resource in any form.

66. Hacking with computer system.

(1) Whoever with the intent to cause or knowing that he is likely to cause wrongful loss or damage to the public or any person destroys or deletes or alters any information residing in a computer resource or diminishes its value or utility or affects it injuriously by any means, commits hack:

(2) Whoever commits hacking shall be punished with imprisonment up to three years, or with fine which may extend upto two lakh rupees, or with both.

67. Publishing of information which is obscene in electronic form.

Whoever publishes or transmits or causes to be published in the electronic form, any material which is lascivious or appeals to the prurient interest or if its effect is such as to tend to deprave and corrupt persons who are likely, having regard to all relevant circumstances, to read, see or hear the matter contained or embodied in it, shall be punished on first conviction with imprisonment of either description for a term which may extend to five years and with fine which may extend to one lakh rupees and in the event of a second or subsequent conviction with imprisonment of either description for a term which may extend to ten years and also with fine which may extend to two lakh rupees.

68. Power of Controller to give directions.

(1) The Controller may, by order, direct a Certifying Authority or any employee of such Authority to take such measures or cease carrying on such activities as specified in the order if those are necessary to ensure compliance with the provisions of this Act, rules or any regulations made thereunder.

(2) ny person who fails to comply with any order under sub-section (1) shall be guilty of an offence and shall be liable on conviction to imprisonment for a term not exceeding three years or to a fine not exceeding two lakh rupees or to both.

69. Directions of Controller to a subscriber to extend facilities to decrypt information.

(1) If the Controller is satisfied that it is necessary or expedient so to do in the interest of the sovereignty or integrity of India, the security of the State, friendly relations with foreign Stales or public order or for preventing incitement to the commission of any cognizable offence, for reasons to be recorded in writing, by order, direct any agency of the Government to intercept any information transmitted through any computer resource.

(2) The subscriber or any person in charge of the computer resource shall, when called upon by any agency which has been directed under sub-section (1), extend all facilities and technical assistance to decrypt the information.

(3) The subscriber or any person who fails to assist the agency referred to in sub-section (2) shall be punished with an imprisonment for a term which may extend to seven years.

70. Protected system.

(1) The appropriate Government may, by notification in the Official Gazette, declare that any computer, computer system or computer network to be a protected system.

(2) The appropriate Government may, by order in writing, authorise the persons who are authorised to access protected systems notified under sub-section (1).

(3) Any person who secures access or attempts to secure access to a protected system in contravention of the provisions of this section shall be punished with imprisonment of either description for a term which may extend to ten years and shall also be liable to fine.

71. Penalty for misrepresentation.

Whoever makes any misrepresentation to, or suppresses any material fact from, the Controller or the Certifying Authority for obtaining any licence or Digital Signature Certificate, as the case may be. shall be punished with imprisonment for a term which may extend to two years, or with fine which may extend to one lakh rupees, or with both.

72. Penalty for breach of confidentiality and privacy.

Save as otherwise provided in this Act or any other law for the time being in force, any person who, in pursuance of any of the powers conferred under this Act, rules or regulations made thereunder, has secured access to any electronic record, book, register, correspondence, information, document or other material without the consent of the person concerned discloses such electronic record, book, register, correspondence, information, document or other material to any other person shall be punished with imprisonment for a term which may extend to two years, or with fine which may extend to one lakh rupees, or with both.

73. Penalty for publishing Digital Signature Certificate false in certain particulars.

(1) No person shall publish a Digital Signature Certificate or otherwise make it available to any other person with the knowledge that-

(a) the Certifying Authority listed in the certificate has not issued it; or

(b) the subscriber listed in the certificate has not accepted it; or

(c) the certificate has been revoked or suspended, unless such publication is for the purpose of verifying a digital signature created prior to such suspension or revocation.

(2) Any person who contravenes the provisions of sub-section (1) shall be punished with imprisonment for a term which may extend to two years, or with fine which may extend to one lakh rupees, or with both.

74. Publication for fraudulent purpose.

Whoever knowingly creates, publishes or otherwise makes available a Digital Signature Certificate for any fraudulent or unlawful purpose shall be punished with imprisonment for a term which may extend to two years, or with fine which may extend to one lakh rupees, or with both.

75. Act to apply for offence or contravention commited outside India.

(1) Subject to the provisions of sub-section (2), the provisions of this Act shall apply also to any offence or contravention committed outside India by any person irrespective of his nationality.

(2) For the purposes of sub-section (1), this Act shall apply to an offence or contravention committed outside India by any person if the act or conduct constituting the offence or contravention involves a computer, computer system or computer network located in India.

76. Confiscation.

Any computer, computer system, floppies, compact disks, tape drives or any other accessories related thereto, in respect of which any provision of this Act. rules, orders or regulations made thereunder has been or is being contravened, shall be liable to confiscation:

Provided that where it is established to the satisfaction of the court adjudicating the confiscation that the person in whose possession, power or control of any such computer, computer system, floppies, compact disks, tape drives or any other accessories relating thereto is found is not responsible for the contravention of the provisions of this Act, rules, orders or regulations made thereunder, the court may, instead of making an order for confiscation of such computer, computer system, floppies, compact disks, tape drives or any other accessories related thereto, make such other order authorised by this Act against the person contravening of the provisions of this Act, rules, orders or regulations made thereunder as it may think fit.

77. Penalties or confiscation not to interfere with other punishments.

No penalty imposed or confiscation made under this Act shall prevent the imposition of any other punishment to which the person affected thereby is liable under any other law for the time being in force.

78. Power to investigate offences.

Notwithstanding anything contained in the Code of Criminal Procedure, 1973, a police officer not below the rank of Deputy Superintendent of Police shall investigate any offence under this Act.

CHAPTER XII

NETWORK SERVICE PROVIDERS NOT TO BE LIABLE IN CERTAIN CASES

---

79. Network service providers not to be liable in certain cases.

For the removal of doubts, it is hereby declared that no person providing any service as anetwork service provider shall be liable under this Act, rules or regulations made thereunder for any third party information or data made available by him if he proves that the offence or contravention was committed without his knowledge or that he had exercised all due diligence to prevent the commission of such offence or contravention.

Explanation.-For the purposes of this section, -

(a)   "network service provider" means an intermediary;

(b)   "third party information" means any information dealt with by a network service provider in his capacity as an intermediary;

CHAPTER XIII

MISCELLANEOUS

---

80. Power of police officer and other officers to enter, search, etc.

(1)   Not with standing anything contained in the Code of Criminal Procedure, 1973, any police officer, not below the rank of a Deputy Superintendent of Police, or any other officer of the Central Government or a State Government authorised by the Central Government in this behalf may enter any public place and search and arrest without warrant any person found therein who is reasonably suspected or having committed or of committing or of being about to commit any offence under this Act Explanation.-For the purposes of this sub-section, the expression "public place" includes any public conveyance, any hotel, any shop or any other place intended for use by, or accessible to the public.

(2)   Where any person is arrested under sub-section (1) by an officer other than a police officer, such officer shall, without unnecessary delay, take or send the person arrested before a magistrate having jurisdiction in the case or before the officer-in-charge of a police station.

(3)   The provisions of the Code of Criminal Procedure, 1973 shall, subject to the provisions of this section, apply, so far as may be, in relation to any entry, search or arrest, made under this section.

81. Act to have overriding effect.

The provisions of this Act shall have effect notwithstanding anything inconsistent therewith contained in any other law for the time being in force.

82. Controller, Deputy Controller and Assistant Controllers to be public servants.

The Presiding Officer and other officers and employees of a Cyber Appellate Tribunal, the Controller, the Deputy Controller and the Assistant Controllers shall be deemed to be public servants within the meaning of section 21 of the Indian Penal Code.

83. Power to give directions.

The Central Government may give directions to any State Government as to the carrying into execution in the State of any of the provisions of this Act or of any rule, regulation or order made thereunder.

84. Protection of action taken in good faith.

No suit, prosecution or other legal proceeding shall lie against the Central Government, the State Government, the Controller or any person acting on behalf of him, the Presiding Officer, adjudicating officers and the staff of the Cyber Appellate Tribunal for anything which is in good faith done or intended to be done in pursuance of this Act or any rule, regulation or order made thereunder.

85. Offences by companies.

(1) Where a person committing a contravention of any of the provisions of this Act or of any rule, direction or order made thereunder is a company, every person who, at the time the contravention was committed, was in charge of, and was responsible to, the company for the conduct of business of the company as well as the company, shall be guilty of the contravention and shall be liable to be proceeded against and punished accordingly:

Provided that nothing contained in this sub-section shall render any such person liable to punishment if he proves that the contravention took place without his knowledge or that he exercised all due diligence to prevent such contravention.

(2) Notwithstanding anything contained in sub-section (1), where a contravention of any of the provisions of this Act or of any rule, direction or order made thereunder has been committed by a company and it is proved that the contravention has taken place with the consent or connivance of, or is attributable to any neglect on the part of, any director, manager, secretary or other officer of the company, such director, manager, secretary or other officer shall also be deemed to be guilty of the contravention and shall be liable to be proceeded against and punished accordingly.

Explanation.-For the purposes of this section,-

(i) "company" means any body corporate and includes a firm or other association of individuals; and

(ii) "director", in relation to a firm, means a partner in the firm.

86. Removal of difficulties.

(1) If any difficulty arises in giving effect to the provisions of this Act, the Central Government may, by order published in the Official Gazette, make such provisions not inconsistent with the provisions of this Act as appear to it to be necessary or expedient for removing the difficulty:

Provided that no order shall be made under this section after the expiry of a period of two years from the commencement of this Act

(2) Every order made under this section shall be laid, as soon as may be after it is made, before each House of Parliament.

87. Power of Central Government to make rules.

(1) The Central Government may, by notification in the Official Gazette and in the Electronic Gazette make rules to carry out the provisions of this Act

(2) In particular, and without prejudice to the generality of the foregoing power, such rules may provide for all or any of the following mailers, namely:

   (a) the manner in which any information or matter may be authenticated by means of digital signature under section 5;

   (b) the electronic form in which filing, issue, grant or payment shall be effected under sub-section (1) of section 6;

   (c) the manner and format in which electronic records shall be filed, or issued and the method of .payment under sub-section (2) of section 6;

   (d) the matters relating to the type of digital signature, manner and format in which it may be affixed undersection 10;

   (e) the security procedure for the purpose of creating secure electronic recod and secure digital signature under section 16;

   (f) the qualifications, experience and terms and conditions of service of Controller, Deputy Controllers and Assistant Controllers under section 17;

   (g) other standards to be observed by the Controller under clause (b) of sub-section (2) of section 20;

   (h) the requirements which an applicant must fulfil under sub-section (2) of section 21;

   (i) the period of validity of licence granted under clause (a) of sub-section (3) of section 21;

   (j) the form in which an application for licence may be made under sub-section (1) of section 22;

   (k) the amount of fees payable under clause (c) of sub-section (2) of section 22;

   (l) such other documents which shall accompany an application for licence under clause (a) of sub-section (2) of section 22;

   (m) the form and the fee for renewal of a licence and the fee payable there of under section 23;

   (n) the form in which application for issue of a Digital Signature Certificate may be made under sub-section (1) of section 35;

   (o) the fee to be paid to the CertifyingAuthority for issue of a Digital Signature Certificate under sub-section (2) of section 35;

   (p) the manner in which the adjudicating officer shall hold inquiry under subsection (1) of section 46;

   (q) 'the qualification and experience which the adjudicating officer shall possess under sub-section (3) of section 46;

   (r) the salary, allowances and the other terms and conditions of service of the Presiding Officer under section 52;

   (s) the procedure for investigation of misbehaviour or incapacity of the Presiding Officer under sub-section (3) of section 54;

   (t) the salary and allowances and other conditions of service of other officers and employees under sub-section (3) of section 56;

   (u) the form in which appeal may be filed and the fee thereof under sub -section (3) of section 57;

(v) any other power of a civil court required to be prescribed under clause (g) of sub-section (2) of section 58; and

(w) any other matter which is required to be, or may be, prescribed.

(3) Every notification made by the Central Government under clause (f) of subsection (4) of section 1 and every rule made by it shall be laid, as soon as may be after it is made, before each House of Parliament, while it is in session, for a total period of thirty days which may be comprised in one session or in two or more successive sessions, and if, before the expiry of the session immediately following the session or the successive sessions aforesaid, both Houses agree in making any modification in the notification or the rule or both Houses agree that the notification or the rule should not be made, the notification or the rule shall thereafter have effect only in such modified form or be of no effect, as the case may be; so, however, that any such modification or annulment shall be without prejudice to the validity of anything previously done under that notification or rule.

88. Constitution of Advisory Committee.

(1) The Central Government shall, as soon as may be after the commencement of this Act, constitute a Committee called the Cyber Regulations Advisory Committee.

(2) The Cyber Regulations Advisory Committee shall consist of a Chairperson and such number of other official and non-official members representing the interests principally affected or having special knowledge of the subject-matter as the Central Government may deem fit.

(3) The Cyber Regulations Advisory Committee shall advise-

(a) the Central Government either generally as regards any rules or for any other purpose connected with this Act;

(b) the Controller in framing the regulations under this Act.

(4) There shall be paid to the non-official members of such Committee such travelling and other allowances as the Central Government may fix.

89. Power of Controller to make regulations.

(1) The Controller may, after consultation with the Cyber Regulations Advisory Committee and with the previous approval of the Central Government, by notification in the Official Gazette, make regulations consistent with this Act and the rules made thereunder to carry out the purposes of this Act.

(2) In particular, and without prejudice to the generality of the foregoing power, such regulations may provide for all or any of the following matters, namely: -

(a) the particulars relating to maintenance of data-base containing the disclosure record of every Certifying Authority under clause (m) of section 18;

(b) the conditions and restrictions subject to which the Controller may recognise any foreign Certifying Authority under sub-section (1) of section 19;

(c) the terms and conditions subject to which a licence may be granted under clause (c) of sub-section (3) of section 21;

(d) other standards to be observed by a Certifying Authority under clause (d) of section 30;

(e) the manner in which the Certifying Authority shall disclose the matters specified in sub-section (1) of section 34;

(f) the particulars of statement which shall accompany an application under sub-section (3) of section 35;

(g) the manner in which the subscriber shall communicate the compromise of private key to the certifying Authority under sub-section (2) of section 42.

(3) Every regulation made under this Act shall be laid, as soon as may be after it is made, before each House of Parliament, while it is in session, for a total period of thirty days which may be comprised in one session or in two or more successive sessions, and if, before the expiry of the session immediately following the session or the successive sessions aforesaid, both Houses agree in making any modification in the regulation or both Houses agree that the regulation should not be made, the regulation shall thereafter have effect only in such modified form or he of no effect, as the case may be; so, however, that any such modification or annulment shall be without prejudice to the validity of anything previously done under that regulation.

90. Power of State Government to make rules.

(1) The State Government may, by notification in the Official Gazette, make rules to carry out the provisions of this Act.

(2) In particular, and without prejudice to the generality of the foregoing power, such rules may provide for all or any of the following matters, namely-

(a) the electronic form in which filing, issue, grant receipt or payment shall be effected under sub-section (1) of section 6;

(b) for matters specified in sub-section (2) of section 6;

(c) any other matter which is required to be provided by rules by the State Government.

(3) Every rule made by the State Government under this section shall be laid, as soon as may be after it is made, before each House of the State Legislature where it consists of two Houses, or where such Legislature consists of one House, before that House.

91. Amendment of Act 45 of 1860.

The Indian Penal Code shall be amended in the manner specified in the First Schedule to this Act.

92. Amendment of Act 1 of 1872.

The Indian Evidence Act, 1872 shall be amended in the manner specified in the Second Schedule to this Act.

93. Amendment of Act 18 of 1891.

The Bankers' Books Evidence Act, 1891 shall be amended in the manner specified in the Third Schedule to this Act.

94. Amendment of Act 2 of 1834.

The Reserve Bank of India Act, 1934 shall be amended in the manner specified in the Fourth Schedule to this Act.

THE FIRST SCHEDULE (See section 91)

AMENDMENTS TO THE INDIAN PENAL CODE (45 OF 1860)

1. After section 29, the following section shall be inserted, namely:

Electronic record.

"29A. The words "electronic record" shall have the meaning assigned to them in clause (t) of sub-section (1) of section 2 of the Information Technology Act, 2000.".

2. In section 167, for the words "such public servant, charged with the preparation or translation of any document, frames or translates that document", the words "such public servant, charged with the preparation or translation of any document or electronic record, frames, prepares or translates that document or electronic record" shall be substituted.

3. In section 172, for the words "produce a document in a Court of Justice", the words "produce a document or an electronic record in a Court of Justice" shall be substituted.

4. In section 173, for the words "to produce a document in a Court of Justice", the words "to produce a document or electronic record in a Court of Justice" shall be substituted.

5. In section 175, for the word "document" at both the places where it occurs, the words "document or electronic record" shall be substituted.

6. In section 192, for the words "makes any false entry in any book or record, or makes any document containing a false statement", the words "makes any false entry in any book or record, or electronic record or makes any document or electronic record containing a false statement" shall be substituted.

7. In section 204, for the word "document" at both the places where it occurs, the words "document or electronic record" shall be substituted.

8. In section 463, for the words "Whoever makes any false documents or part of a document with intent to cause damage or injury", the words "Whoever makes any false documents or false electronic record or part of a document or electronic record, with intent to cause damage or injury" shall be substituted.

9. In section 464,- (a) for the portion beginning with the words "A person is said to make a false document" and ending with the words "by reason of deception practised upon him, he does not know the contents of the document or the nature of the alteration", the following shall be substituted, namely:

"A person is said to make a false document or false electronic record-

First-Who dishonestly or fraudulently-

(a) makes, signs, seals or executes a document or part of a document;

(b) makes or transmits any electronic record or part of any electronic record;

(c) affixes any digital signature on any electronic record;

(d) makes any mark denoting the execution of a document or the authenticity of the digital signature, with the intention of causing it to be believed that such document or part of document, electronic record or digital signature was made, signed, sealed, executed, transmitted or affixed by or by the authority of a person by whom or by whose authority he knows that it was not made, signed, sealed, executed or affixed; or

Secondly-Who, without lawful authority, dishonestly or fraudulently, by cancellation or otherwise, alters a document or an electronic record in any material part thereof, after it has been made, executed or affixed with digital signature either by himself or by any other person, whether such person be living or dead at the time of such alteration; or Thirdly-Who dishonestly or fraudulently causes any person to sign, seal, execute or alter a document or an electronic record or to affix his digital signature on any electronic record knowing that such person by reason of unsoundness of mind or intoxication cannot, or that by reason of deception practised upon him, he does not know the contents of the document or electronic record or the nature of the alteration. (b) after Explanation 2, the following Explanation shall be inserted at the end, namely:

'Explanation 3.-For the purposes of this section, the expression "affixing digital signature" shall have the meaning assigned to it in clause (d) of subsection (1) of section 2 of the Information Technology Act, 2000.'.

10. In section 466,-

(a) for the words "Whoever forges a document", the words "Whoever forges a document or an electronic record" shall be substituted;

(b) the following Explanation shall be inserted at the end, namely:

'Explanation.-For the purposes of this section, "register" includes any list, data or record of any entries maintained in the electronic form as defined in clause (r) of sub-section (1) of section 2 of the Information Technology Act, 2000.'.

11. In section 468, for the words "document forged", the words "document or electronic record forged" shall be substituted.

12. In section 469, for the words "intending that the document forged", the words "intending that the document or electronic record forged" shall be substituted.

13. In section 470, for the word "document" in both the places where it occurs, the words "document or electronic record" shall be substituted.

14. In section 471, for the word "document" wherever it occurs, the words "document or electronic record" shall be substituted.

15. In section 474, for the portion beginning with the words "Whoever has in his possession any document" and ending with the words "if the document is one of the description mentioned in section 466 of this Code", the following shall be substituted, namely: -

"Whoever has in his possession any document or electronic record, knowing the same to be forged and intending that the same shall fraudulently or dishonestly be used as a genuine, shall, if the document or electronic record is one of the description mentioned in section 466 of this Code.".

16. In section 476, for the words "any document", the words "any document or electronic record" shall be substituted.

17. In section 477A, for the words "book, paper, writing" at both the places where they occur, the words "book, electronic record, paper, writing" shall be substituted.

THE SECOND SCHEDULE (See section 92)

AMENDMENTS TO THE INDIAN EVIDENCE ACT, 1872

(1 OF 1872)

1. In section 3,-

(a) in the definition of "Evidence", for the words "all documents produced for the inspection of the Court", the words "all documents including electronic records produced for the inspection of the Court" shall be substituted;

(b) after the definition of "India", the following shall be inserted, namely: 'the expressions "Certifying Authority", "digital signature", "Digital Signature Certificate", "electronic form", "electronic records", "information", "secure electronic record", "secure digital signature" and "subscriber" shall have the meanings respectively assigned to them in the Information Technology Act, 2000.'.

2. In section 17, for the words "oral or documentary,", the words "oral or documentary or contained in electronic form" shall be substituted.

3. After section 22, the following section shall be inserted, namely-

When oral admission as to contents of electronic records are relevant. "22A. Oral admissions as to the contents of electronic records are not relevant, unless the genuineness of the electronic record produced is in question.".

4. In section 34, for the words "Entries in the books of account", the words "Entries in the books of account, including those maintained in an electronic form" shall be substituted.

5. In section 35, for the word "record", in both the places where it occurs, the words "record or an electronic record" shall be substituted.

6. For section 39, the following section shall be substituted, namely-

What evidence to be given when statement forms part of a conversation, document, electronic record, book or series of letters or papers.

"39. When any statement of which evidence is given forms part of a longer statement, or

of a conversation or pan of an isolated document, or is contained in a document which forms part of a book, or is contained in part of electronic record or of a connected series of letters or papers, evidence shall be given of so much and no more of the statement, conversation, document, electronic record, book or series of letters or papers as the Court considers necessary in that particular case to the full understanding of the nature and effect of the statement, and of the circumstances under which it was made.".

7. After section 47, the following section shall be inserted, namely: Opinion as to digital signature where relevant.

"47A. When the Court has 10 form an opinion as to the digital signature of any person, the opinion of the Certifying Authority which has issued the Digital Signature Certificate is a relevant fact.".

8. In section 59, for the words "contents of documents" the words "contents of documents or electronic records" shall be substituted.

9. After section 65, the following sections shall be inserted, namely-

Special provisions as to evidence relating to electronic record. '65A. The contents of electronic records may be proved in accordance with the provisions of section 65B. Admissibility of electronic records. 65B.

(1) Notwithstanding anything contained in this Act, any information contained in an electronic record which is printed on a paper, stored, recorded or copied in optical or magnetic media produced by a computer (hereinafter referred to as the computer output) shall be deemed to be also a document, if the conditions mentioned in this section are satisfied in relation to the information and computer in question and shall be admissible in any proceedings, without further proof or production of the original, as evidence of any contents of the original or of any fact stated therein of which direct evidence would be admissible.

(2) The conditions referred to in sub-section (1) in respect of a computer output shall be the following, namely:

   (a) the computer output containing the information was produced by the computer during the period over which the computer was used regularly to store or process information for the purposes of any activities regularly carried on over that period by the person having lawful control over the use of the computer;

(b) during the said period, information of the kind contained in the electronic record or of the kind from which the information so contained is derived was regularly fed into the computer in the ordinary course of the said activities;

(c) throughout the material part of the said period, the computer was operating properly or, if not, then in respect of any period in which it was not operating properly or was out of operation during that part of the period, was not such as to affect the electronic record or the accuracy of its contents; and

(d) the information contained in the electronic record reproduces or is derived from such information fed into the computer in the ordinary course of the said activities.

(3) Where over any period, the function of storing or processing information for the purposes of any activities regularly carried on over that period as mentioned in clause (a) of sub-section (2) was regularly performed by computers, whether-

(a) by a combination of computers operating over that period; or

(b) by different computers operating in succession over that period; or

(c) by different combinations of computers operating in succession over that period; or

(d) in any other manner involving the successive operation over that period, in whatever order, of one or more computers and one or more combinations of computers, all the computers used for that purpose during that period shall be treated for the purposes of this section as constituting a single computer; and references in this section to a computer shall be construed accordingly.

(4) In any proceedings where it is desired to give a statement in evidence by virtue of this section, a certificate doing any of the following things, that is to say, -

(a) identifying the electronic record containing the statement and describing the manner in which it was produced;

(b) giving such particulars of any device involved in the production of that electronic record as may be appropriate for the purpose of showing that the electronic record was produced by a computer;

(c) dealing with any of the matters to which the conditions mentioned in sub-section (2) relate, and purporting to be signed by a person occupying a responsible official position in relation to the operation of the relevant device or the management of the relevant activities (whichever is appropriate) shall be evidence of any matter stated in the certificate; and for the purposes of this sub-section it shall be sufficient for a matter to be stated to the best of the knowledge and belief of the person stating it.

(5) For the purposes of this section, -

(a) information shall be taken to be supplied to a computer if it is supplied thereto in any appropriate form and whether it is so supplied directly or (with or without human intervention) by means of any appropriate equipment;

(b) whether in the course of activities carried on by any official, information is supplied with a view to its being stored or processed for the purposes of those activities by a computer operated otherwise than in the course of those activities, that information, if duly supplied to that computer, shall be taken to be supplied to it in the course of those activities;

(c) a computer output shall be taken to have been produced by a computer whether it was produced by it directly or (with or without human intervention) by means of any appropriate equipment.

Explanation.-For the purposes of this section any reference to information being derived from other information shall be a reference to its being derived therefrom by calculation, comparison or any other process.

10. After section 67, the following section shall be inserted, namely- Proof as to digital signature.

"67A. Except in the case of a secure digital signature, if the digital signature of any subscriber is alleged to have been affixed to an electronic record the fact that such digital signature is the digital signature of the subscriber must be proved.".

11. After section 73, the following section shall be inserted, namely- Proof as to verification of digital signature.

'73A. In order to ascertain whether a digital signature is that of the person by whom it purports to have been affixed, the Court may direct-

(a) that person or the Controller or the Certifying Authority to produce the Digital Signature Certificate;

(b) any other person to apply the public key listed in the Digital Signature Certificate and verify the digital signature purported to have been affixed by that person.

Explanation.-For the purposes of this section, "Controller" means the Controller appointed under sub-section (1) of section 17 of the Information Technology Act, 2000'.

12. Presumption as to Gazettes in electronic forms.

After section 81, the following section shall be inserted, namely- "81 A. The Court shall presume the genuineness of every electronic record purporting to be the Official Gazette, or purporting to be electronic record directed by any law to be kept by any person, if such electronic record is kept substantially in the form required by law and is produced from proper custody.".

13. Presumption as to electronic agreements.

After section 85, the following sections shall be inserted, namely- "85A. The Court shall presume that every electronic record purporting to be an agreement containing the digital signatures of the parties was so concluded by affixing the digital signature of the parties Presumption as to electronic records and digital signatures. 85B.

(1) In any proceedings involving a secure electronic record, the Court shall presume unless contrary is proved, that the secure electronic record has not been altered since the specific point of time to which the secure status relates.

(2) In any proceedings, involving secure digital signature, the Court shall presume unless the contrary is proved that-

(a) the secure digital signature is affixed by subscriber with the intention of signing or approving the electronic record;

(b) except in the case of a secure electronic record or a secure digital signature, nothing in this section shall create any presumption relating to authenticity and integrity of the electronic record or any digital signature. Presumption as to Digital Signature Certificates.

85C. The Court shall presume, unless contrary is proved, that the information listed in a Digital Signature Certificate is correct, except for information specified as subscriber information which has not been verified, if the certificate was accepted by the subscriber.".

14. Presumption as to electronic messages.

After section 88, the following section shall be inserted, namely: '88A. The Court may presume that an electronic message forwarded by the originator through an electronic mail server to the addressee to whom the message purports to be addressed corresponds with the message as fed into his computer for transmission; but the Court shall not make any presumption as to the person by whom such message was sent.

Explanation.-For the purposes of this section, the expressions "addressee" and "originator" shall have the same meanings respectively assigned to them in clauses (b) and (za) of sub-section (1) of section 2 of the Information Technology Act, 2000.'.

15. Presumption as to electronic records five years old.

After section 90, the following section shall be inserted, namely: "90A. Where any electronic record, purporting or proved to be five years old, is produced from any custody which the Court in the particular case considers proper, the Court may presume that the digital signature which purports to be the digital signature of any particular person was so affixed by him or any person authorised by him in this behalf.

Explanation.-Electronic records are said to be in proper custody if they are in the place in which, and under the care of the person with whom, they naturally be; but no custody is improper if it is proved to have had a legitimate origin, or the circumstances of the particular case are such as to render such an origin probable.

This Explanation applies also to section 81A.".

16. For section 131, the following section shall be substituted, namely-

Production of documents or electronic records which another person, having possession, could refuse to produce. "131. No one shall be compelled to produce documents in his possession or electronic records under his control, which any other person would be entitled to refuse to produce if they were in his possession or control, unless such last-mentioned person consents to their production.".

THE THIRD SCHEDULE (See section 93)

AMENDMENTS TO THE BANKERS' BOOKS EVIDENCE ACT' 1891

(18 OF 1891)

1. In section 2-

(a) for clause (3), the following clause shall be substituted, namely-

'(3) "bankers' books" include ledgers, day-books, cash-books, account-books and all other books used in the ordinary business of a bank whether kept in the written form or as printouts of data stored in a floppy, disc, tape or any other form of electro-magnetic data storage device;

(b) for clause (8), the following clause shall be substituted, namely-

'(8) "certified copy" means when the books of a bank,- (a) are maintained in written form, a copy of any entry in such books together with a certificate written;::: the foot of such copy that it is a true copy of such entry, that such entry is contained in one of the ordinary books of the bank and was made in the usual and ordinary course of business and that such book is still in the custody of the bank, and where the copy was obtained by a mechanical or other process which in itself ensured the accuracy of the copy, a further certificate to that effect, but where the book from which such copy was prepared has been destroyed in the usual course of the bank's business after the date on which the copy had been so prepared, a further certificate to that effect, each such certificate being dated and subscribed by the principal accountant or manager of the bank with his name and official title; and (b) consist of printouts of data stored in a floppy, disc, tape or any other electro-magnetic data storage device, a printout of such entry or a copy of such printout together with such statements certified in accordance with the provisions of section 2A.'.

2. After section 2, the following section shall be inserted, namely-

Conditions in the printout. "2A. A printout of entry or a copy of printout referred to in sub-section (8) of section 2 shall be accompanied by the following, namely-

(a) a certificate to the effect that it is a printout of such entry or a copy of such printout by the principal accountant or branch manager; and

(b) a certificate by a person in-charge of computer system containing a brief description of the computer system and the particulars of-

(A) the safeguards adopted by the system to ensure that data is entered or any other operation performed only by authorised persons;

(B) the safeguards adopted to prevent and detect unauthorised change of data;

(C) the safeguards available to retrieve data that is lost due to systemic failure or any other reasons;

(D) the manner in which data is transferred from the system to removable media like floppies, discs, tapes or other electro-magnetic data storage devices;

(E) the mode of verification in order to ensure that data has been accurately transferred to such removable media;

(F) the mode of identification of such data storage devices;

(G) the arrangements for the storage and custody of such storage devices;

(H) the safeguards to prevent and detect any tampering with the system; and

(I) any other factor which will vouch for the integrity and accuracy of the system.

(c) a further certificate from the person in-charge of the computer system to the effect that to the best of his knowledge and belief, such computer system operated properly at the material time, he was provided with all the relevant data and the printout in question represents correctly, or is appropriately derived from, the relevant data.".

THE FOURTH SCHEDULE (See section 94)

AMENDMENT TO THE RESERVE BANK OF INDIA ACT, 1934 (2 OF 1934)

In the Reserve Bank of India Act, 1934, in section 58, in sub-section (2), after clause (p), the following clause shall be inserted, namely: "(pp) the regulation of fund transfer through electronic means between the banks or between the banks and other financial institutions referred to in clause (c) of section 45-1, including the laying down of the conditions subject to which banks and other financial institutions shall participate in such fund transfers, the manner of such fund transfers and the rights and obligations of the participants in such fund transfers;".